WORLD HISTORY
MADE SIMPLE

WORLD HISTORY MADE SIMPLE

REVISED EDITION

BY

JACK C. ESTRIN, M.A.

Chairman, Social Studies,
Richmond Hill High School, N.Y.C.

MADE SIMPLE BOOKS
DOUBLEDAY & COMPANY, INC.
GARDEN CITY, NEW YORK

Library of Congress Catalog Card Number 68-18120

Copyright © 1957, 1960, 1968 by Doubleday & Company, Inc.

All Rights Reserved

Printed in the United States of America

ABOUT THIS BOOK

There was a time, and it was not so long ago, when we thought of history in local, regional, or national terms. Men's minds seemed limited to near horizons—to their village, their city, their province, their country. Beyond that they could not see—or chose not to see. Two world wars, a mushroom-shaped cloud, and a technological revolution that staggers the imagination have changed all that. We may still reckon distance in county lines, since the mind alters its habitual ways reluctantly, but it is more realistic—as we proceed into the second half of the twentieth century—to regard the whole world as lying on the fringes of our backyard.

It is for reasons such as these that it becomes especially urgent for Americans—who are, whether or not they wish to be, citizens of the world—to begin to think in global terms. In order to do this it is clear that they must come to know something about the world they live in—what it was, what it is now, what it may be in the process of becoming. Confusion is the price of ignorance, and we cannot afford—when the stakes are so high: nothing less than life or death, survival or decline—to be confused or ignorant. Confusion, unfortunately, is very easy to come by in a world that changes with such bewildering speed as ours does; in a world that changes so rapidly that it seems to make itself over every day. We must determine that where ignorance was shall knowledge be, and the best avenue to such an end is, of course, historical knowledge.

This book was written with such a goal in view. My purpose has been to make available to the American reader as much of the history of the world's past as seems most clearly relevant to our interests and needs, and it seemed natural, therefore, to place the heaviest emphasis on the history of Western civilization—the great historical sweep from which we ourselves have emerged and in which we have our roots. I am aware that I have left the great Eastern civilizations comparatively neglected, considering them only where they became involved in the history of the West. This is not because they are in any sense less important—far from it! But only so much can be achieved in a single book, and the scope of this one is already immense. There will be other books, and the East will not remain neglected for long.

Here I am primarily concerned with the sources of our own history, with the total development which has made us what we are. If I have succeeded, then I shall allow myself to hope that the reader will gain from this book a real understanding of our common past, of that long, difficult road which brought us from mankind's earliest stirrings to our present turning point.

—JACK C. ESTRIN

TABLE OF CONTENTS

7

CHAPTER FOUR

CHAPTER FIVE

CHAPTER SIX

CHAPTER SEVEN

CHAPTER EIGHT

CHAPTER NINE

CHAPTER TEN

CHAPTER ELEVEN

CHAPTER TWELVE

CHAPTER THIRTEEN

CHAPTER FOURTEEN

CHAPTER FIFTEEN

CHAPTER SIXTEEN

CHAPTER SEVENTEEN

CHAPTER EIGHTEEN

CHAPTER NINETEEN

CHAPTER TWENTY

CHAPTER TWENTY-ONE

CHAPTER TWENTY-TWO

MAPS

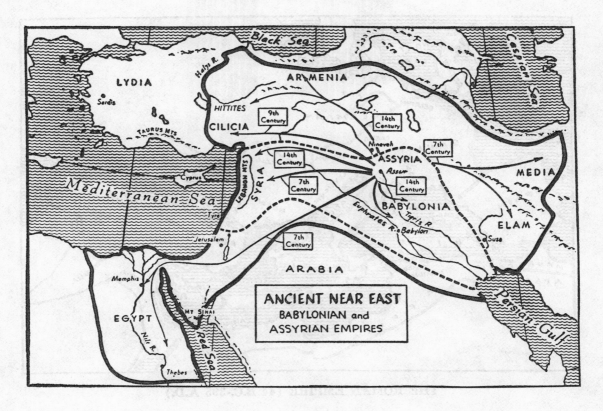

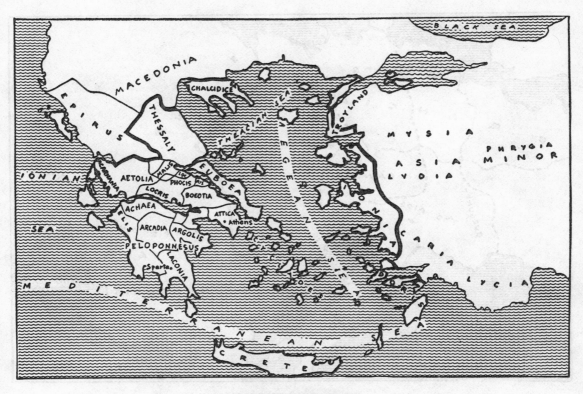

ANCIENT GREECE

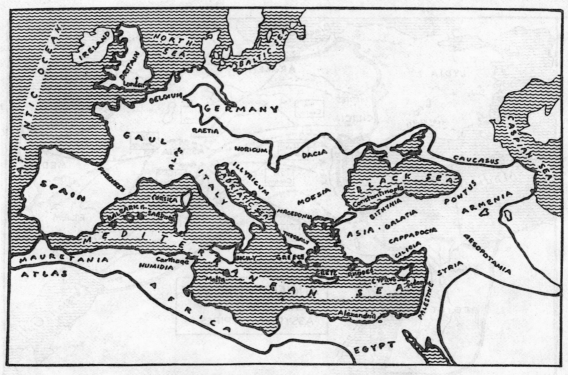

THE ROMAN EMPIRE (44 B.C.-395 A.D.)

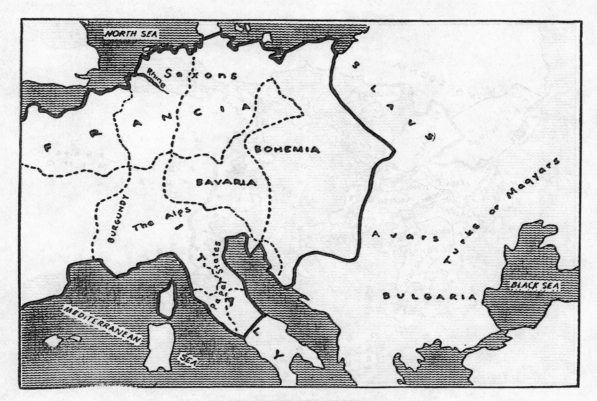

CHARLEMAGNE'S EMPIRE

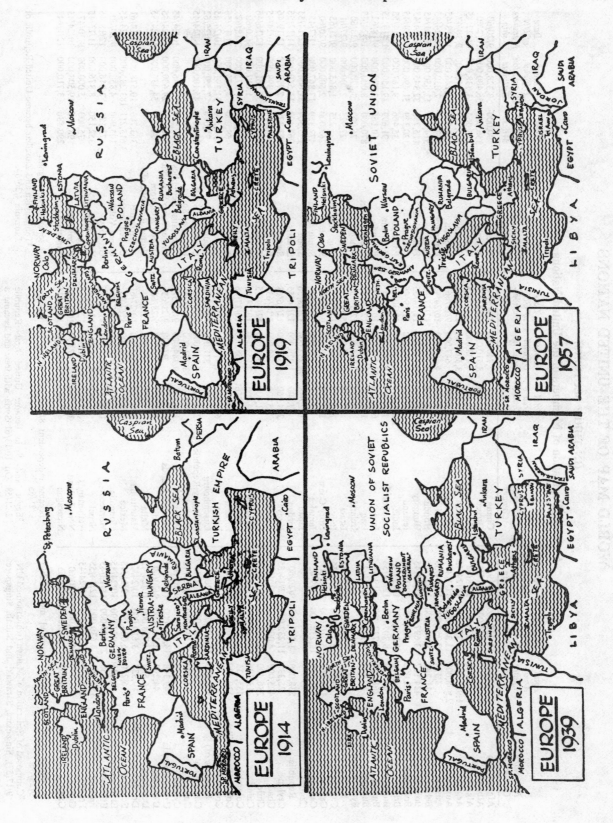

WORLD MAP OF THE UNITED NATIONS

(IN THREE SECTIONS)

Area and Population of Members of the United Nations

Name of Country	Total Area (Square Miles)	Latest Official Population Estimate	Date of UN Membership
Afghanistan	250,000	15,227,000	11/19/46
Albania	11,100	1,865,000	12/14/55
Algeria	919,600	10,670,000	10/8/62
Argentina	1,072,000	22,352,000	10/24/45
Australia	2,968,000	11,360,000	11/1/45
Austria	32,374	7,255,000	12/14/55
Belgium	11,781	9,464,000	12/27/45
Bolivia	424,162	3,697,000	11/14/45
Botswana	222,000	559,000	10/17/66
Brazil	3,286,470	81,301,000	10/24/45
Bulgaria	42,729	8,207,000	12/14/55
Burma	261,789	24,732,000	4/19/48
Burundi	10,747	2,780,000	9/18/62
Byelorussian S.S.R.	80,154	8,054,000	10/24/45
Cambodia	69,898	5,738,000	12/14/55
Cameroon	183,568	5,210,000	9/20/60
Canada	3,851,809	18,238,000	11/9/45
Central African Republic	238,000	1,352,000	9/20/60
Ceylon	25,332	11,232,000	12/14/55
Chad	495,000	4,000,000	9/20/60
Chile	286,400	8,567,000	10/24/45
China	13,886	12,820,000	10/24/45
Colombia	455,335	17,787,000	11/5/45
Congo (Brazzaville)	139,000	900,000	9/20/60
Congo (Democratic Republic of)	904,800	15,627,000	9/20/60
Costa Rica	23,421	1,433,000	11/2/45
Cuba	44,200	7,631,000	10/24/45
Cyprus	3,570	598,000	9/20/60
Czechoslovakia	49,368	14,159,000	10/24/45
Dahomey	44,290	2,300,000	9/20/60
Denmark	16,619	4,758,000	10/24/45
Dominican Republic	19,333	3,619,000	10/24/45
Ecuador	116,270	5,084,000	12/21/45
El Salvador	8,260	2,929,000	10/24/45
Ethiopia	398,350	22,590,000	11/13/45
Finland	130,165	4,630,000	12/14/55
France	212,659	49,157,000	10/24/45
Gabon	102,290	4,612,000	9/20/60
Gambia	4,005	330,000	9/21/65
Ghana	91,843	7,740,000	3/8/57
Greece	51,843	8,510,000	10/25/45
Guatemala	42,042	4,438,000	11/21/45
Guinea	96,865	3,500,000	12/12/58
Guyana	83,000	647,000	9/21/66
Haiti	10,714	4,660,000	10/24/45
Honduras	44,482	2,284,000	12/17/45
Hungary	35,918	10,148,000	12/14/55
Iceland	39,758	208,000	11/19/46
India	1,261,597	471,624,000	10/30/45
Indonesia[1]	735,865	160,000,000	[4]9/28/50
Iran	628,000	23,428,000	10/24/45
Iraq	172,000	8,262,000	12/21/45
Ireland	27,136	2,865,000	12/14/55
Israel	7,993	2,563,000	5/11/49
Italy	116,372	52,736,000	12/14/55
Ivory Coast	127,520	3,750,000	9/20/60
Jamaica	4,411	1,800,000	9/18/62
Japan	142,688	98,282,000	12/18/56
Jordan	37,500	1,976,000	12/14/55
Kenya	224,960	9,365,000	12/16/63
Kuwait	5,800	468,000	5/14/63
Laos	91,000	3,000,000	12/14/55
Lebanon	4,000	2,152,000	10/24/45
Lesotho	11,716	858,000	10/17/66
Liberia	43,000	1,066,000	11/2/45
Libya	679,358	1,617,000	12/14/55
Luxembourg	999	331,000	10/24/45
Malagasy Republic	228,000	6,262,000	9/20/60
Malawi	49,177	3,753,000	12/1/64
Malaysia[2]	128,308	9,384,000	9/17/57
Maldive Islands	112	97,000	9/21/65
Mali	465,000	4,576,000	9/28/60
Malta	122	319,000	12/1/64
Mauritania	416,216	1,000,000	10/27/61
Mexico	758,259	42,809,000	11/7/45
Mongolia	626,000	1,019,000	10/27/61
Morocco	172,104	13,323,000	11/12/56
Nepal	54,362	9,388,000	12/14/55
Netherlands	15,800	12,292,000	12/10/45
New Zealand	103,736	2,647,000	10/24/45
Nicaragua	57,145	1,655,000	10/24/45
Niger	490,000	3,328,000	9/20/60
Nigeria	356,669	56,400,000	10/7/60
Norway	125,064	3,738,000	11/27/45
Pakistan	365,529	102,876,000	9/30/47
Panama	28,576	1,246,000	11/13/45
Paraguay	157,000	2,030,000	10/24/45
Peru	514,059	11,650,000	10/31/45
Philippines	115,758	32,345,000	10/24/45
Poland	120,359	31,496,000	10/24/45
Portugal	35,466	9,167,000	12/14/55
Romania	91,699	19,150,000	12/14/55
Rwanda	10,166	3,000,000	9/18/62
Saudi Arabia	870,000	8,000,000	10/24/45
Senegal	76,000	3,490,000	9/28/60
Sierra Leone	27,925	2,200,000	9/27/61
Singapore	225	1,865,000	9/21/65
Somalia	262,000	2,500,000	9/20/60
South Africa	472,359	17,867,000	11/7/45
Spain	195,504	31,604,000	12/14/55
Sudan	967,500	13,540,000	11/12/56
Sweden	173,378	7,773,000	11/19/46
Syria[3]	72,234	5,399,000	10/24/45
Thailand	200,148	30,561,000	12/16/46
Togo	20,400	1,617,000	9/20/60
Trinidad & Tobago	1,979	975,000	9/18/62
Tunisia	58,000	4,675,000	11/12/56
Turkey	296,500	31,391,000	10/24/45
Uganda	91,076	7,551,000	10/25/62
Ukrainian S.S.R.	232,046	45,100,000	10/24/45
Union of Soviet Socialist Republics	8,337,298	176,846,000	10/24/45
United Arab Republic[3]	386,198	29,600,000	10/24/45
United Kingdom	94,209	54,436,000	10/24/45
United Republic of Tanzania[4]	363,708	10,578,000	12/14/61
United States	3,615,211	183,285,000	10/24/45
Upper Volta	105,900	4,858,000	9/20/60
Uruguay	72,172	2,846,000	12/18/45
Venezuela	352,150	8,876,000	11/15/45
Yemen	75,000	5,000,000	9/30/47
Yugoslavia	98,766	19,508,000	10/24/45
Zambia	290,586	3,710,000	12/1/64

[1]Resigned from UN 1/20/65; resumed membership 9/28/66.

[2]Composed of Federation of Malaya (which joined UN 9/17/57), Singapore, Sarawak, and Sabah. Singapore became independent 8/9/65 and joined the UN on 9/21/65.

[3]Egypt and Syria became United Arab Republic 2/21/58. On 10/13/61 Syria withdrew and became a separate state again.

[4]Tanganyika and Zanzibar became United Republic of Tanzania 4/26/64.

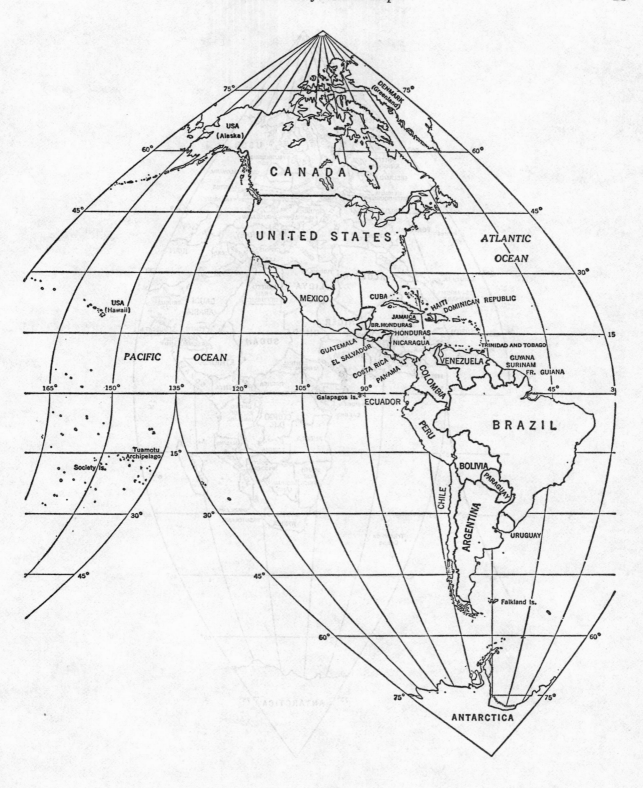

SECTION I

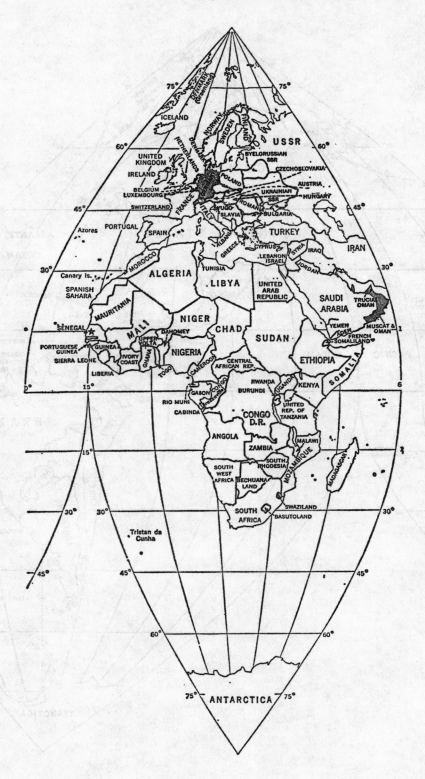

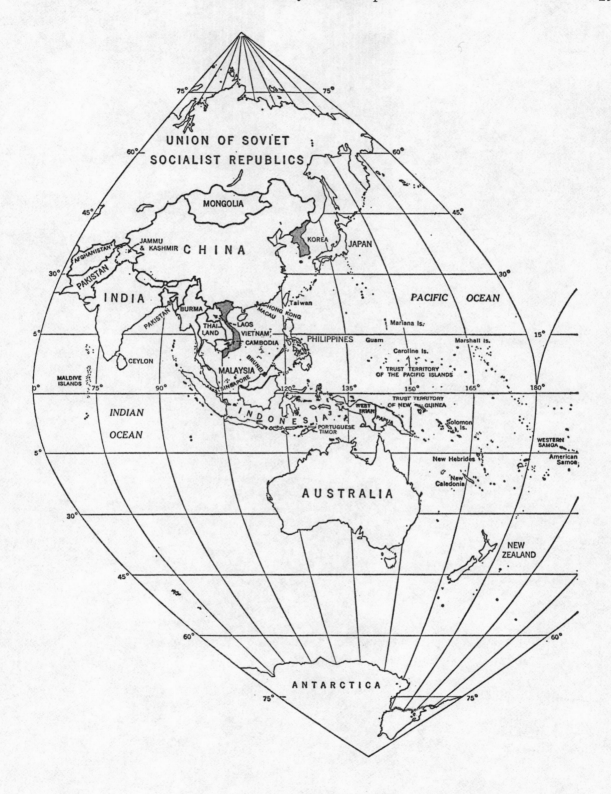

SECTION III

CHAPTER ONE

THE EVOLUTION OF CIVILIZED MAN

HISTORICAL RECORDS

Much of history is the story of what *probably* happened in the remote and more recent past. The qualification "probably" is emphasized because history is based upon **records** which require **interpretation**; interpretation can serve too many masters, unfortunately. Records are broadly of two kinds—**material remains** and **written accounts.** Prior to 5,000 years ago, the records of history are exclusively material—fossils, tools, graves, myth and ritual, art-works, and the like. Such remains will suggest, even to an untrained eye, that the men who left them behind pursued a definite way of life and held some system of beliefs by which they guided their lives. Obviously, the exact nature of the modes of life and thought in pre-historic cultures may never be known as more than scientific deductions and informed guesses based upon prevailing assumptions. Difficulties in the writing of an accurate world history, therefore, abound. Over the years, however, palaeontologists, geologists, archaeologists, biologists and anthropologists have been perfecting the science of inference from material and written records and have provided the historian with an agreed-upon framework of the past development of mankind—however much they differ on the details.

EVOLUTIONARY BACKGROUNDS

The Nature of Man. The cooperation of many scientists was required to locate Man's first appearance on earth and to account for his early development. **Geologists,** studying rock strata, were able to divide earth-history into six eras and to associate with each era some organic, fossilized remains. Man's first remains were then located in the last of these eras. **Palaeontologists** and **physical anthropologists** analyzed these remains of human types, dated them, and arranged them in a series of developments from proto-human (that is, nearly human) to completely human species. They were assisted in this task of arrangement by the **biologists** who provided them with an **evolutionary** scheme of development. Through heredity, variation of

type, overproduction of individuals, struggle for existence and natural selection by survival of the fittest, man developed from a relatively simple and generalized animal to a complex and specialized one. In this process, man retained many links to his animal past and these were evident in his skeletal arrangement, and his processes of nutrition, reproduction, chemistry, neural activity, and so on. His closest relationship was to the primates since both he and they have long embryonic periods, placental and suckling traits, long infancies and similar structural configurations like specialized front legs, five-digited hands with opposable thumbs, stereoscopic vision, furrowed and convoluted cerebrums. But though related to the primates, man was not himself one of them. He was genus—*homo*, class—*mammalia*, family—*hominidae* and species—*sapiens.*

Differentiation of genus—homo. Scientists believe that man-kind descended from the trees during the last climax on earth of mountain building and decreasing temperature and became ground-dwellers and meat-eaters. This event was followed by physical adaptations in man's bodily structure; other adaptations followed upon challenges produced by the glacial periods and by competition with other carnivores for a limited food supply. When the adaptations were completed, humanoids had developed an erect posture, bipedal gait, manual dexterity, increased brain size, a complex nervous system and an expanded vocal power. Brain power and vocal power combined to produce speech; speech, in turn, fed back into the brain selective, abstract and creative thought. Thought-power improved memory and imagination and increased man's capacities for social cooperation and the transmission of culture. If man was still an animal, he was certainly the highest type existing or known to have existed.

Extinct Species. Modern man is the direct descendent of **Cro-Magnon,** a species that appeared some 30,000 years ago. In the course of a million years, the struggle for existence had caused all species of proto-humans to become extinct. Knowledge of these proto-humans is derived from a scattered and fragmentary collection of fossil remains—odds-and-ends of teeth, skulls, jaw-bones, skeletons, foot-prints, etc. Expert **anatomists**, however, can reconstruct whole bodies from these fragments. Thus, they have found that the older the specimen, the closer it is to an apelike appearance—absence of forehead and chin, and presence of prognathous jaw, prominent supraorbital ridges, taurodontism (oversized teeth) and small cranial capacity. The human species developed from the most apelike **Java** and **Peking** men (ca. 750,000 years ago) to the less apelike **Heidelberg** and **Neanderthal** men (ca. 100,000-50,000 B.C.) and finally to the un-ape-like homo sapiens, Cro-Magnon. Since Cro-Magnon only one biological change has occurred, the differentiation of man into races. **"Race" is determined by measurements of skin coloration, hair forms, skull shapes or cephalic indexes, and gnathic or jaw formations.** These measurements are accurate for the *extremes* of racial types only. On the basis of these extremes, scientists classify racial groups as **Caucasian, Mongoloid, Negroid,** etc. But classification is useless for reason of the infinite gradations between the extremes which resulted from the free intermixture of peoples throughout history.

CULTURE AND CIVILIZATION

Only man is capable of producing a culture and his history is inseparable from it. **Culture (in the broadest sense of the term) is the whole of social experience—the knowledges, technics, moral codes, customs and traditions that are transmitted by human groups from generation to generation. Each social group has a unique culture, but cultural anthropologists do distinguish these common elements in culture: the basic patterns are stable but with the years change in details; culture is conservative in its ends, but flexible in its means; it is greater and more enduring than any individual within it, but is realized only through individuals; and it is transmitted by symbols in the form of language, myth, art, religion, etc.** When does a "culture" become a "civilization"? The answer to this question is quantitative. **Culture becomes civilization when it produces an economic surplus, develops mastery over the environment, and has a relatively complex economic organization, a class-system, urban communities, recognized government, systematized law, a form of writing and elevated thought and esthetic patterns.**
Tool Culture. Cultural anthropologists have learned to make a virtue of necessity. The most

numerous material remains of prehistoric **cultures** are the tools and weapons that prevailed. Considerable information about a culture **can** be derived from a tool. Nor can the importance **of** the tool in man's development be underestimated. It sharpened his cortico-motor reflexes, developed his sense of spatial relationships, increased his creative powers, extended his muscle power, introduced his first concepts of the possible mechanization of work, expanded his speech powers in order to transmit the tool-heritage and began the important process of division of labor and specialization of work. That this is no exaggeration can be judged by examining the importance of the tool or machine in our own civilization.

THE AGES OF MAN

Tools provide us with the basis for periodizing the cultural history of mankind.
The Eolithic or Dawn Stone Age. The **Eolithic** or Dawn Stone Age covered the first half million years of proto-human history. It was the time of Java or Peking Man. Its primary tool and weapon was a multiple-purpose ealith (a stone shaped by nature and unaltered by man) which fitted the hand and could be used to stab, cut or hack. In these first days the economy was **collectional**—the gathering of berries, roots, small animals and larvae for food. There is some evidence that spoken language and control of fire appeared at the end of Eolithic—but this is not certain. Nor is there any certainty about the grouping of men. It is assumed that the family was the basic unit of social organization and that kinship groups roamed as hunting packs or herds under the leadership of the strongest and craftiest. Nothing at all is known of the clothing or type of habitation used for shelter.
The Paleolithic or Old Stone Age. Since the **Paleolithic** or the Old Stone Age extended from ca. 500,000 B.C. to 10,000 B.C., and since material remains increase abundantly as times become more recent, it has been necessary to divide Paleolithic into **Upper** which ends about 130,000 B.C., **Middle** which ends about 70,000 B.C. and **Lower** which brought the age to an end about 10,000 B.C. While Java and Peking men may have continued on from Eolithic into Paleolithic, the epoch is predominantly that of Heidelberg and Neanderthal and Cro-Magnon men. Spurred by economic and defense needs, Paleolithic men invented the **manufactured tool.** Two types of stone-tool "industries" flourished during Lower and Middle Paleolithic—the "core" and

the "flake." Core tools were produced by knocking chips off a large lump of flint or volcanic glass until it was reduced to a standard form, the *coup de poing* or "fist-hatchet." Flakes were produced by the Levalloisian technique: the shape of the tool desired was etched on the core; then, by either percussion or spatula-pressure, a flake was detached; the detached pieces were then shaped to desired sharpness by chipping. Earliest Paleolithic tools were undifferentiated. Over the years, however, the core tool became a primary one, that is, designed to produce secondary or specialized tools for perforating, chopping, cutting, scraping or sawing. By the time of Upper Paleolithic, highly specialized tools appeared and took the forms of bone needles, harpoons, pronged fishhooks, dart-throwers and bows and arrows.

Advances. Tooling revolutionized the food industry of primitive men. The mode of economy now became that of fishing and hunting. The fist-hatchet made the stalking and capture of animals safer and more certain. With the invention of the sling, the dart and the bow and arrow, man could capture animals at a distance; he was now provided with a relatively permanent food supply. With the further invention of the harpoon and fishhook, an increase in the food supply took place. Mastery of fire, moreover, gave Paleolithic men a varied food diet—as well as defense, heat and light. Now began an increase in creature comforts. Paleolithic men donned sewn clothing made from animal skins; they initiated the permanent residence, first in caves and then in crudely constructed shelters; and their men and women began to ornament themselves with beads, necklaces and pendants.

Cultural Advances. During Paleolithic, the family grouping of men expanded into larger kinship groups tracing their origin, either matri- or patrilinearly, from a common ancestor. Out of this kinship grouping came the first cultural institutions—economic, political, educational and religious. Men assumed all the duties of the hunt; women concerned themselves with the collectional and household manufacturing activities. Government was probably concerned with the maintenance of internal peace; and the mightiest hunters and the older men probably arbitrated conflicts, enforced taboos and distributed food equitably. Protection of the hunting lands turned the hunters, on occasion, into warriors. All strangers were, therefore, suspect. But good relations existed among neighboring groups of necessity. Often flint supplies gave out and had to be secured outside the locality by trade; or animals were forced by sudden climatic change to new grazing lands; or population decline caused by an imbalance of males and females may have threatened the survival of the group.

Education was for individual survival. Until puberty the child's education was in the hands of the women of the family. Thereafter, men took over the boy's training. He now underwent a severe initiation which included fasting, keeping long vigils and even mutilation; he was instructed in proper behavior to people and to things in the world about him; finally, he was taught to hunt safely and efficiently. Religious guidance was fundamental to the education of both girls and boys for there were many prescriptions and proscriptions to be heeded. Remains of burial and funerary practices make clear that late in Paleolithic men began to experience religious thought and feeling. It would seem that their religious outlook included concepts of a soul or spirit belonging to each individual, and of its persistence after death. Natural forces were regarded as being motivated by a mysterious, supernatural power or "mana." Later this undifferentiated supernatural force took the shape of spirits or ghosts present unseen, everywhere, and in all things in the universe (**animism**). These spirits or ghosts were capable, as was perfectly obvious from the great insecurity in which men lived, of inflicting great harm unless propitiated. To placate these unseen powers, paleolithic men introduced religious rites. They carved female figurines as symbols of fertility with exaggerated sexual organs and worshipped them. They invented sympathetic magic or the practice of destroying an enemy by first mutilating his spirit resident in some effigy of him. They warded off evil by wearing amulets and talismans of beads or pendants. Finally, they created a class of professional religious practitioners called **shamans** who were possessed of powers of healing, divining and casting magical spells.

Though he accepted fully a supernatural explanation of the world of nature, paleolithic man was a close observer of things that mattered most to him. This was evident in his art work. For example, on the walls of caves he carved and painted reproductions of the animals which his band hunted—bison, mammoth, stags, reindeer, wolves. The realism, the naturalistic modeling, the use of light and dark masses, the employment of harmonious or agitated rhythms, the rigorous attention to detail, the ability to suppress detail to create a center of interest, the accuracy and sureness of drawing, the arresting of movement and action, the use of polychromatic effects—any or all of these characteristics of Cro-Magnon art establish the paleolithic artist as a very accomplished one. Nor was his skill limited to murals. He decorated his tools with small sculptures that never interfered with the function of the tool and made etchings that again illustrate his sense of realistic design. Paleolithic art was unquestionably functional in that it served the purposes of sympathetic magic; it was a form of religious ritual. But its esthetic values are timeless and universal.

The Neolithic or New Stone Age. Neolithic men exhausted the possibilities of stone technology. Since surface flint deposits were nearly depleted by 10,000 B.C., a mining industry was begun. Shafts were sunk and chalk veins were tapped with deer-horn picks for the flint they might yield. When required, Neolithic men burrowed long transverse tunnels in their mine pits. All tools were highly specialized now. In addition they were smoothed down to fine cutting edges on whetstones. Handles were attached to all chopping tools and they assumed distinctively modern appearances.

Toolmaking did not account for the profound revolution which occured during the Neolithic Age. Discovery of agriculture and the domestication of animals did. When or how these two epoch-making discoveries took place is not known. There is some evidence for the prevailing belief that women first hit upon the art of cultivation; for many years it was they who farmed the land with picks, digging sticks and hoes while the men continued to hunt and fish. Domestication of animals lessened the need to hunt and fish and permitted the man to settle down as a cultivator.

What were the effects of this agricultural revolution? Permanent settlements along river valleys made their appearance; men experimented with new forms of durable housing—mud and thatch affairs or lake dwellings on high piles. Diets were enriched with large varieties of grains, fruits and vegetables; where rivers overflowed, large scale drainage and irrigation projects were begun; grain surpluses led to increased trade and this, in turn, effected a revolution in transportation on land and water—the wheeled vehicle and the sail were invented. Mankind developed new, civilized habits—a sense of property ownership, patience, industry and planning; soil-rootedness made him conscious of the seasons and the stars; new scientific curiosities led him to inventions such as pottery (for storage and cooking purposes) from baked clay, stone mills to grind grain, etc.

Animals continued, of course, to serve as sources of food, but they also provided man with a new source of motive power, new supplies of raw materials for textiles and a new means of transportation. Because of the availability of animals, plows and wheeled carts were invented; the textile industries of spinning and weaving took root. Civilization, clearly, was beginning to take shape.

Social reorganization followed upon economic revolution. Population increased rapidly and lived longer as the result of more abundant and more reliable food supplies. Though kinship grouping persisted in Neolithic times, it had become a fiction; the reality was the large tribe centered in a fixed locality. Tribal organization took on concrete form. Members of the tribe delegated to either strong men or elders authority to adjudicate an increasing number of disputes over property rights, to interpret tradition in changing circumstances, to defend the village against raids by hungry nomads, etc. This delegation of authority was the rudiment of formal government. Near the end of Neolithic times, representative governments gave way to absolute monarchies, out of necessity. An increase in the number, intensity and dire consequences of war was directly responsible. A lost war resulted in either annihilation, dispersal, subjugation or slavery. To prevent this, Neolithic groups submitted themselves to the authoritative leadership of war-chiefs.

Neolithic men carried religious belief forward from its state of a generalized animism to that of **polytheism.** The vague spirits of Paleolithic belief now became numerous specific gods possessing immortal but human or anthropomorphic personalities. These gods resided in stones, animals, springs, trees, caves and mountains. Methods for appeasing angry gods proliferated and took the forms of human sacrifice, animal slaughter, self-mutilation or torture, sacramental sexual relations or ritual cannibalism. Belief in an after-life also grew more concrete. Burials as a result became more elaborate: chambered tombs were constructed above the graves; into the tombs were piled furniture, weapons, clothing and food for the spirit of the departed. The first form of temple worship was that of worship at monumental stone structures—dolmens or trilithons (two upright stones with a covering slab, post-and-lintel style); or just megaliths, tremendous stones set individually in long rows (some were 70 feet high!); or cromlechs, like the famous one at Stonehenge, England, combining dolmens and megaliths in a circle.

Art declined during the Neolithic Age. Naturalism disappeared and was replaced by abstract representations of concentric lines, zigzags, spirals, dots and chevrons which were scratched or painted as decorative motifs on pottery.

ANCIENT EGYPT

The Land. As history recedes into the remoter past, geography emerges as a dominating, if not quite the dominant, factor. Ancient Egypt was, to a considerable extent, the product of a river, cataracts, delta and desert. "Egypt," said the Greek historian, HERODOTUS, "is the gift of a river." It lay along the Nile and annually that river overflowed to provide Egypt with the only moisture it had and with rich deposits of alluvial soil. Egypt proved equal to the challenge and evolved political, economic and social institutions that enabled her to capture, store and distribute the floodwaters. Canals, dikes and reservoirs appeared early in the history of civilization. The cataracts were in the southern Nilotic waters and created a natural boundary there which acted as a barrier both to expansion and invasion. The desert, too, was a formidable barrier. Geography kept Egypt at peace for centuries. The mouth of the Nile spread into a fertile delta; this region made Egypt the granary of the ancient world and gave her a valuable trading link to the Mediterranean world when she finally emerged from her isolation.

Predynastic Egypt. No written records exist from the period prior to the first families of **pharaohs** (called **dynasties**). Excavations reveal, however, that predynastic Egyptians had made important strides toward civilization. Stone was being abandoned for copper, and Egyptians had already mastered the art of smelting and casting this metal. As a people, the Egyptians were racially mixed, lived in villages as farmers and animal herders, fashioned stone, wood and copper tools, decorated pottery and wove linen goods. They had reclaimed swamplands and had begun local irrigation projects. Political units called **nomes** existed and were ruled by local nomarchs. Powerful nomarchs had effected early union of Upper and Lower Egypt. Some form of preternatural belief existed, for the dead were buried in graves along with their implements and with symbolic figurines.

THE DYNASTIC PERIOD

Sources. Our knowledge of civilized Egypt comes in part from the histories of HERODOTUS who collected legends about Egypt in the fifth century B.C.; from MANETHO, an Egyptian priest of the third century B.C. who drew up lists of pharaohs; and from Romans like DIODORUS, STRABO and PLUTARCH. But these are secondary to the original writings of the Egyptians themselves in the forms of papyri or written scrolls and inscriptions on the walls of pyramids, temples, stelae or stone slabs, etc. Egyptian writing was either in a formal priestly script called **hieroglyphic**, a cursive business script called **hieratic** or a common script called **demotic.** Like other forms of ancient writing, the Egyptian form had passed through the stages of purely pictorial, conventional syllabic and pure syllabic or phonetic writing. In the latter case, an alphabet of 24 signs was evolved—the first in history, but not widely used. Inks, pens and paper were in widespread use. All these written materials, however, were of little use to the Egyptologist until JEAN FRANCIS CHAMPOLLION, after a decade of relentless effort, deciphered the Egyptian language (1822 A.D.). He used for this purpose the **Rosetta Stone** found during Napoleon's invasion of Egypt (1799)—a slab containing an inscription in three languages, hieroglyphic, demotic and Greek. His decipherment founded the **science of Egyptology.** Besides original writing there were many material remains unearthed by the archaeologists—painted reliefs inside the pyramids, temples, mummies, tools, arms, ornaments, furniture, sculpture, in great profusion, for the cold tombs and hot sands were both excellent preservers.

"Menes." Civilized Egyptians left behind no exact chronology since they began their dating anew with each pharaoh's reign. They had a solar calendar of 365 days and occasionally made records of the pharaohs in a dynasty and the dates of their administrations. From these fragments Egyptologists feel fairly certain that the first dynasty of a united Egypt appeared about 3400 B.C. Its founder, and the uniter of Egypt, was the (as yet) legendary MENES. His dynasty and the five that followed constitute in Egyptian history the period of the **Old Kingdom** (ca. 3400-2400).

The Old Kingdom. During the first two dynasties the pharaohs established a centralized authority with themselves as rulers by divine right. Tasks of administration were delegated to an efficient bureaucracy of viziers, superintendents of public works, official scribes or record-keepers and tax collectors. People were divided into classes with priests and nobles in the upper groups. During the third dynasty, the pharaohs moved from the south to the lower edge of the delta at Memphis. One of them, ZOZER, had a step-pyramid built as a tomb for himself. The great pyramid builders, however, followed in the fourth dynasty. KHUFU or CHEOPS, KHAFRE and MENKAURE (beginning about 2900 B.C.) constructed monumental pyramids for themselves at Gizeh—where they still stand. Khufu's tomb embraced 25,000,000 cubic feet; it had no less than 2,000,000 stone blocks each weighing two tons. The labor involved in constructing these massive tombs cannot be estimated. Historians are beginning to reject the theory that the pyramids were built by forced labor. They now feel that the size of the tomb attests to the importance which the body of the pharaoh had in the public mind; those who built the pyramids, it is now held, did so as an act of piety designed to win prosperity from reluctant gods. Pyramid building declined as the power of the pharaohs decreased during the fifth and sixth dynasties. What brought on this decline at the end of a millenium of prosperous rule is not known. Perhaps it was due to the fact that Egypt, which had maintained isolation for so long (except for mining exploits on the peninsular of Sinai and trading ventures into Nubia for gold and silver), now began to make expansionist thrusts north and southward. Foreign adventures invited counter-invasion; invasion precipitated the disintegration of pharaonic control. At the end of the sixth dynasty a kind of feudalism settled over the land during which the power of the local, hereditary nomarch and priest was greater than that of the pharaoh. There are indications, too, of large-scale social revolutions among the lower-class *fellahin*. With political disruption records disappeared and Egypt entered into a "dark age" that lasted for about 400 years.

The Middle Kingdom (ca. 2060-1788). Egypt emerged into the light of recorded history again during the twelfth dynasty when AMENEMHET I effectively curbed the provincial nomarchs and reunited the land with a new assertion of divine pharaonic power. Amenemhet, it seems, reshuffled the class structure to eliminate his feudal enemies by opening the bureaucracy to men of talent instead of men of rank. To crush the power of the feudalized priesthood, he "democratized" religion—as we shall see later. His despotism was benevolent in that he encouraged large scale engineering and architectural works. He made peace with his neighbors. The period of prosperity, begun under Amenemhet I, continued for a brief 200 years. It was ruptured by a resurgence of internal disorder and an invasion by a barbaric foe. Over the borders of Egypt came the Hyksos, a Semitic-speaking tribe, who possessed an absolute weapon in the form of a horse—an animal heretofore unknown in Egypt. The barbarians were able to occupy Egypt for two centuries before they were driven out. Not until 1580 B.C. did the Egyptian, AHMOSE I, begin the reconquest of Egypt for the Egyptians.

The New Kingdom or Empire. Imperialism dominated the last phase of Egyptian independence. AMENOPHIS I and THUTHMOSE I, of the 18th dynasty, fought their conquering way northward up to the Euphrates River. From 1520 to 1480 B.C. there was an interim while HATSHEPSUT, the first woman ruler in the civilized world, converted these imperialist gains into a new domestic prosperity. With THUTHMOSE III Egypt made her widest imperialist expansion and created thereby the world's first empire. The vast booty, tribute and "gifts" collected made possible now a brilliant display of new temples and palaces. For the first time in Egyptian history, a professional standing army appeared and along with it, a military caste. Demands for an enlarged bureaucracy created a new middle-class of scribes and petty officials. Wealth overflowed, too, into the coffers of the priests, who rose in political power. Imperialism and ill-gotten gain carried within themselves the seeds of Egypt's final decline. Defeated enemies recouped and pressed hard on the frontier posts; defense needs drained the treasury; wealth and luxury made Egypt's ruling classes effete and they began to rely upon foreign mercenaries for their defense; as slavery and other forms of bondage increased, the gulf between rich and poor, always wide, became impassable. Steadily the priesthood grew more arrogant. Religious civil war was inaugurated when AMENHOTEP IV or IKHNATON tried to curb the power of the priests. He instituted a brief period of monotheistic worship of the sun but his son, TUTANKHAMEN, restored old forms of worship when IKHNATON died. Egypt momentarily regained eminence under RAMSES II and RAMSES III; they held off their enemies; built more splendid palaces; and crushed the fellahin with new tax burdens. With the death of RAMSES III (1167 B.C.) the priests again assumed command in Egypt; organized government disappeared. Defense of the land became more and more difficult. In 670 B.C. ESARHADDON, the Assyrian, invaded Egypt and so weakened the theocracy that it survived for only 145 years thereafter. In 525 B.C. CAMBYSES, the Persian, conquered Egypt; for the next 2500 years Egypt was to be a subjugated state.

EGYPTIAN RELIGION

The almost incredible stability of Egyptian society and government over a period of three thousand years can best be accounted for by their religious beliefs.

The Ascendancy of Ra. During the Old Kingdom, religion was all-encompassing: pharaohs were gods and their palaces were temples; pyramid building was a devotional act; literature was limited to spell and incantation to be recited in temple and tomb; science was temple-lore; spirits governed the acts and thoughts of men; and great portions of the economy were drained for the support of institutionalized worship. A complex polytheism featured this religion. There were household, tribal and political divinities; only a few were worshiped in common throughout the land. One god might appear in many forms. Gods existed to represent creation, birth, death, wisdom, evil and the like; others presided over human skills like language, letters, numbers arts. Moreover, gods were closely associated with animals of all kinds—lions, hawks, bulls, cobras, rams, pigs, dogs, cats, ibises and jackals, to cite but a few.

Man himself was conceived as possessing—besides his *khat* or body—a spiritual *ren* or name, a *khaibut* or shadow, and *ab* or heart, a *ka* or double and a *ba* or resurrected self. Because these spiritual selves related to each man had independent existences, they could work great harm to their possessors unless placated. Magic spells, therefore, had to be invoked to destroy their evil potencies. The *ka*, for example, lived on after death but continued to function as it did in life. Therefore, it must be fed, watered, kept from loneliness, and so on. That is why Egyptians crammed their tombs with provisions and implements and lined their walls with frescoes reproducing the environment in which the dead man had lived. Mummification to preserve the body was intended to provide a resting place for all of man's enduring spiritual substances. At first it was only the pharaoh, the physical embodiment of the sun-god **Ra,** who was mummified; only he was entitled to immortality. To preserve his blood uncontaminated, he usually married his sister. This man's immortality was of benefit to the whole nation; the resurrected pharaoh would prevent famine, drought and destruction. The pyramid was built out of religious passion to ease the passage of the pharaoh's soul to heaven; it was also an investment in national prosperity. Safe-passage to immortality was

also secured by the use of magical formulae which were inscribed on the walls of tombs, on sarcophagi or on papyrus rolls deposited inside the coffins. If all were properly done, then all would go well with the nation. Obviously, the Egyptian faith did not contain an ethical foundation. Instead Egyptians believed that from the mouth of Ptah there had once issued an established order called *Ma'at,* an order stressing legality, correctness, justice, truth or righteousness, an order binding on pharaoh and fellahin alike. (Ma'at was later personified as a goddess or as a feather against which one's soul would be weighed in a last judgment.) During the Old Kingdom the pharaoh, Ra-on-Earth, was the source of Ma'at and therefore his every pronouncement had to be obeyed if evil and disorder were to be avoided. Thus the popular acceptance of Ma'at not only made the pharaoh the most absolute monarch of all history, but fastened upon the Egyptian mind a rigid conservatism and traditionalism that gave society its incredible stability.

The Rise of Osiris. With the collapse of the Old Kingdom, religion was "democratized" and the cult of Osiris, which was subordinate to Ra during the Old Kingdom, came to the fore. Osiris was a vegetation god who, through his union with his sister Isis, provided the Nile lands with fertility, with birth and rebirth. Set, his brother, and a prince of darkness, slew Osiris. Isis, after a tragic search, found her husband-brother's body and by copulating with its spirit conceived and bore Horus. Horus destroyed Set and a resurrected Osiris became lord of the kingdom of the dead. Through Horus (the pharaoh) on earth and through Osiris after death everyman could now attain to immortality. The hereafter was thus democratized. The idea of heavenly paradise was now elaborated. In reality it was no more than an improved extension of earthly bliss, a land where wheat grew to three cubits' height, hunger was unknown and there were shade trees; a land where fellahin had servants. The way to paradise, however, was filled with countless obstacles—an unknown terrain, terrifying animals, threats of suffocation, lack of means of transport and the like. The so-called "Book of the Dead" (better translated as "Coming Forth into the Day"), which consisted of numerous scrolls originating in the Old Kingdom, was now expanded to eliminate threats to the souls of the dead. It contained spells and incantations invoking the protection of Ra and Osiris, providing the means for eluding the crocodile, serpent, lynx and beetle, keeping the soul from a second death, and supplying it with maps to the terrain, sailboats, ladders, etc., to enable it to arrive at the seat of the last judgment. At the end of this journey, the soul came into the presence of Osiris for a weighing. It was placed on a scale against a feather representing the truth or Ma'at. Prior to this weighing the soul had offered a "negative confession," a series of 42 denials. For example, it asserted

> "I have not done iniquity."
> "I have not committed robbery with violence."
> "I have done violence to no man."
> "I have not committed theft."

and so on through all 42 transgressions. This was a magic ritual to forestall the inquisitive deity.

Religious Revolt and Decline. With increased material prosperity during the Empire Period, the pharaohs were once again able to advance the sun-god concept; this time in the form of Amon-Ra. Suffering terribly from the expense of imperialism, their way to immortality blocked by this new assertion of the priority of pharaonic divinity, the people resorted to gross superstition and their religion became almost exclusively magical. Greedy priests fostered this decline through the wide sale of magical papyri and through encouragement of a growing movement to mummify animals—at a fee, of course, for appropriate "religious" rites. This decline into superstition brought about the attempted reformation of Amenhotep IV. He replaced Amon-Ra by Aton—symbolized in the sun-disk. Aton was the one true god speaking through the pharaoh to re-establish Ma'at in the land. In Aton, Egyptian worship approached monotheism. Amenhotep changed his name to Ikhnaton, established a new capital at Akhetaton, and drove the priests of Amon from the temples. But the new faith failed. It had no popular, ethical base, no promise of redemption; it was coldly intellectual and produced brilliant hymns, but few followers. Ikhnaton's successor, Tutankhamen, restored the priesthood and the worship of Amon-Ra. Ikhnaton's was the last creative spark in the Egyptian faith; thereafter, it declined into a hopeless, pessimistic antiquarianism—a religion fit for slaves and their rulers.

Egyptian Society. Early in Egyptian history the people were differentiated into classes. The royalty, court, landed nobility and priests were a leisured group, divorced from labor and devoted to the task of maintaining their social position in grand style. It was they who fostered the art and architecture of ancient Egypt and provided it with its military cadres and leadership. Below them in the social scale was a wide independent middle class composed of merchants, artisans, bureaucrats, independent farmers, overseers and the like. This group served the pharaohs, particularly those of the Middle Kingdom, as a counterweight to aggressive, feudal nobility and priests. The lowliest were the serfs and slaves attached to soil or master and completely unprivileged. This class division, however, did not freeze into a caste system as it did in India. There was considerable movement in and out of classes over the three-thousand years of Egyptian existence; dominant groups varied in different periods of Egyptian history. Indicative of the flexibility of the social structure was the high position accorded women in Egyptian society. Several queens ruled Egypt; property was inherited through the mother; and all free women were permitted to own and inherit property. However, while individuals moved from one step of the ladder to another, the broad threefold division of Egyptian social existence characterized all of Egyptian history. Ma'at frowned upon social upheaval. Nor did the Egyptian economy encourage it.

Egyptian Economic Life. Agricultural societies incline to be static and conservative, and agriculture was the basis for Egyptian prosperity. Methods and tools for cultivation were extremely crude; nonetheless, Egyptian farmers produced a wide variety of crops and animals and a large exportable surplus. Pharaoh and priest regulated all agricultural production. The pharaoh was responsible for large scale irrigation and reclamation projects, for improving trade lanes and for collecting and distributing surpluses. Planting and harvesting were directed by the priests according to divine revelation—and a keen understanding of nature. Thus the excellent Sothic calendar of the Egyptians (based on careful observation of the movements of the "dog-star" Sirius) was devised to predict the inundation of the Nile; geometry was developed to redistribute the lands after the floods; a "Suez Canal" was dug to facilitate grain shipments, etc. Commerce was secondary to agriculture. It was utilized by the pharaohs to supplement the absence in Egypt of timber, spices, dyes, copper and the like, or to secure luxury articles like Syrian cloth, Aegean pottery or Phoenician weapons. Commerce was regulated; naval patrols protected the trade lanes; and tariffs were collected at all ports of entry. Into the export trade entered Egyptian manufactured goods. Surpluses of metalwork, carpentry, textiles and pottery were produced by independent and enslaved craftsmen who were masters with stone, copper, bronze and wood tools in the forms of sledges, drills, saws, hammers, rollers, etc. They were sold to and disposed of by a free merchant class or by the pharaoh himself. However, neither the merchants nor the craftsmen were able to break the grip which both agriculture and pharaonic control had upon the economy. Because Egypt never became a commercial state, the limits of her progress were narrowly confined.

PRACTICAL AND PURE SCIENCE

Engineering. Egyptian engineering was one of the great achievements of the ancient world. Pyramid building required minute land-surveying and leveling, geometric exactitude, precision stone drilling and solution of the problems of hauling, transport and lifting of 2½ ton stone blocks. Irrigation required the construction of hundreds of miles of dikes, the building of storage basins, timing the cutting of dikes with the rate of flow of the floodwaters. River navigation prompted canal building to eliminate the obstruction created by the cataracts on the south and the land bridge in the north. While the southern Nile canal was only 260 feet long, the forerunner of the Suez Canal extended for 100 miles. Metallurgical engineering was well advanced—the basic ores of gold, silver, copper, mercury, lead and tin were mined; smelting processes perfected; and the use of alloys widened to secure effective hardening.

Astronomy. Egyptian astronomy was functional, not abstract. It was fostered because it enabled the Nile River superintendents to predict with some accuracy the coming of the floods. Early in Egyptian history, the Nile rising was linked with Sirius and on the basis of the movements of Sirius—as well as those of the sun—the Egyptian calendar was constructed. This calendar had a 24-hour day, a 7-day week, 12 months of 30 days and 5 feast-days at the end of the year to make a solar year of 365 days. The astronomical solar year was slighly longer than 365 days; therefore with time, the calendar and the Nile rising failed to coincide. Egyptians noted this and noted too that after a "Sothic" cycle of 1458 years the beginning of the year returned to its original position. This was a remarkable observation and highly indicative of the Egyptian "time-sense." That they were a very time-conscious people is evident also in the wide variety of "clocks" that they used: shadow-clocks like sun-dials and obelisks, and clepsydras or water-clocks. In spite of these

achievements, the Egyptians did not develop a science of astronomy; they knew the stars moved in certain directions, they knew about eclipses—but had no explanation for these phenomena beyond the mysterious actions of sky-spirits.

Mathematics. In this field, too, the Egyptians made some cogent observations, developed some interesting techniques—but failed utterly to produce a true mathematical science. In geometry they had operating formulas for the area and volume of elementary figures; they calculated the value of *pi* as 3.16; and achieved something of a wonder in working out the formula for the area of a truncated pyramid. In arithmetic, they could add and subtract whole numbers and used the same additive method to multiply and divide. They used a decimal system and an awkward method for the addition and subtraction of fractions. They were able to solve linear equations. Their system of notation was like the Roman and made large scale computation almost impossible. They were unable to divide and multiply by more than two and could not use a complex fraction. Their society failed to produce any abstract thought about the theory of numbers. Numbers, too, had magical properties and were the lore of magicians.

Cosmogony. Egyptians substituted fable for fact to explain the nature of the universe. The world was a rectangular box and the sky was supported by four mountains at the corners of a slightly concave earth. A river flowed under and around the earth and the Nile flowed out of it to bisect the earth. The sun was carried on a boat and appeared to cross the sky. The forces of nature were gods—and so on.

Medicine. Egyptians explored anatomy as thoroughly as any of the ancients; mummification is the proof. So, too, is the keenness with which they identified parts of the body, localized symptoms of disease and developed herbal lore. But their medicine was pure demonology. Disease was caused by entry into the body of evil spirits and it was the task of the physician to eliminate them by emetics and purges of the most brutal kind. Therefore, while the record gives an admirable account of their ability to set fractures and to do surface surgery, it cannot be said that they founded a science of medicine.

Why did science fail to develop in Egypt? The divine pharaonic state destroyed all individualism and experimentation; priests enforced the rigid conservatism of the order of Ma'at; scientific knowledge was held exclusively by a small group that converted it into secret lore to be transmitted from father to son; an agricultural economy did not encourage new ventures and fostered magical rites instead of experimental methods; and almost universal illiteracy created poverty of thought and a superstitious world-outlook.

EGYPTIAN ART

Characteristics. Artistic genius flourished in each of the main periods of Egyptian history. It was, however, a group-genius. The individual artist was submerged in the production of conventionalized art works which followed the canons and traditions first set down in the third millenium B.C. Tradition accorded primacy to architecture. Thus sculpture and painting were employed to adorn the walls of temples, tombs and palaces. An architectural spirit invaded the creation of such huge, solid sculptures as the Sphinx, the columns, the obelisks and the colossal statues of the pharaohs. Even the smallest figurine gave the impression of being a large-scale, monumental carving. Since monuments stress the eternal, architects and sculptors alike sought to eliminate all unessential details to capture the enduring likeness of things. Finally, art always was in the service of religion, no matter how secular the subject.

Architecture. Egyptian architecture took the forms of the tomb, the temple and the palace. Representative architecture in the Old Kingdom was the pyramid. Pyramids evolved out of *mastabas*, superstructures over graves. Mastabas had two rooms —a chapel for services to the *ka* and a cellar of a statue of the deceased. Mastaba walls were lined with painted reliefs reproducing the environment of the dead man. When mastabas of diminishing size were heaped one upon another, the step-pyramid, such as that of Zoser at Saqqara, was created. Now the original chapel and cellar were elaborated until they became temples, colonnaded halls, shrines, ceremonial courtyards and the like. In its final form— the pyramid— all of these tendencies were combined into a four-part architectural scheme: the pyramid itself consisting of the burial chamber, true and false chambers and shafts to permit the light of the dog-star and pole-star to enter the burial chamber; the chapel adjoining the pyramid on the east for offering and ceremonial; a covered causeway leading over the cliffs to the pyramid; and a "Valley-temple" the vestibule of the causeway. Guarding this complex of buildings was a great Sphinx, a portrait of the ruler with the body of a lion. The esthetic impact of the pyramid derived from its towering domination of the area, a domination achieved by the principle of contrast of the great height with the flat desert and the low-lying necropolises (cemeteries), of the smooth-faced, iridescent surface of the pyramid with the broken, granulated sands around it. It imposed on its viewers the sense of their own puniness in the face of the eternal; even Caesar and Napoleon were momentarily humbled before it.

Decline in pharaonic power during the Middle Kingdom promoted the construction of the tomb which consisted of chambers dug out of the hills facing the Nile. These excavations took on architectural form when their entrances were adorned with facades of columns, colossi and sphinxes and preceded with the usual complex of temples and gardens. The rock-tomb of Queen Hatshepsut at Deir-al-Bahar is an outstandingly beautiful example of this type of Egyptian architecture.

With the rise of the priesthood during the Empire Period, the temple became the primary architectural form. Those of Amon-Ra at Karnak and of Horus at Luxor are typical of temple style. The style is designated as **pylon**. In a typical pylon temple one proceeded from an avenue of recumbent animals past obelisks and colossi through a gate separating the pylons or facades of the structure into a colonnaded court. The court led to a roofed hypostyle hall (one with many huge columns and lit by light filtering through clerestory windows) and then to a low, dark sanctuary. The court was for assemblage of the masses, the hypostyle hall for a chosen few, and the sanctuary for the pharaoh alone. The temple itself was massive—every inch of wall space was consumed with painted bas-reliefs. Columns with lotus or papyrus capitals provided the main decorative motifs. While the overall design is plain post-and-lintel, Egyptian architects accasionally employed the arch as a substructure. Temples, then, were fit for a pharaoh; the word pharaoh itself means "great white house."

Sculpture. Characteristic of Egyptian sculpture was the colossal statue of the pharaoh—at times more than 60 feet high; theriomorphic portraiture, that is, human bodies with the heads of animals; wall reliefs combining intaglio or incision and cameo or low relief (this combined method is sometimes designated at **coelanaglyphic**); descriptive perspective in relief murals and free-standing statues, that is, each object was drawn from the perspective from which it could be most fully seen: thus, ponds were drawn as seen from above, trees and animals from the profile, the human figure—head from the profile, shoulders from the front, both feet from the inside etc.

The effect is one of motionless eternity. In the Egyptian language a sculptor was "He-who-keeps-alive." How Egyptian sculptors strove for eternal life can best be seen in their sculpted portraits. These fall somewhere between lifeless masks and naturalistic reproductions; there is life in the features but eternity in the abstract geometrical form.

"Minor Arts." Egyptian craftsmen strove for beauty in adornment. Elaborate design, rich color and exquisite workmanship characterized the rugs, tapestries, cushions, furniture, vases, vessels and bowls which adorned the homes of the wealthy. Out of gold, silver, carnelian, felspar, lapis lazuli and amethyst Egyptian jewelers carved remarkable pendants, rings, bracelets and mirrors. Music, too, had a rich development and composers had lutes, harps, sistrums (almost like castenets), flutes and lyres to work with.

Egyptian Philosophy. No record exists of systematic philosophizing by Egyptian thinkers. Senefru's Priest (ca. 2900 B.C.), Ptahhotep (ca. 2600 B.C.), Ipuwer (ca. 2000 B.C.) and the "Eloquent Peasant" (ca. 1800 B.C.) were, at best, practical or denunciatory moralists. They stressed **rules of conduct** which enforced the conservatism, the social status and principle of acceptance inherent in the philosophy of Ma'at; or they denounced the absence of these virtues during periods of public dissatisfaction. The ability of Egyptians to think abstractly was, apparently, confined to their religious theorizing.

CHAPTER TWO

THE LEGACY OF THE ANCIENT NEAR ORIENT

MESOPOTAMIA

The Land. Mesopotamia lay between two rivers, the **Tigris** and the **Euphrates.** In ancient days it was roughly divided by the 34th parallel—Assyria to the north and Babylonia to the south. Of the two, Babylonia was the richer for it lay in the "fertile crescent," an arc of soil extending from the Persian Gulf to the Mediterranean Sea and made productive by annual inundation of the twin rivers. Babylonia was itself divided into Akkad in the north and Sumer in the south. The first civilization in Mesopotamia was in Sumer on the delta, that is, amid the richest deposit of alluvial soil. To this extent, Mesopotamia paralleled Egypt. Unlike Egypt, however, there were no natural boundaries in Mesopotamia to protect it from inroads by neighboring barbaric tribes. Mesopotamia's open geography and her attractive wealth in the south made her a crossroad of conquerors and her tri-millenial history was the scene of the rise and fall of a large number of empires. In spite of this political turbulence, the first culture which arose, the **Sumerian,** imposed itself upon all the nations in the area.

SUMERIAN CIVILIZATION

Politics. Sumeria was a geographical expression rather than a political state. In reality there were a number of "city-states" there—Ur, Lagash, Kish, Sumer—each ruled by a *patesi* or priest-king who directed the worship, defense and engineering works of his tiny kingdom. Patesis built temples, maintained standing armies and organized irrigation projects. Little is known of these enterprising individuals beyond their names—Mesanni-padda of Ur, Mesilim of Kish, Ur-Nana of Lagash, Lugalzagizzi of Erech—and of their petty wars. Imperial possibilities in the Mesopotamian Valley were first probed by Sargon I, a usurper to the throne of Akkad. He reduced the cities in Babylonia to dependencies by conquest or threat of conquest. Then he turned northwestward and brought all of Syria under his aegis. This operation opened a number of protected trade routes leading to Babylonia and resulted in a sharp increase in the wealth of the empire. Sargon's grandson, Naram-Sin, extended the eastern frontiers of the empire. Conquest however, bred resistance and the weaker rulers that followed Naram-Sin were unable to hold back the Gutium, a barbaric tribe from the east. The Gutium ruled Sumeria for 125 years and were overthrown, finally, by Utu-hegal of Erech. A brief revival of Sumerian civilization followed and reached its height under Dungi (ca. 2150 B.C.). However, simultaneous blows by the Amorites from the west and the Elamites from the east destroyed the Sumerian civilization; it disappeared as a national entity.

Sumerian Religion. Mesopotamian religion was, for the most part, an elaboration or modification of the Sumerian faith. Sumerians worshipped many gods: An, god of heaven; Enlil, a wind-and-storm god; Enki, an earth-god; Ninhursag, a mountain-goddess; Shamash or Uti, a sun-god; Sin, a moon-god; Ishtar, a fertility goddess; Marduk, an agricultural-god; Tammuz, a pasture-god; Nergal, a hades-god, and so on. Most of these gods were associated with particular city-states, though they were worshipped "universally." Moreover, each individual had his mediating deity. Gods were conceived as immortal "super-men," an aristocracy that owned all the physical resources of Mesopotamia and ruled over the serfs working their estates. Gods were endowed with human passions; they were therefore unpredictably capricious and capable of good or evil—as the mood seized them. The Sumerian religion, in sum, was polytheistic, anthropomorphic and a personification of the forces of nature.

Man and the Gods. Man was closest to his personal god; and the relationship was that of child-parent. With the higher divinities, the relationship was that of lord-subject. Personal gods stood to higher divinities as mediators. Suffering, the Sumerians felt, proceeded from sin, and sin from the breaking of a taboo. A just man suffers because that which is good conduct to man may still be evil in the eyes of the gods. There were no absolute values to go by; one was completely dependent upon divine mercy and upon *proper* propitiation of one's personal god and *his* power to negotiate relief from suffering with the god who caused suffering. Religion was thus based upon the utter helplessness of men.

Priesthood. Gods ruled their estates and serfs through stewards or priests—a hereditary class that "supervised" the temple community. Priests were either magicians, soothsayers or singers who devoted their energies to satisfying the needs of the divine family which resided in the temple. They alone might anticipate the action of a god by the art of divination which consisted of interpreting the position of a sheep's liver, or bird-flights, or human dreams, or star-and-planetary positions, and the like. They alone could ward off evil by magical incantation and sacrificial rites. They also served as scribes, judges, teachers and physicians. Finally, they were charged with conducting periodic cult-festivals.

Life after Death. There was, for the believer, no substitute for superstition. Man was the last and most worthless spawn of creation; he was derived from Chaos and was formed specifically to relieve the gods of menial tasks. When men died they went to Aralu, a shadowy, dust-filled hole under the earth and became shades living in an eternal gloom. No reward or punishment awaited them in the hereafter.

Fatalism. This dreary faith forced men to accept their fate stoically, without protest or lamentation. The will of the gods was done—whatever man did. The best one could hope for was some slight success or happiness on earth. If one were keen and careful, one could outwit pain and evil and enjoy existence. Life had no moral bounds so long as one did not break the taboos. Pessimism and fatalism in religion bred hedonism, the pursuit of pleasure as an end-in-itself.

Sumerian Literature. Religion inspired Sumerian literature. Epic and liturgical hymn told stories of Creation, the Flood, ascents to heaven and descents to hell. The epic of Creation related the tale of Marduk's (Ea's) conquest of Tiamat and Apsu, the forces of Chaos, and the resulting creation of heaven, earth, the waters, vegetation, animal life and man. Parallels with the Old Testament *Genesis* are remarkably close. Close, too, is the tale of the Flood which appears in the Epic of Gilgamesh. In this tale Utnapishtim and his wife escape a deluge by building an ark and taking abroad two of every living thing. The flood abates on the seventh day and this Sumerian Noah sends forth a dove, a swallow and a raven to test for dry land. He disembarks when the raven fails to return. But the essence of Gilgamesh is not that of Genesis. In Genesis the Flood is a universal catastrophe and part of a divine plan of punishment and redemption; in Gilgamesh the Flood is provoked by divine jealousy for the achievements of man. Noah is spared for his righteousness; Utnapishtim, because he was lucky enough to be a favorite of the gods. Hope springs eternal in Genesis, but in all of the Gilgamesh the hero's quests are doomed to futility and frustration; his search for immortality ends when he learns that the hopelessness of life continues after death. The result was that while the Hebrews looked to their faith, the Sumerians had nothing to look to but whatever joys this life held.

Sumerian Art: Architecture. Serving the this-worldly emphasis of their religion, Sumerian architects concentrated upon palaces and temples rather than tombs. By the third millenium B.C. the main features of their architecture were fully developed. Palaces were elaborately planned—a series of rooms were grouped about three functional centers, each with its own courtyard: the **seraglio** or main quarters, the **harem** or family quarters and the **khan** or servants' quarters. Rooms were ceilinged by corbel-vaulting, a form of arch made by overlapping bricks. There were paneled walls, colonnades, and inlaid wall decoration of human and animal figures. Incorporated into the architectural complex were the temples. The characteristic temple-form was the ziggurat, a stepped or terraced tower crowned at the top with an unadorned shrine. This not only lifted the temple above the flood-line, but was symbolic of the abode of the gods on high.

Sculpture. Sumerian sculptors strove for realistic effects in their portraiture and treatment of flesh and muscle. This careful observation and recording of anatomy gave life to their treatment of animals of all kinds—eagles, ibexes, lions and lionesses. Workmanship on home and personal adornments rivaled that of the Egyptians for design, quality and color. In the art of engraving cylinder seals for personal use, they exceeded—indeed, influenced— the Egyptians.

Sumerian Science. Sumerian temples served as schools. Excavations reveal that students used tablets of soft clay for their lessons. They studied mathematics: multiplication, division and extraction of square and cube roots. This fact alone shows how much more advanced the Sumerians were than the Egyptians in the field of science. By 3000 B.C. the Sumerians had harnessed animals to plows, constructed wheel-draw vehicles, built ships and employed the potter's wheel in ceramics. By the same year they reached the peak in bronze-age metallurgy. Writing, too, advanced rapidly in Sumeria. Priests kept careful account of all the produce turned into the temple for the use of the god-landlords. They were forced to abandon the original picture-sign writing for ideograms based on phonetics. By 2500 B.C. the number of these ideograms had been simplified into combinations of wedge-shaped impressions, from which the cuneiform script evolved. Sumerians developed the first numeral system as well. This system was sexigesimal, that is, based on the number 60; signs for multiples of 60 were given value according to their place in a given number. Multiplication tables were drawn up for the use of mathematics in determining the areas of fields and volumes of solids. Their work with circles and cylinders, however, was weakened by their value of 3 for *pi*. In astronomy, the Sumerians constructed the 30-day month, the 24-hour day and the 60-second minute and 60-minute hour; they gave current names to constellations of stars; they made accurate records of star movements and fairly accurate predictions of astronomical events;

they noted uniformities in solar eclipses and deviations in lunar months. Despite these notable advances in scientific observations, the Sumerians, like the Egyptians, were unable to generalize their experiences into natural law.

THE BABYLONIANS

The Amorites who helped destroy the Sumerian civilization dominated Mesopotamia for three hundred years (ca. 1900-1600 B.C.). They ruled the land out of the city of Babylon. Complete conquest was not achieved until the rule of the sixth king of the first dynasty, HAMMURABI (ca. 1800 B.C.). Hammurabi realized that rule by the sword alone was not enough to consolidate an imperial domain. He therefore gathered existing laws into a unified code and then had them administered by judges closely supervised by his own advisers. This code had a profound effect upon the whole near-Orient world and bears some analysis. (After Hammurabi's death, however, the Babylonian state was weakened by a surprise attack made by the Hittites from Asia Minor. Before it could recover, horse-riding Kassites descended on Babylon and put an end to the Amorites as well as civilized progress for the next four hundred years.)

Foundations. Hammurabi's Code reveals that the Babylonians were the creators of the first great "business civilization." Walled cities were the centers of Babylonian activities. Each city had its own god and its terraced temple. The temple owned land, slaves, animals, and precious stones; it also served as a bank of deposit for the collective savings (the surplus production) of the people. The priest of the temple thus became a businessman and banker. Around the temple were clusters of houses made of sun-dried brick and inhabited by farmers and artisans. Agriculture formed the economic base of Babylonian civilization with production of barley, wheat, fruits, vegetables, cattle and sheep predominating. Artisans wove tapestries and rugs, and fashioned gold, silver and copper goods; they cut gems and manufactured textiles. The surplus of manufactures and agriculture spilled over into trade. Cities were themselves trading posts—depots for goods *en route* by boat or camel caravan eastward to India or China and westward to the Mediterranean lands. Out of this extensive trading grew business practices that were to have a tremendous impact upon future civilizations: legal partnerships, business letters, agreements, lawsuits, the lending of money at interest, precious metals as a standard of weight and measure, personal and real property.

rights represented in deeds, wills, leases, contracts and promissory notes, flood insurance and the like. Out of an attempt to regularize these and other practices came **Hammurabi's Code** (ca. 1680 B.C.).

Hammurabi's Code. Hammurabi's Code was more in the nature of a codification of existing law than an original formulation of law. It was an effort on Hammurabi's part to **unify** his expanding empire. It consisted of about 250 laws regulating property ownership, business practices, flood and agricultural controls, labor and family relations; it codified the criminal law and the law of equity or fair dealing.

Business. The Code regulated ownership and the leasing of land; it authorized legal partnerships; it punished severely dishonest practices; it permitted loans of grain and silver but limited interest to one-third the value of the grain and one-fifth the value of the silver; it protected farm tenants against crops destroyed by flood and against eviction before the termination of the contract; it specifically permitted women to own property, to manage shops and to engage in trade; it also fixed prices.

Labor. Apprenticeship rules were drawn up; wages were fixed; and fines and other punishments were decreed for bad workmanship.

Domestic Relations. Marriage was defined as a legal contract; if one partner broke the contract, the other could sue for violation of contract. Husbands could divorce wives who were undutiful by returning them to their families or by reducing them to the rank of servants; wives could similarly divorce their husbands for cause and take their dowries with them as they left. A man could sell his wife to discharge a debt. Adultery and sexual perversions were very severely punished.

Criminal Law. The *lex talionis* (an eye for an eye) and punishment according to social rank were the two fixed principles in the criminal law. For purposes of law, people were graded as nobles, commoners and slaves. In the matter of the loss, through criminal assault, of an eye, for example: if a man destroyed a nobleman's eye, his was plucked out in retaliation; if he destroyed a commoner's eye, he paid one mina of silver—about a pound; if he destroyed the eye of a slave, he paid the price of the slave. Retaliation often became unduly severe: for example, if a house collapsed killing the owner, the builder was put to death; if the owner's son was killed in the collapse, the builder's son was executed.

Babylonian Religion. The Sumerian faith persisted in Babylonian worship, but the object of worship changed. Business prosperity on earth became the central purpose of Babylonian devotion. Marduk and Ishtar, local deities, came into favored positions in the Sumerian pantheon and were made responsible for winning over the evil spirits that ruined crops and imposed restraints upon trade or the ability to pursue one's vocation (because of ill-health, defaulted debts, etc.). Believing that foretelling is forestalling, Babylonians poured large amounts of wealth into temple sacrifices, divination by priests and the like, for the priests, the worshippers felt, could read the future in winds, storms, drops of oil on water, sheep's livers and the stars. Priests also did a brisk trade in the sale of charms and magical formulae for driving off evil spirits that caused disease.

CHAPTER THREE

FROM THE HITTITES TO THE PERSIANS

THE HITTITES

"Against Samsuditana the men of the Hatti marched, against the land of Akkad." In these words Babylonia chronicled its own fall and the rise of a new imperial power, the men of Hatti or the Hittites; the time was about 1600 B.C. The Hittites had first appeared as conquerors some 300 years earlier; from about 1900 to 1600 B.C. they had gathered in most of what is now Asia Minor; now, under the aegis of King Mursilis they had reached eastward to Babylonia.

The State. The kings of the Hittites were absolute monarchs while they lived and deified when they died. They were, while living, supreme commanders of their armies, the highest judicial authorities, the chief priests and the heads of the diplomatic service. Only the judicial power was delegated to inferiors; all other duties were performed by the king personally. The Queen in the Hittite monarchy enjoyed a strongly independent position and could, for example, conduct foreign relations on her own.

The people over whom these monarchs ruled were divided into the four customary classes: the "Great Family" or the king's kinsmen; the nobility who were the fighters and the landowners; the commoners composed of free peasants and artisans and merchants; and serfs and slaves. The first two of these classes were highly privileged: they collected taxes, held high administrative posts and commanded the lower echelons in the king's army. Rule over the empire was assigned by the king to appointed governors or to puppets from the conquered territories who swore fealty to the king and paid annual tribute for protection. Foreign policy was conducted by intercommunicating embassies, by diplomatic marriages and treaties. A typical treaty, such as that concluded between the Hittite Hattusilis III and the Egyptian Rameses II in 1269 B.C., created a "brotherhood" on the basis of reciprocal dynastic guarantees; provided for an offensive-defensive alliance; guaranteed that the treaty would continue in the event of the succession of a legitimate heir; arranged for extradition of fugitives from justice; and was inscribed in two languages, hieroglyphic and cuneiform.

The Economy. The basic economy was agricultural and subsistence amounts of barley, wheat, grapes and olives were cultivated. Copper and iron ore were mined. It was in iron-smelting that the Hittites became pre-eminent; their fabrication of iron articles was somewhat weak. It is believed that they learned about the properties of iron from tribes in the Danubian regions of Europe. They were, however, the great distributors of iron for the civilizations of the Middle East.

The Hittite Code. The Hittites, unlike the Babylonians, seemed to have avoided codification and permitted law to change according to need. Judicial authority was exercised by village elders, king's officers and the king himself. The king's decision was required in all cases of "sorcery" and those involving the death penalty. Immense efforts were made by Hittite jurists to get the facts in a case by gathering in sworn statements from plaintiffs, defendants and witnesses. In other respects as well Hittite law represented an advance over primitive justice. In primitive societies punishment is often synonymous with revenge; the civil and criminal law tend to merge. Vengeance becomes the duty of the relatives of the injured party and may result in the blood feud. As society advances money payments or other forms of compensation

are accepted by the aggrieved parties. With a growth in organized society, the state endeavored to limit private vengeance; the *lex talionis* was a first step in this direction because it tried to ensure that punishment was limited to the extent of the injury.

Hittite law took a hesitant step in the further direction of substituting restitution for retribution. Only rape, sodomy and defiance of the state were capital offenses for freemen; for slaves, these three and disobedience to the master and "sorcery" were capital crimes. For all other offenses (assault, thefts, property damage etc.) only reparation was required. In most cases responsibility for crime rested with the individual concerned, a very enlightened viewpoint for the times. Alongside this advanced form of jurisprudence were certain primitive practices: in some crimes the entire community, within a "three-mile limit," was made responsible for compensating a victim if the criminal escaped or the whole family of the guilty party was involved in his punishment. In the law of domestic relations, marriage was a rigidly enforced contract, and a form of levirate practice prevailed, that is, a widow had to be remarried first to her dead husband's brother, then to his father and then to his nephew.

Religion. Hittite religion was polytheistic; each tiny community had its own gods. With a growth in the power of the Emperor, religion underwent syncretization (unification) into an orderly pantheon. The characteristic deity was the Weather-God (Teshub) depicted in reliefs as wielding an axe and a symbolic flash of lightning, driving a chariot drawn by sacred bulls over personified mountains. Worship of Hittite deities was in open-air rock sanctuaries, shrines or temples. The temple was regarded as the home of the god; the priests were the god's retinue. They attended to his every need: washed, clothed and fed him and then performed ritual dances to sacred music before him. To the gods were brought propitiatory offerings, especially the first fruits of the land. Human sacrifice was sanctioned. There were numerous religious festivals during which the sacred myths were retold and ritual combats fought. To the Hittites, then, the gods were invisible and immortal but their needs were completely human. These needs had to be appeased for the gods were extremely capricious; moreover they were often so busy with their own concerns that they became inattentive to those of the worshipper if not prodded to do their duty. Misfortunes, however, came because of sinfulness; and the sin could have been committed sometime in the past generations. Magic was used extensively by the priests.

Art. Hittite art consisted of the usual fabrication of animal figurines, jugs and goblets, ornaments, primitive stone idols, polychromatic pottery with geometric decor and the like. Glyphic cylinder seals were beautifully incised. Monumental reliefs were picturesque and vividly narrative. Hittites executed some sculpture in the round and passed the concept of the winged lion on to the Assyrians who elaborated this device into fine art.

PHOENICIA

The impact of tiny Phoenicia upon world civilization was, in the long run, greater than that of the mightier Hittites. Phoenicia was a land of city states—Tyre, Sidon, Byblos and Beirut—joined in a lose union under the hegemony of the king of Tyre. It fronted directly upon the Mediterranean Sea and possessed expert maritime prowess. As a result, the Phoenicians were the first **explorers** in history, the discoverers, for example, of England and its rich tin deposits; they were also the first colonizers in Europe and North Africa. So commercialized a nation had need of an efficient language for record keeping; it was no accident that it was the Phoenicians who first produced a modern alphabet (22 consonants and no vowels). This was their outstanding contribution to civilization.

THE HEBREWS

Foundations. It is believed today that the Hebrews arose from a great commingling of Semitic-speaking tribes like the Aramaeans, Edomites, Ammonites and Canaanites and non-Semitic like the Anatolians and Hittites. According to their own traditions, their ancestors, originating in Babylonian *Ur*, were led into southern Palestine by Abraham and his sons about 1500 B.C. At this time, the Hebrews were nomadic cattle and sheep herders. During a period of Egyptian weakness some Hebrews settled alongside the Egyptian delta, thrived for a while (the Joseph story), were then enslaved —perhaps by Rameses II—and were finally rescued from their rebellious, involuntary servitude by Moses who also led them to the worship of Jahweh and gave them the rudiments of law and social organization. This was about 1150 B.C. After long years of desert-wandering, the Hebrews came to the east bank of the Jordan River; there they wrested the land from the dominion of the Moabites and Ammonites. Emboldened with success, the Hebrews crossed over the Jordan and after long and arduous years of battle defeated the Edomites and Canaanites for the possession of Palestine. Defeat of these two enemies was accomplished piecemeal, tribe by tribe, for there was as yet no unity among the tribes of the Hebrews. In adapting to the new land and an agricultural-commercial way of life, the Hebrews succumbed to many Canaanite influences, particularly that of Baal worship, that is, nature-worship of the gods of fertility. National unity and the purity of their faith were the major problems to be solved at this time (ca. the eleventh century B.C.).

Unity and Purity. Unity was imposed on the Hebrew nation from without. Incursions of Indo-European and Greek tribes into the lands of the eastern Mediterranean compelled a tribe of **Philistines** to move into southern Palestine. The Hebrews were either subjugated by these superior warriors or driven into the hills. About 1025 B.C. the Hebrews regrouped under the leadership of Saul who began the assault on the Philistines; but real success against the Philistines was registered by King David.

David drove the Philistines on to a narrow part of the southern shore; united the northern and southern tribes; completed the conquest of Canaan; extended Hebrew domination east of the Jordan; and founded a new capital at Jerusalem. At Jerusalem the worship of Jehovah was raised to new spiritual heights as is evidenced in the many Psalms composed (according to tradition) by David himself.

Under King Solomon (975-935 B.C.), the central administration of the Hebrew kingdom achieved near-Oriental splendor. Solomon expanded the power of the Hebrews by deft diplomacy and foreign alliance; by controlling all trade routes with fortified points; by wise administration of the kingdom, a wisdom that became proverbial. He strengthened the religious faith of the Hebrews by constructing a temple at Jerusalem out of stone and cedar wood to house the sacred Ark of the Covenant. Temple worship, in turn, stimulated ritualism and priestly domination.

Division and Dispersal. Solomon's luxurious living was achieved by oppressive taxation and forced labor; his Oriental despotism and relaxed moral standards was achieved at the expense of ignoring or suppressing widespread moralistic protest. After his death, discontent turned to revolt and resulted in a suicidal schism of the Hebrew nation into the northern kingdom of the ten tribes of **Israel** and the southern kingdom of the two tribes of **Judah.** The Kingdom of Israel lasted from 933 to 722 B.C. when it was literally obliterated by the Assyrian conqueror Sargon II. The history of this kingdom in these years had been stormy—a history of shifting dynasties, changing capitals, loss and reconquest of territory, religious decline and prophetic warnings of ultimate doom by the prophets Elijah, Elisha, Amos and Hosea. Judah was more fortunate for it persisted until 586 B.C. when Nebuchadnezzar captured and razed Jerusalem and dispersed the kingdom. Except for flashes of rebirth, the political history of the ancient Hebrews ends with this dispersal. Its spiritual history, however, was at the inception of its multi-millenial career.

Hebrew Religion. Hebrew religious doctrines were to persist in the faith of the Jewish people from their inception three thousand years ago until this day; they were to become important influences in the far more numerous faiths of Christianity and Mohammedanism as well. The Hebrews were the first to develop all the implications of a strict monotheistic faith. God, whether in the Yahweh (Jehovah) or in the Elohim versions, was the one and only God; all other gods were rejected as false. God was conceived as the creator of the universe out of chaos or nothing and his creation was continuous; He was the Father of all that was and is—nature, sub-human life and humanity. His relation to His creatures was direct, personal and providential; from the beginning He had ordered all things according to a plan that flowed from His nature, a nature that was omnipotent (all-powerful), omniscient (all-knowing), benevolent, merciful and just. God, too, was righteous, and determined to make his righteousness prevail.

The Chosen People. God had made man in His own image, as proclaimed in Genesis. But the first man and woman had rebelled against Him and had incurred His wrath. This first transgression corrupted humanity. But God, in His infinite mercy, had covenanted with Abraham and his descendants to make the Hebrews a great nation, His "chosen people." Thus, he gave them a Law to control their conduct and commanded them, as their part of the covenant, to love their One God with all their soul, heart and might. The details of this covenant are recorded in the Old Testament.

The Book. The Old Testament—doctrine holds—was a religious revelation dictated by divine guidance. Not only was the Law revealed thus supernaturally, but the sacred history of mankind from its creation to its final consummation was also sketched.

Man. The Hebrews viewed man as co-extensive with the community; the sin of one of its members was suffered by the entire community; the blessing of one was shared by all. Man was a creature with all of the weaknesses of something created; but he was also a thinking being with body, spirit, self, feeling, mind and heart. Because of his power of thought and feeling, man was an ethical person, capable of making moral (or immoral) choices and acting upon them.

Ethics. Out of their examination of moral choices, the Hebrews framed a comprehensive **moral code** from which there could be no departure without the danger of incurring punishment. The ethical code demanded (in part) wise conduct, rectitude, justice, honesty, uprightness, integrity, no exploitation of one's fellow man, no traffic in ill-gotten gains, aid to the needy, no adultery, industriousness, restrained speech, generosity, altruism, obedience to parents, modesty. The moral code, Hebrews felt, was divinely originated; God's justice consisted in the enforcement of His own code. Man was free to obey God's commands; and to disobey.

Sin. Man could sin in many ways: in part, by iniquity, resistance to God, violation of the covenant, blasphemy, unbelief, brutality, oppression of the underprivileged, irresponsibility, stubbornness, arrogance, pride, etc. This was personal transgression; but one could commit both social and cultic transgression as well. Social sin was any sexual, economic, military, hygienic or political act that threatened to destroy the community. Sinful man was not without hope for the Hebrews also viewed God as a God of love, grace, faithfulness, redemption and forgiveness. Repentant, trusting and prayerful man could win forgiveness and redemption.

Eschatology (the Doctrine of Last Things.) Hebraic eschatological thought was based upon apocalyptic utterances of the prophets; these apocalypses were divine revelations of things to come. The future of mankind followed from the Hebrew conception of history. Since God was active in the affairs of men, He was concerned with seeing that His will be done. Hence, Jews looked forward to a culmination of history in a Last Judgment when the good would be rewarded and the evil punished. God would judge his sons as a stern Father, mercifully but firmly. As men had sown, so would they reap.

Finally, the Hebrews believed that the coming of the Last Judgment would be preceded by the arrival on earth of a Messiah or Redeemer. The importance of these ideas for the future religious development of mankind can hardly be exaggerated.

THE ASSYRIANS

In the northern, hilly regions of the Tigris River there arose an extraordinary group of conquerors, the Assyrians. For centuries they had known what it was to be a conquered people; they had felt the whiplash of the Babylonians, Hittites, Egyptians and Aramaeans. About 1100 B.C. it was their chance to scourge. Under Tiglath-Pileser I they gained control of the main trade routes of western Asia. These were held with difficulty for many years. Then, begining in 883 B.C., in the reign of Ashur-nasir-pal II, Assyria began the conquest of the Middle East. They were the first people to make an art of war; they demonstrated military inventiveness with iron weapons, mounted cavalry and siege weapons; they developed military tactics with new types of assault, flanking, siege and reconnaissance operations; they invented "total war" with policies of living off their victims, shifting whole populations, wholesale genocide, blitzkrieg attack and blackmail or the efficient collection of tribute for "protection." Military conquest was followed by tight imperial organization: local wars were suppressed; a public administration was created; local autonomy was permitted but a close watch was kept on governors and subject kings; and communications were improved by extensive road building.

All of the ancient peoples felt the weight of Assyrian arms. Babylon and Damascus fell to Tiglath-Pileser III (745-727); Sargon II (722-705) conquered Palestine and carried off ten of the twelve Hebrew tribes into captivity; Sennacherib (705-681), after exhausting wars against rebellious subjects, destroyed Babylon and founded a new capital at Nineveh; Essarhaddon (681-668) conquered Egypt; Ashurbanipal (668-628) devastated Elam. When the last of the conquerors, Ashurbanipal, died, Assyria stood astride the ancient world. Yet, sixteen years later (612 B.C.) the Assyrian empire disintegrated as the Medes and Chaldeans combined in an eastern and southern assault upon it; Nineveh was razed so that for centuries its name disappeared from history; the Assyrian nation was captured, slaughtered or scattered and it, too, disappeared.

Assyrian Civilization. Conquerors though they were, the Assyrians nonetheless absorbed and to some extent extended the civilization of the conquered. Assyrian religion was Babylonian; but in elevating their own god **Assur** to the top of the pantheon the Assyrians achieved a form of monotheism which had considerable influence on contemporary Hebrew thought. Assyrian art and architecture were adaptations of the Babylonian and Hittite; but they extended the use of stone in the foundations, columns and facings of their buildings and multiplied the use of the Babylonian arch. In their long sculptural reliefs, they did their most original work in the portrayal of the hunt and the agony of the slain lion. They copied Babylonian cuneiform and somewhat later the Aramaean script; they preserved the literature, science and codes of the Babylonians. The oldest known sampling of musical notation comes from Assyrian remains. More than all of their predecessors, however, the Assyrians had a sense of history and, to preserve the past, they established the first royal libraries in the world. That of Ashurbanipal had 22,000 catalogued clay tablets and cylinders containing hymns, legends, works in science, mathematics, records and the like.

THE NEW BABYLONIA

With the fall of Assyria, three powers contended for control of the Middle East. On Asia Minor proper the Lydians ruled, the first nation to begin coinage of money; the name of their king, CROESUS, became a synonym for wealth. Stretching from almost the shores of the Indus River to the Halys River bordering Lydia, was the kingdom of the Medes. In the fertile crescent, a second Babylonian kingdom was founded by the **Chaldeans.** The greatest of the Chaldean rulers was NEBUCHADNEZZAR II (605-562 B.C.). This great ruler eliminated Egypt as a Middle Eastern competitor by defeating the Egyptian Pharaoh Necho II at the Battle of Carchemish (605 B.C.); he conquered Palestine and Jerusalem and carried off the Jewish King Jehoiachin to Babylon appointing Zedekiah as a puppet ruler. When Zedekiah proved to be no puppet by launching a rebellion against Nebuchadnezzar, Jerusalem was destroyed utterly and the Jews taken into their **Babylonian Captivity** (586 B.C.). Tyre was taken after a thirteen year siege. But the poiitical glory of the New Babylonia proved to be that only of its strongest ruler. When Nebuchadnezzar died, the empire quickly disintegrated because of neglect of the empire, weakness in its administration, internal religious difficulties and inattention to the armed forces.

Chaldean Culture. New Babylonia was a magnificent city encased in a thirteen mile circuit of walls. Down the center coursed a beautifully constructed Procession Street which led to the Temple of Marduk. Entrance into this temple was through the renowned Ishtar Gates, a double gateway flanked by towers and decorated with animal figures made of enameled brick. The temple was in classical Babylonian style and contained a mighty ziggurat (about 300 feet high) that served for the Biblical tale of the Tower of Babel. Nebuchadnezzar's palace was vast; it, too, was decorated with enameled brick and variegated columns. The roof of this palace was a terraced garden replete with tropical verdure and as the **Hanging Gardens of Babylon** became one of the seven wonders of the ancient world. The Chaldeans proved to be remarkable engineers:— excavations reveal numerous bridges, piers, a concept of city planning, tenement houses, irrigation canals and the like. As their religion decayed into the rankest forms of superstition, their interest in science seems to have increased. Chaldean astronomers brought the Babylonian lunar calendar into accord with the prevalent solar systems, developed the sexigesimal system by use of a circle of 360 degrees, a twelve hour day, sixty second minute, calculated the length of the year to within 26 minutes of accuracy, accounted for the precession of equinoxes, etc. Late Chaldean science also declined into gross astrological superstition. Before this, however, Chaldeans had passed on to the Persians large accumulations of data on medicine, disease, drugs, grammar, law, etc.

THE PERSIANS

Persia lay on the Iranian plateau stretching eastward from the Tigris River to the Indus River. About 1800 B.C. an Aryan-speaking people occupied the northeastern edge of this plateau. For centuries they were subject to the rule of the Elamites; but Ashurbanipal, the Assyrian, devastated Elam and its capital at Susa (ca. 640 B.C.). When the Assyrians were destroyed in turn, the Medes under Cyaxeres (625-593 B.C.) took over the former Elamite Kingdom. But the Persians now made their bid for power. In 550 B.C. CYRUS THE GREAT took over the Median Kingdom and then continued westward to conquer Lydia and Chaldea. Cyrus's son, Cambyses (530-521 B.C.) added the Egyptian Empire to the Persian. At this point, the empire of the Persians was the largest of all those of the ancient world.

Darius I (521-485 B.C.) added little new territory to this vast empire but devoted his high intelligence to organizing it for efficient administration. His basic principle of organization was centralization through the monarch. Thus he built for himself four capitals with royal residences at Susa, Per-

sepolis, Ecbatana and Babylon. These were interconnected with modernized highways over which flowed normal trade, postal communication and military patrols. The King made a regular circuit of his capitals and while in each he disposed of accumulated local problems. Reporting to him regularly were twenty *satraps* or governors appointed by and responsible solely to himself. (The empire had been divided into twenty *satrapies* or administrative divisions.) Each governor was responsible for the imperial tax and the army levies. In all other matters local autonomy was permitted and everywhere native cultures were tolerated. (Under the Persians, for example, the Hebrews were permitted to return from Babylon to Palestine.) But, to guarantee efficiency and to ward off the evils of bureaucratic corruption, the King appointed official spies known as "The King's eyes and the King's ears" who traveled about the empire incognito and reported back to the King the evils they observed or heard about. The Persian government itself was an absolute hereditary monarchy "by the grace of Ahura-Mazda." There were important limitations on the King's absolutism: he was expected to consult with the nobility, to base his law-making upon the Law of the Medes and the Persians and to be guided by precedents in the law. This was the empire that persisted in the Middle East until 333 B.C. It received its first important setback at the hands of the Greeks at the Battle of Marathon in 490 B.C.; and it was destroyed by Alexander the Great. Its influence, however, continued long after its demise.

Persian Contributions. Conquerors in history often succumb to the culture of the conquered; Persia was no exception. They borrowed and then extended the military and administrative policies of the Assyrians; they took over the Aramaic tongue and the Egyptian calendar; in architecture they used the Babylonian-Assyrian enameled bricks, winged bulls and terraced structure and also the Egyptian horizontal post-and-lintel style and extended colonnade; their medical practices were both Egyptian and Chaldean. Only in religion did they make important original advances. The great prophet of the Persian religion was ZOROASTER or ZARATHUSTRA (ca. 7th century B.C.) and thus spake Zarathustra: There are two divine powers in the world—Ahura-Mazda, the One Creator, Supreme God of Good and Light; and Ahriman, the Prince of Evil and of Darkness. Mazda was surrounded by angels, chief of whom was Mithras, the light; Ahriman, by devils. Between these two powers of good and evil there was ceaseless struggle for the souls of men. Men were free to choose between them; but they were cautioned in their sacred writings, the **Zend-Avesta,** that Mazda would one day conquer Ahriman; on that day there would be a Last Judgment (following the arrival of a messiah); the good would be sent to Paradise, the wicked to Hell. Among the wicked would be those guilty of gluttony, sloth, pride, etc.; the good would have kept their contracts, obeyed their rulers, given alms to the poor, etc.

Persian kings claimed to live by the words of Zoroaster and to rule with righteousness and justice. In their turn, the people worshipped in Zoroastrian temples ruled over by the Magi, or priests. The symbol of Persian worship was the sacred fire kept eternally burning by generations of Magi.

Zoroastrianism was a great advance over previous Sumerian faiths. Polytheism was supplanted by a simpler dualism; religion by ritual gave way to religion by ethical behavior; pessimism and hedonism surrendered to a more optimistic hope for the future and to life guided by principle rather than appetite.

CRETE

Between Persia and Ancient Greece lay the Aegean Sea and around that sea there flourished a number of civilizations which became transitional to the Greek. Earliest of these was the **Minoan** civilization which flourished on the island of Crete and which was revealed to the modern world by the brilliant excavations about 1900 (A.D.) of SIR ARTHUR EVANS. Knowledge of the Minoan civilization is still limited because its language is still undeciphered; what is known is due to archaeological discoveries. From these it is known that Minoan civilization flourished between 3000 and 1200 B.C. In this period, they dominated the Mediterranean sea with their trade and military power.

Their power was manifest in the mighty cities which they built at Cnossus and Phaestus on the island itself. Cnossus, for example, was dominated by the king's palace which was at least two stories high, contained a maze of living rooms, store rooms, workshops, offices, etc., was equipped with plumbing that provided running water and efficient sewage. Attached to the palace were factories which turned out articles for export—pottery, textiles and metal goods.

Unearthed figurines indicate that Minoan worship centered about a snake goddess, a symbol of fertility and of destruction. The dead were buried with their implements of war and livelihood; gods were appeased by sacrifice. There were, however, no temples. Minoan murals are exceptionally revealing: they show the people as unusually sports-loving and engaging in bull fights, boxing, races, etc. Women held an exceptionally high position; they play and work side by side with the men. All this is shown by the archaeological record. This record also reveals that about 1400 B.C. Minoan civilization took root in northwestern Asia Minor about the site of Troy and in a group of Greek islands centered about Mycenae on the mainland. Similar pottery, artistic design and "beehive" tombs prove this. Esthetic analysis of Mycenaean remains, however, shows that the creative flame was gone by 1400 B.C. Minoan art, at its height, is a rare combination of naturalism and spontaneity combined with exquisite delicacy; Mycenaean art is derivative and dull by comparison. The Minoan artist was master of the miniature: the figurine, the painted dagger, jewelry, inlay; Mycenaean is large and crude by comparison. The real influence of the Minoan Cretans was not upon the rough Trojans and Mycenaeans but upon those that conquered them, the ancient Greeks of Dorian and Ionian stock.

CHAPTER FOUR

THE GLORY THAT WAS GREECE

Introduction. Historians rank ancient Greece as the first of the "western" civilizations. In their enthusiasm, however, they sometimes underrate the Oriental contributions to the formation of the Greek mind. Oriental ideas in science, technology, philosophy and religion were imbibed by the Greeks when they absorbed the lands across the Aegean Sea. Greeks adopted and expanded the Phoenician alphabet. They borrowed freely Oriental forms of coinage and credit financing and their existence depended to a great extent upon their economic relationship with the Oriental world. Greek history, in other words, is a good example of the interdependence of peoples.

Nonetheless, there is considerable justification in proclaiming the Greeks a people apart from the Oriental cultural tradition. At the height of their civilization, the cultural values of the Greeks included **humanism, freedom, rationalism** and **idealism**—values otherwise virtually unknown in the world of the ancient Orient.

Humanism stressed the importance of man and his happiness in the here and now, not in some shadowy after-life. This emphasis on happiness led the Greeks to invent many forms of **freedom**—the city-state, the direct democracy, freedom of speech, etc. **Rationalism** led them to reject institutionalized religion and the omnipotence of a self-aggrandizing priesthood and to substitute a spirit of free inquiry in the search for truth and for **moral and rational self-control. Idealism** was linked by them with the quest for perfection, beauty and balance. These values combined to nourish their creative imagination and resulted in the production of **"classics,"** that is, immortal works in art, literature, philosophy, political theory, mathematics and mythology. These "classics" are some of the sources of western culture.

ORIGINS

Greek civilization did not spring full-blown from the soil of Greece. It took a millenium before the Greeks cast off their original barbarism. The earliest Greeks lived in the valley of the Danube; they spoke a common Indo-European tongue. By 2000 B.C., however, their language had become differentiated enough to enable us to divide them into Achaeans, Aeolians, Ionians, Illyrians, Boetians, Dorians, etc. About that time, too, they were uprooted from their homeland and began a folk-wandering southward into the Balkan peninsula; they came, that is, as conquerors.

The first to enter may have been the Achaean Hellenes (ca. 2000 B.C.). Over a period of 700 years these people filtered into central and southern Greece and then into the Aegean islands. They seem to have assimilated with the indigenous Greeks, and absorbed their superior culture; but they imposed upon them the Achaean language and rule. Ionians are found in western Greece as early as 1500 B.C. They, too, settled down, absorbed and assimilated with the natives. But about 1300 B.C. a barbarous tribe of **Illyrians** swept down into Thessaly and uprooted the Achaeans and the Ionians and forced them to scatter into the remoter regions of the peninsula and overseas to Asia Minor. It is quite likely that this upheaval, rather than the legendary kidnapping of Helen, brought the Achaeans under Agamemnon into collision with the Trojans in Asia Minor. This Illyrian conquest was followed by an even more devastating **Dorian invasion** which re-scattered the Achaeans and Ionians. After 1000 B.C. the invasions ended and Greece entered a period of incubation.

Invasion and dispersion were not without positive results. The decadent remnants of Minoan-Mycenean culture were destroyed, paving way for a new culture; the Greek nation differentiated into varied and conflicting types each occupying a fixed territory, and this spurred the growth of individualism; Greek culture became Mediterranean rather than Balkan; overseas, the Greeks came into contact with the civilizing ways of the Near East; and passage over the seas required that the Greeks become "maritime-minded" and oriented to a life of trade and commerce.

The Land. Trade and commerce were vital preconditions for the development of Greek civilization for the Balkan peninsula was a singularly barren land. Criss-crossing mountain ranges covered two-thirds of the land surface; arable plains made up a bare one-sixth. The rivers were non-navigable and varied between winter flood and summer dry-bed. Lakes were rare and inclined, because of poor drainage, to become malarial swampland. Scrubby pasture supported meager flocks of sheep and goats. Deforestation was acute; and there were only thin veins of metals basic to the ancient civilizations—gold, silver, lead, iron and copper. The historian HERODOTUS defined it accurately when he said that poverty was foster-sister to the Greeks. But while geography was, in the main, a barrier to civilization, it did open some opportunities. For example, there were rich deposits of stone and marble and potter's clay; natural harbors abounded along the eastern shore; the Aegean islands were natural stepping-stones to the Asiatic mainland and by occupying them, the Greeks made the Aegean Sea into a Grecian Lake.

The "Homeric" Greeks. Homer's *Iliad* and *Odyssey* are timeless masterpieces of epic poetry; they qualify as such by every standard of literary criticism—by clear, vivid and natural diction; by **epithets** that serve as haunting refrains and impress the *dramatis personae* upon the memory; by an **"heroic" meter, the hexameter;** by suspenseful beginnings *in media res* (in the middle of things) to avoid tedious or interruptive background material; by the music of their language; and by their wide range of human emotions, their varieties of style to fit the scenes, their plenitude of imagery and matchless rhetoric. They are "things of beauty," of "Attic shapes" in motion and as such their influence has not waned in the 2800 years of their lives. In a study of Greek and Roman influences on western civilization (*The Classical Tradition*), Gilbert Highet was compelled to make more than 250 references to Homer's epics. Here we can do no more than note Homer's literary impact. Our interest must be in what he revealed about the "dark age" in the pre-literary history of Greece.

Homer's interest was in his own past; but he was unable to escape his present. So, from between his lines, we are able to piece out that part of Greek history which is called the "Homeric Age."

Primitive Society. Homer's Greeks lived in a relatively primitive society. Their methods of wealth-gathering centered upon crude agriculture, herding and plundering on land and sea. Technologically they had passed from the Bronze to the threshold of the Iron Age. Some specialization of craft had begun for the epics speak of **freemen** who were smiths, potters, saddlers, masons, carpenters and cabinetmakers. Costlier goods, however —objects of art, weapons, fancy raiment and gold beakers—seem to have been imported. Trading was very limited and conducted by means of primitive barter. There was no coinage and wealth was estimated in flocks. The ox served as a medium of exchange. Most manufactured goods were produced in the home by slaves with the assistance of their masters and mistresses.

Private ownership, as an institution, had not yet appeared; landed property was owned by the family with the father as chief administrator. While the father could determine the use of the land, he could not sell it. He had to transmit it, by the common law of **primogeniture,** to his eldest son who became head of the household upon his father's death. The family unit was patriarchal; it was, in fact, a patriarchal despotism for the father could, if he wished, take concubines for himself or offer them to his guests, or commit infanticide, or slaughter his children as sacrifices to the gods. Fathers, however, rarely employed such practices. Homeric families are, for the most part, monogamous; intimacy and affection exist between husband and wife and between father and children; the position of the woman in the household is high and free even though marriage was by purchase. (Women were to lose this high status as Greek society developed.)

Homeric men could and did commit unspeakable barbarities upon one another; but concepts of a common humanity tempered their crudities. They are never far from tenderness, sentiment and tears; deep friendships are common; they show rare hospitality to strangers for they bathe them, clothe them, wine-dine-and lodge them, and then send them off with gifts; slaves have a rare position of equality in the household. On the other hand, they are never far from what we would consider immoralities either. Women are offered as prizes in athletic contests; wanton, cruel sacrifices are made upon funeral pyres; slavery and concubinage follow upon conquest; piracy is an honorable profession and pillage a necessary one; they admire unabashed lying, deceit and treachery. This was their response to an insecure world in which human life was cheap; to survive, a man must have the qualities of Ares, the God of War—strength, guile and deception. Fair was foul, and foul was fair. (These, in fact, are among Odysseus' most conspicuous traits.)

Politics. Political institutions were equally primitive though considerably advanced over Oriental forms as no divine-right absolute monarch existed in Homeric Greece. There was a **basileus or dynastic king** who served as commander in chief, high priest and chief justice. He was, however, a chief among equals. His equals were a landed aristocracy who claimed, as did the basileus, divine descent. They met on important occasions as a council and through this agency they checked any exercise of arbitrary power by the basileus. Within the council the nobility enjoyed complete freedom of speech. As a further check on absolutism there existed an assembly of all freemen who could, in a crisis of war or peace, approve or reject proposals made by the king or nobles. Government was completely decentralized; the power of the king extended, on a "feudal" basis, only as far as his noble retainers obeyed him. For example, while his anger was upon him and he did not choose to fight, Achilles ignored every demand and plea to do so made by King Agamemnon. There was no fixed law but custom; justice was administered by the family-feud—though there is some evidence that justice by trial was beginning to take root.

Religion. Homeric Greeks conceived the ideas that they lived on an earth that was a flat disk floating on Oceanus. Above them was the solid dome of heaven kept aloft by Atlas. Around them the seas abounded with marvels and foreign lands with freaks. Natural forces resulted from the actions of unseen gods who dwelt on Mt. Olympus. Gods were distinguished from men only by their immortality and their extraordinary powers; otherwise they had the shape of humans and all of the virtues and vices of mankind. They fought, feasted, made love, played tricks, lied, deceived, made music, roared with laughter, fell in love with mortals and produced thereby generations of illegitimate progeny. They were, indeed, a capricious lot and therefore had to be cajoled, persuaded or "bought off" by prayers, votive offerings and sacrifices. The head of each Greek family was qualified to conduct these religious rites and therefore there were, among the Homerics, no temples, no organized priesthood. Relations between these Greeks and their gods were earthbound for the Greeks seemed not to believe in underworld ghosts, or spirits, or, in fact, in any last judgment and afterlife punishment. Hence they had only the most rudimentary sense of sin. Life was to be lived on earth and religious devotion was centered upon extending it as long as possible with the aid of favoring gods or by outwitting unfavoring ones through developing the gift of prophecy or omen-reading.

Forces of Unification. During the Homeric "dark ages" certain universal habits and traits among the Greeks led to the formation of a Greek **nation.** Homer was himself responsible for this to a great extent. The *Iliad* and the *Odyssey* were virtually the Greek "Bible"—they gave all Greeks a continuous divine past or common heritage; they inspired all Greek painters, poets, statesmen and philosophers; and they were the basic reader in the Greek educational system. Homer presented the Greeks with a pantheon, with a standard of personal virtue, with a moral maxim ("nothing in excess"), with a concept of an overriding fate that bent even Zeus to its will, with a sense of tragedy that flowed from man's unavoidable fate and with a call to men to fulfil themselves without resort to pride or arrogance.

But besides Homer as a force for unification of all Greeks, there was the Greek language which made all non-Greek speaking peoples "barbarians" (etymologically, "stammerers" or those who cannot speak). Common national feeling was also developed by a number of all-Greek festivals, the best known being the Olympic games which, said legend, were first begun in 776 B.C. The Olympic festival lasted five days and featured athletic contests, beauty contests, drinking bouts and competitions in poetry; victors were awarded the laurel wreath. These games were in honor of Zeus. But all Greeks also patronized the oracle at Delphi which advised them on matters human and divine; and the Greeks

were able to forget their devotion to their native place long enough to organize a Delphic league of Greek states pledged to neutralize and defend this sanctuary in the event of war.

These roots of national unity ran deep; but deeper still ran the roots of **localism, of particularism;** and this was at once the glory of Greece, and her undoing.

The Polis. Aristotle said that a man had to be either a beast or a god to live without a **polis.** Polis was the Greek word for **"city-state."** The polis evolved from the **clan, a large family recognizing a common ancestor and having its own gods, laws, customs and assigned duties.** Defense needs forced various clans to combine into **brotherhoods** and to obey an inter-clan law. These coalesced into **tribes.** Here claims of kinship were tenuous in the extreme; tribes were really bound by common worship and military necessity. When tribes combined they formed an *ethnos* or **nation** which was a **political unit occupying a defined territory and bound by a common language, law and custom.** A "nation" lived in villages grouped around an *acropolis* or fortified height. This territorial grouping then became the *polis* or city-state. Vestiges of each stage in this evolution remained in the polis; thus, members of a polis still claimed descent from a common ancestor, usually divine, and worshipped as "kinsmen" in a common religious cult.

Sparta was the largest polis in Greece; yet it had but 3,360 square miles. The population of a polis was very small. At one time Athens attained the unheard-of number of 50,000 inhabitants. In the polis, citizenship was extended only to freeborn "kinsmen" and all others were considered aliens; naturalization was unknown. Citizenship usually conferred exclusive rights to intermarry, own property and to participate in community affairs. Socrates preferred death to exile. Duties of citizens were carefully defined—service in the government or in the armed forces was strictly enforced. And when a Greek emigrated from his polis to a land overseas, his attachment to it continued; colonists took with them their sacred home fires and the earth of their mother city.

Emigration. Between 800 and 600 B.C. Greeks colonized extensively along the Mediterranean shore. The reasons were many: hunger induced by meager agricultural resources; land hunger coupled with the difficulty of moving into the mountainous north; monopolization of favored lands by the aristocracy; primogeniture, that is, inheritance by the eldest son of all family holdings; desire for adventure coupled with improved methods of navigation; political discontent; the search for commercial outlets or new sources of mineral and timber supplies. Colonies were usually collective municipal enterprises and many overseas colonies were controlled by the homeland. This colonization extended from the Pillars of Hercules (Gibraltar) to the Black Sea. There were settlements in what is now Spain, France (Marseilles), Piedmont, Corsica, most of Sicily (*Magna Graecia*) and southern Italy, Yugoslavia, Constantinople, Egypt, and Libya. The significance of this emigration and colonization can hardly be exaggerated: it meant the extension of Greek or Western Civilization to virtually the entire Mediterranean basin; at the same time, it meant the increase of wealth which followed upon colonization made possible the flowering of the Greek genius. Agriculture expanded; maritime trade blossomed; this in turn encouraged production in Greece of articles for export—pottery, textile, mineral, wool, dye and shipbuilding industries flourished; labor shortages increased slave-gathering; increased trade spread the use of coinage and systems of credit; surpluses of wealth deepened the division between rich and poor but also made the class structure of the Greeks more fluid by creating a middle or commercial class whose wealth did not depend on land ownership. Noble now fought merchant, merchant fought artisan, noble fought peasant; and the result was a social mobility that led to the invention of many new political forms which were handed on to future civilizations.

POLITICAL DEVELOPMENTS IN ANCIENT GREECE

Each city-state had its own complex history; but we shall consider only the history of the two city states that early rose to commanding position—**Sparta** and **Athens.** Their ways of life were so contradictory, their influence on history so diverse that they provide drama as well as centers of attention.

Sparta. One modern historian proclaims the history of Sparta as an "interesting example of arrested development." Yet, when Plato sought a model for his utopian city-state in *The Republic*, he selected Sparta. Sparta's origin was most nearly "pure Dorian," for it was the barbaric Dorian tribes that descended on Laconia (ca. 1100 B.C.) and built a kingdom there. From the beginning, their kingdom was a "closed" or stratified society. Most of the natives were enslaved as **"helots"**; some were made "free neighbors," but were denied political rights or the freedom to enter the ruling class by intermarriage. In these days the Spartans mixed severity with toleration in their rule and out of this spirit of toleration came a Spartan art—fine pottery and delicate ivory carvings, and music such as Terpander's martial meters, Thaletus's patriotic hymns, Tyrtaeus's victory odes and Alcman's love songs. All this happened before the Messenian Wars.

Messenian Wars 736-716 B.C. In 736 B.C. Sparta conquered her neighbor Messenia, using "border incidents" as an excuse. The Messenian population was reduced to "free neighbor" and helot status and the lands of the nobles were confiscated and divided. In 650 B.C., the subjugated Messenians revolted, won the support of a number of Greek city-states, and fought the Spartans to a stand-still for twenty years before they were crushed again. This war brought to the Spartan rulers the terrifying realization that they were a mere 30,000 trying to dominate 120,000 "free neighbors" and 210,000 helots, one for every ten that despised their harsh rule. Hereafter, all of Sparta was placed under severe martial law; and the cretive spark in Spartan life was snuffed.

Lycurgus. Tradition ascribed the creation of the new Spartan state to a lawgiver LYCURGUS (probably mythical). Three castes were created by law and given geographic location. In the center were the **Spartiates,** a pure and simple military caste. They lived under a system of state communism and in constant preparedness for war. Surrounding them were the helots or state **serfs;** as serfs they could not be sold, shifted, freed or put to death by anyone but the state. Their conditions were miserable and their mood was continuously rebellious; therefore, **secret police** watched them continuously and special squads of Spartan youth were authorized to kill any helot whom they suspected of rebellion. In the outer ring, were the **businessmen** and they were placed outside to serve as dams to the helots; they were exempt from military discipline, were given a monopoly of the privilege of trade, but were prohibited from intermarrying with the Spartiates, were heavily taxed and subject, in emergency, to draft into the heavy infantry.

Militarism. Military training of Spartiates began at infancy. Defective infants were destroyed. At seven boys were taken from home and placed in barracks under older youths. They were then hardened by exposure, near starvation and flogging. Lying and stealing were encouraged when successful. At twenty, the survivors married, by compulsion, and began military training. As warrior-husbands they lived and dined in common; they saw their wives occasionaly or by stealth. At thirty they became citizens and full-fledged members of the armed forces. The Spartiates sought to produce hardy warriors by building the bodies of the mothers too; girls got the same physical training as the boys and were famed for their physical prowess and beauty. They were even more famed for the Stoic courage they exhibited in giving their husbands and sons to the war machine. Under such conditions an invincible fighting force was produced and it dominated the military scene for two centuries. Thereafter the system declined rapidly. The remaining 10,000 Spartiates dwindled to 1000; the land system broke down; the treasury was emptied by war. All human values had disappeared —intellectualism, imagination, free thought, free expression, morality and home life. Sparta left posterity nothing but a terrible example of man's infinite capacity for the use of some virtues to destroy all values.

Government. Among themselves, the Spartiates enjoyed democratic rule. Power to legislate was lodged with a popular assembly made up of privileged Spartiates thirty years of age or older. The assembly chose a council and five *ephors*, who served as magistrates, secretaries of foreign affairs, and presiding officers of the assembly. The council had 28 members, 60 years of age or older, and two "kings." They were chosen from a limited group of noble families and served as chief executives and as the supreme criminal court; they could check on the acts of the assembly. The "kings" were council members, priests and army commanders. They were privileged, but powerless. Check-and-balance, then, characterized the Spartan government.

The Peloponnesian League. On the Peloponneus only **Argos** challenged Spartan overlordship; it was Argos that led the allied forces supporting the Messenians in their revolt against Sparta. When the revolt was suppressed, Sparta turned on and defeated Argos. The allies of Argos (Elis, Corinth, Sicyon, Megara, Aegina, Troezen and Argolis) now capitulated to Spartan superiority and made an alliance with Sparta. The resulting **Peloponnesian League** was a defensive-offensive alliance to which members contributed funds and soldiers in time of war. Members met in a congress, and at their meeting, Sparta had as many votes as the others combined.

Athens. Spartanism was as much Greek as Athenianism; but it was Athens that produced the "glory that was Greece." In this "school of Hellas" there appeared within three generations a statesman like PERICLES, tragic poets like AESCHYLUS, SOPHOCLES and EURIPIDES, historians like HERODOTUS and THUCYDIDES, sculptors like PHIDIAS and philosophers like PLATO and ARISTOTLE; and an architecture often matched but never exceeded in qualities of simplicity and beauty. In the achievements of Athens are the true foundations of Western Civilization.

Evolution of a Democratic City-State. Athenian democracy must not be confused with its modern counterpart. It was not based upon equality; at its height, Athenian democracy excluded aliens, women and slaves from a share in government. The active citizen-force in 430 B.C. numbered no more than 30,000 out of a population of about 250,000 free persons. Throughout its history, citizenship remained restricted. Athenian democracy, then, was democracy for the few. For the few democracy conferred the rights of **individual freedom.** In all other ancient societies the individual was submerged in the community; men lived in the mass and as a mass. In Athens, however, there evolved the concept that the body politic existed primarily so that individualized citizens could realize their egos, ambitions, capacities and talents in full. Political institutions were adapted, in the course of centuries, to this end; and when they were fully evolved, by the middle of the fifth century, the Athenians were enjoying the *forms* of democracy. Later ages merely added more substance to these forms.

Origins. Athens advanced to democracy by slow, rational stages. According to Athenian legend, it was Theseus who first united Attica under Athens and in a common citizenship. Her history as a united city-state began with a kingship in the Homeric form; but kings had disappeared some time before the eighth century B.C. and were replaced by an **oligarchy,** the rule of a few nobles who were the largest landowners in Attica. Since the political *forms* by which these landed oligarchs ruled were capable of *democratic* expansion, they are worth some attention. Sovereign power was located in the Council of the Areopagus in which the nobles held life-membership. Executive and judicial power was delegated to an *Archonate* of nine members serving one-year terms only. Five of these archons were lawmakers and responsible to the Areopagus; one was a figurehead king with priestly office; another was a chief justice; and the last was the commander-in-chief of the armed forces. There was also an assembly of all who served in the heavy infantry, called the *Ecclesia;* the power of the Assembly was to elect magistrates from the nobility. The citizen population was divided in two ways. There was a military hierarchy; and an economic division existed as well: the landlords, the urban middle class and the free smaller farmers.

Conflict of Classes. Unlike Spartan, Athenian class divisions were not stratified or static; economic growth caused bitter conflict to flare up; and out of this conflict of classes came the expansion of democracy. About 650 B.C. the oligarchy gave way to a **timocracy.** Both involved rule by the few; but where the oligarchs drew their power from birth and land, the timocrats drew theirs from more generalized wealth. This shift in the base of political power was due to the conflicts generated by economic expansion. The wealth of the urban merchants increased while that of the smaller farmers and city artisans decreased. Small farmers were ruined by population growth which forced a redivision of already small holdings, by foreclosures on high-interest mortgages, by ruinous competition from imports from the overseas colonies and by a shortage of coinage which deflated prices. Many were forced to become tenant farmers or serfs. Artisans found themselves squeezed between a rising cost of living and reduced wages caused by an increasing influx of slave labor.

Fearfully, the landlords and merchants combined against a potential threat of revolt by ruined farmers and artisans. They divided the power of the Aeropagus and Archonate between them; they rearranged society into four economic classes; and one of their number, DRACO, drew up a written code of laws intended to enforce the *status quo* (the state in which things exist at the moment) by drastic penalties for infractions (hence the word "draconian" means unusual severity). The indirect effects of Draco's harsh code protecting property rights were progressive: primitive private feuds were abolished; and the idea of a **uniform, written law** persisted as Athens became more democratic. But the immediate occasion of Draco's Code was the effort on the part of a disaffected nobleman named Cylon to overthrow the timocracy and to establish himself as a *tyrannos* or **absolute dictator** over Athens.

The Tyrannies. Cylon failed; but between 650 and 500 B.C. throughout Greece such ambitious and aggressive men took advantage of timocratic misrule —political factionalism and deep-seated economic discontent—to overthrow the existing governments and to set up **benevolent dictatorships.** Athens was ripe for tyranny. Draco's Code had not suppressed economic protest nor had the efforts of SOLON (ca. 638-558 B.C.) a wise nobleman who had been invested with supreme power as an archon to solve the economic muddle.

Solon tried compromise economic reforms: he abolished enslavement as a penalty for debt default; he cancelled existing mortgages on land to prevent further foreclosures; he introduced a system of coinage to reverse the deflation; and intervened with state aid to stimulate manufacturing and trading. He then extended democracy by giving the poorest class a vote in the Assembly; by creating popular law courts on which *all* citizens might serve; by granting all citizens a voice in the election of magistrates; and by forming a new group, the Council of 400, to discuss and prepare the business for the Ecclesia. But these economic and political reforms did not subdue the turmoil; three new factions appeared: the "Plains" or noble party, the "Hills" or party of the poor farmers, and the "Shore" or party of the merchants. In 560 B.C. PISISTRATUS, a leader of the party of the "Hills" seized the Acropolis and made himself the **tyrant** of Athens.

Benevolent Dictatorship. Pisistratus, with the aid of foreign mercenaries, maintained his dictatorship until his death (527 B.C.). During his one-man rule, however, he made great strides in solving the economic crisis. By fostering the mining of silver, he increased available currency and induced an inflation which spurred both trade and industry; he confiscated the large landed estates of the nobility and redivided them among his followers from the "Hills"; he began an extensive public works program that not only solved the problem of the unemployed but also began the creative period in Athenian art and architecture. To win prestige for his rule, he inaugurated a large number of games and festivals at which athletes and poets competed, and thus stimulated the literary arts among the Athenians. But his absolute power did not please the freedom-loving Athenians; upon his death, a new struggle ensued among the aristocrats led by ISOCRATES and the democrats led by CLEISTHENES (who had the combined support of the "Hills" and the "Shore").

Cleisthenes's Reforms. Cleisthenes sought to extend Athenian democracy; but he realized that this was not possible until the older rival groups and factions were destroyed. He therefore effected a new division of the Athenian citizenry into ten "tribes." The aristocratic Council of 400 was replaced by a Council of 500 made up of 50 delegates from each of the "tribes." Each tribe was expected to provide the army with a regiment and a general; thus the army was "democratized." A direct democracy was instituted: every citizen was expected to serve either in the Assembly which voted on the proposals of the Council of 500, declared war or made peace, voted appropriations, or elected archons; or to serve in the Council of 500 itself, the body which prepared legislation and administered all laws passed by the Assembly; or to serve on citizen juries, each consisting of 501 members (such as that which tried Socrates), which decided by secret ballot on cases brought before it; and, of course, to serve in the army when called. To prevent the return of tyranny, Cleisthenes introduced the procedure of ostracism of those who threatened the peace or democracy of the state. Party strife was reduced, finally, by having all offices filled by lot. Athenian democracy had now reached a high point.

Pericles (500-c. 429 B.C.) This greatest statesman of antiquity who ruled Athens as a "political boss" for thirty years and who introduced the idea of payment for public services could say with justified pride:

> Our constitution does not copy the laws of neighboring states; we are rather a pattern to others than imitators ourselves. Its administration favors the many instead of the few; this is why it is called a democracy. If we look to the laws, they afford equal justice to all in their private differences; if to social standing, advancement in public life falls to reputation for capacity, class considerations nor being allowed to interfere with merit; nor again does poverty bar the way . . . . . . Nor are these the only points in which our city is worthy of admiration. We cultivate refinement without extravagance and knowledge without effeminacy; wealth we employ more for use than for show, and place the real disgrace of poverty not in owning to the fact but in declining to struggle against it. Our public men have, besides politics, their private affairs to attend to, and our ordinary citizens, though occupied with the pursuits of industry, are still fair judges of public matters; for, unlike any other nation, regarding him who takes no part in these duties not as unambitious but as useless, we Athenians are able to judge at all events if we cannot originate, and instead of looking on discussion as a stumbling block in the way of action, we think it an indispensable preliminary to a wise action . . . . . In short, I say that as a city we are the school of Hellas. (Thucydides, *History of the Peloponnesian War.*)

This brief citation, summarizing the goals of the democratic state for all time, was part of a funeral oration delivered on the occasion of memorial services to the Athenians who had fallen in the Peloponnesian War between Athens and Sparta.

THE WARS OF ANCIENT GREECE

The Greek nations were forced to fight their way to freedom because they were caught between the Persian Empire expanding westward from Asia Minor and Carthage expanding eastward from North Africa. The Persian menace first struck the Ionian Greeks who were resident in Asia Minor; by 546 B.C. Cyrus had subdued all the Greek cities there. Mainland Greece was now faced with the possibility that the Persians would cross over the Hellespont into Europe. Already the Persians were seeking to dominate the sea trade on the Mediterranean. When, therefore, Aristagoras in 499 B.C. led the Ionian cities in revolt against DARIUS, Athens risked the fury of the Persians by sending them naval assistance; Sparta refused to send aid. Darius gathered tremendous land and naval forces for an assault on Greece itself.

The Persians first landed at **Marathon** (490 B.C.). This direct threat to the independence of all the Greeks failed to unify them; the Athenian army was left to face the Persians alone. Under the military leadership of Miltiades and Callimachus the Persians were routed and driven into the sea. The results of this victory were immense: it showed that the Persians were not invincible; it delayed a second Persian attack for ten years; it began the Athenian leadership of Greece; it spelled the end of the tyranny as a form of government (for the Persians were fostering this form on the Ionian shore); it inspired the great classics of Aeschylus and Herodotus; it ensured that "western civilization" as opposed to "oriental civilization" would prevail in Europe. Of more immediate value, it forced the Greek cities to unite against the certainty of the second attack.

This attack came in 480 B.C. XERXES, the son of Darius, had gathered a force of 200,000 men for the attack and had selected **Thermopylae** as the battleground. LEONIDAS made his immortal stand against the Persians here and delayed them long enough to permit the evacuation of Athens. The Greeks were unable to prevent the destruction of Athens; nor did they make strenuous efforts to defeat the Persians on land. Greek strategy was to achieve a decisive victory on the sea. They met the

Persians, as planned, at **Salamis** and wiped out the Persian fleet and army there. On the same day Persia's Carthaginian allies were routed. One year later, at Platea, the Persians were defeated on land and driven out of Europe.

The Peloponnesian Wars (431-404 B.C.) The unity finally achieved in the war against the Persians did not last. Capitalizing upon her leadership, Athens, in 478 B.C., organized the **Delian League,** a confederacy of about 200 city-states; then, led by Themistocles and Aristides, Athens converted this League into an imperialist grab-bag for herself. She intervened by occupation and threat of occupation in the internal affairs of the League members; she forced them to pay a tribute to Athens for "protection"; she dominated all their commercial activities. Athenian imperialism forced Sparta, in alliance with Corinth, to take steps against the possible loss of their own independence by strengthening the Peloponnesian League.

Thus matters stood when Pericles came to power in Athens. Democratic at home, Pericles pursued an aggressive imperialist policy abroad: he broke a long-standing alliance with Sparta; he allied with the enemies of Sparta and Corinth (Argos, the landed nobility of Thessaly, Megara, etc.); he helped a group of rebellious helots to colonize in Athenian territory; he began a policy to drive Corinthian trade out of the Aegean. Anticipating the reaction of the Spartans, Pericles completed the fortification of Athens by building the Long Walls connecting Athens with the port of Peiraeus, a distance of four and a half miles.

These preparations were made none too soon for in 431 B.C. Sparta and her allies declared war on Athens. The war lasted 27 years. It was featured, as Thucydides pointed out, by "calamities such as Hellas had never known."

After years of stalemate, the Athenians were defeated at **Syracuse** in the west (413 B.C.) and ultimately at Athens in 404 B.C. The results of the Peloponnesian wars were calamitous in the extreme: the great age of Athens ended; Spartan hegemony was destroyed by the city-state of Thebes under the leadership of Epaminondas; war and confusion prepared the way for a new power rising in the north and readying itself to spring southward.

THE RISE OF MACEDONIA

Philip. At the beginning of the fourth century B.C. Macedonia was a semi-barbarian state on the northern fringe of Greece. PHILIP came to the Macedonian throne in 359 B.C. As a youth he had been taken as a hostage to Grecian Thebes; there he learned to hold Greek culture in great reverence and to disdain Greek politics, which had deteriorated.

Philip, it seems, determined to save Greece from itself by a liberating Macedonian conquest. He would unite her under his single rule and spread her culture abroad. His policy of conquest was to be by devious political fracturing of whatever Greek unity existed and then by direct military assault. With this goal before him, he developed a powerful army and seized the gold mines of Grecian Amphipolis. When the opportunity presented itself he entered a "sacred war" against Phocis on the side of ruling Thebes and this netted him Greek citizenship and a place on the Amhyctyonic Council.

At this time, only one Greek saw through Philip's maneuvering—DEMOSTHENES, and in his **"Philippics"** he warned of conquest to come and urged unity—military and political—upon the Greek city-states. His passionate and eloquent words went unheeded, even laughed at—Philip was such a cultured gentleman who lived so far away! With this advantage Philip defeated Olynthus and neutralized Athens herself. Against the advice of Demosthenes Athens permitted Macedonia to cooperate with her in a second "sacred war" against Amphissa. In the course of this campaign Philip took over all of central Greece. Thoroughly alarmed, Athens and Thebes permitted Demosthenes to organize a counter-Macedonian **Pan-Hellenic League**—which Philip crushed. He was now sole ruler in Greece. His policy toward the conquered Greeks was one of firm kindness; he even offered them an honored place in an expedition against the Persians that he was now planning. But in 336 B.C. he was murdered. His son Alexander succeeded.

Alexander. ALEXANDER THE GREAT was tutored by the great Greek philosopher Aristotle; and no more thoughtful world conqueror ever existed. Better than most, Alexander knew and appreciated the glory of Greek culture. But he knew that no Greek was safe from barbabrian conquest until Greece had conquered all the world. He brought all his genius for military tactics, propaganda and political strategy to bear upon the realization of this goal.

First, Alexander crushed an uprising of Spartans in Greece itself; then, with half his army he went to meet the Persians in Asia Minor. He met them at Granicus in 334 B.C. and at Issus in 333 B.C. and routed them each time. Choosing not to pursue Darius, Alexander turned south and subdued the Phoenician coast; he then descended deeper into Egypt. Here his purpose was revealed fully for he launched a huge public works program to restore all things Egyptian and then recruited thousands of Greek intellectuals and workingmen to build for him a huge Greek city in Egypt itself; this city became **Alexandria,** the first cosmopolitan city in the world, a meeting-place for peoples from all over the world.

This done, Alexander now returned to meet Darius who had regrouped and enlarged his armed forces until they far outnumbered Alexander's; at Arbela, in 331 B.C., Darius was defeated again. Though Darius escaped, he was murdered by his own men; Alexander then assumed for himself the Persian title of the "Great King." He took over Persia's capitals and its treasuries; he assumed Oriental mannerisms and even his Macedonians had to now prostrate themselves before him. In pursuit of the murderers of Darius Alexander now pushed on to conquer Bactria and India; but exhaustion had set in.

Alexander moved on to Babylon, where he contracted the swamp fever and died. He was thirty-three years old; but in his brief lifetime he had changed the face of the world. Alexander's empire died with him. PTOLEMY, a follower, seized Egypt and instituted a pharaonic rule; Seleucus took Syria and the lands of the Persian Empire; Greece degenerated into an internecine war between an Aetolian League and an Achaean League and Macedonia. The world awaited a new unifier and a new peace. In Italy one such was coming slowly to life and power.

Though chaos succeeded Alexander's efforts, what his conquest accomplished was incalculable. He broke down the barriers which had persisted for three millenia between Oriental and Occidental; out of the intermixture of cultures came a new, brilliant Hellenistic civilization; hieroglyphic and cuneiform fell to superiority of the Greek tongue; release of the Persian treasures stimulated trade and commerce to new heights; trade lanes now began to extend from the Pacific Ocean to the Atlantic; new cities grew up and old ones were revitalized all along the trade lanes. He had decisively altered his world.

CHAPTER FIVE

GREEK CULTURE

THE GREEK IDEAL

When one examines Greek culture, one is struck by the persistence of certain ideals in Greek thought. Greek thought was **humanistic,** that is, it was centered on *man*, not the gods. What characterized man, the Greeks felt, was his **rationality** and so Greek thinkers stressed the processes of reasoning and the uses of reason to modify or control instinct and will. **Self-examination** was vital to these ideals; **the unexamined life was not worth living,** said Socrates. An examined life revealed the need for **order, proportion and restraint—nothing in excess.** These cautions, however, were not intended to restrain the human urges for *arete*, or **excellence;** the final goal of intelligent living was **to realize one's full potential,** in body and mind.

Greeks aimed at **versatility.** Greek education reflected these ideals. The best young men were therefore trained in many directions: physical training, health instruction and military science; vocational preparation, chiefly the speech arts since the Greek citizen (in Athens) was expected to take a direct part in the shaping of civic policies; dancing for grace; rhetoric, philosophy and mathematics for sharpening the rational faculties.

GREEK RELIGION

There was no church among the Greeks; no creed nor articles of faith. Priests were public officers assigned to perform religious rites, not to proclaim and enforce official dogma. Yet religion lay at the core of the Greek way of life.

Like all ancient peoples the Greeks sought to live rationally in a potentially hostile universe; they wanted to know the causes of things and events in their environment so they could shape them to their needs. It seemed clear to the Greeks that natural events were determined by spiritual beings or gods. Zeus was the sky; Apollo, the sun; Demeter, the earth; Poseidon, the sea. There were Nymphs in caves and fountains; Nereids in the ocean; Oreads in the mountains; and Dryads in the woods. Human passion, too, was part of nature and the work of gods. Aphrodite was love; Ares, war; Athena, wisdom; the Furies, guilt; etc. These natural and passionate forces, then, were personified; the gods were conceived as larger-than-life mortals, capable of human thought, emotion, and caprice. In fact, they differed from mortals only in their size and immortality. By creative myth-making the Greeks worked out the lives of these gods until they "knew" them intimately. (It is *we* who call these tales of the gods "myths"; to the ancient Greeks they were *facts*.)

Greek Mythology. We cannot here recount the multitude of Greek myths; but we can appraise something of their significance to the Greeks. Greek mythology helped forge social bonds among the Greeks, since many traced their origins from the gods, the half-gods or heroes of antiquity. It provided a common area of worship and strengthened unity among Greeks. It was through common acceptance of such religious institutions as the **Delphinian Oracle** and the sacred oaths which made treaties and conventions valid and through the numerous religious festivals that national unity was fostered. Mythology provided the Greeks with explanations of creation, the past history of mankind, the reason for good and evil on earth, the nature of life and life after death, the limit of man's possible achievement. Men could not imitate the gods without being guilty of *hubris* (arrogance or pride) and suffering extreme punishment, punishment visited upon succeeding generations. Men and gods together were bound in the grip of *Moira* or *Fate*. Fate was all-powerful; what happened, happened.

The Apollonian Cult. Apollo, god of light and patron of the arts, of beauty and of music, was worshipped in temple and oracle. He embraced in his person the principle of rational orderliness; his precepts, inscribed upon the walls of his temples, became moral law for the Greeks. Apollo enjoined his worshippers to live in moderation; to observe the limits set by authority. It was violation of these moral precepts that gave to the Greek dramatists their immortal themes. The Apollonian idea of restraint informed Greek architecture, characterized by cool, balanced symmetry, dignity and calm.

The Dionysian Cult. Opposed to Apollonianism was the emotional, ecstatic, mystical and sensual elements in the Greek character. Greeks who rejected the cult of Apollo turned to the cult of the vine-and-wine god, **Dionysus.** Initiates of this cult believed in the mildly drunken state that brought men closer to the gods through heightened vitality,

creativity and hope. Apollo and Dionysus, however, were not mutually exclusive. By the fifth century B.C. the two cults merged: the Apollonian was practiced in the birthtime of Spring; the Dionysian in the death-time of Winter. Thus the Greeks struck a balance between reason and ecstasy, between restraint and emotion.

Mystery Cults. During the fifth and fourth centuries B.C. the **Orphic and Eleusinian mystery cults** made their appearance. The first was based on the myth of Orpheus. Orpheus lost his Eurydice and was permitted to descend into Hades and bring her back to earth. He did so, but he ignored a warning not to gaze upon her until she was well out of Hades. Once more he lost her. Now he sang his loss upon his lyre so mournfully that the gods forgave him his *hubris* and permitted Eurydice to return to earth.

The religious implications of this myth were numerous; chiefly, however, it enabled the Orphic Greek worshippers to celebrate the **mystery of death and rebirth, of descent into hell and resurrection.** There were intimations of immortality in the myth as well. Influenced by PYTHAGORAS, Orphics developed a **dogma** that mankind was bound to the wheel of life, death and reincarnation. After countless reincarnations the soul might escape from this wheel of birth and rebirth and achieve eternal rest in the Elysian Fields ("heaven"). Believing thus, mystery cults met in secret conclave and conducted rites and sacrifices which were intended to bring them in close contact with their gods. Since they were secret, our knowledge of what went on is meager in the extreme. Eleusinian beliefs were closely related to those of the Orphics. This cult stemmed from worship of Persephone who was stolen from Demeter by Hades but permitted to return to earth during spring and summer when all nature came to life.

Greek Religious Attitudes. In the Greek mind, religion was not concerned with conscience; gods and men were too much alike and the relations between them were external and mechanical. However, since the gods were capricious, each with a will of its own, they had to be propitiated. For this reason, the Greeks developed elaborate systems of sacrifice, prayer and divination. Divination was based on the belief that the gods occasionally gave some sign of their intentions; the flight of birds, celestial phenomena, accidentally encountered people, the shape of animal entrails, and so on any or all might point the direction of man's fate. Even more direct contact with the gods was possible through the oracles. Greeks did not believe that man's nature was corrupt, that the flesh and the spirit were at war with one another. Man was faulty but not wicked. Punishment for fault was passed on through the generations. Atonement, however, was possible, particularly through sacrifice. The Greeks, therefore, had no sense of sin as, say, Christianity understands that concept.

Religious Criticism. Religious beliefs were subjected to sharp criticism by many Greek thinkers. Criticism took two directions: it attacked the idea of polytheism and sought to substitute a belief in one god in its place; or it sought to sweep away all gods and substitute a system of beliefs based upon natural science and philosophy. The humanity of the gods—their loves, infidelities, hates, gluttony, rashness, cowardice—were submitted to critical scrutiny; their immoralities—seductions, desertions, lies—were objected to as unworthy of imitation.

GREEK PHILOSOPHY

The Nature of the Universe. The first Greeks to philosophize about the nature of the universe broke sharply with religious supernaturalism. THALES, ANAXIMANDER, ANAXIMENES and PYTHAGORAS assumed that beneath the multiplicity and variety of the things on earth there must be some single substance. They reasoned that this substance had to be **material** (water, air, physical extension, number), **alive** and **self-moving**; it had to have in its movement some pattern of **order** and **regularity** and was therefore subject to the **basic law of cause and effect.** Man was included in this material order.

These Greeks were obviously quite close to the philosophical concepts of modern science. With the modern scientist they believed that there was a single explanation for many effects; that the simplest explanation—the one involving the least number of assumptions—was probably correct; that nothing came out of nothing; that matter could be neither created nor destroyed; that matter followed some law of evolution from the simple to the complex; that number was expressive of the relations among things.

The Nature of Reality. The first Greek philosophers assumed that reality was alive; change was of the nature of things and needed no explanation. When the search for a single substance underlying reality was momentarily suspended, the problem of **change** came into prominence. Two broad schools developed: those who held that all reality was change, process, flux, a *becoming* and not a *being;* and those who held that change was an **illusion,** that there must be something in the universe which

is immovable, indivisible, continuous and infinite. The problem of **permanence and change** occupied the Greek mind for years and many ingenious efforts were made to solve it.

Of great significance for the future was the solution offered by the **pluralists.** At first they held that the universe consists not of one, but of four substances—earth, air, fire and water—and that all matter was a combination of these four elements. By the time of LEUCIPPUS and DEMOCRITUS the four elements had been further partitioned until they were **atoms.** There were countless millions of these atoms, or particles, in the universe. Each was indivisible. Things were combinations of atoms. Atoms were in continuous motion and therefore the generation of new combinations of atoms was endless and eternal.

The Nature of Man. Greek scientific speculation, without experiment and measurement, led nowhere. Wearied of such speculation a group of thinkers arose who argued that the riddle of the universe was insoluble, and that the proper study of mankind was man. Known as **Sophists,** they argued that **"man was the measure of all things"** because as a thinking being he was capable of moulding the universe to his needs and desires—by right living. The study of **right living** led to the formulation of **ethics** and speculation about right and wrong behavior. Sophists were not all in agreement as to what constituted right living. Some held that men should believe in those ideas that work; whatever works, is true . . . for him who benefits. According to this belief there are no **absolutes** of good behavior; all things are relative to their success or failure. Others held that might makes right and that men should follow that course which gives them power to exert their will on others.

Opposed to these relativistic notions was SOCRATES (469-399 B.C.). He agreed with the Sophists that man was the proper study of man; but he disagreed that the rules for right living could not be discovered. He felt that beneath all diversities, contradictions, ambiguities of behavior and conflicts of opinion lay universal truths which men would recognize as such if they could be made to see them. Men would *do* right if they *knew* right. Knowledge, then, is true virtue. But how are men to be led to knowledge? By having them examine *what they think they know.* Therefore Socrates began to question all sorts of men and by his questioning led them to see the absurdities in their thinking (the dialectic method). Having dispelled their current thoughts, he then led them by a careful series of **deductions from accepted truths** to the rules of right living. These truths are indistinguishable from those of his pupil, PLATO, who recorded them in his *Dialogues*.

THE GREAT PHILOSOPHERS

PLATO (427-347 B.C.)

PLATO was the first of the philosophers to construct a complete philosophical system and to found a university for propagating his ideas. In his "Academy" men met to study mathematics, astronomy, logic and political science. Plato's most famous pupil was ARISTOTLE.

Reality. Plato rejected the world of change as a source of knowledge about the world. Information derived from man's sense organs is simply not stable enough to get accurate knowledge. At best it gives men **opinions.** For true knowledge you have to go behind the world of things to the **form** of things. These forms, capable of being defined in general terms, endure forever. For example, things may have a triangular shape, but they are never perfect triangles; however, the *idea of a triangle* as defined in geometry is real, permanent, indestructible and changeless.

Ideas or Forms. Ideas or forms cannot be seen; they are **mental** concepts. They are present in the mind but their existence does not depend on the mind. They have an independent life of their own. The things all about us can only hint as to the perfect nature of the idea or form of such things as courage, honesty, beauty, health-ness, color-ness, swiftness, mountain-ness, chair-ness, sameness and difference. These are the **eternal essences** of things. These are the models of what all things strive to become. The essence of all essences is **the Good.** It was the Good, in its creative aspect, which imparted truth, knowledge and existence to all the other ideas and forms. (This idea will not be so difficult to understand if we make a loose comparison of the idea of God, the Creator with Plato's The Good the Creator.)

Platonic Love. Plato felt that men aspire to be united with the eternal Ideas and that this aspiration was motivated by Love. **Love** begins as a profane attraction to earthly things; but it ends as Sacred Love, Love for the Good separated from all mundane objects. Those who rise to the love of the absolute and universal and can merge themselves with its timeless essence will have achieved immortality. Thus, there were two parts to man (dualism)—one that remained earthbound and one that could soar above the earth into the eternal.

Utopia. If the Good ruled the universe, **Justice** ruled over the affairs of men. Perfect justice was possible only in the perfect state. In his *Republic* Plato set out to construct the perfect state. There were three types of men: men of Appetite (those dominated by the flesh and its needs), men of Spirit (those dominated by the will and its demands), and men of Reason (those who used intelligence to control their appetites and spirits). In the perfect state the men of Appetite would become the obedient and working masses, men of Spirit would become the military defenders of the state, and men of Reason would become the **Philosopher-Kings.** Each had to be educated to his role in society.

Thus an intellectual elite with the aid of the military would rule over obedient masses, each keeping his place, and the ends of perfect justice would be served.

Knowledge. The perfect state evolved out of man's wisdom, the highest form of knowledge, which few men attained. Plato distinguished four stages of knowledge: random sensations shifting through the mind as **imagining** and guessing; **opinions,** more stable but still unreliable knowledge derived from the senses; **understanding,** the threshhold to conceiving the Ideas; and wisdom or **dialectic,** complete grasp of the "real" world. Men lived, said Plato, as in a cave of flickering shadows (sense data) cast by the real images (Ideas) in the Sun (The Good) outside the Cave (our imprisonment in the world of illusion). Only a few could learn to look into the sun without being blinded. Plato could not deny that knowledge begins in the senses without finding another origin of knowledge. His argument was that knowledge of the Ideas is within us at birth. Then where did these Ideas come from?

Immortality. Ideas came from the soul of man which had existed before he was born. In being born, man forgot his origin. When a human being conceives an Idea, he is *remembering* what he once knew as an immortal soul now returned to earth. Logical reasoning convinced Plato that just as life turns to death, death turns to life. After each death there is a reincarnation of the soul which has continued to live after death. After many such reincarnations, Plato taught, the soul can be freed from any return to life.

Plato and the Idea of God. In his later doctrine the Supreme Good became for Plato the idea of God, the uncreated Creator, who brought a formless chaos into harmony with a group of perfect Ideas operating under the guidance of a World Soul. A chain of being was then created ascending from the lowest level of pure matter to the highest of pure soul. The universe was then set in uniform, circular motion with the earth at dead center. Motion was the striving of each part in the ascending chain of being to achieve its next higher form. The Spirit of God—the Supreme Good—filters through the universe with its righteousness, its rationality, its orderliness.

ARISTOTLE (384-321 B.C.)

ARISTOTLE was a pupil of Plato; like his teacher, he also founded a university, The Lyceum. Aristotle's genius was universal; his learning embraced all that was known in ancient Greece of physics, astronomy, biology, physiology, anatomy, natural history, psychology, political science, ethics, logic, rhetoric, art, theology and metaphysics. Plato's general outlook was idealistic, theistic and mystical; Aristotle's was analytical, scientific and objective.

Critique of Plato. Aristotle felt that Plato was wrong when he divorced the Ideas from objects known through the senses. For Aristotle, there was no disembodied idea; an abstraction could not have an independent existence.

Reality. Reality was in the particular, individual and concrete substance; the universal was simply a convenient classification of a large number of particulars. (In other words, the Idea of an apple comes from seeing a large number of concrete apples.) Every object has two aspects: **matter** or that which makes it an object; and **form** or that which classifies it and distinguishes it from other objects. There is no matter without some form and no form without some matter, said Aristotle. Form and matter stand to each other as **actuality** and **potentiality**; each actuality has some new potentiality (e.g. earth becomes grass becomes nourishment for cattle becomes milk, etc.)

Change. Change takes place when the potentiality in an object actualizes. In this process four "causes" are revealed: a **material cause,** or something to be changed; an **efficient cause,** or that which moves something to change; a **formal cause,** or that which determines the direction of the change; and a **final cause,** or the inner purposes drawing the object to its final goal. In this order of causes, the final is **prior** to the others; the oak tree is already in the acorn; what a thing is to become **determines** the order of the becoming. Thus every object contains an **entelechy** or a motive power to realize itself.

First Causes. Aristotle accepted the universe as uncreated and eternal, a brute fact; but something must have set it in motion. Logically, this first cause had to be an **"unmoved mover,"** something imparting motion but not sharing it, something causing change but not itself changing. If this were so, the first cause also had to be **pure actuality,** something without any **potentiality** and therefore self-existing, self-sustaining and self-explanatory. Beneath the first cause the universe was arranged in a pyramidal form from unformed matter with unrealized potentialities to the human mind which has the least of unrealized potentiality in it. Physical bodies come alive, live physical bodies become conscious, conscious living bodies think and Thought is the nearest thing to Pure Actuality, form without matter.

Physics and Astronomy. According to Aristotle, physical bodies were composed of earth, water, air, fire and ether; these are the first actualizations of the potential. They are characterized by the occupation of space. Space is finite and spherical. Time is united to space by motion. Motion is of three kinds: rectilinear, circular and rectilinear-circular. Following rectilinear motion, earth and water move downward to a center; air and fire move upward to the circumference of the terrestrial sphere. Circular motion characterizes the ether; ether is therefore the substance of celestial bodies. Aristotle's astronomy was geocentric: celestial bodies moved in perfect circles *around the earth*. It was known, however, that some planets did not describe perfect circles; their motion was eccentric. To account for eccentric motions, Aristotle accepted the idea that the universe contains pockets of "crystaline spheres" or hollow containers within containers. Each sphere had two motions: its own oblique motion and that of its container. Any aberration from perfect circularity was accounted for by the oblique paths of the eccentrics. (It is important to describe these erroneous ideas so fully because they ruled the intellectual world for nearly two thousand years before they were overthrown by modern science.)

Biology. Inorganic matter becomes organic when it is infused with *pneuma* or breath and actualizes a soul. The soul, therefore, is the actualization of the body and could not exist without a body. The soul is not a physical substance, but the form which guides the body to realize its potentiality. Realization takes place on three levels: vegetative, sensitive and intelligent. Matter with a vegetative soul experiences nutrition, reproduction, etc.; with a sensitive soul, feeling and perception; with an intelligent soul, thought.

Psychology. The purpose of sensation, Aristotle reasoned, was to actualize in the mind the qualities in the objects outside; hence sensation was not just the receiving of impressions but an active process in which the sense organs participated. Touch was the basic sense and gave to objects their material properties. Sight was next in order of importance; hearing, however, was more vital than sight for thinking. Perception was achieved through a medium—hearing through air, seeing through luminosity, smelling through moisture. Aristotle now assumed that there was a "common sense" which brought together all these messages from the outside so that an object could be presented to the mind; this common sense resided in the heart. Out of the sensitivities of the soul, desire is actualized; out of desire, pleasure and pain; out of pleasure and pain, motivation; and out of motivation, behavior. All behavior is purposeful, pursuing predetermined ends.

The Rational Soul. The intelligent soul has the faculty of reason. Reason can abstract from things their Forms. It operates by judgment or thought. Thought is without matter; its potentialities are all within itself; it cannot change; it can only be absent or present; it is therefore one with what it thinks. How does one think a truthful thought (for thought can often fall into error)? Aristotle now postulated the existence in the universe of an Active Reason. When the Active Reason enters the mind it illuminates it with a sudden insight into the truth. Man's brief encounter with the Active Reason is all that he enjoys of immortality.

Logic. Aristotle was one of the greatest investigators of logic—the "grammar of correct thinking." All thinking, he said, is by categories and these include substance, quantity, quality, relation, place, time, action, being acted upon, state and position. Everything we think falls somewhere in these categories. Categories are joined into sentences or **propositions** which predicate one thing of another (e.g., *Man is a rational animal*). Not all predicates give us an increase of knowledge. Some denote qualities that tell us little of what the subject really is (e.g., *Man is hairy*); others denote important but not definitive properties (e.g., Man runs); still others give us the essential properties (e.g., *Man is rational*). The subject of a proposition has its own distinctive definition, its **species** or that which differentiates it from all other subjects; it may also be identified with its **genus,** which includes it with all other subjects. (Compare "Man is rational" with "Man is living matter": the first is species, the second genus.) Proper definition must precede reasoning if reasoning is to be truthful. Reasoning must also be accurate; it must proceed by correct inference. Correct inference proceeds **syllogistically,** that is from **major premise** to **minor premise** to **conclusion.** (Major Premise: All men are mortal; Minor Premise: Socrates is a man; Conclusion: Socrates is mortal.) (For detailed account of the substance and methods of Logic see **Philosophy Made Simple,** Made Simple Books, Inc.)

Ethics. *Nicomachean Ethics* is Aristotle's great and influential work in the field of Ethics. In this classic Aristotle was concerned to discover what behavior is best for a creature with bodily needs, appetites and passions, reason and intellect in unpredictable admixtures. Human behavior should lead to happiness; but what is happiness. For many reasons Aristotle rejected the hedonist claim that happiness is synonymous with pleasure. Happiness, he felt, is the actualization of man's potentiality for leading a life of reason and a life of balance among his many activities. To live virtuously is to live moderately. Behavior must fall somewhere between over-indulgence and over-inhibition. Virtue is the Golden Mean of balance and restraint.

EXAMPLES OF THE GOLDEN MEAN

EXCESS	MEAN	INHIBITION
rashness	courage	cowardice
self-indulgence	temperance	insensibility
prodigality	liberality	stinginess
ostentation	magnificence	niggardliness
vainglory	greatness of soul	humility

The moral quality of an act is determined by the **intention** behind it; intention involves a preference and results in choice. Our choices should conform with the ends natural to man as a species. In acting we bear the moral consequences of our own acts. Morality is conduct illuminated by intelligence.

The State. In his *Politics* Aristotle examined the actualization of the social potential in the form of the state. He attacked Plato's Utopia—its rigidity, frozen classes, communization of property, women and children. Public interest, he said, is best served by private interest and private interest flourishes best where the individual is free to move. The good state is the one that serves the common interest with greatest justice. The best forms of government are kingship, aristocracy or constitutional democracy—if the rulers are enlightened and benevolent and rule disinterestedly in the interest of all. Disinterested rule is rule by law; under law the happiness of all takes precedence over the happiness of the few.

Rhetoric. In the ideal state all citizens will be politicians. They therefore should master the art of oratory. Aristotle worked out the rules for successful oratory. It should be directed to the emotions and prejudices of the audience. These are best aroused by careful alignment of moral maxims to create the impression that the orator is a man of wisdom. An orator should state his case and prove it; and the best proof is to discredit your opponent.

Esthetics. In his *Poetics* Aristotle examined the role of the fine arts in the ideal state. Art, he said, is an imitation of nature; men respond to art because an act of imitation stimulates their senses and intellect—even if it is a painful subject. The purpose of art is not moral but esthetic; it seeks to give pleasure by stirring the emotions or making us think; it is, above all, recreational. The greatest of the art forms is *Tragedy* which shows human character and conduct in its most universal aspect; which makes use of the ancillary arts of song, dance and choric recital; which arouses pity and fear but purges these of their terror. Great tragedy follows, where possible, the three **unities** of plot, time and place; it tells a complete story and limits it to one day and one setting—where possible.

What is the effect upon the viewer of witnessing the story of men and women surrounded by a fickle, furtive destiny and brought to the depths of unhappiness by the uncertainties of human life? Aristotle argued that the audience experiences pity and terror but that these emotions act as a **catharsis** —that is, a cleansing. Through the tragic hero one cleanses himself of his own predicament; one identifies himself with universal tragedy and by this means makes his own personal tragedy smaller. The end-product is pleasure induced by a release of emotional tension.

Finally, what makes the tragic hero? He is a person of high rank enjoying good fortune; he has some flaw in his character; suffering follows; downfall is sudden and produced by something unforseen; but out of the misery and the downfall there comes an increase in knowledge, a deeper appreciation of human limitations and human possibilities.

LITERATURE

Greek literature began with poetry and the earliest of the poems were the two great epics of Homer, the recital of the deeds of heroic men engaged in heroic actions. As Greek civilization matured, however, a more subjective, romantic and passionate note appeared in Greek verse—the lyric and elegiac were born. Poets now sang of love, war, sorrow, ennui; they composed marriage songs, choric odes and political and personal satires. As reflection matured, there arose the gnomic verse, that is, verse which recited maxims and precepts of wise living; through gnomic verse moral maxims like "Know thyself" and "Nothing in excess" were propagated.

Greek Tragedy. Greek literature achieved its greatest height in the drama, particularly in the tragic drama. Drama evolved from religious ceremonial in honor of Dionysus, beginning probably as a chorus of men dressed as goats or satyrs singing dithyrambs and dancing. THESPIS (ca. 550 B.C.) introduced a speaker who addressed the chorus and thus began the dramatic dialogue. Tradition soon accumulated about these dramatic presentations: they were written for prizes; they were produced in groups of three (trilogies) or four (tetrologies); they used simple scenery, usually a temple façade; actors wore masks; they were produced in amphitheaters; they employed machines to lift actors above and lower them onto the stage; etc.

Tragedy had a five-part structure: a prologue; a parados or entrance song of the chorus; episodes; stasima or choral songs following each episode; and an exodus or finale. Tragedies were based on mythological or heroic characters. The story was well-known beforehand to the audience; they were chiefly interested in the dramatist's treatment of the known. Most of the action was performed offstage. The chief devices for creating and releasing tension were foreshadowing, oracular utterance and *deus ex machina*—a god hoisted by a machine over the stage who resolved the conflict. Characterization was stressed. Poetic meters were severe and stately.

Aeschylus (525-456 B.C.) AESCHYLUS was the first of the great tragic dramatists (*The Suppliants, The Persians, The Seven Against Thebes, Prometheus Bound* and the *Oresteia*—A Trilogy). Aeschylus added a second actor to the Thespian form, reduced the numbers of the chorus, increased the spoken dialogue and originated the trilogy. His plays were concerned with the nature of the gods, the problem of evil, human responsibility and patriotism. In seeking to bring some moral order out of the chaos of private revenge, he stressed the omnipotence of the gods, their justness, the need for men to submit to divine decree by making responsible choices. He pointed out that when men sin—through pride or murder—they must expiate their sins through suffering; but suffering is worthwhile if it brings wisdom in its train.

Sophocles (495-406 B.C.). (*Ajax, Antigone*, the *Oedipus Trilogy, Electra, Philoctetes*). SOPHOCLES added another actor; increased the amount of dialogue; and reduced the chorus to a relatively subordinate role. He concentrated his plays upon single, central issues. He made excellent use of dramatic irony where the audience knows that which the actor does not know and his characterization was increasingly realistic. Sophocles contrasted characters and revealed their inner motivations. He therefore reduced the role of the gods in human affairs and concentrated upon the individual or family flaw that resulted in tragedy. He, too, believed that tragic suffering results in wisdom.

Euripides (480-408 B.C.). (*Alcestis, Medea, Ion, The Trojan Women, Electra, Iphegenia in Tauris*). EURIPIDES added a third character to the *dramatis personae* and further reduced the role of the chorus; he made the prologue an address to the audience; he introduced romantic love; he experimented with musical "bridges"; he made use of sensationalism, melodrama, mad scenes, comic relief, etc.; he utilized subplots; and most important, he treated human beings **realistically.** Euripides's creed was pessimistic; he had lost faith in the orthodox gods, in the ruling democracy, in women and in the possibility of ever attaining happiness.

Comedy. Extant Greek comedy is limited to ARISTOPHANES (448-380 B.C. (*The Archarnians, The Knights, The Clouds, The Wasps, The Birds, The Frogs, Lysistrata*). Greek comedy served many purposes: as satire on topical events and personages; for ribaldry and buffoonery; as wit; as flight from reality and the like. Aristophanes was a rigid political conservative and through his comedies attacked all innovations in contemporary Greece—new manners, new religious beliefs, new philosophies, etc. He regarded these as dangerous symptoms of degeneracy and sought to restore the Greeks to old-fashioned sanity. Thus he opposed the Peloponnesian War, democracy, Socrates, the jury system and Athenian imperialism, Euripides, Sophocles and Aeschylus—in fact, most of mankind.

GREEK ART

Greek art was to a great extent a projection in stone and clay of Greek religious and philosophical thought. For example, the influence of the Greek religion is evidenced in the fact that most of Greek architecture was temple building, and much of Greek sculpture was pictorial representation of gods, heroes, myths and legends. The artistic equivalent of "nothing in excess" is present in the remarkable proportion and balance of Greek structures and in the idealized portraiture of Greek sculpture. The essential worldliness of the Greek outlook can be seen in the naturalism of Greek modeling and in the application of scientific and psychological principles to achieve the most realistic and esthetic effects. Above all, Greek architects and sculptors followed an *order* of performance, an order transmitted to posterity as "classic." Within this order, however, the Greek artist was permitted great leeway for individual expression. In the free air of Ancient Greece, Oriental anonymity died and the individual rose from the mass.

Architecture. *Order* in Greek art was expressed as *orders* in Greek architecture. These orders were threefold: **Doric, Ionic** and **Corinthian**—simple, ornamental and elaborate. The orders can best be identified from the **capitals** used in the **columns.**

The most noted Greek temples were **Parthenon** and **Erechtheum** both constructed on the Acropolis of Athens. The Parthenon was the focal point of a sacred way that led from the heart of the city to the summit of the Acropolis. Entrance was through the colonnaded **Propylea,** made of white Pentelic marble, into a sacred area where stood the statue of Athena Promachos. The Parthenon was on the right. Essentially it was a **cella,** a central room housing the cult statues, surrounded by a colonnade. The order was **Doric** and was based on a simple post-and-lintel construction. Three steps led up to the **stylobate**—the ground on which the columns rested. The columns were **fluted** (grooved) and curved so that they tapered at the top. Topping the column was the **capital,** upon which the **entablature** rested. Part of the entablature was the **frieze** which was divided for decorative purposes into grooved **triglyphs** and sculptured **metopes.** Crowning the structure was the triangular **pediment** with painted, free-standing sculpture.

Less imposing but equally attractive was the Erechtheum—also colonnaded with **Ionic** columns. But one porch, the Porch of Maidens, was supported by **caryatids** or sculptured figures. Basic to both these classical structures and to most others were these principles: no straight lines were used, corrections being made to secure optical illusions of straightness; unity and variety, vertical and horizontal were brought into balance; monotony was eliminated by judicious decoration, design and sculpture; space was enclosed and humanized by intervals, repeated patterns, spacial progressions, and suggestions of distance; everywhere there was proportion, reserve, restraint and order.

Sculpture. Sculpture was independent or ornamental—free-standing or high or low relief; carved in marble or cast in bronze; painted or natural. Earliest or **Archaic** sculpture bore resemblance to the Egyptian: rigid figure frontally disposed; clenched fists close to the body; one foot advanced; "archaic smiles"—more like grimaces. Female figures were heavily, even puritanically, draped. Gradually the Archaic limitations dissolved and in the classical period under the leadership of Polykleitos, Myron and Phidias sculptured figures stressed abstract beauty of form, philosophical detachment, anatomical perfection, arrested movement, perfect balance, etc. During the fourth century B.C. sculptured figures became more relaxed; portraiture was less idealized; grace replaced strength; nudes made their appearance; human themes were exploited. Praxiteles and Lysippus were the giants of this period. In the Helenistic Period restraint gave way to emotionalism, formal canons to eclecticism (a mixture of styles), heroic themes to tales from the streets, Greek types to exotic types, stoic acceptance of suffering to portrayal of the agony of suffering.

Music. Greek music was the handmaiden to all the other arts. It served to evoke moods and for each mood there seems to have been a musical mode: virile and bellicose—the **Dorian Mode**; majestic—the **Hypodorian**; pitiful—the **Mixolydian**; agitated—the **Phrygian**; nimble—the **Hypophrygian**; mournful—the **Lydian**; voluptuous—the **Hypolydian**; etc. Vocal music was stressed over the instrumental. Music was basically melody and rhythm; harmony was not known. Music followed the metric rules of poetry rather than its own and without its own rules variety was achieved chiefly through a wide collection of tones.

HISTORY

Awareness of the past as it shaped the present characterized all Greek thought; out of this awareness the **science of history** was born. In the hands of HERODOTUS (484-425 B.C.) "*Father of History*," it was a poor science. Herodotus's *History* proposed to tell the story of the Greeks from their origins to the Persian Wars. But his work had more of epic in it than history. It was uncritical, used hearsay and legend, accepted supernatural causation, was anecdotal and moralistic, romantic and imaginative, naive and credulous. Nonetheless it gave a detailed picture of the society Herodotus knew; it was often impartial; and it told a good story.

Of far greater significance to the historical science was the work of THUCYDIDES (470-398 B.C.) *The History of the Pelopponesian War*. Thucydides's viewpoint was materialistic; he rejected intervention by the gods; he sought for the causes of human events in human character. He believed in the doctrine that "history repeats itself." He tells his story coldly, carefully, and bases most of it upon available sources. Bias is singularly absent from his account.

This was hardly so with XENOPHON (434-355 B.C.) who left an interesting history of a military retreat in *The Anabasis*, an historical "novel" in *The Cyropaedia* and a series of memoirs of Socrates. Xenophon was pro-Xenophon, pro-Spartan and pro-Persian. He was uncritical; but he, too, told a good tale by a careful marshalling of facts.

PHYSICAL SCIENCE AND MATHEMATICS

The Greeks achieved only moderate success in science because they preferred intuitive reasoning to experiment and exact measurement. As far as it was possible to advance intuitively, they did so. Thus they began the study of matter; formulated the principle of cause and effect; suggested the basic principles of the evolution of nature and the atomic division of matter; discovered the sphericity of the earth and the possibility of its movement around the sun; noted the properties of magnets; stated the law of the conservation of matter; classified aberrations in the movements of the planets; identified animal species and noted that there were correlations in the structures, that organs seemed adaptive, that the embryo goes through well-defined stages; named and classified numerous species of plants. In medicine HIPPOCRATES (460?-377? B.C.) grounded a theory of health and disease in a **physical** (not demonological) system of "humors" —the melancholic, sanguineous, choleric and phlegmatic—any imbalance of which caused disease. He made a careful note of the symptoms and the course of many diseases and based his therapy upon "natural" cures (sunshine, rest, nutrition, etc.).

Since mathematics responded more to intuitive investigation, Greek achievement in this field of science was immense. THALES and PYTHAGORAS founded the science of geometry. The Pythagoreans then went on to distinguish and name various kinds of numbers, to work out arithmetic and geometric progressions, to compile tables of squares and cubes. The Sophists produced studies on the quadrature of the circle, the trisection of angles, theorems on circles, the volumes of pyramids and cones. Systematization of these separate studies began when NICHOMACHUS wrote a basic text on all that was known of arithmetic and EUCLID produced his famous and still used The *Thirteen Books of Elements* in geometry.

Possibly the greatest of all the Greek mathematical thinkers was ARCHIMEDES whose genius led him to formulate the first possibilities of an infinitesimal calculus. Not far behind Archimedes was APPOLONIUS who foreshadowed both projective geometry and analytical geometry. This by no means exhausts Greek achievements in mathematics which extended to work on parabolas, spirals, conic sections, spherical triangles and the like.

Applications of geometry carried the Greeks to important discoveries in geography, physics, astronomy and engineering. By means of geometry Eratosthenes measured the earth and derived remarkably accurate results. Posidomius theorized that tides were caused by the pull of sun and moon. Archytus founded the science of mechanics and Archimedes brought static mechanics, hydrostatics, the principle of equilibrium of weights, of the center of gravity, of the pulley-wedge-lever-and screw, of floating bodies (specific gravity) to considerable heights. Hero, a remarkable engineering genius, produced, for example, siphons, fountains, water-clocks, jet-propulsion and air pumps. Greek astronomy was unfortunately tied to the geocentric notions of Aristotle. Within this limitation, however, geniuses like PTOLEMY were able to apply geometry to celestial movements with exceptional predictive accuracy using the concept of epicycles to explain aberrations.

This was about as far as man could go by using his "common sense" and intuitive reasoning power to solve the riddle of the nature of the universe.

CHAPTER SIX

ROME

THE BASES OF ROMAN CIVILIZATION

Geography. The mountains of Italy were not obstacles to political unification as were those of Greece; while precipitous, they terminated in the broad plains of Latium—large and fertile areas capable of intensive cultivation. The Appenines, however, forced the Romans to face westward, away from the civilizations of the eastern Mediterranean; and this gave the Romans the isolation they needed for independent development. Italy's peninsular form made it inevitable that, when able, the Romans would concentrate upon domination of the Mediterranean Sea. The open land areas, the easy invasion of Italy from northern lands and surrounding seas, forced the Romans on the defensive from their earliest days; militarism became synonymous with survival. Finally, the situation of Rome itself atop seven hills commanding the Tiber River gave her a powerful position on the peninsula.

People. The original Italian peoples are lost in the mists of the past. When the Romans emerged they were a linguistic, cultural and racial mixture of Samnites, Umbrians, Latins, Gauls, Greeks and Etruscans. Greek influence was particularly strong; but most profound was that of the **Etruscans,** an Oriental people whose high civilization was absorbed by the Romans. The earliest Romans were subject for many years to the overlordship of these Etruscans. Etruscan practices of many kinds seeped into Roman life and remained long after the Etruscans themselves had vanished.

Political Institutions. Because they began as a conquered people under absolute monarchy, the Romans created political institutions to defend themselves from the exercise of arbitrary power. When they became a free people, they placed supreme power in the hands of two political bodies —the **Assembly** and the **Senate.** The Assembly included all male citizens of military age. It was basically a ratifying body and as such had an absolute veto on executive decrees in matters of war, peace and justice. The Senate was a council of elders whose membership derived from traditional clans. Senators comprised, for the most part, a conservative, landowning aristocracy; they were charged with choosing successors to the monarchy and with safeguarding the **law of custom** from invasion by either the King or the Assembly. Such were the **checks and balances** that characterized the Roman government when it began its independent existence in 509 B.C.—the year the Etruscan kings were finally expelled.

Socio-Economic Institutions. The family was the basic unit in primitive Roman society. Its sole legal personality was the *pater* (father) who had the power of life and death within the family. Custom and the position of the Roman matron acted as restraints on the absolutism of this *paterfamilias*. The social group was separated by rigid class divisions: there were **patricians** or large landowners of noble birth, a privileged class who served in the Senate, monopolized army offices, and conducted public religious ceremonials. Then there were the **plebeians,** a free citizenry drawn from the small farming and artisan classes. They served in the Assembly and enjoyed the right of trading, property holding, and judicial self-defense. But they were barred from entry into the Senate, they could not intermarry with the patricians, and had no recorded bill of rights. **Clients** or tenant farmers and slaves completed the class structure; they were without freedom or rights.

Religion. Religion cemented Romans of all classes. There were no priestly castes; religion was related to civic activities. However, specialists in religious knowledge did exist: *haruspices* who inspected the vital organs of sacrificed animals; *augurs* who interpreted omens.

Household and farm deities predominated: Janus, the Spirit of the Doorway; Vesta, The Spirit of the Hearth; the Penates, the Guardians of Household Stores; the Lares, The Guardians of Family Property; and the Genius or Guardian Spirit.

Religious devotion was quite materialistic: it was based on bargaining and contracting with the gods and such bargains and contracts were enforced by law, duty and taboo. Late in the monarchical period national gods made their appearance: **Jupiter,** the sky-god and chief over all; **Juno,** Jupiter's spouse and protector of matrons; **Minerva,** the artisan's divinity; and **Mars,** god of war. With national deities asserting themselves, the gods left the Roman household and entered into temples; worship became cultish.

The Roman Ideal. Where the Greeks found their ideal within themselves, the Romans looked back to their founding ancestors for theirs. For it seemed to Romans that these founders were worthy of worship. They had set the ideal of "sterling integrity, stern dignity, stoic endurance, rugged simplicity, hard economy and sturdy industry" for all posterity. They were unselfish patriots, austere puritans, practical utilitarians—without philosophy, imagination or culture.

FROM CITY-STATE TO NATION-STATE

From 509 to 265 B.C. the small city-state of Rome expanded its dominion until it was master of the whole Italian peninsula. This 250 year expansion was piecemeal and resulted from the efforts of the Romans to make themselves defensively secure against hostile neighbors and to solve their problem of a landless population at the expense of their neighbors.

The Fifth Century B.C. Etruscan power declined steadily during the fifth century B.C. and released a large number of Italian tribes for war and expansion. Rome was threatened by engulfment by any one or all of them. Cities in Latium had formed a **Latin League** and were pressing upon Rome. After many years of defensive battling, Rome brought the Latin League to terms by a tremendous victory at **Lake Regillus** (486 B.C.). Members of the Latin League were forced into an offensive-defensive alliance with Rome, an alliance that held for 150 years in wars against the Etruscans, the Aequi, and the Volsci. Aggressive advances by the northern Sabellians had set the Aequi and Volsci in motion against Rome. Under the leadership of CORIOLANUS the Aequi were vanquished; and under that of CINCINNATUS, the Volsci. Momentarily secure on her farther borders, Rome attacked and eliminated an Etruscan stronghold at Veli—twelve miles to her North across the Tiber. This latter victory enabled Rome to double her territory and to emerge as the leader of the Latin League.

The Fourth Century B.C. The fourth century B.C. opened with a disastrous invasion by barbarous **Gauls** which ended in the sack of Rome and the impoverishment of its people. Under Camillius the Romans painfully rebuilt their razed city, built strong walls around it, reorganized their army into more flexible units, introduced iron weapons, and revised their requirements for Roman citizenship.

Chastened and strengthened, the Romans were occupied for most of the rest of the century with eliminating the strong threat of the Samnites, warlike mountaineers who were threatening Rome's fertile lands in Campania. A victory over the Samnites had the effect of stirring Rome's allies in the Latin League to attack her; she was becoming too big and powerful for the security of other Italian states on the peninsula. But Rome defeated their combined effort. The Latin League was dissolved; its cities were isolated by separate treaties; some were made colonies; others were given a suffrageless Roman citizenship.

Rome became the capital of all Latium and the protector of all under her dominion. Colonies of Roman citizens were settled within the conquered territories to relieve the pressure of the landless upon Rome's land. The Samnites, defeated but not conquered, now (327 B.C.) attempted to organize all of the conquered people into a federation for independence. To meet this new threat, Appius Claudius made further reforms in the army, built a navy, broadened the base for both military and tax levies, and constructed the first of the great Roman military highways (**The Appian Way**). The result was the complete defeat of the Samnites and their allies at the Battle of **Sentium** (296 B.C.). All Italy was within the grasp of the Romans.

The Conquest of Italy. The remainder of Italy was taken in the third century B.C. This was southern Italy where Greek cities predominated. When war between the Greek cities and Rome threatened, the city of Tarentum called upon King Pyrrhus of Epirus (in Greece) for aid. Pyrrhus responded and at Heraclea (280 B.C.) won a bitter and costly victory—hence the phrase "Pyrrhic victory." Pyrrhus's advantage came from the use of terror-spreading elephant cavalry. Rome now allied with her powerful North African neighbor, Carthage, in a defensive alliance against Pyrrhus. By 275 B.C. Pyrrhus was forced to leave Italy, and Tarentum fell; all of southern Italy now succumbed. Rome occupied Italy from the toe to the Po River.

Why Rome Conquered. Many reasons are given for Rome's success. Her enemies were disunited and Rome's policy of divide and rule was effective; Rome's allies were weakened by continual wars with *Rome's* enemies; Roman statesmen kept internal strife at a minimum by generous land grants, liberal division of the spoils of war and extension of democratic rights. Rome's victims were forced to place their armies at her disposal. Highway trunk-lines were built with each new conquest, colonies and garrisons were placed at all strategic outposts, bilateral treaties militated against new combinations against Rome.

Most important, however, was the use made of Roman citizenship.

Conquered peoples fell into four classes: **citizens, municipia, Latin Allies** and **Italian Allies.**

Roman citizens had full rights and privileges of citizenship.

Municipia had Roman citizenship *without* suffrage rights; they enjoyed local autonomy and the rights of trade; they served in the army and paid taxes.

The Latin Allies had no citizenship but still enjoyed the rights of trade; they furnished Rome with foreign legions and had some local autonomy.

The Italian Allies were Roman protectorates; they sent troop levies to Rome, levies that were supported at Roman expense and shared in the war booty.

Though the bulk of the Italians thus lost their independence, were bound to do Roman military service and had to pay numerous special taxes to their Roman rulers, Roman rule brought them many advantages: a *pax Romana* (Roman peace), an end to inter-tribal warfare, defense against external aggression, partial freedom and the possibility of full citizenship, economic unity, the use of Roman public works (aqueducts, roads, bridges, etc.) and a share in the new prestige that Rome had won for Italy.

Effects on Rome—Military, Economic, Cultural. The Roman army took on permanent form. It was a paid, national militia based on universal conscription of all property holders for service at home or abroad. The military unit was the phalanx of heavy and light infantry; the sub-unit was the centuriate (100 men). During the fourth century a more flexible form of legion (4000 infantry) was adopted. It was divided into 120 maniples for maneuverability. Larger units of cavalry were added and by the middle of the fourth century the Romans had a navy as well.

The Italian conquest extended the importance of agriculture in Rome's economy, since large tracts of arable soil were added to her holdings. Labor power for these expanded estates was provided by the slaves who were taken as war-prisoners. From the conquered people new techniques of farming were borrowed and applied (particularly in wine and olive production). War profits increased the demand for foreign luxury goods; trade expanded and with trade there came a money economy. Trade brought the trader—a new class of rich men that began to press for a larger share in government.

Latin translations of Greek works began to spread through Italy. Greek gods were adopted and given Roman "citizenship." Hellenistic philosophies began to capture the imagination of the intellectuals and to undermine the traditional beliefs.

POLITICAL DEVELOPMENTS IN THE ROMAN REPUBLIC

The Aristocratic Republic. It was the patricians who made the revolution of 509 B.C. that resulted in the overthrow of the Etruscan monarchy. The government they designed to replace the monarchy was republican in form and aristocratic in substance. Absolutism was abolished by creating two executive heads, the **Consuls**, each elected annually. Each had the absolute veto over the acts of the other; both were charged with judicial, financial and military duties and for these purposes were equipped with the necessary police powers. In time of crisis a **dictator** with unlimited authority might be appointed for six months or for the duration of the crisis.

The Senate consisted of 300 aristocrats appointed by the consuls. Consular legislation was laid before the Senate for its *recommendation* only; only the Assembly could pass on legislation. However Senatorial ratification was required before a bill could become a law. The Centuriate was an assembly of citizens organized by hundreds and divided according to military rank and wealth. It could not initiate laws, but could pass on them. Vote-rigging gave the aristocrats control in the Centuriate and the result was that the plebeians, who served in the military, paid taxes and were represented, had no voice at all in the governing of Rome. This led to a perpetual "struggle of the Orders"—patrician versus plebeian for political power. In this struggle the plebeians used one weapon with great effectiveness, the strike against military service—particularly when the enemies of Rome were closest to the city.

The Development of Roman Democracy. With each extension of political power to the plebeians, Rome became more democratic. The succession of laws which accomplished this were as follows:

—509 B.C. **The Valerian Law.** This was the *habeas corpus* act of ancient Rome for it permitted plebeians to appeal death sentences by the consuls delivered in peace time to the Centuriate Assembly.

—494 B.C. **The Tribunate.** Two tribunes were to be elected annually to protect plebeian rights; they were given police powers and an ab-

solute veto over legislation or executive decrees harmful to the plebs.

—494 B.C. **The Icilian Law.** This made the persons of the tribunes inviolate.

—471 B.C. **The Publilian Law.** This created a new assembly—the comitia tributa—*for plebs only*. It could not pass law but could vote *plebiscites* or recommendations for laws to the Senate and Centuriates. The fight now became to secure legal validity for the plebiscites.

—449 B.C. **The Valerio-Horatian Law.** This law provided for the Twelve Tables, a codification of existing criminal and civil law which were inscribed on twelve wooden tablets. Written codification limited partician monopoly over the judicial branch. The Twelve Tables became the foundation of Roman Law.

—447 B.C. Consular aides were to be elected by the comitia tributa and not appointed by the consuls.

—445 B.C. **The Canuleian Law.** This extended the right of state marriage to the plebs. They were free to intermarry with the patricians and the children of such marriages were legitimized.

—367 B.C. **The Lucinio-Sextian Reforms.** This law made mandatory the tenure of one annual consulship by a pleb.

—356 B.C. The office of dictator was opened to the plebs.

—351 B.C. The office of censorship was opened to the plebs.

—337 B.C. The praetorship was opened to the plebs.

—313 B.C. **The Poetelian Law.** This exempted debtors from being hurled into slavery because of bankruptcy.

—287 B.C. **The Hortensian Law.** This law gave legal validity to the plebiscites of the comitia tributa; ratification by Senate or the Centuriate Assembly was *not* required.

Rome had come a long way from aristocracy to democracy. But the transition was orderly, gradual and constitutional; it was reform by evolution, not revolution.

ROMAN IMPERIALISM

Masters of Italy, the Romans began in 265 B.C. a policy of conquest that ended in world domination. They were not consciously, as yet, pursuing an imperialist policy; it seemed to the Romans that their wars outside Italy were *defensive*, just as those inside Italy had been.

There were, however, other forces pushing the Romans into foreign adventures. Their foreign trade was extensive and freedom of the Mediterranean was vital to their national needs. Maintenance of a large standing army required continuous sources of booty for soldiers and taxes for the state. Population growth brought pressure for new lands. Increased use of metal for armaments required new mineral resources; and increased ownership of large landed estates required additional supplies of slaves. Such, then, were the underlying factors that drove Rome into the Punic Wars (265-221 B.C.).

The Punic Wars. Carthage, located in North Africa directly across the sea to the south of Sicily, was viewed by the Romans as a threat to their security. For one thing, Carthage had made the Mediterranean into a "closed sea." Its powerful navy patrolled the waters; its navigation acts, trade restrictions, customs duties made competitive trade almost impossible. For another, Carthage ruled an empire that extended into Italy. She had founded cities and trading posts all along the coast of North Africa from Libya to Gibraltar and in the Mediterranean islands—notably Sicily, Sardinia and Corsica. With her vast wealth, Carthage was able to hire fighting mercenaries to defend her position. Moreover, when the Romans conquered Southern Italy, Carthage dropped her friendly policy toward Rome. When Carthage moved to take over enough of Italy to control the strategic Straits of Messina, Rome was ready to take up the challenge.

In the **First Punic War** (264-251 B.C.) Rome aimed to secure control of Sicily. With Greek aid Rome crossed over the Straits of Messina into Sicily and defeated the Carthaginians in major battles. Hastily constructing a fleet, the Romans were able to hold off Carthage long enough to seize Sardinia and Corsica. An attempted attack on Carthage itself failed; but in western Sicily, the Romans were successful. At this time (251 B.C.) a Carthaginian fleet was destroyed. Carthage sued for peace; Rome accepted. Sicily was turned over to Rome and became her first imperialist conquest.

Carthage did not accept her defeat graciously. Under the leadership first of HASDRUBAL and then after 221 B.C. of HANNIBAL a military base was created in Spain. Rome was helpless to prevent Hannibal's advance to the *Pyrenees* for she was bitterly engaged in defensive wars with the Gauls on land and the Illyrian (Greek) pirates on sea. In order to protect his rear in the Spanish advance, Hannibal was forced to attack a Roman city (Sagentum). Rome promptly declared war but was equally promptly faced with a Carthaginian invasion from the north for Hannibal had pushed over the Alps to descend on Rome. En route he had picked up the Gauls as allies. Reinforcements from Carthage were due in southern Italy to complete the encirclement. Hannibal's hopes rose high as a result of victories on the **Ticinus,** on the **Trebia,** at **Lake Trasimene** and at **Cannae** (216 B.C.). Moreover, Macedonia, sensing the kill, moved in to threaten Rome on the east. Some of Rome's allies began to desert.

But the Latin Allies held firm. Every Roman—freeman and slave—was drafted for military service. Under QUINTUS FABIUS the Roman army refused open battle and waged hit and run warfare. Meanwhile the Roman, SCIPIO AFRICANUS, moved into Spain and crushed Hannibal's rear support. Philip V of Macedon was stymied by a Roman inspired Greek coalition against him; Sicily too was neutralized. Now the Romans sprang the trap that Hannibal had built for himself. Offensives forced Hannibal to the coast. Scipio landed in North Africa for an assault on Carthage. Hannibal was recalled to defend his homeland. At the **Battle of Zama** (202 B.C.), however, the Carthaginians were destroyed.

Carthage was reduced to a small African dependency. Under the insistent demands of CATO THE ELDER, who made famous the slogan—"Carthago Delenda Est" (Carthage must be destroyed)—Rome was maneuvered into taking a final step against Carthage in 146 B.C. For no apparent reason but revenge, Carthage was razed. She disappeared from history after this most unnecessary of Punic Wars.

Illyrian piracy and Macedonian aid to Carthage convinced the Romans that there could be no peace until Greece, too, became a Roman province. Aided by the Achaean and Aetolian Leagues, Rome advanced against Macedonia and defeated her (200-197 B.C.). This was followed by the defeat of Antiochus III, King of Seleucis in Asia Minor. Rome's imperium now extended from Spain to Asia Minor. Her empire was vast; but her problems of empire were vaster.

THE CONSEQUENCES OF EMPIRE

Conquered territories were divided into provinces ruled by governors appointed in Rome for one-year terms. Governors ruled by army-enforced decree; they were aided by magistrates sent from Rome. Conquered peoples all had to pay extraordinary taxes to Rome. The collection of these taxes was turned over to private tax contractors (the **publicans**) who were permitted ten per cent maximum profit above the assessment. Corrupt practices were punishable in the courts. In the first days of conquest, cases were few. But temptation was large since both judges and governors were drawn from the same class of people and had only a short time to reap any rewards from office. Not many wealth-making opportunities existed in Italy itself.

Rome's economic foundation was agricultural and in the export trade the balance of trade was against Rome. The wealth of some Romans was, of course, enormous; booty (theft) and tribute (extortion) created a class of new-rich—the equites or knights. It was they who handled the tax-contracts and the contracts for public works in the provinces. And it was they who finally corrupted the governors and magistrates there with bribes for shutting their eyes to fraudulent tax collection. Over-taxation forced large numbers of conquered peoples into debt from which they were then "rescued" by money lenders at fearful rates of interest. When the Roman Senate threatened investigation and exposure, they too were bribed. Corruption thus worked its slow poison into the blood-stream of Roman society.

Imperial booty flowed into the hands of the Senators. But they were forbidden to contaminate themselves with business ventures. Therefore they invested their booty in land, which was to a great extent purchased from small farmers who had been ruined by the Punic Wars. Senatorial *latifundia* (large estates) were worked by slave labor. The displaced yeomen drifted to the big city as unemployed workers. Most were citizens and could vote. They were therefore a potential menace to the ruling oligarchs—unless their votes could be bought. Herein was the origin of "bread and circuses," that is, public distribution of free food and public presentation of free spectacles—to distract the hungry and bored workers from more violent amusements. Roman workers did not want bread and circuses; they wanted land; and they began to demand that the latifundia be broken up and redistributed.

LAND REFORM

The Gracchi Brothers. When TIBERIUS GRACCHUS was chosen tribune in 133 B.C. he undertook a program of reform. Behind this attempted reform lay these conditions: the increasing corruption and land monopoly of the ruling group; the increase in slaves and their increased restiveness as reflected in numerous uprisings; the struggle of Rome's allies to secure Roman franchise; the decrease in the number of freemen eligible for military service.

Seeking mainly to reform the army, Tiberius proposed a land division which would result in an increase in the number of peasantry eligible for army service. The *comitia tributa* passed a law confiscating all land above a fixed amount and distributing the surplus among the landless. Two warring camps appeared—the rich and the poor. The power of the rich was in the Senate, and the Senate vetoed the Gracchian reform. When the King of Pergamm willed his country to Rome, Tiberius seized it on behalf of the *comitia tributa*, although custom dictated that it was the Senate's privilege to dispose of such bequests. When Tiberius now also came out with the proposals to reduce army service, reform the jury system, and make it easier for the allies to get the vote, the Senate accused him of seeking to establish a tyranny and had him murdered.

Tiberius's brother, GAIUS, became tribune in 123 B.C. Bravely he proposed an even more extensive reform. He first sought to convert Rome into a democracy by transferring from the Senate to the Assembly all important business. Land confiscation and redistribution was continued with this addition —the provincial as well as Italian estates were to be taken. Plans were drawn up to establish Roman colonies far and wide through the provinces. Franchise was to be given to both the Latin and Italian allies. A number of reforms for the army were drawn up; juries were to be opened to other groups as well as the Senators; and, finally, a grain law was passed providing that the state could sell corn to citizens below the market price.

Senatorial opposition to these reforms was violent; by demagoguery and playing upon popular superstition they turned the Roman populace against Gaius. He fled, and when he was overtaken, he committed suicide.

The heritage left by the Gracchi Brothers to Rome was a wide cleft between the Optimates (rich) and the *Populares* (poor) that brought the Roman Republic to its eventual destruction and ushered in the period of Roman absolutism—Caesarism.

THE REPUBLIC DESTROYED

Civil War. The Optimates and Populares sought military support for their programs. MARIUS, a military conqueror who took up the cause of the Populares was chosen consul for three years in succession. He divorced army recruitment from landholding and enrolled large numbers of the

Populares into service, an act which professionalized the army. In his *sixth* consulateship, Marius seized the provinces for colonization by his army veterans. Moreover, the Marian party pushed through a franchise extension to all the Italian allies. When the Senate rejected this, the Italians rose in revolt in the **Social Wars** (91-88 B.C.), wars that were terminated only as a result of a new threat to Rome from Mithrades VI of Pontus in Asia Minor. The franchise was granted.

Marius and Sulla. In turning to the problem of the Mitharaditic threat, the Optimates and Populares split on the matter of command of the Roman armies. The Optimates chose LUCIUS CORNELIUS SULLA, a consul; the Populares naturally wanted Marius. Each had his own army. The result was bloody civil war and in the end Sulla conquered. (Marius had died a natural death.) Mithradites was crushed. Sulla then ended the policy of cheap grain; limited the powers of the tribunate and the comitia curiata; restored all magistracies to the Senators; increased the powers of the Senate until it ruled the state; raised the age-limit for office-holding; and made all executives subservient to the Senate. Sulla carried out his restoration as a dictator chosen for the duration of the crisis. His support rested upon his army which had been rewarded with the lands confiscated from Sulla's enemies.

The Sulla Aftermath. Sulla retired from political life; but the hatreds he had inspired persisted. There were the personal hatreds of the survivors of those who had been massacred; hatreds of those who had lost their lands; of those who had been deprived of political power. New discontent arose among the veterans, the slaves and the conquered peoples. New threats appeared from Spanish tribes; from Mithradates again. Populares regrouped under LEPIDUS and made a bid to restore the tribunate. Then, out of Capua in Italy came the slave revolt led by SPARTACUS, a Thracian gladiator. On the sea, pirates in alliance with Mithradates harrassed Roman shipping. The merchants at home were bitter: the slave revolt had destroyed their stores; pirates were taking their shipped goods; Senatorial prerogatives had cut into their political rights. People were looking for a new leader; candidates appeared.

POMPEY and CRASSUS had eliminated foreign enemies and the Spartacus revolt. When they returned home they demanded that the Senate surrender its new won power over the executive and judiciary to them. To reinforce their demands both commanders allied with the merchants and the Populares, whom, under Sulla, they had helped defeat! The Senate was forced to agree and in 70 B.C.

Pompey and Crassus became consuls. The Sulla reforms were scrapped. Pompey then went off to foreign wars in Pontus, Judea and Syria.

JULIUS CAESAR AND CAESARISM

Caesar. Between 70 B.C. and 46 B.C. JULIUS CAESAR rose from an ordinary soldier to Roman dictator to dominate Roman history. His first bid for power came when, together with Crassus and CATALINE, he plotted to overthrow the Senate. When CICERO exposed the Catiline conspiracy, Caesar went to Spain to escape complicity. He bided his time until Pompey returned from the wars; then, with Crassus and Pompey, Caesar helped form the **First Triumvirate** (60 B.C.). Caesar became a consul and as such pushed Pompey's cause against the Senate vigorously; he had no army of his own—yet. Since the Gauls were becoming troublesome, Caesar suggested that he be made the governor of Gaul and given an army to subdue the Gauls. This was readily granted and Caesar fought his **Gallic Wars** and recorded them brilliantly in his *Commentaries*. Circulated in Rome, the *Commentaries* built Caesar's reputation as an invincible conqueror.

By 49 B.C. the fruit was ripe for plucking. Crassus had been killed in battle; Julia, Caesar's daughter and Pompey's wife, who had been a cementing force between them, died; conditions inside Rome became so anarchic that Pompey had established a military dictatorship. Still Caesar waited for Pompey to make the first move. When, in 49 B.C., Pompey deprived Caesar of his command, Caesar "crossed the Rubican" for a decisive battle. Pompey fled to his army in the east; Caesar pursued and defeated him utterly in the **Battle of Pharsalus**. Pompey himself escaped to Egypt but was murdered before Caesar landed there. Caesar turned his military attentions to the conquest of Egypt, and his amorous attentions to Cleopatra whom he established as the ruler of Egypt. Then came Caesarism.

Caesarism. The program of Caesarism was developed between 46 B.C. and the "Ides of March," 44 B.C. Caesar rested his power upon a broadened army base which was now extended over the breadth of the Empire. At home he kept only a praetorian guard of picked men. Widespread land reforms endeared him to the veterans.

Caesar recognized that the old forms of government had become obsolete; but he also knew that he must observe the *form* in changing the substance. In substance the government had to become one with his own absolute and undisputed power. Thus, he made himself dictator—for life; he secured, legally, the powers of the consul, the tribune, the chief priest and the censor for himself; he was *voted* the right to appoint all magistrates, to make war and peace, to command the armies, to expend public funds and to rule by executive decree. It was all perfectly proper. The Senate and Assembly continued to meet—to confirm Caesar's edicts. So close was Caesar to monarchy, that he willed his nephew, GAIUS OCTAVIUS, as his heir and successor. When a popular movement developed to deify him, Caesar thoroughly approved and supported it.

Reforms. It was in Caesar's interest to make wide reforms in the Roman state and empire. He began to extend Roman citizenship and franchise to inhabitants in the provinces; he restored Carthage as a commercial center; the Senate was made representative (without power) of the whole empire and Rome was converted from the capital of Italy to the capital of the empire.

Other reforms followed: the calendar was corrected for errors and modernized; civil and criminal courts were reformed; codification of the law was begun; the imperial bureaucracy was reorganized; provinces were removed from the control of the Senate; grain doles were reduced and those on relief were encouraged to take up land; imprisonment for debt was abolished; interest on loans was fixed at 12 per cent; installment payments for debt were legalized; market inspection to protect consumers was launched; direct taxes were reduced; reclamation projects were begun; slaveowners were encouraged to free their slaves so that the percentage of slaves in the total population might be reduced.

Caesarism aroused deep hostilities in the aristocrats now stripped of power; in ex-Pompeyites; in the bureaucrats who found opportunities for extortion in the provinces curtailed; in democrats and republicans who saw through the forms of Caesarism to its actual substance—absolute dictatorship. Under the leadership of CASSIUS and MARCUS BRUTUS a band of senatorial assassins slaughtered Caesar on the Ides of March. Caesar died in the shadow of the statue of Pompey which overlooked the Senate chamber.

THE ROMAN EMPIRE

Rise. Caesar had willed his rule to his nephew OCTAVIUS. Octavius had to fight for his bequest against MARC ANTONY and LEPIDUS—both Caesar's friends and both commanding effective military power. All three, however, had a common enemy in the republican forces led by Cassius and Brutus.

A **Second Triumvirate** was therefore formed which consisted of Octavius, Antony and Lepidus. At **Philippi** the republicans were overwhelmed. Antony moved on to Egypt and to Cleopatra while Octavian (Octavius) returned to Rome to consolidate his position. When Antony divorced Octavia (Octavian's sister) to marry Cleopatra, Octavian declared war. At the **Battle of Actium**, 39 B.C., his fleet won a decisive victory over Antony and Cleopatra. Octavian was now without opposition.

The Principate. Julius Caesar had sought to transform Roman society; **Octavian** sought to re-establish it—within a new order. Octavian, for example, forced Caesar's appointees from the Senate if they were not descended from the highest Roman nobility. He decreed that no Roman citizen could marry a freeman, or outside his rank. Old Temples were restored—in marble. Republican forms were scrupulously observed. When Octavian acted it was *through* the Senate and Assembly. In 27 B.C. Octavian laid down all his extraordinary powers and it was the Senate that granted them to him anew by popular acclaim. Thus by senatorial proclamation Octavian became

Princeps—the head of the Senate and first citizen of the State

Imperator Caesar Divi filius—commander-in-chief of the armed forces and son of the Divine Julius (hence he could become the object of religious worship)

Augustus—restorer and augmenter of the state (a title formerly bestowed on certain gods).

In these bestowals the Senate recognized that the old order was gone; new times, new governmental forms. After a century of civil war the great desire of all Romans was peace and order. And Augustus Caesar was the one to give it to them.

Reforms. Augustus brought the *Pax Romana* to the Romans and to the world. The Roman army, recruited from the ranks of Roman citizens and officered by men from the aristocratic classes, stood guard at all the frontiers and within all troubled areas in the Empire. In Rome Augustus kept for himself a small praetorian guard. A standing navy was added to the armed forces. Military affairs were made the exclusive prerogative of Augustus himself. Competence over the provinces was divided: those pacified and near at home were granted to the Senate; others were administered by the Imperator.

Within all provinces Augustus decided upon all military matters. To meet the rise in state expenditures for the military, for public works, for grain distribution and the like, Augustus made tax collection a state function; taxes were now collected efficiently and new import taxes were introduced. To keep expenses down, no new foreign conquests were undertaken—particularly after the resounding defeat suffered by the Romans under Varus at the hands of Arminius, a Germanic barbarian.

Height. Augustus died in 14 A.D. and his stepson TIBERIUS was nominated by the Senate as his successor. Tiberius abolished the *comitia tributa*, transferred certain provinces from the Senate to himself in order to reform them, suppressed two great mutinies in the ranks of the legionnaires and many personal plots against himself. He died unpopular in 37 A.D.

CALIGULA (37-41 A.D.) who succeeded him was insane and managed to dissipate the treasury in drunken revels and bizarre celebrations. The Praetorian Guard disposed of him. It was they who named Claudius as successor.

CLAUDIUS (41-54 A.D.) ruled well. He reoccupied Britain; reformed the bureaucracy by instituting special divisions; he completed the construction of two aqueducts and improved the great harbor at Ostia. Because she plotted against him, Claudius had his wife, Messalina, executed. He then married his niece, Agrippina, who bore him a son Nero. Agrippina then disposed of Claudius by poisoning him.

NERO (54-70 A.D.) was probably insane. His administration was filled with plot and counterplot, with assassination and execution, with persecution of the Christians who were made the scapegoat for a fire that swept Rome in 64 A.D., and with border revolts extending from Britain to Judea. When the Senate finally condemned Nero, he committed suicide.

VESPASIAN (70-79 A.D.) proved a wise choice: he reformed the tax structure, recovered large tracts of public lands from extortionists, introduced rigid governmental economy, increased the income of the state, restored discipline in the ranks of the army and kept the peace. His successor, TITUS, ruled for two years only (79-81 A.D.) and was followed by Domitian.

DOMITIAN (81-96 A.D.) built the lines of forts between the Germanic and Roman lands where no natural boundaries existed. This established peace in the northeast. Murder and assassination, including his own, featured Domitian's rule.

NERVA'S (96-98 A.D.) brief rule produced an interesting agricultural scheme: to encourage agriculture in Italy a revolving fund was set up by the state; farmers could borrow from the fund at low interest rates; upon repayment, the principal was returned to the fund, and the interest was used for relief for indigent widows and orphans. Nerva began the adoptive system of imperial succession when he adopted Trajan as his son and successor.

TRAJAN (98-117 A.D.) was the first provincial to become an emperor. He was a brilliant military commander and during his rule he brought the Roman Empire to the Tigris and Euphrates Rivers —its widest extent. He also made important reforms in the imperial administration. He adopted Hadrian as his son.

HADRIAN (117-138 A.D.) was a most unmilitary ruler. His interests were in languages, literature, philosophy and art. To avoid the bother of empire, he ceded Mesopotamia and Assyria to the Parthians; granted independence to Dacia; completed the northern forts; built a wall in Britain between Roman and Celtic lines; destroyed Jerusalem and scattered the Jews far and wide through the Empire. Internal administration was reformed and the praetorian edicts were codified. Hadrian's Tomb (The Castle of Saint Angelo) on the banks of the Tiber is a most fitting memorial of this most esthetic of the Roman emperors.

ANTONINUS PIUS (138-161) ruled long and peacefully; his successor MARCUS AURELIUS (161-180) ruled long, was a man of peace, but lived through troubled times. There were local wars against the Parthians, Germanic tribes and others; there were severe persecutions of the Christians. These external exertions were in direct contradiction to the inner life of Marcus who, in his famous *Meditations*, a treatise on Stoicism, revealed himself as simple, conscientious, retiring, philosophical and ascetic.

COMMODUS (180-192) was a true son of Marcus Aurelius, at least in the flesh. The spirit of Commodus—cruel, sensuous and cowardly—was far removed from that of his father. With Commodus begins the decline of Rome.

THE DECLINE OF ROME

Rome's decline extended over centuries; it had no sudden fall. Many factors contributed to the decline. Science and technology did not keep pace with Roman expansion and Romans found that they were unable to handle efficiently the food, tools and transport problems that arose. The immense size of the empire was also a factor. It was impossible for the best-intentioned emperor to cope with the ceaseless problems of rising nationalisms, border attacks, graft and corruption in the provinces, inefficient bureaucracy, gross waste of limited resources. The drain on the public treasury was continuous. The wider the empire became, the less intense became the degree of patriotism; loss of patriotism engendered corrupt political behavior. The army was sensitive to the decline particularly as it lost its Roman character and became increasingly provincial. With decline in emperor character, the army became a prime political force. It began to make and unmake emperors so frequently that one can say accurately that between the rule of Commodus (d. 192 A.D.) and the rise of DIOCLETIAN (284 A.D.) military anarchy prevailed in the Empire.

Political decline hastened the factors making for economic decline. Small farmers, the backbone of the Roman Republic, virtually disappeared or rather were absorbed into the immense estates as semi-slaves. The purchasing power represented by these small farmers disappeared and helped to ruin the city artisans who had produced manufactured goods for sale to the small farmers; besides, an important source of tax revenue also disappeared. With the ruin of the small farming and artisan classes, the state became the primary producer of goods, a factor which destroyed the initiative of the Romans. Resulting shortages of goods produced a steady inflation. Coinage began to disappear; what remained was debased and became worthless. The result was a reversion to barter. This had a tremendous impact upon the trading or middle classes who had become the backbone of the Empire. Foolish imperial decrees hastened the decline of this group. They were made responsible for the collection of taxes in the municipalities. Whatever they did not raise of the quota assigned them, they had to pay out of their own pockets. They could not meet their quotas because the artisans had been ruined with the decline of the small farmers. Soon the middle class followed the artisans into ruin.

Some social factors entered the picture too. Population declined all during the imperial period. War, epidemic and plague were chiefly responsible; and, as times grew harder, natural birth rates declined among the poor as well as the rich. Of equal importance was the failure of nerve which accompanied physical decline. This was revealed in the search for security above enterprise, in the widespread superstitions that developed, in the rush to join mystical cults that guaranteed, at least, some reward in the hereafter, in the loss of patriotism, in the wild and bestial indulgences of the rich, etc.

The Fall. Several strenuous efforts were made to halt the decline of the empire. Most notable was that of DIOCLETIAN (284-305 A.D.). Diocletian tried to augment the powers of the Emperor by introducing Oriental features of absolutism into his rule. He reformed the army; tried to halt inflation by instituting both price and wage controls; and made significant changes in imperial administration. This latter was most important for the future of European history. The Empire was divided in two, a western and eastern half and Diocletian ruled from the east. This division became permanent when CONSTANTINE (306-337) made Constantinople into a second Rome. When the fall came, it was the western half that collapsed; **the eastern half continued for more than a thousand years to preserve and disseminate the culture of the Roman Empire.**

THE GRANDEUR THAT WAS ROME

The Conquered Conquerors. In the sphere of culture the Romans themselves accepted the Greeks as their superiors. Greek influences, particularly in their Hellenistic or Alexandrian forms, determined the form and substance of Roman culture. Romans borrowed freely from Greek architecture, engineering, religion, literature and philosophy. Oddly, however, in spite of the reliance of the Romans upon the Greeks for a "classical education," modern civilization has relied upon the Romans, not the Greeks, for its classical training.

Latin. Compared to the Greek, the Latin tongue is inflexible, and lacks subtlety; it is not a language of fine distinctions. It is terse, precise, clear—an admirable instrument for science, engineering, business and law.

Roman Law. Probably the greatest cultural achievement of the Romans was its system of law. Roman law originated as a law of custom and religious taboos. In the **Twelve Tables,** however, the law became secularized into a **civil law.** To the laws in the Tables there were added those passed by the Senate and the Assembly. These laws were interpreted by special jurists called praetors. Before announcing his edict (decision), the praetor would pronounce the legal principles upon which his edict rested. These relied heavily upon precedent. Praetorial edicts were collected into a systematized code by Hadrian in his "perpetual Edict." As Rome became an empire a new law, the **law of nations** developed. Eventually this became more important than the civil law. Influenced by the Stoics, Roman jurists began to search for basic principles that underlay all law, a law of nature. This thoughtful approach to legal matters produced a law that was exact, impartial, liberal, humane.

The job of the judge was justice and justice was "the steady and abiding purpose to give every man that which is his own." If justice were to prevail, then the law itself must be simple and available to any who could read. Romans concerned themselves frequently with the problems of simplification and codification of the law.

The most notable achievement in this field was that of JUSTINIAN (527-565 A.D.) an eastern Emperor. Justinian created a commission headed by TRIBONIAN to simplify and codify all extant Roman law. Tribonian's commission first produced the **Code,** a collection of the recorded decisions of judges and writings of famous jurists. These were summarized in the *Digest*. Since the length of the summary was still forbidding, Tribonian reduced them into the book-length *Institutes*. New laws by Justinian were then put into the *Novels*. All together these made up the famed *Corpus Juris Civilis* which had such great influence in medieval civil and canon law and in the secular law of national states until the end of the 18th century A.D.

Religion. We have seen that the original Roman religion was far less anthropomorphic than the Greek. In fact, Jupiter, Juno, and the other gods did not become divine *persons*, possessing human attributes, until the first wave of Greek influence swept over Rome. As in the days of Hellenistic influence, the Greek faith itself succumbed to orientalization, to cult and mystery, to initiation and emotion, the Romans experienced an invasion of many new Oriental cults which challenged their prevailing beliefs. Common to these mystic faiths were beliefs in immortality, purification of the soul, redemption, rites and ceremonies, initiations, priesthood and community worship.

Especially popular was the **Mithraic cult,** a derivative of **Zoroastrianism.** Accepting ZOROASTER'S basic premise that two forces contended in the world, Light and Darkness, Mithra worshippers added the premise that Mithra, a sun-god, was sent to earth to redeem mankind from the force of darkness. Mithra had no human mother; he emerged at birth from a rock in a stable; a few shepherds were witness to this remarkable birth. Mithra waged war on evil, was slain and then was resurrected; he rose to heaven and it was there his followers went after death; the wicked went to hell. Mithra sat in judgment on each soul. One day he would return for a general judgment of all mankind. Some of the Mithraic rites included: worship in candlelit caves; baptism; the eating of consecrated bread and wine; the celebration of December 25th as Mithra's birthday; elaborate initiation rites during which the candidate passed through seven stages to a final abode among the blessed. Membership in the Mithraic cult was restricted to men.

Philosophy. Mithraism appealed to army men, lower classes and slaves; the Roman elite preferred emperor worship or philosophy. A considerable vogue was enjoyed by **Stoicism,** a late Greek concept inaugurated by ZENO of Citium (c. 300 B.C.) and which attracted such noble minds as those of Cicero, Seneca and the Emperor Marcus Aurelius. Stoicism postulated a Divine Reason which was identical with universal natural law (pantheism). Through study of nature men came to God. In translating natural law into ethics, Stoics proclaimed the doctrines of the World State, equality of men, and natural brotherhood of all men. Stoics rejected all gods; for them man stood independent in the universe; each man was an individual pursuing an ideal. This ideal was compounded of many elements: indifference to one's personal fate; service, unpaid, to mankind; a belief in the here-and-now only; self sufficiency; the virtues of resolution, fortitude, willingness to die for one's beliefs, devotion to duty, contempt for pleasure or pain. Stoics argued that man owes allegiance to no one or no thing but his conscience; however, to avoid emotional distress, one ought to accept the *status quo* confirmed in the belief that all men will gradually grow more reasonable and work to bring the Divine Order, the rational scheme of things, on earth.

Quite opposed to Stoicism was **Epicureanism.** The Roman LUCRETIUS made a beautiful and excellent summary of this doctrine in his *De Rerum Natura*. Epicureanism was founded in atomism as developed by Democritus and was therefore a thorough-going materialism. Atomism, we have seen, was destructive of all belief in gods; all things were reducible to material particles. Man was formed of particles too and for one purpose—the pursuit of happiness. Happiness was nothing more than freedom from pain and enjoyment of pleasure (hedonism). Epicurus taught that pleasure is maximized when men reduce their wants to a minimum: the possession of friends; good talk; satisfying appetites; avoiding pain-bearing responsibilities; gathering rosebuds while one may; eating, drinking and merriment; study, for an increase in knowledge is a fruitful source for discovering new pleasures.

SCIENCE AND ENGINEERING

In spite of a general ignorance of pure science, Roman technology was the most advanced of the ancient world. They were master civil engineers: their roads, bridges and tunnels—still surviving—are evidence of their impressive knowledge of construction techniques, tooling, metallurgy, practical hydraulics and siphoning. They were master craftsmen in mining, glass and glaze works, dyes and textiles.

ARCHITECTURE

In Roman hands the Greek building became grandiose, colossal—and more practical. The Romans added to the Greek heritage the art of the administration building, the public bath, the theatre, the amphitheatre, the race-track (Colisseum) and the monumental structure like the triumphal arch and the commemorative column. To secure proper height Roman architects abandoned the simple post-and-lintel system of the Greeks and utilized the arch, the vault and the dome. To secure proper ornamentation, they adopted and elaborated the Corinthian column. But columns ceased to be functional; they were added purely for decorative effect. Roman architecture was tasteless, but imposing. An original contribution was the **basilica** with a nave, aisles and clerestory windows—a form successfully adapted later by medieval church builders.

LITERATURE

In The Days of the Republic 240-27 B.C. In the formative days of Roman history literary art was imitative of the Greeks. In the drama PLAUTUS (c. 254–185 B.C.) and TERENCE (185–159 B.C.) towered above all others, writing brilliant comedies, satires, farces.

In CATULLUS (84-54? B.C.) the Republic produced an exceptional lyric poet.

Julius Caesar and Sallust produced creditable histories during this era. But the major prose figure was CICERO. His collected works include treatises on rhetoric, orations, political essays, moral essays, theological treatises and letters. Cicero was an unoriginal thinker but his prose set the pattern for "classical prose" for centuries to come with its emphasis on pure vocabulary, precise idiom, straightforward speech fluent rhythm and emotional appeal.

In The Days of the Principate 27 B.C.-14 A.D.

Augustus brought peace and wealth to Rome; art now reflected Rome's new pride.

The giant of this era was VIRGIL (70-19 B.C.) Virgil first composed the *Bucolics* and *Eclogues* —pastoral poems.

The *Georgics* were essentially propaganda designed to get the Roman back on the farms. But these were exercises in preparation for the epic to follow, the *Aeneid*. This great epic of the founding of Rome was imitative of Homer; nonetheless it was peculiarly Virgilian in its perfection of diction, rhythm and style; in its brilliant reportage; in its unity of theme around the central character Aeneas, brave, pious, temperate, wise, and, above all, devoted to duty.

Second in stature only to Virgil was HORACE (65-8 B.C.), a master of many poetic forms. Throughout all of his works there ran a strain of hedonism, of stoicism and of Aristotle's concept of the golden mean. His was the perfected style— witty, direct, and always polished.

During this same period OVID produced his erotic lyrics and the *Metamorphoses*, on the lives of the Roman gods. The histories of LIVY were notable for color and enthusiasm, but they were overconcerned with celebrating Rome's greatness and success.

In The Days of the Empire 14-200 A.D. In the hands of SENECA (3 B.C.-64 A.D.) Roman drama turned from comedy to tragedy. Seneca got his stories from the Greeks, but in his hands the noble and restrained tragedies of Aeschylus and Sophocles became tales of horror and violence exploited for the sake of sensationalism instead of edification.

Satire became more bitter, more direct in the hands of PETRONIUS (*The Satyricon*) and MARTIAL (*The Epigrams*). PLINY THE ELDER left a masterpiece (*The Natural History*) exposing Rome's ignorance in the fields of science; PLINY THE YOUNGER, however, wrote nine books of charming letters which are a mine of information about contemporary Roman life.

In LONGINUS, the Romans produced a highly original thinker in the field of esthetics. Longinus contributed the affective theory of literature in his essay *On The Sublime;* his argument was that the value of a literary work was not in its moral value as Plato had held, or in its form as Aristotle maintained, but in its ability to move the reader into a state of ecstasy or sublimity by the grandeur and passion of its art.

In the field of History the era was fruitful for it produced TACITUS, SUETONIUS and PLUTARCH. Tacitus (55-117 A.D.) wrote history in almost a colloquial vein; his themes were the Roman emperors and the Germanic tribes. His aim was to compare the corrupt state of the Roman rule, with the innocent and pure state of Germanic custom. His histories, dominated by morality, are somewhat unreliable therefore. Suetonius was far more objective. In his *Lives of the Caesars* he relied upon factual detail impartially related. In the person of Plutarch, a Hellinistic Greek, (46-120 A.D.) historical biography reached a great height. Plutarch's *Parallel Lives* are biographies arranged in pairs: one Greek compared with one Roman. Pride in Greek achievement and fairness to the Roman characterized his presentations. Psychological insights abound in his studies in spite of the fact that he always sought to draw moral implications.

CHAPTER SEVEN

THE ORIGIN AND THE TRIUMPH OF CHRISTIANITY

INTRODUCTION

As Rome declined, the outlines of a new civilization began to form. The process of decline was reflected in the minds of men as a shift of values. Disruption of the traditional way of life brought with it a sense of insecurity and pessimism in the submerged classes and a sense of apathy in the ruling groups; Gilbert Murray's phrase, "the failure of nerve," sums it up well. Men searched for some relief of suffering and turned in greater numbers to religious faiths that promised a blessed hereafter, some "heavenly city."

One such religious movement swept through the Jewish communities in the Near East in the last years of the first century B.C. and in the first years of the first century A.D. It was believed, and preached, that a Messiah, an "anointed one," was about to come to deliver mankind from sinfulness. Shammai-ites, Hillelites and Essenes awaited momentarily the destruction of the Roman Empire by some universal fire and the establishment through the Messiah of a Kingdom of Heaven on earth. St. John the Baptist recognized Jesus Christ as the Messiah.

THE MESSAGE OF JESUS CHRIST

Jesus Christ left no writings. His sayings, however, were collected by the authors of the **Four Gospels**—Matthew, Mark, Luke and John—and are incorporated as part of the **New Testament**. The sayings of Christ have been the subject of considerable interpretation, but there is wide agreement on their literal content.

God. Christ placed emphasis on the omniscience of God, Who, for example, knows what one needs before asked in prayer for it, or can see the deeds done in secret, or can penetrate to the intent of some external act. God, too, was omnipotent and had the intent of bringing every man to the bar of judgment. God was Father of all that is; His providential care was motivated by His love for all that is and His mercy for all that sin and suffer.

Ethics. Christ's sayings are deeply imbued with ethical content. Ethically, His sayings stem from two commandments that He considered primary:

"The Lord God is one God and thou shalt love the Lord thy God with thy whole heart, and with thy whole soul, and with thy whole mind, and with thy whole strength."

"Thou shalt love thy neighbor as thyself." Or, a variant of the same: "Therefore, all that you wish men to do to you, even so do you also to them. . . ."

How, then, shall this love for God and neighbor manifest itself in conduct or behavior? On this matter Christ placed considerable emphasis on the inner attitudes of men, on their unseen states of mind and heart. Thus among those he considered blessed were those who were the poor in spirit, the meek, those who mourn, those who hunger for justice, and those who are peacemakers. He believed firmly that one must love one's enemies and from this derived two corollary beliefs: it is not enough to obey the injunction that Thou shalt not kill, one must not even be angry with one's brother, one must come to terms with one's opponents quickly, one must not resist the evildoer, one must turn the other cheek, and the like. More positively, one must forgive men their offenses. The state of one's intent requires self-examination and men were warned not to judge lest they be judged, not to lust inwardly for to look with lust at a woman is to commit adultery in the heart.

Many of the ethical precepts of Christ stemmed from His conviction that Judgment Day was imminent. He called upon those who have faith to prepare for this event by immediate reformation and repentance, to lay up treasures in heaven, to give up trying to serve God and Mammon, to forego the flesh, pride and earthly glory—particularly worldly riches—to beware of following false prophets, to sell what they had and give to the poor—for it would be difficult for a rich man to enter the Kingdom of Heaven—and to do good as did the Samaritan.

Some of His sayings gave support to the ethics of asceticism. He called upon the faithful to give no thought for the morrow and pointed out that God, Who cares for the birds in the sky and the grass in the field, must certainly have equal care for those who seek His Kingdom.

In sum, then, Christ proclaimed his doctrine with finality; He demanded obedience to His teachings. Sinfulness was disobedience to the law of God. The key to the law of God was love—love of man for the Lord and love of man for man in the Lord. This love was based on faith, childlike wisdom, mercy, forgiveness, peacemaking, humility and meekness. The direction of these ethical precepts was toward making each man precious through his kinship with the Heavenly Father.

Legalism and Hypocrisy. Part of the message of Christ was a wholesale condemnation of those who abided by the strict letter of the law, or who paid more mind to outward manifestation than inward purity. He argued that He did not come to destroy the Jewish law but to fulfil it. But the strict letter of the law is the blind guide of blind men; and demonstrative prayer and sacrifice without pure intention was the device of hypocrites. Christ centered his attack upon those whom He called Pharisees, Scribes and Sadducees.

Eschatology. Christ painted in broad strokes the nature of the Last Judgment. He asserted that there would be a period of preparation for this day when false prophets would abound and there would be wars, rumors of wars, famines, earthquakes and other physical catastrophes. During this period the true believers would undergo a period of trial and tribulation. Then Jerusalem would be destroyed. On the very last day, the sun and moon would be darkened, the stars would fall from Heaven. A sign of the Son of Man would then appear in Heaven and this would be followed by His appearance. The angels would trumpet a great sound and the final election of the blessed would commence.

THE MESSAGE OF THE GOSPELS

The Gospels are *about* Jesus and the primary concern of the Gospel writers was to announce the news of the arrival in human form of the long-predicted Messiah. With His arrival the time had come for a new type of worship. Thus, the Gospels are the foundation of the religion of Christ.

Prophecy. For Matthew, Mark and Luke the new religion had been foretold in the Old Testament Hence a considerable part of the New Testament is devoted to relating the facts of the life of Christ to previous prophecies. For example, the Gospels trace the geneology of the family of Christ to David; the prophecy was that the Messiah would be of the house of David.

Miracles. Additional proof of the divinity of Christ was His reported ability to work miracles. Most of these miracles, as recorded in the Gospels, were of a medical nature: thus Christ cured leprosy, paralysis, dementia, a withered hand, haemophilia, etc.; on one occasion he restored the dead to life. There were other reported miracles: walking on water; compelling the sun and wind to obey; feeding five thousand people with but five loaves of bread and two fishes.

Other Signs Of Divinity. Each sign of Christ's divinity—as believed in by His followers—became the basis for future worship of Christ. These were among the many: Mary's immaculate conception; the virgin birth of Christ; the incident of the Magi and the star of Bethlehem; God's direct intervention in the flight to and return from Egypt; the transfiguration of Christ; Christ's foreknowledge of His betrayal, crucifixion and resurrection; the resurrection itself; the reappearance of Christ to his disciples following the resurrection; etc.

In sum: the figure of Jesus Christ, His life and sayings, His miracle workings and the supernatural events that were believed to have attended His life became the basis for a new faith propagated by His chosen Apostles, twelve in number, and those whom they converted. In its inception the Christian religion was but one of many that competed for the faith of the people of the Roman Empire. Many factors contributed to ensuring that this faith, of all, should triumph. Not the least of these factors was the work of ST. PAUL who elaborated Christian doctrine into the idea of redemption.

CONTRIBUTION OF THE APOSTLE PAUL

The Moral Heritage. Paul of Tarsus was a Jewish convert to Christianity and, following his conversion, became a practical organizer of the Christian religion and the first to set up Christian communities outside of Palestine. In his preaching, Paul continued and even deepened the Judeo-Christian stress upon one, all-embracing, all-powerful, all-good, merciful God; upon God's special relationship with a universal body of the faithful; upon the dire fruits of sinfulness and the rich fruits of lawfulness; upon the need for personal and social perfection, particularly of the spirit. These preachings filled the need of the time for something more enduring than the ecstatic oriental mystery cults. Paul, however, introduced a new note into this tradition by stressing the conflict between the flesh and the spirit—flesh was material and evil, spirit was non-material and good.

The Supernatural and the Mysterious. Essentially Christianity was a supernatural belief and rested upon faith in the mysteries and miracles of Christ. Paul heightened and deepened these elements by linking them with the principal mystery—the Redemption. To be released from sin and saved for eternity, a believer had to identify himself, through faith, with the death and resurrection of Christ. He had to believe that Christ's death and resurrection were in the nature of atonement for the sins of mankind. The inward act of faith, preached Paul, had to be coupled with participation in the external acts of baptism and eating the bread and drinking the wine of the Eucharist. By this means, supernaturally and mysteriously, the Body of Christ became indwelling in the believer and thus a share in eternal glory was vouchsafed.

Eschatological. Paul linked the judgment of last things with the origin of first things in a drama of salvation. In the beginning was the Creation and Adam's sin and fall. Adam's surrender to the devil had corrupted all mankind. God had foreseen all this and had prepared the way to salvation through the divine being incarnate in Christ. Through Christ mankind can be redeemed.

The Law. Among the early Christians there were those who insisted that the entire Jewish law was valid and in force for all Christians. Paul championed the cause of complete freedom from the Law. This insistence paved the way for the spread of the Christian gospel into the very heart of pagandom, Rome itself.

WHY CHRISTIANITY TRIUMPHED

When the first millenium opened Christianity was a small struggling sect in a vast sea of contending beliefs. By 392 A.D. it was the only legal faith in Europe. How does the historian account for this?

Conversion of the Mediterranean Peoples. Early Christians set themselves the goal of carrying their faith to all men. As a result of Paul's activities, congregations were founded in Jerusalem, Antioch, Philippi, Thessalonica, Corinth and Athens. Tradition holds that Peter evangelized Rome and was followed there by Paul. Early successes were greater in the east than in the west, and in the cities than on the farms. Evidence points to conversion first among slaves, impoverished freemen and women, though at all times a few of the well-to-do were attracted to the new faith. The common people were obviously attracted to Christianity by such features as its humanity, its feeling for brotherhood, its care for the poor, the widowed, the orphaned.

Syncretism. Residents of the Roman Empire were practitioners of many faiths; Christianity had to overcome their devotion to these competing faiths. Conversion of Jews became possible when Christianity incorporated into its doctrine beliefs in one God, the story of universal creation and the divine plan of history, the moral code of the Ten Commandments, the concept of sin, a hereafter, and redemption through a Messiah. Manicheans were attracted by Christian otherworldliness; the doctrine of the conflict between matter (evil) and spirit (good), and Christian asceticisms. *Gnostics* were committed to the stress upon spiritual knowledge through intuition and the doctrine of the Primal Man who would come to redeem mankind. Worshippers of Mithra who followed many of the rites practiced by Christians (e.g., baptism, a holy meal, December 25th); neo-Platonists and neo-Pythagoreans, who could accept Christian ideas of the creative Logos, of intermediary spirits like powers and angels, etc.; Stoics, who also preached universal brotherhood—all found something with the Christian doctrine and ritual that won their consent.

Roman Persecution. Romans were normally tolerant of foreign religions; they acted on the principle that all gods are true, including those of the Romans. Christian insistence that no God was true except their own, and that worship of Roman gods was pagan and doomed such believers to hell, caused the Roman state to retaliate by persecution. This persecution increased when the Christians denounced military service, gladiatorial contests, immorality, slavery, etc. The secret meetings of the Christians, at night and in caves, gave rise to charges that they were engaged in immoral and subversive activities.

In the first two centuries, Christians suffered more at the hands of the Roman populace than at the hands of the Roman emperors, though the persecutions of Nero, Trajan and Marcus Aurelius were severe. In the third century A.D. imperial persecutions become systematic. Decius (c. 248 A.D.) killed and banished hundreds of Christians who refused to appear before the magistrates and make a sacrifice to the Roman gods; Valerian (253-260) intensified persecutions to prevent many of the upper class Romans from joining the Christian order; Diocletian, in 303 A.D. purged the army of Christians, burned Christian books, removed all Christians from public office and prohibited the freeing of Christian slaves.

Persecutions had an effect contrary to that expected by the Roman rulers. It increased the feeling of "apartness" among Christians; it gave to the Christian Church a group of martyrs who were considered to be witnesses to the faith; it won to the faith many adherents who objected to persecution; and it convinced many that the Christians were indestructible when the faith survived in spite of persecution.

Christianity Becomes Legal. Toleration was extended to the Christians by an edict of GALERIUS in 311 A.D. Galerius, who had persecuted Christians severely, sought their aid-through-prayer for a malignant disease he had. CONSTANTINE (306-337) also sought such aid from Christians as he entered the Battle of Milvain Bridge (312) in his war against the Eastern Emperor Maxentius. His men bore Christian devices on their standards and shields. He was victorious and in gratitude he issued the **Edict of Milan (313)** which granted Christians freedom of worship, the removal of all legal disabilities, and the restitution of all confiscated property.

Constantine's pro-Christian policy accelerated conversion among the upper classes of Roman society. Constantine also took steps to convert the conservative peasantry upon whom paganism had its strongest hold. He made observation of Sunday obligatory, built new churches, dedicated the new city of **Constantinople** to the Blessed Virgin, granted alms to poorer congregations, exempted Christian priests from political obligations and compulsory labor, participated actively in Church councils and helped to enforce the decisions of these councils. Under Constantine it became increasingly difficult to be anything but a Christian. Constantine's successors, with the exception of JULIAN (361-363)—whom the Christians labeled "the Apostate"—took more direct steps against paganism: the death penalty was invoked against any who performed pagan sacrifices; temple properties were confiscated and given to the Church; "heretics" were driven into exile; pagan priests were deprived of exemptions and privileges; "heretics" could not make wills or inherit property; etc. Finally, under THEODOSIUS I (379-395) Christianity became the *only* legal religion, and Catholicism the *only* orthodox faith.

The Christian Priesthood. The success of Christianity was determined to a great extent by the consolidation of its organizational forms. The first Christian leaders were the Apostles who traveled about the Roman Empire founding congregations. Within these congregations the presbyters or elders and the deacons became the leaders. Presbyters were instructors in the faith and deacons carried on the charitable works. To govern large numbers of congregations the colleges or collection of presbyters appeared; they, too, were aided by deacons and had the function of keeping the faith pure, guarding morals, administering sacraments and the like. Christian leadership became an **episcopate** with the rise of the **bishop** as the chief functionary of the Church. Bishops derived from the belief in the primacy of Peter as leader of the Apostles and from the idea of the **apostolic succession.** Socially, the power of the bishop increased because of the great increase in administrative work as the numbers of Christians grew, the need for centralization in such matters as performance of the Eucharist, installing new priests, etc., the geographical separation that began to appear between the parish and the diocese and the religious conflicts that swept the Christian communities in the first three centuries. A provincial meeting of bishops was called a **synod**; a general meeting of all bishops, an **ecumenical council.** By the end of the third century, after considerable debate and struggle, it was established that there could be no salvation outside the church and that no one could be in the church who did not accept the bishop, successor of the Apostles, as the spiritual head of the church.

The Supremacy of the Roman Papacy. For many years the Bishop of Rome claimed supremacy over all bishops. This claim was based upon the

Petrine Doctrine. The Petrine Doctrine rested doctrinally upon this verse in Matthew 16:18: "Thou art Peter, and upon this Rock I will build my Church." Because of this statement it was argued that what Christ gave to the other Apostles, he gave *through* Peter. Peter was therefore the prince of the Apostles and "rules personally those whom Christ rules supremely." The claim for the supremacy of the Roman bishop was based historically upon the tradition that Peter himself had established the Roman bishopric.

Needless to say, this claim was bitterly contested by the **patriarchs** and **metropolitans** of other areas. Many factors account for the fact that western Christians came to accept the claims of the Roman bishop: Rome's traditional position as the center of a universal empire; the removal of imperial political authority to the east after 330 A.D.; the barbarian invasions, which often left the Roman bishop as the sole temporal (political) power in the west; the succession of very able bishops at Rome; the unvarying orthodoxy of the Roman bishops, etc. POPE LEO I (440-461) made the primacy of Roman bishops a fact when he persuaded the Emperor, Valentinian III, to decree that Rome was to be the chief seat of ecclesiastical power for Christianity, and that the decrees of the Roman bishop were to have the force of law for the entire church. An ecumenical council at Chalcedon in 451 sustained Valentinian's decree.

Monasticism. Monasticism developed from the Christian ideal of moral perfection. This ideal became linked with the belief that moral perfection could only come through a renunciation of all wordly goods, needs, desires and ambitions; it was through this worldliness that corruption and sin made their entry into the human spirit. To flee temptation, some Christians began to make a physical withdrawal from the world: they went to live solitary lives in the desert, or in caves, or in the wilderness. They grubbed for food, spent long hours in prayer and meditation, mortified their flesh by fasting and physical punishment and avoided all contact with other people. In a sense, they were continuing the tradition of Christian martyrdom and came to be regarded by surrounding Christians as very holy men. Secular clergymen, that is, the bishop and priest who worked *with* people appreciated the holy intent of these hermits but felt that it would be far safer for the church if withdrawal from the world were done in a more organized fashion. The result was that a movement began to establish communities of "monks."

The monk AMMON (c. 200 A.D.) was the first to gather together a group of hermits to live together *as a community*. Each of his membership lived in a home quarried from rock; prayed, meditated and mortified the flesh; and engaged in some kind of work. PACHOMIUS (292-346) built upon this foundation and formulated the first rules for monastic living: lonely living; work; memorization of the New Testament; no washing; head covered when eating; etc.

Because of the political and economic disorders of the fourth century monasticism grew swiftly and the need for regulating these communities increased. ST. BASIL of Caesera (330-379) in Asia Minor adapted monasticism to the organized life of the church and his rules were widely adopted in the east. Basil was opposed to the self-inflicted austerities of the early hermits. He realized that to be a successful monk, one had to be tested and trained; he therefore introduced the **novitiate** into monasticism, a probationary period during which the beginner was systematically trained. Thereafter monks devoted their lives to organized study, prayer, meditation, charity and work.

In the west it was BENEDICT (480-543) who formulated the rules for monastic life. His monastery established at **Monte Cassino** in Italy. The novitiate was carefully planned to test the true desire of the entrant to give up the world. When admitted, the Benedictine monk took vows of absolute poverty, obedience and chastity; he ate, prayed, worked and slept in common with his brothers; he suppressed all idle gossip; he followed a set and rigid schedule; he could undertake no special austerities without permission; he ate no flesh of quadrupeds; he engaged in many prescribed fasts; he could be flogged for violation of the rules.

Monasticism, then, created a clear division between the **secular clergy**, the sacred hierarchy that worked in the world, and the **regular clergy**, those who lived according to rules that withdrew them from the world. Both branches of these spiritual elite served as important stabilizing forces in the "Dark Ages" that were to come after the fall of Rome.

The Forging Of Orthodoxy. From the first Christianity had to cope with the problem of what was the **right or orthodox** doctrine as opposed to the **heretical or self-chosen and wrong** doctrine. In the second century, for example, Gnostics like Valentinus tried to force upon Christianity the ideas that Christ was the *Logos*, the mediator between God and man, the source of light and life, and

therefore no person; Christ as a person would have had to have contact with matter which, said the Gnostics, was pure evil. Valentinus (d.160 A.D.) and Marcion (fl. ca.144 A.D.) both tried to divorce Christianity from all connection with the Old Testament and to link it only with the New Testament. Montanus (150-180) argued that God's revelation was continuous, that it was vouchsafed to inspired prophets, and that therefore only inspired prophets should be permitted to the priesthood. Furthermore, since women too can be inspired, they should be permitted into the priesthood.

Such interpretations of Christianity were fought by apologists for the orthodox faith and were eventually rejected as "heresies." In the struggle with these heresies, however, orthodox Christians were compelled to begin **theological speculation** on the relation of Christ to universal processes of creation and salvation, on the validity or non-validity of the body of Christian writings, on exactly what is the true, fixed, universal (catholic) doctrine. As a result of the work of IRENEUS (130-200) and TERTULLIAN (155-225) and others by the middle of the third century the books in the New Testament were fixed and the first formulation of the **Apostle's Creed** was made.

New pressures on the doctrines of Christianity came when the educated classes were converted during the fourth and fifth centuries. Political rivalry between Rome and cities in the Near East helped to spark new intellectual controversies that now arose from the educated Christians. It is calculated that by 325 A.D. there were as many as ninety Christian sects extant. In the main, however, their differences had to do with disagreements about the **unity of God,** the **freedom of the human will** and **the nature of Christ.** Lesser differences centered on Church organization, discipline and ritual.

The greatest of these quarrels centered around the teachings of ARIUS (310-336) and ATHANASIUS (298-373). Arius denied the divinity of Christ; Christ was made of a substance *similar* with that of God, but not *identical.* Christ was created and therefore not eternal and not God. To this, Athanasius opposed the **doctrine of the Trinity.** The Trinity consisted of three persons: God, the Father Almighty; Jesus Christ, the Son of God; and the Holy Ghost. Each of these three persons was an essential principle of a **single substance.** This fundamental issue was settled for the orthodox at the first ecumenical council called by Constantine in 325 A.D. and held in Nicea. The **Nicene Creed** there adopted favored the position of Athanasius.

Controversy did not end with adoption of the Nicene Creed. **Nestorians** raised the question, How could Christ at one and the same time have both a *human* and a *divine* nature at the time he was incarnate? How could Mary be the Mother of God if she were a human being? **Pelagians** denied that Adam's sin had affected the whole human race; man therefore could be sinless and could go to Heaven without being redeemed. **Monophysites** argued that Christ was God and never man. Each of these "heresies" found enough followers to create its own church and to persist in spite of severe persecution. For western Europe, the end of the era of theological controversy did etablish a core of orthodox creed. This included the following dogmas, that

God is one substance and three persons (the Trinity);

Adam's sin of disobedience doomed the whole human race to corruption (the Fall);

God became man as Christ to redeem sinful man (the Incarnation);

God as Christ was miraculously born of the Virgin Mary (the Virgin Birth);

At one time Christ was both God and completely man (the Dual Nature of Christ);

God as Christ died as man to redeem the whole human race (the Atonement);

God as Christ rose from the grave to bring those who believe in Him immortality (the Resurrection);

God as Christ founded the Church as the *only* means of redemption (the Divine Foundation of the Church);

Through his Love, God gives man spiritual aid in his effort to escape from sin (Grace);

God as Christ will return to earth, resurrect the dead, save the blessed and damn the wicked (the Second Coming).

The Latin Church Fathers. The early Latin Church fathers (Lactantius, Arnobius, etc.) were more concerned with practical matters concerning the supremacy of the faith and ecclesiastical organization than with philosophical and theological speculation. During the fourth century, however, Latin Churchmen began to give more attention to the "theory" of their faith. AMBROSE (340-397), Bishop of Milan, wrote copiously to prove that Christian ethics were superior to pagan, that ecclesiastical authority is supreme over secular, that the Bible contains figurative and allegorical meaning, etc. JEROME (340-420) was a great scholar and his contribution to Latin Christianity was a translation of the Bible, known as the **Vulgate,** which became the accepted translation of the Roman Church. Ethically, Jerome leaned to severe, ascetic morality.

The greatest of all the Latin Church Fathers, however, was AUGUSTINE (354-430), the Bishop of Hippo. In his works, *On The Trinity, Confessions,* and *The City of God,* he provided Catholic Christianity with its first all-embracing synthesis. He sought to give final formulation to the relation of men to divine control and the relation of the Church to the salvation of men. In the course of his speculations, he formulated theories which embraced theology, philosophy, psychology, ethics, esthetics, etc. Not all of these theories have been accepted by the Roman Catholic Church, but his contributions to the Christian world-view of the fifth to twelfth centuries was immense.

THE FIRST CHRISTIAN SYNTHESIS

God was pure spirit—uncreated, unchangeable, omnipotent, omniscient, omnipresent, immortal. **He was perfect**—holy, just, merciful, truthful; He was independent of all other beings. He was the Creator of all things and all purposes; **He was One in substance and Three in persons**—as the Father He created the world and designed its activities, as Christ He re-established relationship between fallen man and Himself, as Holy Ghost He performed works of charity and love and grace. Signs of grace were many: speaking with wisdom, knowledge and "tongues"; the gifts of healing, miracle-making, interpreting speech and discerning spirits. **God was knowable**—primarily through **revelation** for this gave man supernatural knowledge, then through **introspection** of the state of one's heart and mind, and lastly through **reason** which can demonstrate the presence of God in the design of Nature.

Creation. The orders of created beings were three: plants and animals, men and angels. The first were incapable of achieving immortality. The second had been originally created in the image of God—with reason, intelligence and immortality; but Adam's sin brought death to the body and sin to the soul. Man, nonetheless, could still attain to immortality if he used his free will to choose between good and evil, if he exercised his capacity for faith. Angels were arranged in orders or choirs:

    a. angels, archangels and princedoms;
    b. powers, virtues and dominions;
    c. thrones, seraphim and cherubim

Good angels aided God in working for man's salvations; bad angels, led by Lucifer, were the enemies of man.

Redemption. Man could be redeemed if he atoned. In suffering death, Christ had atoned for Adam's fall; man could share in this atonement and win redemption through the established Church and through fulfilment of its sacraments and through good works of faith, hope and charity. Sacraments were supernatural mysteries: through baptism one's original sin was cleansed and the way was opened to a spiritual life; through the Lord's Supper one came into communion with Christ and prepared oneself for eternity.

Eschatology or Last Things. Christianity taught that there is a life after death for the souls of men. Each soul would undergo a **last judgment.** Souls free from sin would go to Heaven, live in supreme bliss, and enjoy the beatific vision or contemplation of God. Souls that were damned were sent to hell for eternal punishment. The unbaptised souls and those that were of men born before Christ became incarnate would dwell in **limbo**; while those that had committed venial sin were cleansed in **purgatory.** There was to be a **Second Coming** which would be heralded by celestial signs and earthly disaster; at this time Christ would judge the living and the dead and distribute rewards and punishment.

Ethics. God did not create evil; evil is a privation of good, that is, an incomplete good or a failure of good to fulfil itself. God created man with free will, freedom, that is, to choose to complete his nature or not. If man, by free choice, separates himself from his creator, he sins; if man loves himself rather than God, he sins. Adam's fall doomed all mankind to sin from which there was no escape except through the grace of God. Sinful acts flowed from succumbing to temptation of the devil or giving way to one's lower (animal) nature. In sinning man committed two kinds of acts: willful transgressions or **mortal sins** (pride, avarice, lust, sloth, murder, adultery, apostasy, etc.); and incidental transgressions or **venial sins.** To avoid sinning, man had to obey the moral law which derived from that revealed by Moses and that revealed by Christ. The purpose of the moral law was to point the way to union with God through purity of heart and active brotherly love; signs of moral behavior were meekness, humility, obedience and virtuousness. There were three orders of virtues:

theological—faith, hope and charity.
moral—prudence, temperance, fortitude and justice
religious—obedience, profession of faith, prayer, performance of vows and duties

Truth. Revelation was a source of truth. Through revelation God "spoke" to man. Man received this revelation as a voice from a burning bush, through divine inspiration, or by means of vision, trance, dream, etc. Scripture was revealed truth; it could not contradict human reason; the function of reason was to explain what appeared to be contradiction between revealed truth and experience. Faith preceded understanding.

Allegory was a source of truth. Allegory was an aid to discovering the meaning of revealed truth. Thus, any Biblical verse might have a literal or historical meaning, a moral significance not directly expressed, a prophetic declaration incorporated, or a revelation of life in the world after death. **Authority** was a source of truth. Authority flowed from the need, which arose often, to make a final decision between what was truth and what error. At this time in Church history, authority proceeded from the Church council to the bishop. Penalties for refusing to accept authoritative pronouncements were severe in the extreme. **Illumination** was a source of truth. This was the way of the **mystic**. One might rise to an illumination by various paths: through **quietism** or the avoidance of all physical activity; or through mortifying the flesh so that only the spiritual part remains; or by **ecstasy**—the attainment of utter happiness through complete loss of the self.

Philosophy. Augustine made philosophy into a handmaiden of theology. Plato was useful in defining God as a spiritual reality and Platonic Ideas or Forms became the emanations from the mind of God that became the things of the universe. Aristotle's doctrine of essences as the material embodiments of forms were also employed to establish original emanations from the mind of God. Aristotle's concept of the substance that underlay the diversity of things was utilized to resolve the problem of the Trinity. The Neo-Platonic Logos was used to demonstrate the means by which things came into being from spiritual origins. Stoic ideas of universal natural law became the distinctive markings of sinful and sinless behavior. PLOTINUS provided Christians with a sense of the conflict between spiritual and material, the goodness of the one and the evil of the other. Socratic rationalism was employed to demonstrate the existence of God. Augustine reasoned that God must exist because creation demands a creator, because there is evidence of design and purpose in the universe, because mankind consents to the existence of God and because thought itself is proof of the divine essence in mankind.

Psychology. Man's nature was inevitably examined by Christian thinkers of this early period for it was necessary to demonstrate the existence of a soul. Evidence for the existence of a soul was found in the soul's activities—providing the body with life, making possible sensation, perception, reasoning, meditation, and aspiration, the act of will, and the like. Augustine followed Aristotle in his belief that the soul had two parts: an irrational and rational. The former was concerned with vital activities and impulses, the latter with memory, reasoning, imagination and understanding. Location of these activities within the body, however, produced a completely erroneous physiology. Religious reasoning also produced theories of the nature of sleep as a kind of death, of dreams as messages, of insanity as possession by demons and so forth. In fact, most scientific data was given a moralistic interpretation. Men read God's purposes into zoological, biological, cosmological and historical data.

Society. Church and State. The State was a necessary instrument to curb the corrupt tendencies of sinful man. Social practices like marriage, property, slavery, law and government were intended as checks to violence, greed and immorality. The State obviously had divine sanction and it was the duty of men to obey. But the rulers of the State were men. As men, rulers were subject to the word of God as were all other men.

The word of God was incorporated in the church to which all men, regardless of political or social status, belonged; the Church then was clearly above the State in all matters coming within its jurisdiction (marriage, morals, beliefs, etc.). Its priesthood was by nature a *privileged* class, obedient to a higher law. What was more, the State was obliged to use its power against the enemies of the church whether these were pagans, Jews, heretics or schismatics (those who remained Christian but split from the Church). Early Christian emperors were most zealous in enforcing persecutions against pagans, Jews, Manicheans, Montanists, Donatists, and other groups and sects outside the Church.

Economic. By divine law, property belonged to God; by natural law, to all men; by positive law to some men and not to others. Private property was justified because of the sinfulness of men; but it entailed responsibilities as well as rights. The use of private property had to be Christian in its intent. Where property encouraged avarice and self-indulgence its use was sinful. All men had the obligation to work; all work had equal value—chiefly moral and disciplinary. Some work led men into sinfulness, for example, work involving speculation, or usury, or trading. Men who gained from work were obligated to apply some of their gains to almsgiving and other works of charity. But the division of mankind into social and economic classes—even the existence of slavery—was accepted by the church.

Social. Christian charitable works were extensive. Church activity centered upon betterment of the lot of the poverty stricken, the poor, the widowed, the orphaned, the disabled and the sick. These were given food relief, work and medical care. Not only the stricken, but the homeless and wandering were also cared for and sheltered for the period of their stay.

Nor did charity end with relief. The church did its best to improve the conditions under which men labored as both freemen and slaves; it tried to introduce humane practices into master-servant relationships. Thus, while sanctioning slavery, it fought such practices as enslavement because of debt and immoral practices with female slaves.

EARLY CHRISTIAN LITERATURE

War against paganism included war against pagan arts. However, Christians employed literary forms in the effort to transmit religious doctrine and emotion to the masses.

Eventually, each of these literary arts incorporated pagan forms of literature. Thus the poem became the **hymn** and the Christian **epic,** the tale became the biographical account of the **lives of saints,** oratory became the **sermon** and exposition became **exegesis** (explanation of texts). Though on occasion the emotional content of the hymn, usually accompanied by music, raised it above creed into poetry, the occasions were rare. The epics and the lives of the saints are not primarily interesting as literature, nor were they intended to be. They were instructional in purpose. Augustine's *Confessions* is the great exception; it is a highly personal account of an individual search for the meaning of life. The *Confessions* is a great classic in the Greco-Roman sense.

EARLY CHRISTIAN ART

There has been a considerable revival recently of interest in early Christian art as a result of imitations by the modern artists. The purposes of early Christian art were twofold: to tell a tale that pointed a moral and to symbolize the articles of faith. Christian arists cared little for naturalistic reproduction; careful copying of nature would give the wrong emphasis to their beliefs, namely, a this-worldliness. What they sought was an other-worldliness in its abstract and symbolic forms. It is precisely this abstraction and symbolism which attract the modern artist.

Earliest Christian painting was in the Catacombs and took the form of murals, frescoes and inscriptions. As churches were built, the painting arts were brought in as allies to architecture. The chief motifs in early Christian art were Biblical scenes, natural symbols (lambs and doves, loaves and fishes, etc.), priestly processions, saints and martyrs and the Christ image. Perspective was ignored; spiritual significance determined size; attitudes of piety, glory, penance became fixed; color took on symbolic meaning. Artists tried to fix eternity into their panels.

EARLY CHRISTIAN ARCHITECTURE

Church architecture evolved slowly by tentative stages. The first form of building was called a basilica and had no distinctive features. Then, in the East, experimentation began with the use of arch and column, the barrel-vaulted roof, the dome placed on a square base, the dome placed on arches across the squares of the base, the apse, the portico, the nave and aisles, the semicircular apse containing the altar. By the sixth century, the Western Church had made its selection of style: the building was to have the form of a cross, a long central aisle—the nave and two side aisles, a barrel-vaulted roof with a dome and porticos. Columns and arches were adorned with sculptured figures and plants; spaces were filled with paintings or mosaics of Biblical motifs, Christ images, saints, and other religious images. Thus, the interior of the church had a single purpose, to lift the heart upward to the dome of heaven and to keep heaven before the eyes of the congregation even when they were leveled. Though the purpose was religious, the result was art.

CHAPTER EIGHT

TEUTON, BYZANTINE AND MUSLIM

THE TEUTONS

North of the Roman Empire in Europe lay the land of the Teutons or the Germanic tribes. More to the east were the Goths, Vandals and Scandinavians; to the west, the Franks, the Alemani, the Burgundians, the Frisians, the Anglo-Saxons and the Dutch. When the Romans first encountered them they were a primitive people. They dressed in animal skins, lived in crude huts, engaged in sheep-and-cattle herding and some primitive agriculture and used tools and weapons made of stone and iron.

Social Characteristics. Teutonic social patterns were as primitive as their economic. The family was the most important social unit; but it was severely patriarchal. The father had secured his wife by purchase or capture; he had unlimited authority over the children. He could sell into marriage or slavery both wife and children. Kinship was traced for the most part through the male and determined many of the Germanic customs, among them marriage purchase and blood feuds.

In time, family kinship evolved into the tribe and some of the more savage practices were refined. Payment of compensation in goods replaced blood feuding; tribes regulated marriage practices, took over abandoned or illegitimate minors, supported the aged or needy and arranged for defense against enemy attack.

German society was caste-ridden; there were the nobility, the freemen, the semi-freemen and the slaves. Only the nobility and freemen enjoyed political and legal rights and could own land. Semi-freemen were without these privileges but could contract marriages and acquire property.

Religion. Religion among the Teutons was primitively animistic, that is, the unseen world was peopled with spirits that accounted for such things as fertility, death, natural phenomena, war and peace, physical health and disease. These spirits were invested with the human characteristics of physical activity, pleasure and pain, thought and emotion. Freya was the goddess of fertility; Wotan or Odin, of stormy weather; Thiu, of war; Thor, of thunder. (It is from the names of these deities that we derive the names of the days Tuesday, Wednesday, Thursday and Friday.) Spirits were either good or evil. From his abode in Valhalla, Thor led the good spirits against the evil. Man, caught in this eternal struggle between the two, had no choice but to buy the favor of the one and ward off the malevolence of the other by a carefully regulated system of rites and incantations. There was no priesthood among the early Teutons; the head-males performed the services and sacrifices that were required.

Political Institutions. During the nineteenth century it was the accepted belief among most historians that Anglo-American republicanism and democracy derived from the political practices of these early Germanic tribes. Closer examination shows this to be an exaggeration. The basis for this belief was the fact that among the Germanic tribes there existed the practice of submitting tribal problems to an assembly for decision. The assembly chose its kings or princes, declared war or made peace and acted as a kind of court in civil and criminal cases. This assembly, however, was dominated by a council of aristocrats who initiated legislation. Kings and princes had a military following, all of whom lived in their leader's house. This has little of the republican or democratic about it; it was more closely related to the medieval institution of feudalism.

Roman and Teuton. In the period of the Roman Empire, scattered Germanic tribes coalesced into larger political units and began to press against the boundaries of the Empire. Chief among these were the Goths, the Franks, the Saxons, the Frisians, the Bavarians and the Thuringians. Land hunger and envy of the rich realm to the south were the primary driving forces. Entry into the Empire was at first made by the Germans through infiltration. As the Empire expanded, the Emperors began to employ German bands as allies within the Roman army. In the later Roman period, whole tribes were granted admission into the Empire provided they served as border-guards. Many individual Germans rose to officer rank and were permitted to command large Roman forces; some rose even to high political position. Intermarriage between Roman and German became fairly common.

The "Barbarian" Invasions. As a result of this

commingling, the Teutons underwent civilizing—just as the Romans underwent barbarizing. At the end of the fourth century, however, the pressure of the Germans could no longer be resisted. The Empire was exhausted; its frontier defenses were sapped; Germanic tribes were both inside and outside the Empire; additional pressure now came from the East from the Slavs and Huns. The Huns—an army of wild riding Chinese—were the immediate cause for the Teutonic invasion of the Empire. The East Goths (Ostrogoths) had been defeated by the Huns; the West Goths (Visigoths) asked for sanctuary within the Empire. Emperor Valens granted them permission to cross the Danube in 376. Over a million Visigoths moved in. Exploited and abused by the Romans, they turned on their hosts and in the significant **Battle of Adrianople,** 378, defeated them. Thirty years later, under the leadership of ALARIC (408) the Visigoths invaded Italy and took Rome in 410. After plundering the city, they moved on and finally settled in Spain and southern France.

Close behind the Visigoths were the Vandals. They, too, moved into Spain but were forced out by the Visigoths. They went overseas to North Africa. By capturing Carthage they established their hold on the Mediterranean Sea. In 455 they too sacked Rome. Their domination lasted until they were destroyed by the Byzantine general, Belisarius. This, then, was the general pattern of occupation. Burgundians were in the upper regions of the Rhone by 440; Bavarians settled in Pannonia about the same time; Angles, Jutes and Saxons took the westerly route into England; the Lombards followed the line of the Elbe and in the sixth century invaded northern Italy.

The Teutonic destiny of Europe was threatened most by the Tartar-Mongolian Huns. After almost eliminating the Ostrogoths from history, they pursued the Visigoths along the lower reaches of the Danube. Soon they were threatening Rome; but the Emperor Theodosius II was able to buy off ATTILA, the Hun leader. Having spared Rome, Attila began a westward march that carried him into Gaul. There, however, in a turning-point battle at Chalons (451) the Roman general Aetius supported by the Visigoths stopped Attila and forced him to retreat. Attila's death in 453 ended the Hunnish menace. It was a narrow escape for Europe. Defeat of the Huns paved the way for a brief reunification of the Roman Empire under Theodoric; but it was only a last gasp.

Clovis and the Franks. Between the sixth and the ninth centuries Europe was dominated by the Franks, a Gaulish people, whose power was first established by their leader CLOVIS (486-511). The Franks were conquerors more than invaders, for they never lost contact with their home base in northern France and Germany. From this base they expanded until they held most of Gaul and the land on both banks of the Rhine. In the course of this conquest, Clovis created in part the concept of kingship: he established orderly processes of government, issued decrees and enforced them with his army and supplied a measure of justice through himself. More important for the future was the fact that Clovis was the first of the great Germanic leaders to adopt Christianity in its orthodox form; in fact he became the military arm of the Roman Church in its war against the Arian heresy, a heresy freely adopted by most of the German leaders before Clovis.

Teutonic-Romanic Amalgam. The merging of Germanic and Romanic elements produced new institutions, a fusion of both. Monarchy featured the rule of the German kings; however, there was a new tendency toward dynastic succession. The territory ruled was regarded as a personal possession to be transmitted to one's descendants. Latin remained the official tongue; Roman administrative apparatus was retained as were the forms of local government. The code of law remained, for the most part, barbaric.

Germans fastened the economic institutions of declining Rome upon Europe. Rulers took for themselves great estates and villas along with the resident tenant farmers and slaves. A few contacts with trade on the Mediterranean were maintained, but this declined sharply from its height during the Roman Empire. Industry languished and the great Roman cities became increasingly depopulated.

With the passing centuries the concept of Roman imperial power passed. Arianism as an opposition creed disappeared. The Germans were increasingly Christianized and Latinized. As a substratum to this fusion, however, were the Roman institutions that persisted, not only in the "romance" languages that were beginning to emerge, but in the Roman law which underlay both church and secular law, in the dream of a universal empire that lingered on, particularly inside the Church, and in the political institutions that never quite disappeared.

THE BYZANTINE EMPIRE

Under the impact of the Barbarian Invasions, Roman civilization in Western Europe crumbled and the people of that area had to evolve new forms of civilization in order to survive. Collectively, these new forms became the Feudal System.

The situation in Eastern Europe and Asia Minor was quite different. In an effort to halt the decline in the Roman Empire, Diocletian (285-304) had divided its administration among four co-rulers. For his own seat of government Diocletian selected the eastern part of the Empire, a part which took in Asia, Thrace and Asia Minor. Constantine (306-337) had, in 324, built a new capital city, Constantinople, for the whole Empire; Rome's significance as a capital of the Empire declined. In 395 Theodosius I officially divided the Empire into two legal divisions. As pressure from the Teutons mounted, Emperor Honorius removed the western capital from Rome to Ravenna. It was from this site that Odoacer, an Ostrogoth, removed Romulus Augustulus in 476. This removal dropped the curtain on the Roman Empire in the West; but that in the East continued strong for 1,000 years more. *Rome* fell; but the *Roman Empire* had simply shifted its locus.

A Mixture of Civilizations. The substance of the Empire changed with this change in place. **It became predominantly Greek in language and culture.** Greek became the language of the court and the schools; Greek classics formed the basis of the curriculum of the schools; Greek art influenced Byzantine architecture, painting and sculpture to a marked degree. This Greek element, however, was **grafted upon the Roman institutions which were retained:** chiefly, the legal and administrative systems, the army and navy, commercial practices, the system of taxation, the engineering and design of the cities. Moreover, now that Rome had moved East, **Oriental** practices became more manifest; absolutism by divine right in government, pomp and ceremony in court and church, increased emotionalism in art, mysticism in religion and pessimism in philosophy. Thus the Roman Empire became the Greco-Roman-Oriental Empire: collectively, the **Byzantine Empire** (from **Byzantium** on whose site Constantinople was built.)

Political Development. Expansion-decline-revival-expansion cycles marked the epochs of Byzantine political history. In the fourth century Teutonic invasions caused the Eastern Empire to totter along with the Western. In 378 the Visigoths killed Emperor Valens at the Battle of Adrianople; a century later, Theodoric, the Ostrogoth, almost took Constantinople. The city's impregnable position saved the Empire. In the sixth century, Justinian the Great led a revived imperial corps out of Constantinople in a majestic effort to retake the entire Empire of old. His brilliant generals, Belisarius and Narses, took almost all of North Africa, the Balkans and Italy. Further conquests were then made eastward into Asia Minor. After Justinian's death the Empire crumpled under blows delivered by barbarian Slavs, Avars (a Mongolian people), Bulgars and Mohammedan Arabs and by the eighth century it had shrunk to its smallest size. Then, under Leo III, the Byzantine forces broke the Muslim power and regained control of the Mediterranean Sea. Leo's demise was followed by further decline until in the ninth century Basil I, ably assisted by Generals Nicephorus Phocas and John Tzimisces, once again defeated the Bulgars, Russians and Muslims. This was repeated by Basil II in the tenth century.

The most serious threat to Byzantium, and, indeed, to all Christendom came in the eleventh century with the rise to power of the Seljuk Turks. Recognizing the threat, the Christians of the West came to the aid of the beleaguered Byzantines. But in 1204 western **Crusaders** themselves occupied and sacked Constantinople. This blow considerably weakened the Byzantine kingdom, but it lingered on for two centuries. Finally, in 1453, the Ottoman Turks took Constantinople. It became and remained Mohammedan. Western Europe had lost its control over the Near East and had to wait four centuries to regain it partially.

BYZANTINE CONTRIBUTIONS TO WESTERN CIVILIZATION

Absolutism. The influence of Byzantine civilization upon Western Europe and, indeed, upon world civilization, is in the process of current reappraisal by historians. For decades it had been dismissed—following the lead of Gibbon's *Decline and Fall of the Roman Empire*—as of no consequence in the history of western civilization. This estimate of an otherwise able historian was false in the extreme. From the Byzantine Empire came the concept of **divine-right absolutism** that prevailed in Europe during the 17th and 18th centuries. Diocletian first established an Oriental despotism in the Roman Empire in imitation of Persian models; thus, men prostrated themselves before him as they approached the throne. Constantine continued this practice and added Christian-religious overtones to it. By the time of JUSTINIAN THE GREAT (527-565) the practice was institutionalized. The ruler of the Byzantine Empire ruled without check. He was God's regent on earth; his acts had to be accepted as divinely inspired; to oppose his decrees was to commit sin. To match his "divinity" the Byzantine Emperor produced a court unequaled in history for grandeur and splendor.

Church and State. The Greek Catholic Church became an arm of the state. The Emperor was the titular head of the Church; he was the *direct* representative of God. His rule over the Church, however, was indirect. The direct ruler was the **Patriarch of Constantinople** who was chosen from a list of three candidates submitted to him by a synod of metropolitans. If none of these candidates pleased the emperor, he substituted his own. Church bishops resided at court as a Holy Synod. Thus Emperor and Patriarch cooperated in producing combined politico-religious policies. In a sense this union of politics and religion was a reflection of popular opinion in Constantinople. The Byzantine masses, unable to give vent to political protest, turned their criticism into religious channels. It was a contemporary by-word in Constantinople that the Byzantine butcher and baker would and could, at the drop of a hat, discuss complicated theological aspects on the Arian creed, the use of leavened versus unleavened bread in the Mass, etc. Inevitably sharp dissension characterized Byzantine religion, dissensions that created "parties" within the Empire and eventually forced an important schism with Western Catholicism.

Schism. Eastern ecclesiastical practices and beliefs had begun early to diverge from those of Roman Catholicism. Latin became universal in the Western Church; the Eastern Church, on the other hand, permitted the use of Latin, Greek or **vernacular** (the popular language)—depending upon the composition of the parish. In the East parish priests could marry before they were ordained; civil servants could be given bishoprics because of their administrative talents; regular clergy were preferred over secular for advancement to higher positions; church ritual was far more elaborate and Orientalized; there was less stress on the New Testament and on the personality of Christ; religious dissension was more frequent and more bitter and more violent.

These differences between East and West were sharply emphasized in the dispute that arose over the use of religious images—the **Iconoclastic Controversy (725-843).** Some of the purists among the Byzantines felt that the use of icons (carved and painted religious figures) had become idola-

trous and superstitious: large numbers of people, they protested, had begun to invest the icons with miraculous powers and so they kissed them, prostrated themselves before them, lit candles to them, and the like. Emperor Leo III agreed with this point of view and forbade the use of icons in the East and tried to have them banished in the West as well. Byzantine monks rallied to the defense of retention of the icons and organized a religious party opposed to the Emperor and his iconoclastic party. This was in effect a *political* protest. The Emperor, ruler by divine right, was accused of an abuse of his arbitrary power, of denying Christ's personality; the Emperor in turn accused the monks of deserting from industry, agriculture and the armed forces to enjoy the cloistered life. The icon party won. In the course of the struggle, however, relations between the West and East worsened.

Rome disapproved of these hairsplitting theological dissensions. No matter how pressed, the Greeks refused to accept the Petrine Doctrine of papal supremacy. The whole atmosphere of Greek Catholic practices was now foreign to Roman prelates. The inevitable came in 1054. The Roman pope pronounced Greek Catholics as excommunicated; the Constantinople Patriarch excommunicated the Roman pope. Religious unity was ended.

Economic Institutions. Byzantine economic practices profoundly affected the course of economic development in Europe. They kept alive and extended the basic industries which had been developed in the course of Greco-Roman civilization. These had virtually disappeared in the west. Leather and metal trades, fashioning of precious stones and their settings, the textile industry featuring silks and brocades, the carpet and rug industry, dye and glass manufactories—these were some of the "luxury" items manufactured in the large Byzantine cities for the export trade.

Continuation of Roman trading practices was the second contribution of Byzantium to world economic civilization. Byzantium kept open the lanes to the Far East and the silks and spices and drugs that originated in that area of the world. Trade routes to the Far East—the overland route by way of the Black and Caspian Seas; the Syrian-Red Sea route, mostly by water; the overland Syria-Tigris-Euphrates-Persian Gulf water route—were kept open all during the Dark Ages in Europe. Maritime power, both merchant and naval, was highly developed.

Finally, Byzantium set the pattern for economic centralization under the control and supervision of the State. Manufacturers were organized into **pro-**

ducers' guilds; laborers into workers' guilds. Control of both guilds was in the hands of the State bureaucracy which promulgated **codes of practice** for each. Thus, manufacturers were regulated in the prices they charged, the kind of raw materials they could use, the quantity and quality of the goods they manufactured, the areas of distribution, and the like. Workers were regulated in the amount of wages they could receive, their type and terms of employment, and the like. The State itself owned and operated dye, textile, mineral, and armament concerns. Agriculture was, for the most part, unsupervised with the exception that in the fourth century the emperors fastened serfdom, a form of semi-slavery, upon farm laborers employed on the estates of both nobility and Church.

Society. Byzantine society was riven by a strange contradiction. On the one hand, the monkish recluse and ascetic was the social ideal. Men who gave up the world to retire to some monastery on Mount Athos and to live by strict rules were greatly admired. Patriarch and bishop were usually chosen from monastic ranks; gifts and endowments were showered upon the monasteries. On the other hand, Byzantium produced one of the most corrupt and immoral societies in the history of civilization.

Wealthy landlords and merchants made up the elite. For the first time in history the tradesman and manufacturer was freely admitted into the aristocracy. Both of these types of nobility were superbly cultured, for the Byzantines placed a high value on liberal education. Teachers were well-trained and well-paid. Education began at 6 with instruction in reading, writing, spelling and grammar. Homer and the classical poets were taught early and large sections of these works were committed to memory. From 7 to 18 adolescents were trained in rhetoric, arithmetic, geometry, music, astronomy and philosophy. Thereafter, a student might enter a university and pursue law, medicine, theology, classical literature, advanced mathematics or advanced philosophy. At all levels religion was taught by trained monks.

BYZANTINE CULTURE

Scholarship. Byzantine scholarship was preservative rather than creative. Considerable energy was devoted to the collection of the best texts available of the works of Greek scholars and artists; to writing learned commentaries upon these texts; to making digests of them for easy memorization; to cataloguing works for libraries; to the editing of encyclopedias and anthologies. Some originality appeared in the works of JOHN OF DAMASCUS (8th c.) who is considered by some to be the "father of Scolasticism" because he attempted a reconciliation of Aristotle and the Scriptures; and in the work of MICHAEL PSELLUS (11th c.) who attempted a reconciliation of the thought of Plato and Aristotle. But this is a meager output for 1,000 years of existence.

Literature. Sterility was equally characteristic of Byzantine literary efforts. Writers composed in Attic Greek which was no longer the language of the people; their styles were elaborate, rhetorical and artificial; most of their writing was theological disputation. Only Procopius in the field of History and Romanos in poetry achieved some stature as literary artists.

Art. Byzantine contributions to art were immense.

In the fields of art they drew upon a wealth of source material. From the early Christians they took their themes and symbols; from the Greeks the principles of balance and clarity; from the Romans skill in engineering the arch and vault and in using marble, cement, stone, fabric and jewels; from the Orientals, color, mosaic, grandeur and mystery.

The **Church of Hagia Sophia** (6th c.) was the masterpiece of Byzantine art and architecture. It rose 179 feet to the high point of its 107-foot-diameter central dome, a dome immense enough to house forty windows at its base. This height was achieved by brilliant use of compounded pillars, arches and vaults which rested upon a cruciform base; the relationship of dome to arch and vault was engineered (for support, stress and strain) to perfection. Hagia Sophia was intended as a symbol of the interior life of man and therefore the exterior of the structure was kept bare and unattractive. However, glory itself burst upon the viewer as he stepped inside, for light poured in through the dome-windows upon masses of blue and gold decoration, upon richly colored mosaic upon mosaic, upon marble facings and sculptured, graceful, elaborate columns and pillars, upon abundant gold-leaf and tinted glass and sparkling gems. The interior height was breath-taking. When it was completed, Justinian remarked, "I have surpassed thee, O Solomon." He was not boasting.

Mosaic was preferred over painting by the Byzantine artists. These artists specialized in the "stained-glass attitude," that is, the figure of Christ or the Madonna without a touch of realism. Conventional poses—exaggerated and distorted—were utilized to secure eternal effects of piety or humility or any of the other religious virtues. The Byzantine artist was a master in the symbolic use of color, again exaggerated to strike a religious rather than a realistic note. One exception to this general analysis must be noted, however. When they dealt with the subject of the crucifixion of Christ, Byzantine artists dwelt realistically with His pain, agony and sorrow.

The Impact of Byzantine Culture. Europe slept while Byzantium flourished and awoke when it declined. Therefore, the impact of Byzantine culture upon Western Europe was in the form of a delayed shock, a re-discovery. Western discovery of the compilations of Byzantine scholars provided the impulse for the creative burst of medieval scholarship in the 13th century. Byzantine scholarship was the primary stimulus to the great Renaissance in Europe in the 14th century. Byzantine contacts with Venice and Milan and the Far East laid the foundations for the Commercial Revolution that burst upon Europe in the 15th century. Architects of the medieval Gothic cathedrals borrowed liberally from Byzantine models. Byzantine painting influenced European painting from El Greco to Picasso. Justinian's law code entered into the substance of the civil and canon law of Europe. Byzantine monks brought civilization and Christianity to the Slavic peoples of Europe: they created a Slavic (Cyrillic) alphabet based on Greek forms (and a Gothic-Ulfilas-alphabet based on Roman forms); they introduced into Slavic Europe Greek Catholicism, Byzantine monasticism, art, music, mysticism, theology and political absolutism. This is but a partial listing of the impact of Byzantium on European history. One equally long could be drawn up for its impact upon Mohammedanism.

MOHAMMEDAN CIVILIZATION

During and after the 7th century A.D. there rose up between the Byzantine civilization and that in Western Europe a new civilization which originated in the teachings of MOHAMMED (569-632). This civilization was both a threat and an inspiration to western culture. On the one hand it was a warring and conquering civilization; on the other, it was an accumulative and transmittive one—accumulative of the best in the old and current cultures, and transmittive through its extraordinary breadth of trade and commerce. Of the three civilizations that existed during the "medieval period" of European history, the Muslim was by far the most superior.

Mohammed. Mohammed was born in Mecca, a city on the trade route from the Mediterranean to the Red Sea and the center of an area in which dwelt Bedouin, Berber or Arabian tribes. The city itself was cosmopolitan. Visitors from many lands brought with them variable winds of doctrine which stirred considerable intellectual ferment there. Arabians were still, for the most part, in the polytheistic stage of religious development. Their religious interest centered in Mecca because it contained the K'abah, a black stone sacred to them. A small minority of Arabs had already conceived of a single, supreme deity—Allah. It was Mohammed's destiny to elevate Allah above all other gods.

Mohammed entered into the caravan trade, did well at it, but paid as much attention to religious disputation as to business. He was also extremely sensitive to the extreme misery of his countrymen. At age 25 he married a wealthy widow and thereafter devoted his life to religious studies and ascetic practices. At age 40 he began to receive visions in which the angel Gabriel announced that he, Mohammed, had been singled out by Allah to be the prophet of a new faith. The substance of this new faith was also given to Mohammed in the form of visions. As he received these revelations, Mohammed had them recorded; the book of these recorded revelations is today the Holy Book of Islam, the **Koran.**

Mohammed began preaching the new faith among the Arabian masses collected in Mecca. He converted his wife, his cousin Ali, a prominent Meccan named Abu Bakr and an intelligent youth named Omar. But the masses did not respond. In fact, conservative Arabs raised such opposition to his teachings that Mohammed left Mecca for Medina. (This period of separation from Mecca— 622 A.D.—is known in Islamic lore as the *Hegira.* Muslim calendars are dated A.H., *anno hegirae.*) The Hegira lasted eight years while Mohammed created a following in Medina. In 630 he returned to Mecca and converted the city. He died there two years later.

Mohammedan Conquests. ABU BAKR (632-4) and OMAR (634-44) established the first Muslim caliphates, literally, successors of the prophet. Both these caliphs preached a Holy War to extend Muslim supremacy over Arabia. Within a year Arabian opposition was reduced and offensives were begun against Syria and Persia. Neither Persia nor Byzantium offered much opposition to this offensive for they had been exhausted by war with one another. Syria and Mesopotamia having been conquered, Caliph Omar took Egypt in 642 and Persia in 651. Success bred conversion; tens of thousands of Arabs now poured into this new, victorious faith that had lifted the impoverished Arab from the status of nomad to that of world conqueror. Following Omar's death, the Ommiad Dynasty removed the capital from Medina to Damascus in Syria, substituted territorial for religious kingship, produced a bureaucracy based on Byzantine models and made succession to the caliphate hereditary.

With this secular reorganization, conquest was resumed. Naval supremacy was established over the Mediterranean Sea; Constantinople was isolated and detached from its North African possessions; North Africa was then seized and converted; and the way was open for conquest of southern Europe. In the year 711, Moorish armies crossed the waters into Spain. They were led by Gebel Tarek—who gave his name to Gibraltar. The Moors destroyed the Visigothic Kingdom in Spain and within seven years had crossed the Pyrenees into central Gaul. Near Poitiers (732) they were met by Charles "Martel"—a Frank of the rising Carolingian House —and defeated. This ended the Muslim advance into Europe; they retreated over the Pyrenees and settled down to consolidate their position.

Divided Empire. Brilliant as conquerors, the Muslims proved unable to weld their heterogeneous lands into a single imperial form. The result was that in the latter half of the eighth century a number of independent Muslim states were created. In Spain the Caliphate of Cordova was set up under the remnants of the Ommiad Dynasty; in the city of Baghdad, the Abbassid Dynasty created a second caliphate; still a third was founded by the Fatimids in Kairowan in North Africa. However, when the empire was thus divided into smaller units, it proved to be remarkably stable and enlightened. Few conquerors have been more generous to their conquered. With the exception of a compulsory tax, fairly levied and efficiently collected, the conquered were free to move, to believe as they wished and to take advantage of the many commercial and cultural opportunities available.

Of the many peoples in the Muslim empire, two predominated: the Arabs and the Turks. During the first period of conquest it was the Arab or **Saracenic** element that prevailed (7th to 11th c.) In the eleventh century the **Seljuk Turks** came to power. It was they who held off the Christian Crusaders. When the Mongols under GENGHIS KHAN crushed them, the Ottoman Turks rose to take their place. It was these Turks who successfully overthrew the Byzantine Empire in 1453.

MUSLIM CIVILIZATION

Islam. Islam, as taught by Mohammed and recorded in the Koran, was a severely monotheistic faith. "There is only one God, Allah, and Mohammed is His prophet." Since the Christian Trinity was viewed as polytheistic, the orientation of Islam was to the *Old Testament*, not the *New*. The Koran cited the *Pentateuch* and the *Psalms* with approval; it accepted the revelation given to Moses as divinely inspired; it considered all the Old Testament patriarchs as inspired by Allah; but above all it claimed to have revived the *uncorrupted* religion of Abraham and to have derived from Abraham's son Ishmael. Islam rejected Christ's *divinity* but acknowledged that Christ was a divinely inspired prophet. Through Moses and Christ a partial revelation of the true faith was given to mankind. Now, through Mohammed, the revelation was made complete.

The Faith. Allah was absolute—one, omniscient, omnipresent, omnipotent, the single creative force in the universe, the agent behind and within every event in the universe. Muslims say, "It is the will of Allah; I am content with His decree."

Allah was pure spirit—no image could reproduce Him and image-worship of any kind was idolatrous. Between Allah and His creature Man were mediating **angels and devils.** Angels were the forces of Good, God's messengers, the source of prophecy, recorders of man's activities, receivers of the souls of the dead, and witnesses at man's Last Judgment. Devils were those who rebelled against Allah and continued their rebellion by leading men to sin and damnation.

Of great importance to Islamites was the Last Judgment of all mankind. It would open with a blare of trumpets, the heavens would gape, physical destruction would strike the earth, graves would open and all the living and the dead would rise to heaven to be judged. The blessed would be sent on upward to Paradise where there were gardens and running waters, lovely maidens and abundant food and drink. The damned would be sent below to hell to suffer unspeakable tortures for eternity. It behooved believers, therefore, to abide by the injunctions of the Prophet concerning the right way to blessedness.

The Right Way. Islam demanded set forms of prayers. In the course of the day there were to be five separate prayers. Before each, the worshippers were to wash their hands, face and feet with water or sand, face Mecca, and recite their prayers in

Arabic. On Friday at noon, the faithful would gather in the Mosque (temple) for special prayer; there the *Imam* or prayer leader would conduct the service. **Islam had no priesthood.** They followed the leadership of those who were obviously consecrated and learned in the ways of Allah and the Koran. **Islam had no sacraments.** The relationship between God and Man was direct and unmediated. The right way was also through alms-giving. This took the form of a religious tax, a "loan to Allah" which Allah would repay manifold. Monies collected through alms were set aside for charitable and religious purposes only.

The right way was by observance of the month of *Ramadan*—a month of fasting for no food or drink could enter the mouth of the faithful between sunrise and sunset. The right way was by a *pilgrimage* (made at least once in a lifetime) to Mecca where one might meet and commune with all one's brothers in the faith from all over the world. Finally, the right way was unqualified acceptance of the basic creed: "There is only one God, Allah, and Mohammed is His prophet."

It is important to note how simple and direct was the faith of Islam—without complicated dogma, without an hierarchical priesthood, without an extensive ecclesiastical machinery; its simplicity and directness accounted in part for its tremendous success as a missionary faith among the poor, illiterate and downtrodden.

Taboo and Injunction. As in many other religions, Islamites were enjoined against certain actions. They were forbidden to use wine or pork, to gamble, to collect usury, to make graven images, or to engage in crimes like murder, theft, slander, etc. Islam was an **ethical faith;** it stressed right living by means of the vitrues of temperance, humility, tolerance, generosity, etc. Courage was the required personality characteristic of all Islamites for they were, through their faith, pledged to a Holy War against infidels and he who died in a Holy War was ensured immortality in Paradise. Certain aspects of Islam were permissive: where danger might ensue, prayer and fasting could be relaxed without fear of punishment; men could take four wives and an unlimited number of concubines—if they could afford them.

Political Forms. Muslim law proceeded from the Koran; political and religious rule were completely merged. Allah ruled through caliphs. Caliphs were, therefore, divine-right kings, absolute in their power but for one thing—they could not violate the precepts of the Koran. The Koran thus became the written constitution of the Muslim state, interpretation of which was in the hands of the doctors of law. Theoretically absolute, the caliphs were unable to assert their rule over all areas; they therefore permitted powerful rivals to set up independent rulerships as **sultans;** sultans were happy to pay lip-service to caliphate over-lordship. With the passage of years, the caliphate became an historic shadow; the sultan was the actual ruler.

Economic Forms. From the 7th to the 12th centuries Muslim supremacy rested upon its power in trade and manufacturing, though agriculture was the prevailing economic mode. Commerce was extensive because of the vast stretch of Moslem-held land—from Spain to Malaysia; the multitude of products and resources in this land; the maritime power of the Moslem middle-classes; and the freedom in Islamic law for free economic activity.

Muslims set the patterns for international trade: "traffic," "tariff," "bazaar," "caravan"—these are Arabic words. They advanced the use of business organizational forms like the partnership and the trade association and they invented anew many instruments of international credit like the bill of exchange. Intrepid exploration preceded trade and expert geography followed it. Old and new lanes of commerce were laid out, serviced and policed. The entrepot (a city for the deposit and redistribution of goods) was fostered. Baghdad, Basra, Aleppo, Aden and Alexandria were the New York, London, Amsterdam and Marseilles of their day.

Western Europe was bound to feel the effects of Muslim commercial expansion. Through Spain particularly, Europeans made their acquaintance with Far-Eastern spices, dyes and unguents; from the Muslims the Europeans acquired knowledge of the compass (first discovered by the Chinese c. 1093 A.D.); stories of faraway places abounding in gold and silver, silks and spices, were brought back by Muslim traders, explorers and travelers and circulated by word-of-mouth through Europe.

MOSLEM CONTRIBUTIONS TO CULTURE

Synthesis. Muslim civilization provided the basis for the highest development of culture during Europe's Middle Ages. Arabian contribution to this culture was slight even though the Arabic tongue was the chief medium of expression; a tiny minority of scholars were Arabs. Muslim civilization was the best atmosphere for cultural advance because of its exceptional tolerance of other religions and cultures, because of its positive encouragement of science and scholarship and because of its true respect for the accumulated cultural heritage of the ancient Greeks, the Hindus and the Chinese.

Baghdad became the first great center of Muslim learning. Here were gathered scholars who devoted themselves to translating into Arabic the works of Plato, Aristotle, Euclid, et al. and the mathematical treatises of the Hindus. Arabic translation of Hindu mathematical lore produced "Arabic numerals," the employment of zero in the number series, algebra, etc. When, in the 10th century Cordova in Spain became the cultural center, it was visited by many Christian and Jewish scholars who brought this "new learning" back into Europe.

Scholarship. Muslim culture was basically one of collection, compilation, translation, editing, commentary upon and publication of the great works of other peoples. The unique destiny of the Muslims was to set established learning into circulation for other people to use creatively: in **mathematics,** arithmetic, algebra, geometry and trigonometry; in **astronomy,** instruments for observation and records of celestial movement—the astrolabe, the sextant, the observatory and the concepts of longitude, latitude, chronology and calendar; in **physics,** studies in optics and the use in these studies of prisms, mirrors, lenses, etc.; in **chemistry,** familiarity with such products as alum, sal ammoniac, mercury chloride, alcohol and the like; in **medicine,** Hippocratic and Galenic practices, clinical study and surgery; in **language,** the production of dictionaries, grammars, philologies, etymologies.

Creative Thought. In some fields Muslim scholars were creative. In the field of History, Ibn Khaldun (1322-1406) made one of the first modern efforts to recapture the past by an examination of the evidence in sources of the past. But Khaldun did not limit his examination of past records to religious or political documents; instead he related history to geography, anthropology and sociology as well as to religion and politics. It took centuries before western Europe caught up with the ideals of Khaldun's historical research.

In philosophy Muslims revived and extended Aristotelianism. One of the profoundest of the Aristotelian scholars was Ibn Rushd (1126-1198)—known to Europeans as AVERROES. His impact on European thought was through the Christian philosophers Albertus Magnus and Thomas Aquinas and through the Jewish philosopher Moses Maimonedes.

Literature. Arabic poets exploited all the known forms of poetry and produced some of the world's greatest love, nature, death, war and wisdom poems and ballads. In AL-FIRDAUSI (935-1020) the Arabs developed a major writer of epics. His *Book of Kings* centering about the exploits of the hero Rustum ranks with the *Iliad* and the *Aeneid* in world literature. Firdausi is, unfortunately, known to but a few scholars in the western world today; but OMAR KHAYYAM (c. 1100) is widely known through the English translation of Edward Fitzgerald. Omar's *Rubaiyat* provided many poets with both theme and form. Equally familiar to the western world is the *Arabian Nights,* a collection of fables, exploits and tales.

Fine Arts. Muslim architecture was a borrowed art; Byzantine and Persian influences predominated. Mosques were places of worship, yet somehow this-worldly. Their exteriors were slight and delicate; they were often topped by domes that moved quickly past the bulge to a graceful and prayerful point. Around some of the mosques were courts and arcades; some had minarets (slender towers) from the top of which the *muezzin* called the faithful to the five prayers. In some areas the bulbous dome was abandoned for a flat-topped roof and the praying arch for a horseshoe arch.

In fact, Muslim architecture varied widely with locale and produced five styles: the Syro-Egyptian or Arabic, the Moorish or Spanish, the Persian, the Indian and the Turkish. Since their religion prohibited the carving or painting of images, the interiors of the mosques were bare of pictorial representation. This did not prevent the Muslim artist from projecting his highly developed sense of beauty into architectural decoration involving many motifs: latticework, stellaform, gilding, colored tiles and the like. Decoration spread from architecture into pottery and glass work, inlaid metal products, elaborate woodworking, carpets, damasks, silks and laces.

Mohammed had ordered instrumental music out of Islam with the result that vocalization became the chief form of music-making. In defiance of the Prophet's command, however, Muslims introduced accompanied vocalization. When this won religious sanction, Muslim genius was turned to the production of an infinite variety of instruments of accompaniment—the lute, the harp, the tambourine, the flute, the reed pipe, the cymbal, and many others.

EUROPE

While these great advances were being registered in the Byzantine and Muslim worlds, how was Europe faring?

Merovingian and Carolingian. The Christian Church, as we have seen, singled out Clovis and the

Franks of the Merovingian family as its secular arm. This was open recognition of the strength of the Germanic component in European civilization. Germany, in fact, became the seat of political power in Europe. For one hundred years Merovingian monarchs conducted themselves as did Clovis: they practiced an absolutism in government, waged war against their neighbors, treated their kingdoms as personal property, made forcible conversions to the orthodox faith, and dominated both the policies and personnel of the Church itself.

By the middle of the 7th century, however, the spark of courage and conquest went out of the Merovingians. They became "do nothing kings." This was hardly the time for Europe to be left leaderless for Catholic Europe was still surrounded by a sea of unconverted pagans; the rise of Mohammedanism had begun to restrict Mediterranean commerce; the link with Byzantium was steadily weakening; the economy was dissolving into more primitive forms of barter and agriculture for self-sufficiency; government was becoming increasingly decentralized. Counts, dukes and patricians were beginning to rule over small territorial units as independent lords. The Merovingians existed as long as they did because they were still able to reap the benefits of old Roman commerce, manufacture and trade. But a do-nothing policy encouraged the trend toward disintegration.

It was inevitable, then, that groups of powerful nobility at the Merovingian court would strive to seize the power from these ineffective rulers. The most powerful of the king's advisers was the "mayor of the palace." Beginning with PEPIN OF LANDEN (639) the mayor of the palace began to take over the powers of the king. CHARLES MARTEL, hero of Poitiers, was one such. The last of the Merovingians was deposed by PEPIN THE SHORT (741-768) in 751. Pepin began the **Carolingian Dynasty** which took its name from CHARLEMAGNE (Charles the Great).

The Carolingian "Renaissance." Charles the Great came to the throne in 768. His aim as king was to restore the old Roman Empire and to include in it the lands north of the Danube. He therefore made war on the Saxons to the north, the Slavs in the east and the Mongolian Avars in the mid-Danubian region. When completed, his conquests produced a territorial empire equal in size to that of the old Roman Empire in Europe.

It was now important to unite these conquests into an administrative whole. Charlemagne used a number of methods to achieve this: he added vast domains to his personal estate to ensure a source of revenue; he built up a personal army based upon contributions of men and arms from the wealthy nobility, conscription of the richer freemen, and contribution of arms by the poorer freemen. Strongly fortified frontier posts were created. Administratively, the system of counties and duchies that had grown up following the barbarian invasions was retained and the counts and dukes were expected to keep law and order within their domains; they also had to swear allegiance to the king, who in turn enforced allegiance.

Church and State. Charles linked the Church to the State by "converting" pagans at the point of the sword, by dictating Church policy and practice even in matters of ritual, by employing churchmen as state administrators, etc. These actions met with the approval of the reigning popes, particularly Leo III. Leo had met with considerable opposition in Rome, so considerable that he was forced to flee over the Alps to Germany to seek the help of Charles. Charles took Leo back to Rome and re-instated him; Leo's enemies were scattered. The Pope showed his gratitude on Christmas Day in the year 800. As Charles was kneeling in prayer, Leo placed on his head a crown and hailed him as "Augustus, crowned of God, great and pacific Emperor of the Romans." Tradition has it that Charles was considerably annoyed at having thus received his secular power from the hands of a churchman; future emperors were to make even more violent protests.

Combined with efforts on behalf of the Church, Charles began an educational revival within and through the Church. Schools were set up in the palaces and cathedrals of the land and leading European scholars like ALCUIN OF YORK were brought in to teach in these schools. Meanwhile the monks made manuscript copies of the ancient classics—copies that were to spark the revival of learning in high medieval times.

THE FINAL DECAY OF EUROPE

Had Charles's work been continued there is some likelihood that the Saracens may have been expelled from Spain, that the Mediterranean may have remained open and contact with Byzantium renewed. For the Saracen power had weakened considerably in the ninth century. But Charles's work was not continued. These were the reasons:

After his death the Empire was divided by the **Treaty of Verdun** (843) into three territories roughly corresponding to France, Germany and Italy. This division became more pronounced and permanent as "nationalizing" forces of language, custom, history and tradition developed.

With the Iconoclastic Controversy, the break between Byzantium and western Europe became deeper. Meanwhile, the Moslem seizure of the Mediterranean had severed the direct contact of the two related civilizations.

Barbarization of Europe was triply ensured when a new group of barbarians, this time from Scandanavia (hence, Northmen or Norsemen), violently invaded the settled areas of Europe to accelerate the tendency already under way toward decentralization and decomposition. These **Vikings** were fear-less seamen and warriors. Danes and Norwegians invaded the British Isles, the North Atlantic French coastal areas, Rome, Ireland, Spain, Sicily and Southern Italy; their Swedish confreres took the easterly route into Russia. Westward sailing Vikings discovered Greenland, Iceland and North America (492 years before Columbus). The immediate effects of these raids was to hasten the feudalization of Europe, to destroy all the literate arts, to accelerate the division of Europe into "nationalities," and to cast Europe into a brief Dark Age. In the long run, it was these same Norsemen who helped, because of their driving energy, to bring Europe out of the Dark Age into the noonday of Medieval Civilization.

CHAPTER NINE

THE FOUNDATIONS OF MEDIEVAL CIVILIZATION

INTRODUCTION

The **Medieval** or **Middle Ages** of European History are those that lie between the Greco-Roman Age and the Age of the Renaissance—approximately from 476 A.D. to about 1350. These Middle Ages reached their height between the 11th and 13th centuries. Our concern in this chapter is with Medievalism at its height and with only the broadest aspects of its civilization and culture.

FEUDALISM

A distinguishing feature of the Middle Ages was the **Feudal System,** a system that pivoted upon a **personal, contractual relationship** between two nobles—a **lord and a vassal.** A nobleman became a lord when he made a grant of a fief (a section of land with its peasant inhabitants) to another nobleman in exchange for the latter's services, chiefly military. A nobleman became a vassal when he accepted the fief and swore homage and fealty to his lord. It is important to remember that both the lord and the vassal were noblemen and freemen.

Origins of the Feudal System. Both Roman and German influences contributed to the creation of the Feudal System. It was not unusual in Roman times for a freeman to attach himself to a wealthy or influential man as a "client." In exchange for services, the client received protection. In more troubled times the practice of **commendation** arose. A client would "commend" both himself and his land to a patron in exchange for protection. In reverse, it was also a common practice for a wealthy landed patron to grant a client a *precarium* (land with precarious or uncertain tenure); in time this became a *beneficium* or a grant of land for a fixed period of time, say, a lifetime or two generations, in exchange for services. This land-services practice became merged with the Germanic practice of establishing a personal military relationship between a chief and his freemen-warriors. The Germans also introduced a practice of "immunity-grants" whereby powerful noblemen were granted free, unsupervised sovereignty over fixed territorial areas.

The Fief. In the tenth century the practice became fixed to **invest** a warrior-vassal with a fief. The fief might be a single, small holding or an entire duchy of many holdings. It was an *hereditary* holding and was transmitted by succession through the eldest son. Within the boundaries of the fief the vassal exercised sovereign rights: he collected taxes, coined money, exploited the resources, raised armies, provided for the public defense, administered justice, established and regulated markets and the like. The investiture of a fief was often recorded in a written contract. In the written contract was also included a listing of the services which the vassal would render to his lord. A fief could be *sub-infeudated* or divided among sub-vassals.

The Services of the Vassal. The basic obligation of the vassal to his lord was military service; in time this came to be limited to about forty days of military action. The number of fully equipped men that each vassal contributed depended upon the number of sub-vassals that he controlled. Vassals were also expected to help garrison the lord's fortress or castle and to engage in administrative activities. A vassal, then, might be chief administrative agent of fief and household; a constable or commander of the castle; a marshal or supervisor of the horses; a butler or supervisor of the wine supplies. Vassals were expected to attend the lord's court and to serve as judges in inter-vassal disputes, thus giving rise to a "trial by one's peers."

Feudal aids or monetary payments accompanied the personal services of the vassal; occasions for such payments were numerous. If the lord was captured in battle, the vassal had to contribute to ransom him back; if the lord planned an expensive undertaking in the nature of a pilgrimage or crusade, the vassal had to provide monetary assistance; if a vassal died, the inheriting son had to pay an inheritance tax. To protect himself against the possibility that an enemy would take legal possession of a fief, the lord secured the right to himself to veto a marriage proposal made to the vassal's daughter or widow; to assign custody over minors, who had inherited a fief, to a male regent. If a vassal failed to deliver his services, he could be forced to forfeit his fief and if he died without an heir, the fief would revert to the lord.

Feudal Hierarchy. Medievalism was patterned on the needs of these broad social groups: the peasants, the military nobility, and the clergy. These three groups formed **estates** and the first was the clergy, the second, the nobility, and the third, the peasantry and other producers (the townsmen did not fit easily into this medieval pattern—as we shall see).

In theory, the feudal hierarchy was carefully pyramided. At the top, as lord of all vassals, was the king; counts, dukes, and viscounts followed; beneath them were the barons or seignors; and knights or chevaliers made up the lowest rank. The Church held a special position in the hierarchy. In the 9th and 10th centuries many churchmen gave military service for feudal allotments and when this was prohibited on moral grounds, church fiefs were usually sub-infeudated among lay knights who could fulfil by proxy the Church's military duties.

Within the hierarchy, the king was potentially powerful but actually limited in his power to his own estate. Theoretically he owned all the land; in reality it was in the inalienable possession of the powerful nobility. Theoretically—as in Germany—the king ruled by divine right (The Holy Roman Emperor); in reality, he was an *elective* monarch chosen by the nobility and the clergy. Theoretically, the king commanded the allegiance of all his subjects; in reality, they obeyed him to the extent of their oath of allegiance and feudal contract. The point of this comparison is that the seeds of royal absolutism were buried in the medieval order and could be released the moment the power of the feudality weakened. This is precisely what happened by the 15th century.

Feudal Life. While feudalism prevailed, violence and turbulence characterized the life of the nobility as they contended over matters of inheritance and succession, of lay and ecclesiastical supremacy, of infractions of the feudal contract and the like. With war as an almost constant condition, feudal lords were forced to convert their homes into fortresses. The castle was a fortress. Its thick walls, crenelated towers, deep donjons, inner and outer battlements, surrounding moat, iron-toothed portcullis and drawbridge made it virtually unassailable by feudal armies except by seige and starvation.

The state of permanent war conditioned the education of youth. Feudal youth were trained to become knights or warriors. Like his Spartan prototypes, the feudal youth was removed from parental care at the age of seven or eight and sent to another feudal household for upbringing. He served as a page until he was sixteen and as a squire until he was twenty-one. Throughout these early years, he was made to live a hard life in the course of which he was taught the use and care of arms and horses. When he was battle-ready, he became a knight. This occasion was an impressive religio-feudal ceremony during which the knight-to-be knelt before another knight and received an *accolade* which was originally a sharp blow with the flat of a sword intended to knock the initiate out but was later modified to a slight tap on the head or shoulder. Once knighted, the warrior spent his time in war or warlike games which took the forms of hunting and tournaments or jousts.

The Church and Feudalism. During the Middle Ages the Church was a superstate within a state; its powers were both **temporal** (political-economic and social) and **spiritual** (religious and moral). It owned vast areas of land secured through pious donations. As a landed proprietor within the feudal system, the Church itself became a feudal overlord. Its properties were made into fiefs and as fiefholders, clergymen swore fealty and homage, collected feudal dues, produced and marketed goods, employed serf labor and enjoyed sovereign political rule through grants of jurisdiction, immunity and special privileges. Unlike the feudal landlords, however, the Church nobility (bishops and abbots) retained *perpetual* control over their properties; they paid no reliefs or inheritance taxes, since, it was argued, though churchmen died, the Church did not and therefore there was never, really, any transfer of property.

Of considerable importance to both Church and lord was the problem of investiture. If the Church was a feudal landholder, was it the right of a lord to invest a bishop with land? This amounted virtually to giving the lord the right to dictate who should be the bishop. Churchmen resisted this claim to "lay investiture" vigorously arguing that even though clergymen were vassals or lords temporal they were also bishops or lords spiritual and their status as churchmen placed them above any feudal lord. Only a churchman, they said, could invest a churchman.

Though the conflict over investiture was sharp, it was modified by the fact that the Church commanded the devotion of the feudal nobility as a whole. Church teachings were accepted for the most part without question. Sins were committed, but repentance and atonement followed quickly. Feudal lords built monasteries on their estates, helped to erect church buildings, gave large endowments of property to church and monastery, etc. Because of its intimate connection with the Feudal System, the Church was able to infuse it with some of its own goals.

For example, the Church—and particularly the Papacy—was opposed to the violence of feudalism. It tried to restrain warfare by moral command. Through Church Councils a "Peace of God" was proclaimed, a command reinforced by an official curse designed to protect the unprotected (the poor, the merchant, the Church itself) from robbery, pillage and assault. The Church also proclaimed a "Truce of God"—a command reinforced by threat of excommunication forbidding warfare from sundown Wednesday to sunrise Monday as well as during specified holy days during the year. (Church restraints were directed, of course, to wars of Roman Catholics upon each other; wars of Roman Catholics against heretics or infidels, on the other hand, were wholeheartedly approved.)

Chivalry. Church influence was considerable in the formation of the feudal code of **chivalry.** Chivalry—in essence, a code of ethics—had secular, religious and courtly components. It consisted of accepted ideals of virtuous behavior for the class of warrior-knights. As a warrior, the knight was expected to be loyal to his plighted word, to be brave in battle, to give an opponent a fair chance, to treat a captive as an honored guest (until he was ransomed), to release a captive in exchange for a hostage so he could collect his ransom, and to fight for *honor* in tournament and joust.

As a *Christian* warrior the knight was expected to be "a very perfect knight"—to protect the Church and its faith, to help the weak and the poor, and to battle the heretic and the infidel to the death. As a *courtly* knight, the warrior was expected to glorify women in the ideal (no matter how brutally he treated her in reality!), to adore them in song and poem, to woo them in a chaste and holy spirit, to fight for them, to wear their tokens in joust or battle, to be in love with love, and always to show the "courtesy." The origins of chivalry have been traced to various sources. To the castles there came wandering troubadours—minstrels who composed and recited tales of knightly adventure and poems of courtly love. In their stories, delivered before the assembled knights, they created ideal warriors fighting for ideal causes and thus moved their auditors to imitation.

Troubadours, who originated in the south of France, were also professional entertainers who composed love lyrics and helped create the tradition of woman-on-the-pedestal-worshipped-from-afar by a lover who had no thought but to please her, to win her smile or die for the lack of it. Reinforcing this idealization of womankind was the rise of the cult of the Virgin Mary, who, it was believed, would intercede with her Son on behalf of troubled mankind. Courtly love was institutionalized by ELEANOR OF AQUITAINE (1124-1204) who became a patroness of troubadours and other men of letters. Following their mother's example, RICHARD THE LION-HEARTED (1157-1199) and MARIE OF FRANCE (ca.12th c.) similarly fostered literary circles at their courts.

THE MEDIEVAL CHURCH

In view of the tremendous influence of the Church, we ought to pause to examine its structure when it reached its medieval height.

Church As State. The medieval Church consisted of all who professed Christ, partook of the sacraments and accepted the government of legally appointed priests who were in turn subject to one visible head, the Pope. Thus the organization of the

Church was **monarchical.** It was also **hierarchical** because from the Pope there descended successive ranks of officials.

At the top of the hierarchy was the Papacy which consisted of the Pope and his assistants, the cardinals and the officials of the papal court at Rome. The papal bureaucracy contained a *Sacred Penitentiary* to execute excommunications, interdicts, dispensations, etc.; a *Roman Rota* to hear appeals from bishop's courts and to try cases involving canon law; an *Apostolic Signatura* to hear appeals from the Rota; a *Datary* or secretariat; and an *Apostolic Camera* or treasury. The Pope held office for life and was elected after the eleventh century) by a college of cardinals. Bishops (elected by the clergy) ruled over dioceses from a cathedral center; the seat of the bishop's authority was called the **see.** A number of bishoprics formed an archdiocese and was headed by an **archbishop.** Just as the archbishop ruled over the bishops, so the bishops ruled over **parishes.**

Parish priests made up the lowest rung of the ladder of authority. They were usually "presented" to the bishop by the lord of the manor and then appointed by the bishop. Parish priests dealt directly with the communicants, administered the sacraments, gave instruction and established parish houses and churches. They derived their income from any land attached to the parish or from **tithes** or church taxes collected from the peasantry.

The Sacraments. The sacraments were seven: baptism, confirmation, penance, Holy Eucharist, matrimony, extreme unction and holy orders.

Baptism removed the stain of original sin. At the ceremony of baptism, godfathers and godmothers promised for the infant that which he would promise when he was adult. **Confirmation** came when the communicant was old enough to understand the teaching of the Church and to receive the Holy Spirit. **Penance,** or **confession,** consisted of examining one's conscience, feeling true repentance for sins committed, confessing them orally to a priest, resolving never again to commit the sin, and accepting such penance as the priest saw fit to administer. (**Absolution** discharged a penance.)

The **Holy Eucharist** involved the body and blood of Christ in the bread and wine of the Mass. The Mass was an effective repetition of the sacrifice of Christ for the sins of the world. The bread and wine in the course of the Mass underwent a mysterious **transubstantiation** into the body and blood of Christ. (Using Aristotle's distinction between the "appearances" of a thing and its *substance,* medieval theologians explained this transformation as a change in the *substance* of the bread and wine.)

Matrimony was holy; and no marriage was valid if performed outside the Church. The last sacrament in man's life was **extreme unction,** performed at the death bed. *Holy orders* or ordination was the means by which priests were set aside from ordinary Christians. Ordination made all the other sacraments valid.

The Age of Intolerance. Not only was it believed in the Middle Ages that the *only* road to salvation was through the Sacraments of the Roman Catholic Church, but that any other road—Christian or non-Christian—was a menace to the community. Christians who chose other paths to salvation were heretics and were in the grip of diabolic forces. They had to be destroyed, so reasoned the community, to prevent the pestilence from spreading; and they were destroyed by fire. Non-Christians were a similar danger, but since most resided outside Europe and were well armed, destruction could come only by missionary conversion or by force of war. Fears for their safety caused the inhabitants of medieval Europe to make the Middle Ages one of the most intolerant in history. However, in spite of the terror visited upon the misbeliever and unbeliever, heresy did rise in the Middle Ages.

Albigensians and Waldensians. It was inevitable that, in an organization so vast as the medieval Church, evil practices should arise. Some clergymen lived truly scandalous lives; **simony** or the sale of church offices, was rife; churchmen used their positions to extort unreasonable fees for their sacramental services and to levy extortionate fines in the church courts; a number of churchmen held numerous positions, etc. Thoughtful men resented these practices and subjected them to severe criticism. One wing of this criticism led to the Cluniac cleansing, a cleansing designed primarily to reduce the role of churchmen as lords temporal and to increase their spirituality. Such criticism was tolerated and even welcomed by the Church. Frequently, however, criticism continued until it became heresy— a challenge to Church doctrine rather than practice. Two such heresies appeared in the twelfth century —the **Waldensian** and **Albigensian.**

Revolted by immoral practices among the clergy, PETER WALDO (c. 1170), a prosperous merchant, gave away all his property and began to follow an "apostolic" way of life. He began to preach in the countryside (without having been ordained) a perfect Christian life as he interpreted that life from the New Testament. When he was ordered to stop this practice of preaching without permission of the bishop, Waldo ignored the order and began to attack the Church itself *as unnecessary for salvation.* Waldo taught that any Christian could find salvation by learning from the New Testament what Christ commanded and by living accordingly; the sacraments, he taught, were useless. In 1181 he and his followers were condemned as heretics.

Albigensians believed in a revived form of Manicheanism; that not one, but two deities ruled the Universe—God and Satan, good and evil. Things spiritual were God's; things material, Satan's. To eliminate as much as possible of the Satanic from life, Albigensian priests practiced absolute celibacy, ate no animal food, owned no property, etc.

Because they despised things material, the Albigenses taught that material creation came from evil forces, that the God of the Old Testament was evil, that Christ could not have adopted the human form, that the Eucharist was a false sacrament because Christ could not appear in the materials of bread and wine, that marriage is an evil, that the Pope was the successor, not of Peter, but of Constantine since he was associated with the temporal universe, etc. Eternal damnation was rejected and a doctrine of reincarnation substituted. Suicide was advocated as a means of freeing the soul from its material prison.

Church Discipline. How to cope with a rising heresy was a major problem for the Church. Reform of abuses was undertaken vigorously. Argument and persuasion were tried. These having failed, more forceful means were available. The canon law provided for **excommunication, anathema** and **interdict.** Excommunication could remove the heretic from all legal and spiritual association with the Christian community. Anathema, usually added to an excommunication, was a remarkably detailed curse placed upon the heretic and upon all his acts. The interdict was a suspension of all or most religious services for all the people in an area (both the guilty and the innocent) in the hope that the innocent would compel action against the heretics. If the heresy persisted, then the Church could apprehend the heretics, jail them and submit them to a Holy Inquisition.

The Albigensian heresy was exterminated by the **Inquisition.** During the course of the heresy, the Pope and the Emperor Frederick Barbarossa had ordered the clergy to proceed to the infected areas and to conduct inquests. If they found any who would not be "instructed" by them, they were to turn them over to the secular authorities for punishment. The penalty was to be banishment and confiscation of property. This was a relatively humane punishment since the common people were putting heretics to the torch.

Frederick II ordered in 1224 that heretics were to be punished by fire and mutilation; this barbarous practice was then endorsed by Pope Gregory IX. Pope Innocent IV then legalized the use of torture to secure recantations. In the thirteenth century the Inquisition was turned over to two new organizations, the Franciscan and Dominican Friars. They gave to it an orderly procedure. The primary object of the Inquisition was to save the soul of the heretic. For this purpose he was confronted with the accusation (not the accuser), asked to confess and to do penance. If the heretic recanted, he was punished by temporary imprisonment, banishment, property loss; or he was forced to go on a pilgrimage. If he was stubborn, he was then subjected to torture of the cruelest kind to force a confession from him. This failing, he was turned over to the secular arm for burning or mutilation.

It would be wrong to view the Inquisition with the eyes of the more tolerant Twentieth Century. The Inquisition was a product of its own times, times that did not understand the meaning of tolerance in matters of religious belief. Certainly it had the approval of the majority of the people. It was aimed at what was considered the most horrifying of crimes, heresy. It did seek to reform before it punished. But, these qualifications having been noted, it is still an historical fact that the Inquisition was a monstrous evil. It has overcast so much that was wonderful in the Middle Ages and discouraged thousands from reading the history of this period with an objective eye. It created a pattern of inhumanity to man—accusation without accuser, torture to enforce conformity, death for free-thinking. *It did not abolish heresy for long* and so failed in its primary purpose.

Widespread heresy could be met by the ultimate weapon only—the **crusade.** When Innocent III took papal office, the Albigensian and Waldensian heresies were rife in Toulouse, in the southern part of France. He tried persuasion through dispatch of preachers into the region, but to no avail. Raymond VI, count of Toulouse, was tolerant of these heretics (while formally a Catholic) and refused to use force against them. He was therefore excommunicated. Raymond ignored the excommunication. Innocent had no choice but to preach a crusade against Toulouse. He did so and in 1209 Philip Augustus of Paris (who was more interested in Raymond's land than his faith) led an army southward. Frightful slaughter was inflicted upon the inhabitants of Toulouse, both the heretics and the innocent. The battle cry was, "Kill all . . . . for God will know his own." The heretics were in this manner exterminated.

The Friars. Peter Waldo was not alone in his desire to live an apostolic life. FRANCIS OF ASSISI was the son of a wealthy merchant whose youth was typical of carefree, urban existence. Experiencing a sudden conversion, Francis gave up all worldly possessions and began to devote his life to preaching, praying and tending to the needs of the ill and the poor. Francis's message was love for all God's creation—man, plant, animal and inanimate matter and a faith linked to joy. It was not long before Francis had many followers who traveled as his brothers (friars) through the countryside as mendicants or beggars, and doing good works wherever they went.

Francis and twelve of his disciples went to Rome in 1210 to secure permission from Innocent III to create an order. Though troubled and hesitant, Innocent approved. Thus was created the Friars Minor, an order devoted to living an apostolic life and to wandering in the world to do good for the needy. (A feminine counterpart appeared in the Second Order or Poor Clares, after St. Clare; a lay counterpart was the Third Order—the Tertiaries—or Brothers and Sisters Of Penance.) The order grew and in a short time became an established monastic order with vast properties and organized rules—something rather distant from Francis's original concept of poverty, mendicancy and wandering-preaching. (One group, the Spiritual Franciscans, seeking to cling literally to their founder's principles suffered widespread persecution as heretics, for they too entered on to the path of defying the secular clergy.)

The **Dominicans** (or Soldiery of Christ) took their origin from the life and work of ST. DOMINIC who also practiced absolute poverty and mendicancy. Dominic was inspired to found an order of wandering preachers by the rampant heresy in southern France. Where Francis hoped to aspire by example and exaltation, Dominic sought to instruct by debate and precept. His order was sanctioned in 1215 and became known as the Black Friars to distinguish them from the Franciscan Grey Friars. Since their objective was preaching, the Dominicans established a number of schools to train preachers. From these schools Dominicans, trained in the arts, in nature study and in theology, wandered about the continent of Europe defending the Church against heresy.

Growth of the Papacy. Until the 11th century, the Popes of Rome struggled, and not too successfully, to assert their spiritual ascendancy over Christendom. Barbarian invasions had cut them from many of their ecclesiastical subjects and the result was that pronounced regional differences in Christian practice began to appear. For example, this was a period of intense missionary activity among the pagan Europeans. In 432 SAINT PATRICK began a thirty-year mission which converted Ireland to Christianity. Following their conversion, the Irish themselves became Europe's leading missionaries. Saints Brendan, Columba and Columbanus carried the Christian message to Scotland, England and Saxony which were in turn converted; and so it went.

But the remoteness of Ireland from Rome encouraged regional differences in Christian practice that led to bitter controversy. Ireland and Rome quarreled over the degree of Christian asceticism permitted, the correct dates of Easter, the proper tonsure (hair-cut) for monks, etc. Geographical remoteness, then, was one cause of the weakness of the Popes. Another was the fact that the papacy was too often a pawn in the international feudal wars of the Carolingians and then the German and Italian Kings and Emperors. Papal election became dependent upon royal approval. Moreover, there were times when more than one pope claimed the papal crown and in such cases the popes became direct appointees of the emperors. By the tenth century there was a crying need for papal reform.

Leadership in the movement for papal reform was taken by the **Abbey of Cluny.** Founded in 910, Cluny had organized about 300 monasteries throughout western Europe. Cluniac monasteries chose their own abbots, rejected all lay controls and upheld the doctrine of the supremacy of the Pope. Since, contrary to Benedictine practice, Cluniac monasteries were centralized under the direct supervision of the central Abbey of Cluny, it was possible for the abbots of Cluny to begin and carry through an extensive reform of the corrupt practices that had crept into so many of the ecclesiastical organizations. Cluniac reforms were imitated everywhere; but at the heart of this reform movement was the insistence on the absolute independence of the Pope. A model of papal independence had been set during the sixth century by Pope Gregory I (the Great).

From the sixth to the eleventh century no pope attained the stature of GREGORY I. In a time of famine and disease Gregory had brought succor to the sick and food to the hungry. When the barbaric Lombards had descended on Rome, Gregory had bought them off with revenues from the papal estates. During more peaceable times, Gregory had built churches and houses. He had asserted the primacy of Rome over Byzantium. At the same time he kept a scrupulous watch over the papal estates and the income of the Church. He fostered many missions—particularly that of St. Augustine that led to the first conversion of the English. He preached and wrote extensively and produced two religious classics—*The Pastoral Rule* (thoughts on conducting an episcopal office) and *Moralia* (a commentary on *Job*); he set the liturgy in order; and (possibly) he established the "Gregorian" chant as part of the liturgy. As Cluny reformers viewed it, this was the model of a pope.

Results of the Cluniac Reforms. The Abbey of Cluny and its 300 priories had considerable influence on the course of papal history. A group of churchmen arose devoted to the spiritual cleansing of all ecclesiastical institutions; as preachers they were able to bring about something of a religious revival among the laymen, including some of the nobility; as independent churchmen beyond the reach of the feudal nobility they were able to agitate for the separation of state and church, but only in matters affecting the church.

Out of Cluny came Hildebrand who rose to be POPE GREGORY VII and who instituted the so-called Gregorian reform. While the abolition of simony, nepotism, incelibacy, etc. were important in the Gregorian reforms, Gregory's chief concern was to establish the independence of the papacy. Previously POPE LEO IX (1048-1054) had made the final break with Byzantium and had freed the Church to concentrate upon its position in the West. Then POPE NICHOLAS II (1059-1073) broke away from German control by linking the fate of the Church with the Normans of South Italy. Thus secured, he issued a decree that henceforth the pope would be elected by a College of Cardinals. Since cardinals were chosen by the pope for life, continuity of policy was assured.

A new church officer, the papal legate, was established. He was the personal representative of the pope and took precedence over any clergyman in the country to which he was sent. When abroad, the legate could act in the name of the pope, make the pope's pronouncements, excommunicate, interdict, etc.

The Rule of Gregory VII. Gregory found theoretical support for the policy he pursued in two documents, later revealed to have been forgeries. The first was the **Donation of Constantine** in which the first Christian Emperor supposedly had given to the papacy the rule over the whole Western world and absolute authority over its clergy; and the second was the **Isidorian Decretals** (now known as the "False Decretals") which made explicit the degree of papal control over the clergy and established that the Church was the superior of the State.

Gregory's announced policy was precisely that outlined in these documents. He proclaimed himself as spokesman for God on earth, responsible to no power but God's and therefore deserving of obedience from all the lay rulers in the world. These ideas were set forth in a proclamation called *Dictatus Papae* and legates were sent through Europe to make them known to kings, nobles and clergymen. When certain German clergymen refused to obey these orders, they were excommunicated. In 1075 Gregory took the decisive step of prohibiting lay investiture of bishops.

German bishops owned rich tracts of land in trust for the German emperors. The election of bishops was very carefully controlled by the emperors. A bishop was nominated by clerics; but land and secular immunities was secured from the emperor (lay investiture). It was thus virtually impossible for a bishop not pleasing to the emperor to be elected. It was this practice that Gregory made illegal. The German Emperor at this time was Henry IV. When Henry learned of Gregory's order he promptly retained the excommunicated clergy in office, invested new bishops in Germany, named an archbishop for Italy, branded Gregory as "no Pope, but false monk," and ordered Gregory to descend from the papal throne and "be damned to eternity."

Gregory retorted by depriving Henry of his kingdom and releasing all Henry's subjects from obedience to Henry and excommunicating him. Gregory's position was far the stronger: Henry was unpopular with the feudal lords because of his efforts to centralize the German state; one feudal lord, Rudolph of Swabia, fully supported the Pope; the proclamation of excommunication genuinely frightened the German people. Henry's nobles seized him and demanded that he make peace with Gregory. Henry did so but in a manner that led to the ultimate defeat of the Pope. He crossed the Alps dressed in a coarse woolen garment and went barefoot to Canossa where Gregory was. There he stood outside the castle in the snow and begged forgiveness. Gregory, a priest as well as a Pope, had no choice and forgave him when Henry promised to give satisfaction.

Henry returned to Germany and the Emperorship knowing full well who his enemies were. His power restored, he struck hard at the feudal nobles who had deserted him; Rudolph was killed. Gregory promptly excommunicated Henry again but it did not have the same effect. Henry now gathered an army and an antipope and marched into Italy. Gregory, beaten and deposed, fled and died in exile. Henry died a year later.

The Concordat of Worms. In 1122 the matter of lay investiture was finally compromised and embodied in the **Concordat of Worms.** Under this agreement the emperor was to invest the clergy with their lands and secular authority; the pope invested them with spiritual authority. Thus each could veto the appointment of the other; stability depended upon effective cooperation between pope and emperor.

Papal Supremacy. In the twelfth century the struggle of emperor and pope took on a new form. In Germany the family of Hohenstaufen revived Otto's ambition to establish a Holy Roman Empire in Europe. Leader in this movement was FREDERICK BARBAROSSA (1152-1190). Barbarossa succeeded in uniting Germany; his aim was to bring Italy within the German fold. This move was bitterly opposed not only by the pope but by the towns of Italy that had arisen as a result of the Crusades. Those who opposed imperial ambitions took the name of **Guelph;** those who favored it, the name of **Ghibelline.**

Barbarossa launched his campaign by insisting that the towns pay him feudal dues and at the Diet of Roncaglia (1158) decreed that imperial nominees be assigned to collect these dues. Towns that refused to pay were attacked and razed. Since the pope, ALEXANDER III, sided with the towns, he was deposed and an antipope was set up. With Alexander's assistance, the towns then organized a defensive union, the Lombard League, and at the Battle of Legnano (1176) defeated the cavalry of Barbarossa.

In 1183 Barbarossa sued for peace and at Constance signed a treaty which gave the towns virtual independence. Thus the Pope had made a fortunate alliance. Henry VI of Germany almost succeeded where Barbarossa failed but he died suddenly, leaving a three-year old son as ruler. Young Frederick Hohenstaufen now became the ward of the most remarkable pope in history, INNOCENT III, under whom the papal power reached its supreme height.

Innocent III. Innocent's first aim was to prevent forever the possible union of Germany and Italy. When the German nobility elected Philip of Swabia king in 1198, Innocent entered the lists against Philip and supported Otto of Brunswick. When an unexpected train of events placed Otto on the throne and Otto revived the policy of German-Italian union, Innocent excommunicated Otto and turned to Frederick II (now grown) as a replacement for Otto. Thus did the Pope keep German politics in ferment and prevent any effective unity from evolving.

Innocent's second aim was to make all feudal monarchs aware of the supremacy of the spiritual over the temporal power. When Philip Augustus of France put aside a Danish wife to marry another, Innocent forced him, at the point of an interdict, to take her back. When John of England decided to ignore Innocent's approval of Stephen Langdon as Archbishop of Canterbury, Innocent, using an excommunication, an interdict and a threat of war led by Philip Augustus, forced John to turn all of England over to the Pope as a fief, to do homage to the Pope and to pay him heavy feudal dues as the Pope's vassal. This represented the papal power at its height.

The Crusades. Innocent III preached three crusades—Holy Wars against heretics or infidels. The most important of the infidels were the Muslims. Crusading against the Muslims preceded **The Crusades.** Spanish and Italian Christians had been engaged since the ninth century in efforts to oust the Mohammedans from their strongholds in Spain, Sicily, Corsica and Sardinia. The Crusades began when the Seljuk Turks defeated the Byzantine army at Manzikert in 1070 and then proceeded to conquer all of Asia Minor, including the Holy Land of Jerusalem. Byzantine emperors importuned the Roman Popes for assistance. POPE URBAN II (1088-1099) took positive action.

Urban's motives were mixed: he wanted to free the Holy Land for unmolested pilgrimages; he was eager to extend Roman Catholicism eastward; he foresaw a possible reunion of the Greek and Roman Churches; he wished to enhance papal prestige. So, on November 25, 1095, Urban preached the First Crusade at the Council of Clermont.

He told the assembled clergy and knights of the plight of the Christians in the East and called upon them to put aside their petty feuds for a holy war. He promised those who went remission of sins and guarantees of paradise. The multitude responded enthusiastically, shouted "God wills it!" and with red crosses sewn to their shoulders, knelt before the Pope for a blessing. Urban had hoped that this would be a strictly disciplined baronial affair. But control slipped from his hands as other preachers —notably Peter the Hermit and Walter Sansavoir —brought the cry for a crusade into the countryside and stirred the penniless knights and peasantry to join in.

The motives of the Crusaders were as mixed as Urban's. The Pope had assured salvation and blessedness to any who went and this had a powerful appeal. Others sought to do Christian service. Serfs could hope to win their freedom; debtors, their freedom from debt; the landless and impoverished, a chance to repair their fortunes; the Italians, profits and trade by marketing booty and ferrying men and horses and provisions over the Mediterranean Sea. Motivations in sweeping historical events are endless. In the breasts of the Crusaders there mingled the "causes" of God, Glory, Grandeur, Gold. In the course of two hundred years, eight major crusades were launched.

Results of the Crusades. The results of the Crusades were meager in the extreme considering the cost, the time, the numbers and the pain and agony consumed in their execution. The Italians benefited materially; their profits and trade increased as did the volume of shipping facilities; eventually they were able to establish their supremacy in the Mediterranean. Knowledge of Oriental civilization increased European demand for luxury goods and this accelerated the free market in town and country which was already under way before the Crusades began. Two military Orders were created— the **Knights Templars** (1119) to protect pilgrims and to wage war on infidels; and the **Knights Hospitalers** (1131) to aid the sick and the poor. (Diverted from their original purposes, these Orders grew wealthy and powerful, so wealthy and powerful, in fact, that they were destroyed later in the Middle Ages by the kings who envied them and hungered for their wealth.)

The power of the monarchs increased owing to the prestige they acquired in leading the Crusades and the death of many of their enemies. The wealth of the Church increased since many of the crusaders willed their properties to the Church in the event they did not return; and very many of them did not return. But the prestige of the Church declined: the Crusades did not retake, in the long run, the Holy Land and many came to question the efficacy of the Catholic Church; indulgences and remissions of sin, when granted wholesale, lost their potency;

contact with foreign civilizations broadened the intellectual horizons of many, who returned to Europe in a questioning mood. Finally, the Crusades left for posterity a treasure trove of romantic tales of heroic adventure and adventurers.

Some Highlights of the Crusades. The first crusaders, under the leadership of Godfrey of Bouillon, Robert, Duke of Normandy, Raymond of Toulouse and Tancred of Apulia, did take Jerusalem and organized four Latin states based on the Feudal System. When one of these states was retaken by the Muslims, a second crusade was preached by ST. BERNARD, himself one of the most colorful personalities of the medieval period. (Bernard was of the Cistercian Order and one of the most searing critics of the age. Himself a mystic and ascetic, he attacked with rare fury the secular clergy, the laxity of monks, church architects for their excessive decoration, Abelard for his faith in reason, etc.). The second crusade failed utterly.

The Third Crusade became necessary (1187) when SALADIN, the great Muslim leader, retook Jerusalem. This one brought together three of the great leaders in medieval Europe—Frederick Barbarossa, Richard the Lionhearted and Philip Augustus. Philip and Richard quarreled and Philip withdrew; Barbarossa was drowned en route; Richard took Acre in a gallant battle but failed to take Jerusalem; on his return to Europe, Richard was captured and held for ransom. No Crusade was more "glamorous" than this one!

No Crusade was less glamorous than the Fourth. It started for the Holy Land but stimulated by the blind Dandolo, the Doge of Venice, it turned instead upon Constantinople and demolished this *Christian* center.

In 1212 came the tragic and pitiful **Children's Crusade.** It occurred to some preachers that armies of sinful and sinning knights were hardly the instrument of God's justice against the infidel. Where the sinful failed, the innocent would succeed. Two youths, Stephen and Nicholas, began to preach a crusade of young innocents to the Holy Land. They were to be armed only with God's protection. Thousands of children left their homes and headed southward. Hundreds starved and died en route but many did get through to Italy. They did not expect trouble in crossing the Mediterranean for Nicholas and Stephen had told them that God would part the waters for them as he had for the ancient Hebrews. Since the miracle did not occur, obliging Venetians furnished the children with ships of passage. Once they were captive on board, the

Venetians ferried the children to Egypt and sold them into slavery there.

The Decline of the Medieval Church. The decline of the medieval papacy is evident even in the extraordinary career of Innocent III. Philip Augustus obeyed Innocent in the small matter of a marriage, but disobeyed him on all other and larger issues like the Albigensian Crusade and the command to stop absorbing English territory in France. England became a fief, but no threat of Innocent could control the English feudal lords who, defying Innocent's specific prohibition, forced John to sign **Magna Carta.** Innocent could preach a crusade, but could not win the obedience of the crusader to his commands not to act sinfully. Innocent suppressed heretics, but not heresy. Innocent fostered the Inquisition but could not force England or Scandanavia to adopt it. Innocent trained youthful Frederick II to be a model Christian prince and he became almost the worst enemy of Christendom.

Frederick II. No one can question Frederick's intellectual brilliance. He was master of many languages, a creator of universities, a theologian, political scientist and economist, a profound biologist. In theology, however, he was a **freethinker** and, if anything, more sympathetic to Mohammedanism than Christianity. In the field of political science he denied the secular authority of the papacy and supported instead the doctrine of **divine-right monarchy.**

Contrary to papal desire, he united Germany and Sicily. He refused for many years to go on a crusade when ordered to do so; when he was excommunicated for this refusal, he did go and won back the Holy Land by negotiation with the Muslim ruler. Here indeed was a mocking irony: where the most devout failed, an excommunicated prince succeeded.

On his return, Frederick fought and defeated papal armies. Frederick, then, created a pattern of contempt for the temporal power of the popes and his example was imitated by the rising kings throughout Europe.

Royal Assault on the Papacy. By the fourteenth century a number of forces were opposed to the Pope's pretensions to temporal power: the growing national states, the alliance of local clergy with the princes in demanding a curb on papal power, national patriotism from below, increasing heresy, mounting opposition to church taxation, growing royal envy over the wealth of the Church, the rise of an urban middle class drawing its wealth by trade with the non-Christian world. When the kings began to attack the popes, the popes found themselves with few friends.

Philip IV of France and Edward I of England placed state taxes upon the clergy (1296). Pope Boinface VIII issued the famous bull "*Clericis laicos*" in which it was reaffirmed that the state could not tax the clergy without consent of the pope; any king who did would be automatically excommunicated. Edward outlawed all disobedient clergy and Philip forbade the export of all monies to Rome. Boniface responded with the bull "*Unam Sanctum*" (1302) and pointed out that all Christians, both Kings and commoners, were subject to the Church. Philip thereupon sent William Nogaret to Rome to kidnap and jail Boniface! The maneuver failed but the low state of papal authority was clearly evident.

In 1305 Philip dictated the appointment of a Frenchman as pope (Clement V). Clement became Philip's tool: he removed the papacy from Rome to Avignon in France where it remained from 1309 to 1377 (and is known in history as the "Babylonian Exile"); he revoked Boniface's bulls against Philip; he granted Philip permission to destroy the Knights Templars and to confiscate their wealth.

To assure continuation of *French* papal supremacy, French cardinals replaced Italians. Avignon popes were no less determined than their Italian predecessors to build the power of the Church with the aid of the French monarchs. They continued to oppose the unification of Germany and Italy. To build a papal center at Avignon, they increased church taxation ruthlessly: the payment of one year's income was required for an appointment to a benefice; the **tithe** was converted into a tax payable to the papacy; **procurations** had to be paid to bishops who made tours of inspection; taxes were levied upon papal bulls and decrees; delinquent taxpayers were excommunicated.

Criticism became loud and bold. JOHN WYCLIFFE in England began a new heresy by denouncing the divinity of the papal office and the sanctity of the sacramental system. DANTE (*On Monarchy*) pleaded for the separation and state. WILLIAM OF OCKHAM wrote upholding the supremacy of kingly authority. Franciscans demanded that the popes return to evangelical poverty.

The most important of the protests, however, came from the pens of MARSILIUS OF PADUA and JOHN OF JANDUN (1324). In a closely reasoned pamphlet they asserted the supremacy of the royal power and its independence of the Holy See. They argued that excommunications and interdicts were without effect; that secular authorities could tax or confiscate ecclesiastical wealth; and that the sovereign power in Christianity lay not with the papacy and its hierarchy, but with a council of clergy and laity, with elected representatives of all of Christendom. Such a council would have the power to reform the pope and the clergy and to alter church institutions with the times. The kings were to be defenders of the peace (hence the title of the pamphlet, *Defensor Pacis*) and the executive arm of the council. Kings would see to it that the pope and clergy were deprived of special privileges and would perform limited but useful duties in the sphere of religion. *Defensor Pacis* provided powerful arguments for the **Reformation** to come.

The Great Schism (1378-1417). To escape an English attack on Avignon, Gregory IX, an Avignon pope, returned to Rome in 1377; he died in 1378. The cardinals elected Urban VI, an Italian, as pope. When Urban refused to return to Avignon, a new set of cardinals chose Clement VII as pope. Now there were two popes, each with its papal bureaucracy, each with its legates, each taxing all of Christendom, each excommunicating the other, each commanding the allegiance of separate kings (who acted, of course, in their own national interest). Christians everywhere were scandalized and discouraged.

In 1409 there were still two popes, Benedict XIII and Gregory XII. A council was therefore called at Pisa to heal the schism. There the Avignon and Roman parties compromised on the cardinal of Milan, a Greek, who thereupon became ALEXANDER V. But the other two popes refused to accept the compromise with the result that Christendom now had three popes, each excommunicating the other. The papacy had reached its nadir. The **conciliar movement** was invoked again by the Emperor Sigismund to meet at Constance in 1414. Delegates came as the representatives of nations. This Council lasted four years and when it was over all popes were deposed and a new Roman pontiff, MARTIN V, began a new line that has been uncontested since. The Great Schism was healed but the future lay with another action of the **Council of Constance.** To its sessions came JOHN HUS (1369-1415) on a safe-conduct pass to present his "heretical" views on the papacy. The Council listened, demanded that he recant and when he refused burned him. The line from the martyred John Hus to Martin Luther was direct and short.

CHAPTER TEN

VILLAGE, TOWN AND STATE

THE SEIGNORIAL SYSTEM

Agriculture. The economic base of feudalism was self-sufficient agriculture, that is, farming which produced no surplus for sale. The unit of economy was the village or hamlet, mostly the former. Villages were clusters of families surrounded by arable land which was located near a manor-house or castle and which contained a common meadow, a woodland, a wasteland, a mill, a smithy, a wine press, an oven and a church. In more backward areas the arable lands were divided on a two-field basis—one planted, one fallow; in more progressive regions the three-field system was used—one planted with winter grain, another with spring grain, and the third fallow. Both systems employed, obviously, the most primitive form of field rotation since other forms of fertilization were unknown. Planting was done in narrow strips a furlong long.

Each household had its individually owned strips, use of the common pasture and woodland (depending on the number of animals owned), and a private garden patch. Perforce, cooperative rather than individual farming characterized medieval village life. Plowing, harvesting, threshing, pasturing and the like had to be done together to secure the maximum efficiency. Maximum efficiency produced little enough since the level of productivity was extremely low owing to very primitive farming methods and to the need to set land aside for animal fodder. What little was harvested had to serve for drink and seed as well as food.

Thus bare subsistence distinguished the life of the villager. His fare was meager and simple and consisted mainly of bread and ale or wine as staples, some fruits and vegetables in season, and very little meat or fish. Villagers lived in mud and thatch huts that serve as home and barn; their clothes were crudely fashioned and made of coarse textiles. They lived and died within the narrow precincts of the village—unless they were freemen. Family, church and village festival provided them with their few joys. This bare existence of the villager was made barer by his obligations to a lord or **seigneur.**

Serfdom. Medieval labor can be classified broadly as peasant labor. Peasants, however, varied in their social status from freemen to slave. **Freemen** held land by military tenure or by contract; they had less onerous burdens than the serf or slave; they could use the king's court in an appeal for justice. **Cotters** were semi-free day laborers who owned the plots on which their cottages were built and hired out as day-laborers.

Most of the peasants, however, were unfree agricultural workers called **villeins** or **serfs** (slavery died out *during* the Middle Ages). It was the serfs who supported the non-producing classes of nobility and clergy. Like feudalism, serfdom can be traced back to German and Roman origins. In Roman times latifundia were cultivated by *coloni.* Coloni were granted cottages and small landholdings in exchange for labor on the landlord's estate. They were not permitted to leave the estate without the landlord's permission. The invading Germans brought with them their "mark system," a system characterized by land owned by a free village community and worked on a communal basis. In the course of time these German villages lost their freedom to seignorial landlords on a coloni basis, but retained their communal agricultural life. Free farmers had little choice in the troubled times of the Dark Ages but to surrender their freedom to some powerful noble in exchange for military protection. Surrender of freedom was always in terms of labor on the lord's land and giving up the freedom of movement.

The Demesne. The lord's land was part of the arable soil of the village and was called the **demesne.** The demesne consisted of the demesne proper worked by special serfs and day laborers; the "lord's close," or part of the demesne rented to freemen or serfs; the villagers' own land scattered in strips; the land belonging to the village priest; and the meadowland and woodland.

Villagers were obliged to work the demesne as they did their own strips; to sow, cultivate, harvest and hay it; and to pasture the lord's cattle and swine in the common meadow. This unremunerated labor consumed from two to four days of the week, on the average. Besides the regular labor, there was

"boon" or extra work on special occasions. With growth in the power of the lords, many more obligations were heaped upon the backs of the serfs and freemen.

Seignorial Dues. There was the *corvée* or forced labor in clearing the lord's woods and wasteland, in draining his marshes, in building his roads, raising his dikes, etc. There were special taxes: the head (poll) tax for each member of the family; the land tax; the produce tax; the church tax; forced purchases of salt or wine; fees for fishing or hunting; taxes for the use of the lord's (monopolized) oven, mill, smithy, or wine press; "fines" for permitting a son to enter the church or a daughter to marry someone who lived outside the lord's jurisdiction; inheritance taxes when sons took over their deceased fathers' strips; gifts "freely" given on the occasion of knighthood for the lord's son or marriage for the lord's daughter or ransom for the lord himself.

It is estimated that these enforced payments—not counting the labor spent on the lord's demesne—consumed about two-thirds of the serf's produce. Nor was there any way for a serf to escape his lot. Failure to meet his obligation met with swift and merciless punishment at the lord's hands; he could not leave the village, a bankrupt, and seek his fortune elsewhere; if he did secure the lord's consent to leave, he could take nothing with him since all his personal property belonged to the lord.

In spite of these many restrictions dues and obligations, the serf was not a slave. He could not be removed from his parcel of land. He could be sold or given away, but his land was part of the transfer of ownership. Moreover, the lord had clear obligations to the serf, obligation to furnish him protection in time of war, food in time of famine, and the utilities (mill, press, etc.) required for a self-sufficing community.

There were other mitigating factors in the serf's poor lot. Feudal dues tended to become fixed and customary and to remain so even though the lord's living costs rose and he had the power to increase dues at will.

The Manorial System. Some villages belonged to one lord alone; others were shared by two or more lords. The serf's obligations similarly might be to one or to many lords. Properly speaking, then, there was a difference between the lord's demesne and his manor. The latter represented the basic unit of the lord's administration whether his holdings were concentrated in whole villages or scattered through many. Manorial administration was in the hands of a steward who supervised many demesnes and a bailiff who was resident manager of one.

Manorial Courts. The manorial system made its influence felt through the lord's tax collectors or through his justices. By the eleventh century the most powerful nobility and clergy had won immunity from the king's jurisdiction and had become fully sovereign within their own manors. As sovereigns they could legislate and could enforce the laws they made by punishing violators to the extent of capital punishment.

Manorial courts were instituted to try cases between tenant and tenant or between tenant and lord. (These were in addition to courts which judged between lord and vassal and church courts which heard cases involving persons in religious orders.) Manorial courts applied a barbaric code of justice. Plaintiff and defendant were both jailed pending trial and decision; decisions were arrived at by **trial by ordeal** or **trial by combat**; penalties were severe —the pillory, stock, beheading, flogging, galley slavery, branding, mutilation, hanging, burial alive, depending on the nature of the crime.

The Decline of Serfdom. The village—the base of feudalism—was an independent unit with very little contact with the outside world. There was almost no trading in it, and what trading there was was on a barter basis. All dues were paid in produce. By the fourteenth century this static, fixed center had virtually disappeared after a steady decline during the twelfth and thirteenth centuries.

Several factors account for this decline. During the twelfth century a movement began to reclaim deserted villages, forested areas and marshes. Landed nobility began to encourage "frontier" settlements by offering free farmers and serfs attractive terms —chiefly reductions in feudal dues. Monasteries and abbeys similarly engaged their monks in reclamation projects. With an increase in arable land, the lot of both the serf and the lord improved. At about the same time the towns made their appearance or re-appearance in Europe. It now became profitable to produce a surplus over subsistence to sell to the townsmen. Townsmen had already begun the practice of using money as a medium of exchange and it was inevitable that money should invade the village. When it did the lords began the practice of permitting serfs and other debtors to discharge their obligations in money payments.

As the lords began to receive money for rents, they found it more profitable to release serfs from working on the demesne and renting demesne lands for additional monetary returns. The logical next step was emancipation of the serf. Emancipatory moves were made throughout the Middle Ages as acts of charity; by the fourteenth century, however, it became profitable to release serfs from bondage. Emancipation not only freed the serf from the rule of the lord; it also freed the lord from his obligations to the serf, an obligation which could become costly in difficult times. Money, then, became the dissolvent of the seignorial system, and, to shift the metaphor, the midwife of a new order of free enterprise in land.

Peasant Revolts. Emancipation of the serfs was a gradual process; not all feudal lords responded to the possibilities of increased profits; conservatism and tradition were strangleholds upon even those lords who saw the benefits of the new system. When such was the case, the peasants often took matters into their own hands to force emancipation. This led to a number of peasant revolts in England and France during the fourteeth century. Such revolts often developed extremely equalitarian objectives. The revolt led by WAT TYLER (1381) resulted in a widespread attack on the properties and persons of the English nobility. The peasant rhyme asked:

> When Adam delved and Eve span,
> Who was then the gentleman?

These peasant uprisings were crushed with great brutality; but they did hasten the process of emancipation.

THE GROWTH OF TOWNS

Throughout history cities have been the promoters and carriers of high civilization. Urban dwellers have proved to be more receptive to new ideas and to change than their rural neighbors. Townsmen have been interested in wealth accumulation and the use of wealth for better living; they have been the instigators of freedom since they were a "middle class," that is, a class without tradition and the conservatism bred of tradition. Moreover, urban centers have been market places, areas where goods were exchanged, deposit points for merchant fleets or caravans. Cities are linked to commerce; ruin of commerce or trade will doom a city to extinction. This is what happened from the fifth to the ninth centuries A.D. European urban centers dwindled and almost disappeared because of the increasing hazards to safe-trading on the Mediterranean Sea brought about by the Barbarian and Muslim invasions.

Money—as a medium of exchange—was itself the

product of town economy; so long as some town life persisted after the fifth century even the barbarous Franks had to coin currency. But the Germans were themselves responsible for the ruin of urban centers. At first they sacked these centers and drove the population into the hinterlands where they might eke an existence from the soil. When they became the rulers of Europe, the German kings failed to take the measures required to insure preservation of town life and they permitted roads and bridges to fall into disrepair; where these were usable they placed heavy tolls upon them; they set heavy tariffs upon goods entering their domains; they provided no police force for traveling merchants; they themselves played the roles of robber barons. Until the eighth and ninth centuries some commerce persisted in spite of these handicaps along the rim of the Mediterranean Sea. When the Moslems took possession of the Sea, these towns also suffered a decline. By the tenth century European urbanization and commerce were at their lowest point. The European economy settled down to the long sleep of feudalism.

Revival. Revival of trade and commerce came in the eleventh century. The causes for this revival are still obscure. Some historians take this revival back to the ninth and tenth centuries because at that time local trade made its appearance in the region of the castle and, more especially, the monastery.

Monasteries were actively engaged in land clearance and improving agricultural productivity. They were experimenting with such technological innovations as the multiple yoke for oxen, an improved harness for horse, horseshoes, water-and-wind mills and irrigation. These experiments resulted in an increase of production or surplus which could be exchanged for other goods or cash. Some historians claim that the credit goes to **Venice** in Italy which had never lost its contact with Byzantium in spite of Muslim control of the Sea. Still others trace it to the conquest of the Baltic Sea and the river lanes in Russia by the Varangian Norsemen.

Whatever the origin, by the eleventh century a degree of specialization had begun in Europe. **Flanders** was the first region in Europe to develop as an industrial and commercial center. Her stock-in-trade was woolen cloth of which she produced a surplus. To secure raw materials Flanders began a three-way trade: her woolen goods were exchanged for far northern furs and hunting hawks and these were traded in northern France and **Germany** for raw wool. As the demand for wool

rose, English lords—inspired by the example of the Cistercian monks—began to specialize in sheepherding to supply the Flanders market. England also became the center for an active metals export-trade and a wine import-trade.

But the more important development did take place in Italy. Venice, Genoa and Pisa began to build ships for a growing commerce between Italy and ports on the Western Mediterranean. Venice, moreover, was pressing the Byzantine trade and since Moslem control of the Mediterranean was the main barrier to expansion, military expeditions were launched against Corsica and Sicily, both in Moslem hands. The Italians welcomed the Crusades.

The Crusades and Commerce. The First Crusaders achieved their objective and created a feudal state in Palestine and Syria. This gave the Italians their golden opportunity. They gathered their vessels together and shipped—for fantastic prices—European supplies into Asia Minor; they ferried individual crusaders and pilgrims—for fantastic prices—over the Sea. In the area of Asia Minor they set up trading centers and secured from the feudal knights monopoly privileges over trade and trade routes. Empty vessels were now loaded for the return voyage with silks, spices, dyes, gems, medicinals, rugs, etc. From Italy these goods were distributed throughout Europe. Flanders-Italy now made up a trade axis about which Europe began to revolve.

Results of Commerce. Trade created its own imperatives. Eager for luxury goods, churchmen and feudal barons began to improve the lanes of commerce; roads were cleared and mended; rivers were carefully policed; bridges were rebuilt. Mining for silver and gold was intensified. A distinct merchant class appeared and along with it urban centers at river landing or crossroads where homes and warehouses were built. Around these clusters of merchants grew the medieval towns. As such, they fitted nowhere into the feudal-seignorial-ecclesiastical pattern: they wanted to pay for the lands they rented in money; they demanded protection against robbery; they insisted on contracted sales and the means to enforce a contract once it was signed. From these many demands there evolved the **town charter** which restricted the freedom of the barons and the clergy. But these latter were quite willing to barter some of their sovereignty for the luxury goods offered by the merchants.

The Town Charter. Merchants secured town charters at a price, usually a large fixed sum of money plus an annual payment. Such charters were regarded as contracts. In most of the charters the lords agreed to make the land rented to merchants **free land;** town members were to become freemen after a residence of a year and a day in the town. Rentals were to be in the form of money payments. Lords undertook, for a fee, not to debase the local coinage. Merchants could form guilds or corporations to deal with the lords; they could create special courts to hear cases involving commercial law; they could exercise local police powers and elect local officers—mayors and aldermen—to carry out town regulations; finally, they could organize a local military for defense. (Many of these charters had to be fought for and won before they were granted and the struggles of the towns for charter rights became an important factor in the three-cornered fight that developed in medieval times among the Church, the nobility and the kings.)

The Rise in Town Population. For many reasons the population of the towns increased rapidly once they were founded. Large numbers of serfs fled to the towns to become freemen. Moreover, the town increasingly offered security in a world torn by feudal war. By building thick walls around them and hiring mercenaries to defend them, the towns were able to withstand assault by the feudal lords. Since they had many interests in common, towns combined into leagues of defense. Towns had much to defend for their wealth grew rapidly. Increasing wealth produced increasing opportunities; these, in turn, encouraged the production of large families. Threatened by overpopulation, the towns expanded in size.

Problems of Town Government. Towns were governed, usually, by a council of burghers elected annually—the first type of representative government to develop in modern Europe. These councils were responsible for matters of defense, public works, markets and social security. Their problems were immense. Streets were unpaved, unlighted, narrow, houses were flimsy firetraps, water polluted, the filth incredible, the crowding a menace to public health, the air foul-smelling. Not until most recent times were these problems reduced to manageable proportions. In spite of these handicaps, the towns did manage to achieve dignity and beauty. Townsmen were inordinately proud of their locale and eager to beautify it by construction of elegant townhouses, townhalls and cathedrals.

The Medieval Fair. All these were secondary purposes in the life of the town; its primary purpose was to do business. Merchandising was at first little more than peddling. Merchants went from castle door to church door hawking their goods. An unusually favorable route lay in the Champagne region of France. It was almost an all-water route by means of the Rivers Rhône, Saone, Moselle and Seine.

In the twelfth century the powerful count of Champaigne, Henry the Liberal (1152-1181) took advantage of this favored waterway to create sites where sellers and buyers could meet for mass trading; these were called "fairs." Henry himself undertook, for a price, to guarantee the success of the fairs. He set up booths-for-rent, money-changing booths for rapid conversion of multiple currencies and commercial courts for rapid disposal of commercial disputes. Besides rentals, Henry levied a sales tax for services rendered. All along the routes to the fair merchants were protected by the Count's vassals who were given a share of the profits. Once successfully launched at Champagne, the idea of the fair—the large-scale wholesale and retail market fully protected—spread throughout Europe. Spread of the fair led to institutionalization of some of its features: the development of commercial law and of special courts to apply it; the use of bills of exchange, letters of credit and money as means of exchange; standards of weights and measures and the like.

The Hanseatic League. Fairs succeeded only when princes or kings were both strong and cooperative; they failed when princes and kings were weak or (more often) over-greedy. To protect themselves against the weak and greedy rulers, a number of the free towns in Germany—Cologne, Lubeck, Danzig, Hamburg—formed themselves into a **Hanseatic League** (ca.13th c.). Thus organized they established permanent trading stations in other nations. (One such, Steelyard, gave London its start and originated "sterling" as a means of exchange.) They constructed, operated and maintained their own navy for war on piracy. They policed the trade routes. To unify their policies, they maintained a representative assembly or diet. Until the fifteenth century, the Hanseatic League held a virtual monopoly of the Baltic herring fisheries, all trade out of Russia, and trade with England and the Low Countries.

The Merchant Guild. Within the towns merchants formed a distinct class, those who controlled the imports and exports of the town. The greatest threat to the survival of these merchants came from alien rivals. Therefore the merchants of the town set up iron-clad regulations that would ensure them monopoly control over the town's imports and exports. Alien merchants were forced to pay special tolls and taxes; they had to charge a "just" (fixed) price; they could not compete with the town's merchants by buying cheaply outside the town, by cornering the market of any commodity, or by charging more than the wholesale cost without having made any change in the product. They had to meet standards of quality, weight and measure before they could even offer goods on the market.

Membership in the merchants' guild was kept at a minimum. Since merchants were more often than not also members of the town council, the town's police powers were exercised in their behalf. He was fortunate indeed who could become a member of the merchants' guild since the guild made itself responsible for helping those who lost their money, for securing release of imprisoned merchants, for supplying burial expense and survivors' insurance for its members and by building guildhalls, holding secular and religious festivities, and undertaking wide works of charity for the sick and the poor.

The Craft Guilds. Far more numerous in the towns were the artisans or craftsmen. The content as well as the means of trade had expanded vastly by the thirteenth century. Towns were centers of large-scale and varied manufacturing—butchers, bakers, textilers, sword-and-armor makers, blacksmiths, tanners, booksellers, etc. Though numerous, the artisans were without political power.

To challenge the power of the merchant guilds, the artisans therefore organized their own craft guilds. These took their origin from the production of a single type of commodity. Craftsmen were concerned, like the merchants, to eliminate competition. They therefore drew up a great number of regulations concerning the quantity, quality and price of the goods sold; the hours of labor; the number of apprentices, etc. Faulty workmanship was heavily fined; and faulty workers, if repeated offenders, were punished in the pillory or by banishment.

A second goal was to limit the number of artisans that could engage in the trade. Before a new member was admitted to the guild he had to follow a long course of apprenticeship. A youth would be "bound" by his parents or guardian to a master. He would serve for years as an apprentice and receive board, lodging and clothes as wages. His apprenticeship completed, the young man would become a journeyman or hired day-laborer. As a journeyman he could work for any master in town. The wages, hours and conditions of work of journeymen were fixed by the guild. The journeyman's goal was to become a master and to set up shop for himself. This was impossible, under guild

regulations, until he had made a "master's piece" which won the approval of the officers of the guild. Obviously, if the field was overcrowded, no masterpiece was approved; in fact, custom began to dictate that only the masterpieces of the sons or sons-in-law of the masters could gain approval.

It should be apparent that the tendency of even these town institutions was toward the fixed and static so typical of all medieval life. Future capitalists, pressing onward toward free and wider enterprise, were going to find it necessary to destroy the power of the guilds as well as that of the feudal nobility and the hierarchy.

MEDIEVAL MONARCHIES

Medieval feudalism came to a close when the feudal lords were crushed by national monarchs and their fiefs were reabsorbed into the national state. This event did not occur overnight but was hundreds of years in the making. Monarchs had first to establish themselves and their families and win recognition of this establishment from the feudal lords and the clergy. Then they had to create an administrative organization within their own realms which could be expanded with territorial increase. Expansion of territory was vital to their success and for this purpose they required large sums of money to finance superior fighting forces. Above all they needed allies and these could only come from the peasantry and the middle class. Here we shall trace these developments within a number of developing national states.

ENGLAND

England was brought into the compass of European civilization by the Romans. In the fifth century A.D., however, the Romans had to retire before the onslaughts of the barbarian Angles, Saxons, Jutes and Frisians. The chaos which resulted was brought into some kind of order as a result of the missionary work of the Irish and Roman clergy. In 664, at the Synod of Whitby, Roman Catholic Christianity was officially adopted by the ruling tribes.

These tribes were divided into seven kingdoms, the so-called **Heptarchy.** By the ninth century, the kingdom of Wessex rose to power and produced one of England's great leaders, ALFRED THE GREAT (871-901). Alfred was able to establish a working relationship with the Danes who were threatening Anglo-Saxon England with extinction and then to initiate in England something of a "renaissance" of learning. He established schools and fostered the translation of Latin classics (e.g., Boethius' *Consolation of Philosophy*, Venerable Bede's *Ecclesiastical History of the English Nation*). He himself helped produce the *Anglo-Saxon Chronicle* and inspired the work of CAEDMON and CYNEWULF, founders of English literature. By codifying the laws and by remarkable defense of his realm, Alfred gave the English a tradition of strong kingship that soon became legendary. His work was undone by weak successors and by the conquest of England by KING CANUTE, the Dane (1016-1035). Canute's invasion forced many of the Anglo-Saxon nobility to flee to Normandy in France.

William the Conqueror. One such who fled was EDWARD THE CONFESSOR who in 1042 returned from Normandy to the throne of England. Edward brought with him many Norman advisers. Great rivalry developed between the Anglo-Saxon earls and these Norman nobles. When Edward died, the Witan (Council) selected Harold the Saxon (of Wessex) as king. WILLIAM, DUKE OF NORMANDY opposed this selection saying that Edward had promised the kingdom to him. In **1066** William invaded England and at the **Battle of Hastings** defeated Harold and his Anglo-Saxon forces. All of England fell as a feudal fief to the Conqueror.

Showing rare wisdom, William kept the government institutions he found in England and infused them with a new life. William destroyed the Anglo-Saxon earldoms, dividing them into smaller administrative units; over them he placed officials directly responsible to himself. Thus he merged Anglo-Saxon institutions with Norman institutions.

William's intention was to build a strong, centralized monarchy in England. His position was unique for he held all of England as a fief and could therefore make every landholder his vassal; every landholder had to serve in William's army. To further strengthen his position William kept a private standing militia for his use and prohibited private warfare. He issued a uniform royal currency. Even more remarkable for his time, William based his taxation upon the Domesday Survey (1085-1086), a national census of property holders and property! To defend his realm, William built castles everywhere and armed them with his own retainers.

Henry I (1100-1135). When William died the nobles tried to disrupt his plans for centralization. HENRY I consolidated his position by creating a permanent council of advisers—a bureaucracy of professional civil servants—and a group of "circuit" judges who traveled about the kingdom bringing the king's justice to all parts.

Henry II (1154-1189). Following Henry I's death, feudal and civil wars reduced England to a state of anarchy. Order was eventually restored by HENRY II, one of the greatest of all English kings. Henry was founder of the **Plantagenet dynasty** and ruled a land that extended from Scotland to the Pyrenees; his wife was the brilliant Eleanor of Aquitaine.

During the course of his reign, the English monarchy was considerably strengthened, particularly in the arena of judicial control. Henry's judicial reforms entered not only into the blood stream of the English nation, but into that of the United States as well. In the Assize of Clarendon of 1166 Henry did more than strengthen the king's justice. He initiated the participation of the people in the lawmaking process. The Clarendon Assize established the circuit judge as a permanent part of the English judicial system. When the circuit came to town, it was the duty of the sheriff to call up witnesses to give the judges information of existing wrongs. This practice created the **grand jury** which made "presentments" to the judges. In time these presentments were turned over to a **petit jury** ("twelve good men and true") to hear the presentments and pass judgment. He enlarged the jurisdiction of the King's Bench by permitting—contrary to feudal practice—civil as well as criminal cases to come before the circuit judges. This reduced considerably the power of the local, feudal baronial court.

Henry also resolved to reduce the power of the church courts by limiting the claim of "benefit of clergy" to major officials of the church. In this he was opposed by THOMAS A BECKET, the Archbishop of Canterbury. When Henry promulgated in 1164 the **Constitutions of Clarendon** which ordered that church officials accused of a crime should be taken before a royal court, Becket ordered churchmen to ignore the decree. After six years of dispute, at Henry's instigation a group of his followers murdered Becket.

The church and baronial courts having been curbed, the king's justices were free to consolidate English law and practice and out of their procedures there grew up the great system of **English Common Law.** Unlike Roman Law, the Common Law was never codified; it consisted of **customs and precedents.** In spite of this, it is wholly proper to call Henry II the "English Justinian."

Magna Carta (1215). Centralization of monarchical power suffered greatly under the rules of RICHARD THE LIONHEARTED and KING JOHN. Richard spent his father's bequest fighting as a knight errant in the Holy Land. John, whose goals of a centralized monarchy were consistent with Henry's but whose abilities and character were far inferior, became involved in a war with the feudal nobility and in a terrible quarrel with Pope Innocent III. As a result of his quarrel with Innocent, he lost all of his kingdom to the pope as a fief; and as a result of his war with the nobility, having been defeated in the **Battle of Runnymede,** he was compelled to sign the **Magna Carta** which placed severe restrictions on the power of the king in matters of taxation and judicial trial. At the time it was signed, Magna Carta served the interests of the feudal system. Only later did it become the **"charter of English liberties."** To cap this sad climax to the efforts of Henry II to establish the royalty in England, John proceeded to lose all of England's French possessions.

Edward I (1272-1307). When he came to the throne, EDWARD I resumed the reforms that were begun by the two Henrys. He further weakened the baronial and church courts; he strengthened the civil service; he gave strong impetus to a new institution, the English Parliament; he began the union of all the British Isles under one crown by conquering Wales (and creating a post of Prince of Wales as successor to the Crown) and Ireland. His work with Parliament deserves special mention since herein was the "wave of the future."

The Development of Parliament. Parliament is traced to the Anglo-Saxon Witan, a council of prominent nobles. William the Conqueror converted this into a Grand Council of nobles which served him in a judicial and advisory capacity.

Parliaments became popular in Europe during the second half of the thirteenth century as kings sought for revenues outside feudal dues to carry out their programs of national aggrandizement. It became customary to convene an assembly of three "estates," the lords, the clergy and the townsmen (bourgeoisie) as a means of raising money. Spain had its **cortes,** France its **Estates General,** Germany its **diet** and England its **Parliament.** In 1265 SIMON DE MONTFORT had convened, on behalf of the feudal lords, the first British Parliament. But it was Edward I who convened the "Model Parliament."

Edward's purpose was to reduce his dependence upon the nobility for moneys and he therefore agreed, in 1297, that certain taxes would be levied only with the consent of Parliament. By the 14th century, this Parliamentary "power of the purse" was ingrained in English practice—to the considerable regret of the monarchs who followed Edward.

Not only had this custom begun to prevail, but it also became a custom for the lords temporal and lords spiritual to sit together as the House of Lords, while the others sat separately as the House of Commons.

Furthermore, when Parliament met, it became the practice of the House of Commons to submit to the king a "list of grievances" which had to be taken care of before any money was voted. When England became involved in the Hundred Years War, and the financial drain became severe, the House of Commons began to insist on directing how the funds should be spent. For this to be legal, it became further necessary for the Commons to draw up a law which stipulated the way the money should be spent. Thus, in the Middle Ages, grew up one of the primary forms of modern democracy.

The Hundred Years War (1337-1450). The wars between England and France in the years between 1337 and 1450 were largely inspired by the desire of the kings of England who followed Edward to repossess their French holdings. As a result of these wars, England was driven permanently off the continent and forced to concentrate upon the British Isles. British kings became more and more dependent upon Parliament. Parliament became more and more independent in such matters as freedom of Parliametary debate, extension of suffrage for Parliamentry members, the right of all money bills to originate in the House of Commons and not the House of Lords. The kings' power having been weakened by war and parliament, the power of the nobility rose.

The Wars of the Roses (1453-1485). The English baronial class split into two factions, **Lancaster** and **York**—Lancaster of the "Red Rose," and York of the "White Rose." (their emblems). Both factions struggled for control of the monarchy and of Parliament. The result was a lengthy civil war known as the **War of the Roses** (celebrated in Shakespeare's History Plays). As a result of this civil war, the feudal nobility virtually exterminated one another and permitted Henry VII of the **House of Tudor** to come power. With Henry VII, England moves from the Middle Ages to modern history.

FRANCE

The concept of royal absolutism in France was the work of a remarkable line of kings, all members of the **Capetian dynasty.** This dynasty remained in office for 341 years—from 987 to 1328. A considerable amount of luck entered into the Capetian succession. Over the three hundred years the family never lacked for a male heir and since the eldest son was elected (by the nobles) and consecrated during the reign of the father, the French grew accustomed to the idea of hereditary succession. The Capetians, moreover, had the support of the Church and capitalized on the claim that they were the direct descendants of Charles the Great. While the Capetians placed heavy reliance upon the feudal nobility, they did not ignore the middle class in the towns and as a result had extra levies of taxes and troops at their command. Finally, Capetian kings had the administrative genius that characterized their English contemporaries.

Capetian Kings. HUGH CAPET (987-996), Count of Paris, founded the dynasty. LOUIS THE FAT (1108-1137) suppressed the disobedient vassals in the terrain of the Ile de France and placed the royal power on a firm basis there. PHILIP AUGUSTUS (1180-1223) strove to restore the might of Charlemagne in all of France. He secured about half of the Plantagenet possessions in France for his own state; he created an effective royal administration; he recruited a corps of personal servants from the lawyers of Paris steeped in the Roman (not feudal) law and from the monied middle class; he organized law courts to put the new concepts of royal sovereignty into effect. Before he died, Philip had created a central government for France that was winning the loyalty of many Frenchmen.

LOUIS IX (1226-1270). Louis' religious activities won him sanctification; it won for French kings that followed him a dignity and presence that they would not have commanded without him. Louis created the impression among the French that the king was the supreme fount of justice and charity. He did not, however, place his sole reliance upon inspiration. He employed spies who served as the king's eyes and ears and held local officials to strict accountability; he created a broad system of national royal courts and forced the nobility to abandon private warfare in favor of legal settlement.

PHILIP THE FAIR (IV) (1285-1314). This Philip was the last of the Capetians. By means of craft and violence he built the wealth and power of the monarchy at the expense of the nobility and the papacy. He was France's first absolute monarch.

THE HUNDRED YEARS WAR

The **House of Valois** succeeded the House of Capet and was the immediate cause of the **Hundred Years War (1337-1453)**. The English king, Edward III, claimed that he was the legitimate heir through his mother. According to the French Salic Law, however, no woman could inherit estates or transmit them to a son. When the French nobility rejected his claim, Edward began the conflict. There were other causes operating as well as the dynastic one. The English sought to recover their French possessions. The French were eager to take over one remaining English possession in Gascony. The French were striving to take over the English wool market in Flanders while the English were trying to eliminate French ships from the northern seas.

Battles. The Hundred Years War produced a number of military incidents that have delighted students of history since. First was the **Battle of Crecy** (1347) in which a smaller English force decimated the French and proved the superiority of a new weapon, the longbow, over the traditional short crossbow. The fact that the arrow from the longbow could pierce a knight's armor gave new importance to the role of the infantry in medieval war. As a result of Crecy, northern France and Calais fell to the English. A ten year truce followed out of necessity for in 1348-1349 the "Black Death" (bubonic plague) swept over Europe.

In 1356 the Black Prince Edward entered the fray and led the English to a tremendous victory at **Poitiers**. In the Peace of Bretigny which followed the English surrendered their claims to the French throne and to Normandy in exchange for Poitou, Guienne, Gascony and Calais. The Black Prince ruled these provinces oppressively and the French rose in indignation to the attack again. They were defeated at **Agincourt** (1415) and in the **Treaty of Troyes** arrangements were made for English succession to the French throne.

At this low point in the life of the rising French nation there appeared on the scene JEANNE D'ARC (Joan of Arc). The story of this marvelous girl, her youth in the village of Domremy, her visions, her efforts to secure a hearing and a military command—all have been sufficiently celebrated in history, novel, poem and play. Here it need only be pointed out that as a result of Joan's activities the French experienced a resurgence of national spirit, the Dauphin was crowned at Rheims as Charles the VII, the English armies were driven from France (except Calais) and the Hundred Years War was brought to a close. Captured by the British, deserted by the man she made king, Joan died a martyr's death in 1434. In the twentieth century she was at last sanctified as Saint Joan.

Results. The Hundred Years War brought the French to the point of national unity. Large numbers of nobility were destroyed in battle and thus removed as a challenge to royal power. The French kings experienced an increase in power as they secured direct control over the armed forces and resorted more and more to direct taxation. England was cleared from the continent of Europe. (Of great importance for the future of the feudal system was the fact that during the seige of Calais the first cannon made their appearance in warfare.)

SPAIN

In the period under consideration (ca. 1000-1450) Spain was engaged in a re-conquest of the Iberian Peninsula from the Moorish Moslems established at Cordova. Leaders in this move or crusade to oust the Moslem were the Spanish states of Leon, Castile and Portugal. The great and legendary hero of this Spanish crusade was RODRIGO DIAZ DE BIVAR ("El Cid").

By the end of the 13th century Moorish power was relegated to one center in Spain, Granada. Complete unification did not come until that fateful year 1492 when the Moors were driven from Granada. Meanwhile the foundations of Spanish nationalism were laid in 1469 when Isabella of Castile married Ferdinand of Aragon. These rulers were most adept at building up the royal power. They converted La Santa Hermandad, a holy brotherhood, into a strong police force; they crushed all unruly nobles through the Holy Inquisition; they destroyed the *cortes,* one of the oldest of European parliaments. Few monarchies in Europe were as absolute as the Spanish.

THE HOLY ROMAN EMPIRE

While other European nations took the path of national unity, Germany and Italy did not become united nations until the nineteenth century. The reasons for this failure were numerous. German emperors dissipated their energies in an effort to unite Germany and Italy, a policy that was opposed, as we have seen, by the papacy and the powerful Italian towns. The popes were particularly effective in preventing this union. They openly interfered in imperial elections within Germany and kept that nation split in perpetual war between Guelph and Ghibelline, they used their extensive powers of excommunication and interdict against such strong rulers as Barbarossa, Henry VI and Frederick II, and, when these failed, they invited foreigners like Charles of Anjou (1265) to make war on the Germans.

The Germans themselves made a unified nation nearly impossible by measures continually adopted to weaken the Emperor. For five hundred years thereafter there was no Germany—just a series of archduchies, margravates, counties, duchies and free cities known as the Germanies.

Italy suffered the same fate. The lead in preventing the unification of the Italian states was taken once more by the popes who feared for their vast possessions in Italy and by the short-sighted Italian cities. Constant invasion plagued the Italians as well. Following the decline of the Carolingian power Italy was invaded by the Normans who settled in Sicily. The Normans provided Italy with models of intelligent rule: laws were codified; a parliament was created (1225); trade and commerce were fostered. Because it threatened their power, the popes invited the French Angevins into Italy as conquerors. So bitter was the Italian resentment against the French that in 1282 at Palermo they rose up, at the hour of vespers, and murdered every Frenchman they could find. (This massacre is known in history as the "Sicilian Vespers.") When the French left it became the turn of the Spaniard Alfonso of Aragon to conquer Sicily and Naples (1443). In 1494 Charles the VIII of France invaded Italy . . . but by this time Italy's will to exist as a nation was destroyed.

Out of this failure in government a new state was born—Switzerland. While Frederick II was King he permitted two Swiss cantons to become self-governing—subject to his overlordship. A habit of independence was born. When in 1291 Rudolph of Hapsburg, the German ruler decided to remove their independent rights, the Swiss cantons formed a Perpetual Compact or alliance directed against Rudolph. Their resistance was successful. In 1315 the frustrated Hapsburgs moved an army against the Swiss and were soundly beaten by boulders rolled down the declivities of the cantons. Their success encouraged the Swiss to organize a confederation. In 1394 the Hapsburgs compromised with necessity and recognized Swiss independence. Out of this struggle came the legend of **William Tell.**

EAST EUROPEAN SUMMARY

During the Middle Ages the Scandinavian countries were first beginning to stir. Denmark was the first state to rise to some power. In the Union of Calmar of 1397 she became the ruler of Norway and Sweden. Danish influence was swept out of Sweden by 1533. After many years of independent existence the Czechs (Bohemians) fell successively under Polish, Hungarian and finally Austrian rule. The Poles were dominated by the Lithuanians and at one time formed the largest state in Europe. Hungary was the land of the Magyars and created a model of an intelligent, progressive Christian state until they were destroyed by Turkish on-slaughts. Finally, the Russians were a tribal folk until the Norse invasion created the first kingdoms.

Principalities were established at Novgorod and Kiev. Links to Byzantium promised an early ad-vance in the Russian state, but this advance was crippled by Mongolian invasions. Not until IVAN THE GREAT (1462-1505) did Russia emerge from her captivity.

CHAPTER ELEVEN

CULTURE IN THE MIDDLE AGES

INTRODUCTION

Everyone living in the Middle Ages in Europe felt the impact of the Catholic Church upon his life daily.

The Church, as we have seen, was a holder of vast estates; it conditioned and at times dictated the roles played by secular governments; it was a monarchical state within a state; it lived by its own canon law which in 1142 was codified by GRATIAN in his *Decretum;* it had its own law courts to try those who had "benefit of Clergy" or cases arising over conflicts involving wills, sworn contracts, marriage, blasphemy, sorcery, etc.; it was the pri-mary guide to the moral life of men and women. In this latter role it dictated that wealth was a great temptation to sinning; that individual business competition was morally dangerous; that price manipulation, the charging of interest for loans, outbidding, outbuying, monopolizing and the like were outlawed activities; that work was dignified and worthy of Christians; that men and women must accept their status in life as trials of their virtue.

The Church defined the relationship of sexes. Woman was a potential source of evil; chastity was glorified. Marriage as a holy sacrament sanc-tioned sexual relations, but for procreative pur-poses only. Divorce was prohibited. Within the family the husband was dominant. Finally, whatever social security medieval men knew—in hunger, sick-ness, old age—came from the hands of the Church. This overwhelming power of the Church was in-evitably reflected in the culture of the Middle Ages.

MEDIEVAL THOUGHT

The Dark Ages (5th-9th c.) Christianity was itself a force in the decline of Greco-Roman civil-ization; its attack upon "paganism" involved not

only the physical destruction of the works of the classical masters, but a transformation of their modes of thinking into Christian forms. Chris-tianity determined that the orientation of thought should be turned to the otherworldly, the super-natural, the miraculous, the revealed and the au-thoritative aspects of knowledge. Where rational modes of thought or direct observation of phe-nomena could serve these aims, they were used.

Great reliance had to be placed, however, upon the methods of **allegory** and **symbolism.** Through allegory churchmen could argue that the point of a Biblical story or statement is figurative and not literal, is implied and not stated. By means of symbolism all kinds of secondary and tertiary meanings could be found in the phenomena of nature. In this manner what seemed contradictory or impossible or unworthy of the conduct of good Christians could be satisfactorily explained and fitted into the general corps of knowledge.

It was clear to medieval churchmen and laymen that all that happened was part of a divine plan moving in the direction of a Last Judgment. Reason, when properly used, could find some of the pur-poses of this divine plan as they affected man and his institutions. In their search for purposes in the universe, churchmen did not rule out the possibili-ties of divine intervention through the miraculous. The fundamental groundwork of medieval thought, then, was *faith,* faith in what had been revealed and faith in what established authority said was con-tinuing to be revealed.

Philosophy in the Dark Ages. Between the fifth and ninth centuries Christian philosophy pro-duced no masterwork to equal that of St. Augus-tine. But though the period was uncreative, it was not entirely unproductive. The primary task of the intellectual in a dissolving world was to preserve and transmit and scholars devoted themselves to compiling and classifying what remained of Roman-Christian civilization.

During the Dark Ages in Europe grammars were written, translations were made of the works of Aristotle and Porphyry, and encyclopedias of information (filled with error) were compiled. Of considerable importance for the future was the establishment by Martianus Capella and Cassiodorus of a curriculum of study. "Seven Liberal Arts" were established and then divided into a **trivium** (grammar, rhetoric and logic) and a **quadrivium** (arithmetic, geometry, astronomy and music). The works of BOETHIUS (d. 524) were also of considerable importance. In his writings on Christian themes Boethius was the first to try to fuse the philosophy of Aristotle with Christian theology. Moreover, he supplied philosophic discipline with a Latin vocabulary. His most widely read and translated work, *The Consolation of Philosophy*, was, however, neo-Platonic and Stoic rather than Christian in its de-emphasis of the problems of sin and salvation.

Scholasticism. Beginning with the Carolingian Renaissance a philosophical rebirth took place. Charles had founded palace and cloister schools and had brought Alcuin from York to introduce the trivium and quadrivium into them. Such schools spread rapidly into urban centers in England, France, Germany and Italy. Teachers at these schools were called "schoolmen" and their approach to the subjects in the trivium and quadrivium was known as scholastic. As this approach grew into a philosophy, it became known as **Scholasticism.** However, Scholasticism never became *one* philosophy, based on *one* method; it included a number of philosophies and a number of methods each depending on initial premises, and many arriving at different conclusions. Debate, often violent, featured scholastic thought in the Middle Ages.

Yet scholastic philosophy is distinguished from non-scholastic philosophy by a number of criteria. It was the philosophy of a Christian society and as such was based upon accepted **authority** in the forms of tradition and revealed religion. Tradition bound the scholastics to the systems of Aristotle and Plato as adapted to Christian thought. The problems to which the scholastic thinkers applied themselves were controlled by **theology**; rational interests were never permitted to push religious pre-occupations aside. Put otherwise, philosophy was always subordinate to theology.

Scholastic methods were based on Greek logic; concern was with deduction, systematization and formal logic. To Greek logic Scholastics added a unique pedagogical device which involved eight distinct steps:

1. State the question or proposition.
2. Give a succint listing of the negative arguments.
3. Make a brief statement of the affirmative and give a citation of authority.
4. State the principle difficulties and doubts which inhere in the proposition.
5. Now give a detailed presentation of the negative.
6. Follow with a detailed presentation of the affirmative and include refutation of the negative.
7. Explain and solve the inherent doubts.
8. Summarize by once more disposing of the negative.

In their logic, Scholastics made considerable use of the "Tree of Porphyry." From Aristotle on, thinkers had sought to arrange all knowledge into a hierarchy of "forms." Porphyry's arrangement was as follows:

	Substance	
Corporeal		Incorporeal
	Body	
Animate		Inanimate
	Living Thing	
Sensitive		Insensitive
	Animal	
Rational		Irrational
	Man	
	Individuals A,B,C etc.	

This tree enabled one to determine quickly that any human individual is a rational, sensitive, animate, corporeal substance. In other words, it provided thinkers with their initial premises on which to build a syllogism. For example, from the Tree we secure the **major premise**—

Man is a rational animal.

This leads to the **minor premise**—

Plato is a man.

From these two premises the conclusion follows—

Plato is a rational animal.

In the medieval mind the major premises were provided by fixed and unalterable belief derived from faith in revelation and authority; hence the main concern of thinkers was with minor premises and conclusions. One could not safely question the validity of the major premises until the Church lost its power to punish free thought. (When men arose to test, observe, weigh, and challenge the major premises of the Scholastics, the scientific revolution was in the making.)

SCHOLASTIC PHILOSOPHY

Within the framework described above, scholastic philosophy made tremendous strides. It was forged in the heat of debate. In the ninth century an original and daring thinker, JOHN SCOTUS ERIGENA (Duns Scotus), had produced a work which raised reason above revelation and authority and which dissolved all of nature into a pantheistic reality. Substance, bodies, living things, animals and men were all emanations from a single source, God, and in essence were indistinguishable. A little later, BERENGER OF TOURS had raised many questions about the "reality" of transubstantiation. This problem of the "reality" of that which was not given directly to the senses became the so-called "problem of universals," which is central in the history of medieval thought.

The Problem of Universals. Plato and Aristotle had earlier differed here. Human beings perceive many *particular* objects—these trees, those rocks, etc. They also use *general* terms for all trees and all rocks—these terms being simply "tree" and "rock"—without reference to a particular object. For Plato the idea or form of a rock or tree had more reality—both in logic and in being—than any particular specimen. Aristotle insisted that the mind gets the *idea* of any particular from the visible object itself. For Aristotle the universal was a classification made by the mind; for Plato it was the truer reality.

Belief in the one or the other of these propositions converted medieval scholastics into **"Realists"** (those who agreed with Plato) and **"Nominalists"** (those who reduced universals to the *names* of things). ST. ANSELM headed the former, and ROSCELLINUS (c. 1050), the latter.

This was no pointless quibble. Nominalists said there was no transubstantiation in the Eucharist since the bread and wine remained *visibly* unchanged; there was no Church *Universal* apart from separate and individual church groups; there was no Unity in any Trinity, etc. In other words, Nominalists challenged any concept for which visible evidence was lacking. Anselm pointed out that this challenge was but a short distance from heresy; Roscellinus was, in fact, convicted of heresy in the matter of the Trinity and he was forced to recant his views.

PETER ABELARD (1070-1142) produced a compromise in his doctrine of **Conceptualism.** His compromise was that a universal has no objective existence as such; it exists as a concept in the mind.

The mental concept, however, is derived from observation of particular things and from taking note of the similarities or identities in their qualities. From these real identities the concept is made. In this sense it has objective reality.

Abelard. Abelard was typical of the "new man" that was arising in the Middle Ages. He was a troubadour poet and composer, a bold lover (his love for Heloise is famous as one of the world's great love stories), a fearless and brilliant scholar, a ruthless debater and logician, a free and inquiring spirit. Abelard came into conflict with St. Bernard who was his complete opposite—ascetic, relying completely on faith, distrusting reason. Against Bernard, Abelard argued that thought must begin in doubt for doubt leads to inquiry and inquiry to the truth. For his own satisfaction Abelard composed the *Sic et Non,* a book which proposed 158 questions concerning faith and reason. About these questions, Abelard collected arguments for (Sic) and against (Non). He attempted no reconciliation of the opposites, but others did (PETER LOMBARD in the *Sentences;* THOMAS AQUINAS in the *Summa*). The significance of Abelard's work was that following him there could be no reliance any more on faith alone.

The Revival of Aristotelianism. Abelard's insistence on logical rigor gave an impetus to the study of Aristotle. The time was ripe, for from Moslem lands the works of Aristotle were being imported into Europe and translated into Latin. Once acquainted with Aristotle's writings, ALEXANDER OF HALES, JOHN OF FIDENZA and ALBERTUS MAGNUS began the task of fusing his teachings with Christian theology and philosophy. ST. THOMAS AQUINAS (1225-1274) was a pupil of Albertus Magnus and set himself to the task of creating a synthesis or *summa* of all knowledge—rational and revealed. In his monumental *Summa Theologia,* Aquinas made the major summary of the Christian synthesis. He is the greatest of the medieval thinkers.

The Thomistic System. St. Thomas was a theologian and his work in philosophy must be regarded in the light of its relation to theology. His problem was to introduce philosophy into religion without corrupting the essence and nature of theology. Theology treated of the revealed, and the revelation must remain intact. But some truths in theology (e.g., God's existence) can be ascertained without revelation.

Thomism is essentially realistic and concrete. Metaphysics studies the nature of being; Thomas studied it as *existent* being. He started with the existing world and asked what its being is, how it exists, what is the condition of its existence, etc. At the same time he concentrated upon supreme existence, on Being that is its own cause. By placing his emphasis upon existence Thomas advanced philosophy beyond Plato and Aristotle who emphasized essence rather than existence. God, of course, was both essence and existence; any other existence was a creation by God. Concentration upon existence made Thomas begin with sense-experience from the visible world. Even in his proofs of the existence of God, Thomas began with the visible world.

The theologian accepts God as Creator as an unquestioned assumption; the philosopher argues or reasons his way up to God the Creator. One proceeds from a revealed premise, the other from a reasoned conclusion. Thomas produced five famous proofs for the existence of God:

> **Proof from motion:** Whatever is moved has a mover; but motion must have begun with a first mover that was itself unmoved. This cause of initial motion was God.
>
> **Proof from causation:** Similarly there must have been a first cause for all efficient causes. This First Cause is God.
>
> **Proof from contingent being.** Beings depend upon one another *ad infinitum*. There must therefore be one being that does not depend on any but itself. This Self-Dependent Being is God.
>
> **Proof from the stages of perfection.** In the world things are arranged in more and more perfect series. The Most Perfect is God.
>
> **Proof from teleology.** The universe exhibits purpose and design. Purpose and design imply a directing will. That Will is the Will of God.

By such reasoning Thomas sought to prove that God is eternal, pure act, without matter, identical with His own essence, absolutely perfect, the highest good, complete unity, an intelligent being, a being with will, a loving being, etc.

The human intellect cannot apprehend God directly. It comes to knowledge through the senses. Outside are corporeal objects that act on the senses and produce **particulars**. The particular proceeds to the intellect which has the capacity to make an abstraction and derive a **universal**. There are no innate ideas in the mind; all knowledge begins with sense perception. The human mind cannot therefore, in this life, attain knowledge of immaterial substances that are not the object of the senses. But sense impressions can suggest, by analogy and logic, what immaterial substances may be like.

Everything seeks to fulfill its potentialities; such fulfillment is perfection. Evil is relative to good and is the failure of a thing to reach its proper form. Since all things come from God they are either actually or potentially good; evil is negative, a deficiency in being, an incomplete realization of its potential. Evil exists but it is not real since it is not *a part of* but the *absence* of being.

God created man in His own image. Men direct themselves through free will to their appointed ends. Man and angel alone are capable of sin. Man and angel have definite places in a universal hierarchy, the chain of being. Man's happiness does not consist of bodily pleasure, honors gained, glory, wealth—these are means to moral ends. Man's greatest happiness is understanding God and attaining to virtue.

The universe is evidently governed by law—natural, human and divine. The laws of nature are the laws of God at the level of inanimate nature; the law of reason in personal and social morality are the laws of God at the human level; the divine law is revelation of the laws of God at the spiritual level.

The Decline of Scholasticism. Attacks on the Thomistic synthesis came from within the ranks of the Scholastics. DUNS SCOTUS (1270-1308) found flaws in Thomistic logic and suggested that major premises needed some other form of examination. WILLIAM OF OCCAM (1280-1349) drove a sharp wedge between faith and reason, revived Nominalism and brought European thought close to the experimental method of investigation. The reasoning of post-Aquinas scholastics became so tortuous that men were repelled by philosophy in general and began to seek other means of acquiring knowledge. By the 14th century Scholasticism was clearly outmoded; it was far too static for the dynamic forces that had been released by the first winds of the Renaissance, the Commercial and Scientific Revolutions and the Reformation.

MEDIEVAL UNIVERSITIES

Universities began to form in the twelfth century. In its inception a university stood for a kind of guild or corporation; later it became particularized as a guild of learners and teachers. In this form, universities began to receive charters from royal and ecclesiastical authorities giving them special rights or immunities. Bologna was an early university center. Students flocked to that town to study civil law. At first the university at Bologna was controlled completely by the students. It was they who organized living quarters, qualifications for teaching, standards of teaching performance, courses of study, etc. The masters, however, were permitted to decide in the matter of granting degrees. To Paris came students who wished to study theology. Before long, however, the university there how been divided into separate faculties of arts, canon law, medicine and theology. Customary degrees granted were Bachelor of Arts, Master of Arts, Doctor of Laws, Doctor of Theology and Doctor of Medicine. The standard undergraduate curriculum was the trivium and quadrivium. Slowly graduate schools began to specialize. Paris remained the center for theology and Bologna for law; for medicine, however, one went to Salerno or Padua in Italy, or Montpellier in France.

MEDIEVAL LITERATURE

Latin Writings. Latin remained the language of scholarship well into the seventeenth century; it was also the language of some delightful and moving religious and secular verse. During the Dark Ages religious verse was closely related to rounding out the form of the liturgy in the church services or to the recitation of prayers in the Benedictine monasteries. In the hands of such figures as Abelard, St. Bernard and St. Francis religious verse emerged into the open air. Latin was employed for secular themes too. Ekkehard produced an epic, the Song of Walter, that described the terrors of the Hunnish invasion. In the twelfth and thirteenth centuries appeared the "goliardic" poems composed by wandering monks, teachers and students. These creations are most curious. They dealt broadly with nature themes, with chivalric love, with extremely profane love; they were at once ecstatically religious, mockingly irreligious and even pagan. Some histories were written in Latin, those of Gregory of Tours, Cassiodorus and the VENERABLE BEDE being most notable—not so much as history, but as interesting insights into the Dark Ages.

Vernacular. After the ninth century vernacular tongues rose to challenge the supremacy of Latin. Two broad groupings of vernacular appeared, the Romance and the Germanic. The former embraced Italian, French, Spanish, Portuguese and Rumanian; the latter took in German, the Scandinavian tongues, Dutch and English. Out of these vernaculars came a great literature.

French. One of the most popular productions of the French vernacular tongue (employing the *langue d'oil* or dialect of the northern part of France) was the **chanson de geste.** This was an epic of legendary heroes that centered about the life of Charlemagne. The *Song of Roland,* describing the wars of Charlemagne against the Spanish Moors, remains to this day a "children's classic." Its chivalric ideals of heroism have an eternal fascination. So, too, have the Arthurian Romances, the tales of the Round Table and its many knights, which were also a product of northern French vernacular bards. Romance was a favorite theme; some dealt with classical subjects, others with love themes. *Aucassin and Nicolette* is a particularly good example of the French romance of this period.

Southern France produced a "Provencal" literature under the influence of the troubadours and utilizing the *langue d'oc* dialect. Provencal was less stately, less formal than the northern literature and dealt lightly and gayly with worldly subjects. Realistic and satirical writing donned the cloak of concealment in the form of animal fables and allegories. The most noteworthy allegory was the *Roman de la Rose* combining a tender love story with a biting exposure of the evils of the age. Finally, Villehardouin produced a brilliant history of the Crusades in his *History of the Conquest of Constantinople;* and Joinville wrote a classic *Life of St. Louis.* Both of these volumes enjoy wide reading to this day.

German. Most people know the *Nibelungenlied,* a product of medieval vernacular German, through the operas of Richard Wagner. This epic is of Siegfried and Brunhild and takes place in the time of the invasion of Europe by Attila the Hun. Von Eschenbach in his *Parsifal* rounded out one part of the Arthurian cycle. Von Strassburg gave to the world the immortal tale of Tristan and Iseult. Walter von der Vogelweide, a minnesinger (troubadour) wrote charming lyrics, worthy of his French models.

English. England, too, produced a number of Arthurian cycles, fabliaux, romances, lyrics, epics and allegories. But vernacular had greater difficulty in England than elsewhere because of the Norman invasion. Polite society after the invasion spoke Norman French; the common people spoke Anglo-Saxon. It took considerable time before the two languages merged. The man who gave shape to the merger of the two tongues was GEOFFREY CHAUCER (1340-1400). Chaucer's work, however, belongs more to the Renaissance than to the medieval period of English literature.

England's peculiar contribution to medieval literature was the ballad and the drama, both folk productions. The ballads were sad, popular songs about heroic figures. The dramas were related to church festivals. In their earliest forms they were **miracle plays,** plays where problems were resolved by divine intervention; later they became **mystery plays** placing greater stress upon human solutions of human problems. Irish contributions to the English literary heritage were two cycles: one centering about the heroes Finn and Ossian and the other about the heroes Conchobor and Cuchulain.

Spanish. Spain was not behind the others in production of gifted troubadours, romancers and historical writers. Her outstanding contribution to medieval literature, however, was the *Poema del Cid*, relating the heroic adventures of Rodrigo Diaz de Biyar in his campaigns against the Moors.

Italian. In the person of DANTE ALIGHIERI (1265-1321) medieval literature reached its greatest height. Into his writing of the *Vita Nuova* (New Life), the *Convivio* (Banquet) and the *Divine Comedy* Dante poured the essence of the philosophical, moral, and intellectual lore of the Middle Ages. He was the first to write in the Italian vernacular and in this language he wrote the *Divine Comedy*, one of the world's great masterpieces.

MEDIEVAL ART

Medieval art was devotional, man's way of proclaiming the glory of God. Its function was to provide places of worship and to instruct communicants in Christian traditions.

Gothic cathedrals were the supreme creation of this period. Whole armies of stonecutters, masons, carpenters, woodworkers, metalworkers, glassworkers and sculptors were involved in their creation over many generations. Architects began with what was at hand, the Romanesque church—low-lying, massive, gloomy, idea-less. Their aim was to lift it heavenward, make it lighter, airier, more beautiful, more mysterious and more radiant. This effect could not be achieved without height and to secure height they used a vaulted ceiling supported by curved stone ribs which in turn rested upon heavy pillars that reached upward to the roof. The weight of the roof threatened the stability of the walls and pillars. To contain this outward thrust additional pillars or buttresses were built outside the church and then joined to the outer walls by means of braces or flying buttresses. With these inner and outer supports for the roof, the wall became self-supporting and was embellished. Wherever possible ogive (pointed) arches looking like hands in prayer were inserted to give grace and attitude to the façade. The groundplan of the church was cruciform. Within, all along the apse and the aisles were chapels, choir areas, carved stalls. Almost every inch of space was utilized for decorations—traceries, pinnacled spires, statues, receding arches, gargoyles and the like.

Medieval sculpture was handmaiden to architecture but beautiful in its own right. Religious symbolism dominated sculpture. Figures representing Biblical tales or saints' lives were free standing and usually erect. Proportion was ignored for importance. Yet sculptors avoided the extremely mannered and lifeless figure. Painters, on the other hand, imitated Byzantine modes. They produced conventional and lifeless figures in stained glass attitudes surrounded by scenes devoid of perspective. In tapestry work and book illumination, however, medieval artists attained to greater naturalism. Perhaps this was due to the fact that they dealt more often with secular scenes of the hunt and the manor and were therefore somewhat freed from conventional restrictions.

Music. Church music was chiefly in the form of the **plain chant** which was used in the singing of masses. Thus music became linked with the liturgy of the Church. Plain chant was a single line melody without harmony or counterpoint. In the **Gregorian chant** melody patterns were classified according to one of eight modes, each a segment of the C-major scale. In the later Middle Ages came the rise of polyphonic music. This in turn prompted the use of exact notation. It was inevitable that the Mass should be affected by this move to polyphony. The musical setting of the Mass was divided into five parts: Kyrie, Gloria, Credo, Sanctus and Agnus Dei. Out of the Mass for the Dead came the musical Requiem with its many prayers and its awesome and solemn section *Dies irae* (Days of Wrath)—the musical depiction of the Last Judgment.

Science. Pure science could not flourish in an age when primary emphasis was placed upon authority. Nonetheless some progress was recorded during the Middle Ages in mathematics, in observational techniques and in practical engineering. In mathematics Arabic numerals, the decimal system, algebra and geometry became widespread. Astronomy was wedded to the Ptolemaic System and getting itself ever more involved in epicycles as men became more cognizant of eccentric movements of celestial bodies. In geography, the travels of many Europeans like Marco Polo began to dispel many of the fabulous notions that people held of lands overseas. Physics and chemistry were still chained to the theory of the four elements and made very little progress. Medicine, too, was limited by Galen's theory of the four humors. What progress there was came from the barber-surgeons who performed dissections and who experimented with anesthetics of one kind and another. Leprosy was effectively controlled and the practice of quarantining people with apparently contagious diseases was begun. There were many practical inventions: e.g., mariner's instruments, new types of rudders, masts, spars and rigging, the cannon, windmill and watermill.

Looming large in the modern mind, though bothersome to the medieval, was the work of ROGER BACON (1214–1294). Bacon made interesting studies in optics, geography, astronomy and mechanics. These studies led him to advance the opinion that knowledge could only be advanced if men put aside authority and custom and substituted a method of experimentation and mathematical measurement. If they were to do this, said Bacon, they would one day ride in machines that would navigate rivers without oars, in automatic cars (chariots), and in flying machines! Bacon was dismissed by his contemporaries as a fanatic dangerously close to heresy. Actually, however, Bacon was no startling innovator. Frederick II and Albertus Magnus had already suggested similar approaches; and the experimental approach was implicit in the whole school of Nominalists.

CHAPTER TWELVE

THE ECONOMIC TRANSITION TO MODERN TIMES

THE COMMERCIAL REVOLUTION

Statistics of the growth of European commerce between 1350 and 1650 are not available; but some indication of the growth is reflected in the fact that by the latter date there were an estimated 2,000,000 tons of shipping afloat. We are concerned with this fact because with each increase in Europe's trade **the power and position of the middle class grew.** Fixed capital such as landed property began to take second place to fluid capital in the form of money. Manufacturing was becoming a competitor of agriculture for available investment capital. There still were many medieval shackles upon the free flow of trade—feudal tolls and tariffs, religious prohibitions, guild restrictions, and the like. But these were being shaken loose by the rise of **national states** under *national* monarchies, by the wave of humanism and new learning sweeping Europe, and by the religious reformation. Taking advantage of these dissolvents of the medieval order, the middle class began to develop forms of manufacturing that evaded the boundaries set down by the guilds. In the mainstream of all these charges, however, was the revolution in commerce that made itself felt by the fifteenth century.

Trade and Commerce. By 1400 European markets were no longer restricted to the luxury trade from the Near East. These still commanded an imposing position in the trade picture, but trading was as much concerned now with new European foodstuffs, textiles, shipbuilding materials and tools. Markets were no longer restricted to a few favored areas since goods could now travel along the king's roads protected by the king's police and the king's courts. The supply of money had increased; European deposits of gold and silver were dug with intensified fervor and North African mineral sources were tapped. When the Americas were discovered —just as European deposits were almost exhausted— a flood of gold and silver bullion re-entered the trade stream.

Manufacturing. Traders clamored for manufactured products to be sold abroad in exchange for luxury goods and for foodstuffs. Throughout these early years, in fact, the drain of gold and silver out of Europe was very heavy. Europe suffered from an almost continual unfavorable balance of trade which kept her prices low (deflation) and her debts high. When the political power of the guilds declined, entrepreneurs (early capitalists) appeared who discovered and invested in a new mode of production of manufactured goods, the **domestic** or "putting out" system.

Under this system the entrepreneur contracted with many craftsmen to supply them with raw materials and to pay them for the goods they manufactured out of the raw materials. The entrepreneur then disposed of the manufactured goods in the local or international market. This was a very attractive offer to the craftsman. He already owned his own tools, he could do the work at home (hence domestic), he did not have to worry about purchasing raw materials and selling his products, he could keep a garden patch and do some farming to supplement his income from manufacture.

To the entrepreneur this system was still not ideal: the cost was high since the craftsman made the whole product and insisted in producing quality goods, the entrepreneur depended upon the craftsman who owned the tools, the small number of craftsmen kept wages high, production was limited, invention of new tools was discouraged since craftsmen could not afford to finance them, etc. Over the years, the attractiveness of the craftsman's position brought many new workers into the field. Entrepreneurs took advantage of this situation by lowering wages considerably. The lowering of wages had the effect of increasing the dependence of the craftsman upon the entrepreneur. To get more money, the craftsman had to give up his farming and put his wife and children to work. Under pressure to make more, the craftsman became less concerned with the quality of the product. The entrepreneur, in turn, got poorer goods and found it increasingly difficult to supervise many workers in their homes. The time soon came when a more radical innovation in manufacturing processes would have to be made. For this period, however, the domestic system served admirably to build up the quantity of trade, the wealth of the entrepreneurs and to destroy effectively the power of the guilds.

Finance. Financing by means of money grew side by side with commerce and manufacturing. Professional money lending was an old practice by 1400. As early as the 10th century monasteries began to engage in extensive money lending, generally to local peasants and landlords. Political loans were on occasion made to Emperors, Popes and high feudal lords. Later, the knightly orders (Templars, Hospitalers, etc.) played the part of kings of finance and supplied credit needs.

In the medieval cities the role of professional lenders fell to the Lombards, Jews and money changers. Medieval Jews, prohibited from becoming farmers or artisans, had been among the first to engage in commerce. The rise of Christian merchants forced them out of this business and into the business of money-lending since they were not subject to church prohibitions and money-lending was a necessary function in an expanding economy. Christians permitted them to settle in specified areas *only if they would make loans;* Jews paid with their lives *if they refused to make a loan when security was offered.* Jews, then, won "toleration" so that Christians might evade the church's prohibition of "usury"—though the latter of course reaped the rewards of usury.

Soon, however, the Italian Lombards became active competitors of the Jews. Their loans went out to the urban merchants, feudal lords and handicraftsmen. The Lombards discovered that they might lend out more money than they had (since some was always being paid back)—but not safely. Therefore, they began to solicit interest-bearing deposits (a practice forbidden to the Jews). This was the origin of commercial banking. Other methods—such as bills of exchange, bank drafts and bank acceptances—were soon instituted.

Business Organization. Forms of **partnership,** family and non-family, had developed in the Middle Ages and were continued into the modern period. So too was the **regulated company**—an association of merchants created to monopolize and exploit some branch of trade. It received its charter from the government. Each associated merchant worked as an individual entrepreneur but contributed to a common treasury to finance a central body which maintained foreign trade centers, gave protection to the membership and laid down the rules for the proper conduct of business.

But the most modern of the forms developed in this period was the **joint stock company.** The others were a union of persons; this was a union of capital. A number of investors put their money into a venture and then chose a board of directors to conduct the venture; they then shared the profits and the risks.

When joint stock companies came to be linked to regulated companies, they were called **chartered commercial companies.** A good example of one such was the famous English **East India Company.** Its capital was derived from shareholders but it did more than engage in commercial ventures. Its charter granted it monopoly rights to trade anywhere in the Pacific and Indian Oceans; to buy land in unlimited quantity; to deal with foreign potentates; to wage war and to make peace treaties. With these freedoms permitted to it, chartered companies began to colonize the world on behalf of the mother country.

DISCOVERY AND COLONIZATION

Colonization was first attempted, unsuccessfully, by the Crusaders. The germ of the colonial concept was also present in the trading posts which were set up in Europe and the Near East by the Venetians and the Hanseatic League in the 13th and 14th centuries. But these ventures were in relatively settled and civilized areas. Modern colonization began when a vast new world of either sparsely settled or barbarous regions were suddenly discovered, explored and found more than useful. The first burst of such exploration and discovery came in the half century between 1450 and 1500. Why at that time?

Causes. Many factors combined to produce the burst of overseas exploration in 1450-1500. Nations along the Atlantic coast were growing desperate for gold and silver with which to offset the unfavorable balance of trade with the Near East. They resented more and more bitterly the stranglehold which the free cities of Italy had upon that area and upon the Mediterranean Sea. Momentarily the Italian monopoly had been threatened when the Ottoman Turks in 1453 had captured Constantinople and overthrown the Byzantine Empire. (Indeed, they had advanced deep into Europe itself and had overrun Serbia, Wallachia, Bosnia and Greece.) The Turks, however, anxious to keep the favorable balance of trade with Western Europe, had renewed Venice's privileges in the Near East. Even had there not been this political domination of the Near East, the price of Far Eastern commodities was extremely high since the price reflected the great distances by sea and overland that the goods had to come, the tariff that had to be paid en route, the brigandage that lined the whole trade route, etc. It was clear to thoughtful merchants that there was but one answer to this distressing problem: some all-water route to the Far East—either around Africa or by a westward sailing.

Successes. MARCO POLO and other travelers had returned to Europe with the news that Far Eastern lands were washed by some mighty water. Why could it not be the same mighty water that washed the Atlantic shores of Europe? Europeans became convinced that it was and began the systematic conquest of this water—which held so many terrors for the uninformed.

By 1450 improvements in seafaring were far advanced. The magnetic compass was in general use; the astrolabe to measure latitude out at sea was perfected; new scientific maps were in circulation; shipbuilding had advanced toward larger and more powerful vessels. With the invention by JOHANN GUTENBERG of the printing press, geographical, maritime and astronomical information was diffused over wide areas. In particular it became better and better known that the earth was a sphere and that one could reach east by sailing west.

Southward and westward sailing were in the minds of many men by 1450. National states were well advanced by that time and the monarchs hungered for more revenue with which to counter the feudal nobility; dispossessed nobles hungered for a new chance to recoup their fortunes. Individuals stirred by the Renaissance stress on man sought new adventures and new glories. Men looked to Africa and to the Far East as vast potential fields of conquest.

Now Europe needed bold and fearless navigators to try the dangers of the unknown sea. One who did not fear the sea was Prince HENRY THE NAVIGATOR, son of King John I of Portugal. Motivated by a zealot's hatred for the Moslems and a desire to conquer them by outflanking them in the south of Africa, Henry organized a navigational center on the southern tip of Portugal facing the Atlantic. Here captains were trained in the making of maps, the reading of them, the use of navigational instruments, etc.

Their training completed, Portuguese navigators began to edge cautiously down the western coast of Africa. In 1488 (twenty years after Henry's death) BARTHOLOMEW DIAZ reached the Cape of Good Hope. Ten years later VASCO DA GAMA sailed around Africa to India. The southward route had been breached. Six years before da Gama's feat, however, the Western route was opened by the world-shaking voyage of CHRISTOPHER COLUMBUS (1492). Some years had to pass before Europeans came to realize that Columbus had discovered a huge continent that blocked the way to the Far East. The first to see the ocean on the other side of the New World was VASCO NUNEZ DE BALBOA; and the first to circumnavigate the globe by sailing westward was FERDINAND MAGELLAN and his crew (Magellan having been killed in the Philippines). By 1522 the Mediterranean Sea route to the luxury items of the Far East had been circumvented in two directions. Hegemony over Far Eastern Trade now passed to the nations on the Atlantic shores. The Commercial Revolution was complete.

THE RESULTS OF
THE COMMERCIAL REVOLUTION

Spain. From the outset the nations who succeeded in discovering and exploring new lands were intent upon their conquest. This led immediately to rivalry between Spain and Portugal over division of the spoils of discovery. To prevent bloodshedding, Pope Alexander VI in the Treaty of Tordesillas divided up all discovered lands between Spain and Portugal. To Spain went those lands that lay 370 degrees west of the Cape Verde Islands; to Portugal, the remainder.

Spain promptly began to subdue the lands awarded her. From the mainland there streamed a small army of *conquistadores* (conquerors) and missionaries taking over for themselves backward areas—in the name of Spain. Ponce de Leon (1513), Balboa (1513), Herman Cortes (1519), Ferdinand Magellan (1521), Francisco Pizarro (1531), Hernan de Soto (1541), Francisco Vasquez de Coronado (1550)—conquered for Spain the Floridas, Central America, Mexico, the Philippines, Peru, the Mississippi Valley and the United States Southwest. These became jumping-off places for the eventual conquest of all of South America except Brazil, all of Central America, most of the West Indies and most of the United States west of the Mississippi River. In control of the largest territorial empire the world had yet known, the Spaniards should have emerged as Europe's greatest power. This did not happen.

The reasons for Spain's failure to capitalize on her conquests were many. Spain failed to build up in her country a thriving middle class that could make effective use of the inpouring capital; instead it was frittered away in high living by generations of spoiled nobility. The expulsion from Spain of the Jews in 1492 had removed a thriving and progressive group that might have given Spain leadership in this direction. When the flow of gold and silver bullion from the colonies diminished, the Spanish economy collapsed. In spite of government aid to commercial ventures, most of them failed in competition with those of other nations. Spain did make an effort to centralize control of her colonial possessions in the hope of promoting settlement overseas. This did not result because of restrictions placed upon free trading, because settlement was limited to Roman Catholics and because the Spanish government was too weak and corrupt to protect settlers from foreign powers.

England particularly invaded Spanish domains and without much check after the defeat of the Spanish Armada in 1588. In spite of these many defeats, the Spaniards retained their empire well into the nineteenth century when the revolutions led by SIMON BOLIVAR freed most of South and Central America and when the United States forced her to give up her territories either by sale or war.

Portugal. In the New World Portugal was able to colonize only Brazil. But she did capitalize upon being the first to round the Cape of Good Hope and soon built up a vast empire that included territories in Africa, India, China, Japan, the Malayan Archipelago and East Indies. Through control of native rulers, Portugal established a virtual—but temporary—monopoly of the trade of the Far East. Her downfall came as a result of invasion of Portugal by the Spanish King Philip II in 1581.

Spain held Portugal for sixty years in the course of which Portuguese commerce declined to a vanishing point. Spanish rule was partly to blame. Other reasons, however, were that Portugal, with a population of only two million, had neither the wealth nor strength to rule an empire numbering hundreds of millions; the wealth that poured into Portugal created a devastating inflation; she found it difficult to dispose of her goods profitably; and unlike Spain the Portuguese never developed effective centralized administration of the empire. Dutch, French and British companies—well armed and well financed—tore the Portuguese empire to shreds. Portugal managed to retain Angola and Mozambique in Africa, Brazil until 1822 and Goa and Pondicherry in India.

The Dutch. Dutch commercial prosperity began when Holland successfully won her independence from Spain (1566-1609). As part of her war on Philip II, the Dutch, in 1596, seized the East Indies from the Portuguese. **A Dutch East India Trading Company** organized in 1602 capitalized on this conquest and began to exploit the resources of Ceylon, Sumatra, the Spice Islands and Java. A **Dutch West Indies Company** hoped to duplicate this feat in the New World and managed to settle New Amsterdam there, as well as some of the West Indies and portions of Brazil.

In the early part of the 17th century, the Dutch were the greatest commercial power in Europe and Amsterdam became the financial center of the world. Dutch religious toleration had much to do with her success for it attracted the dissenting Christian and non-Christian middle classes from all countries to her land. But her success did not last because narrowly conceived mercantile policies discouraged settlement overseas; she, too, had too small a nation for so large an empire; and, finally, she lost to England in a series of wars that occurred late in the seventeenth century. She was able, however, to retain her possession of the "Dutch" East Indies until after the second World War when she had to succumb to the wave of nationalism that swept over the Far East at that time.

French. Not until midway in the 16th century did the French awaken to the possibilities of colonial expansion. They had been interested in the new world previously, but only for its fisheries. Under King Francis I (1515-1547) she underwent an awakening only to find the world outside Europe divided between Portugal and Spain. France began to send explorers and priests into the New World. GIOVANNI DE VERRAZANO, JACQUES CARTIER, SAMUEL DE CHAMPLAIN, ROBERT CHEVALIER DE LA SALLE, LOUIS JOLIET *and* JACQUES MARQUETTE gave to France its claims over Canada and the Mississippi Valley.

At a later time the French sought to establish control over India in the Far East. A French imperial empire did not result from these efforts. Very severe government restrictions on free enterprise and trade in the New World, a prohibition upon all but Catholics to settle there, failure of the government to give support to its settlers and the bitter hostility of the British to all French moves in the colonial empire led to the collapse of all her ambitions overseas in the 18th century. In the nineteenth century these ambitions revived.

England. The victor in this first modern race for imperialist power was England. England, too, was indignant at Pope Alexander VI's arbitrary assignment of the world to Spain and Portugal and in 1497 defied the papal decree by sending JOHN CABOT (an Italian) on an exploratory mission. Cabot established England's claim to the northeastern part of North America. At this time England was not interested in the conquest of New World territory; what she sought was a **northwest passage** through the New World. In the course of this search, Martin Frobisher, John Davis, Henry Hudson, William Baffin, and others, extended England's claims to Canada and the territorial United States.

More important even than finding a passage, was the need to reduce Spanish power, particularly after Henry VIII led England out of the fold of the Roman Catholic Church. One effective way was to attack Spanish merchant ships. This was done by a remarkable group of "Sea-Dogs"—legalized pirates —(e.g., SIR JOHN HAWKINS, SIR FRANCIS DRAKE) who were granted the right to prey on Spanish commerce. They traded with forbidden areas and "highjacked" Spanish gold-carrying galleons on the high seas; for which they were knighted by Queen Elizabeth. Spain had to retaliate to survive; she built her awesome armada; and in 1588 it was destroyed by the smaller, swifter, more maneuverable English fleet. This was the turning point in English maritime and colonial history for now she became interested in securing colonies all over the world.

Her success was phenomenal. After failures by Sir Humphrey Gilbert and Sir Walter Raleigh, she made a successful settlement of the territory of the United States at **Jamestown** in 1607 and before long had established thirteen colonies along the coast. Defeat of the Dutch in three wars (1652-1654, 1664-1666, 1672-1674) brought her great possessions in the Far East as well as additional territory in the New World. Her crowning achievement, however, was the defeat of the French in the **Seven Years War** (1756-1763) as a result of which she secured possession of all of Canada and India. Meanwhile she occupied many islands in all the seas to serve as naval bases for ships en route to her far-flung possessions. Why was England so successful where the others failed?

The answer would seem to lie in the fact that Englishmen were willing to go overseas in large numbers and settle the conquered territories. No religious bars were placed on settlers; settlers took with them the "rights of Englishmen"—that is, the basic freedoms; the English government fostered free enterprise within mercantile restrictions; considerable local autonomy was permitted overseas settlers; the government took a direct interest in the defense of her settlers against hostile native or foreign powers. Above all, England established and maintained herself as "mistress of the seas."

The Mercantilist System. A second major result of the Commercial Revolution was the growth and development of the system of **mercantilism**. Mercantilism was both a theory and a practice. Its theory stemmed from the belief that a country's wealth depended upon the amount of gold and silver bullion in its possession. How can a country increase its supply of bullion? It can steal it from others (Humphrey, Drake); it can occupy backward areas, mine precious metals; or it can accumulate it by maintaining a favorable balance of trade since the balance of payments would have to be made in gold or silver. The slogan became: "Encourage exports, discourage imports."

What mercantilism was in practice can be seen with great clarity in the work of JEAN BAPTISTE COLBERT (1619-1683), Louis XIV's finance minister. Colbert first set the French national house in order; he cut government costs, simplified its financial structure and then filled its coffers by increased direct and indirect taxation. With finances on hand to support his projects, Colbert now proceeded to create great mercantile monopolies or trading organizations (an East Indies Company and a West Indies Company) to capture the world's markets. To increase France's ability to sell, he built model factories with state funds and encouraged productivity by subsidy, internal improvements (roads, canals, etc.). To discourage imports (the spending of any money overseas) he placed a high protective tariff on all incoming goods, constructed a merchant marine and fostered colonization in backward areas to discover cheap sources of raw materials. Had these practices succeeded, no gold would have left France while from purchases abroad gold would have poured into France. The theory was admirable but it did not work out in practice—it proved immensely expensive and wasteful, and resulted in a stagnation of the economy.

Economic Consequences. As a result of the Commercial Revolution commerce became worldwide. The Mediterranean Sea shrank in importance as a commercial lane and doomed both Italy and Turkey to role of second-rate commercial powers. The Baltic Sea—second only to the Mediterranean in late medieval commercial importance—declined and brought down with it the economic power of the Germanies, the Scandinavian countries and Russia. Commercial power now rested with the states bordering the Atlantic Ocean and in their great port-cities.

Changes in the types of commerce followed. With open-sea passage to the Far East, silks, spices, etc., ceased to be luxuries and became staples of commerce; their prices declined drastically. New products like indigo, china, porcelain, cocoa, tea, coffee, cotton, dyewoods, and tobacco entered the trade stream. The slave trade, begun by the Portuguese and developed by the Dutch, grew in importance.

An interchange of domestic animals, fruit trees and vegetable seeds was now begun. Diffusion of manufactured goods was equally widespread, making for greater abundance and variety.

The influx of gold into Europe resulting from discovery of mines overseas had very important consequences. A price revolution occurred in the form of inflation; in a hundred years prices nearly tripled; wages rose too but lagged behind prices. Many dislocations accompanied the steady rise of prices: landlords raised rents; landowners began intensive cultivation to get more grain per acre; where small landowners could not do this they were forced to sell their properties to the new middle class; lag between wages and prices created the severest hardships for laborers and considerably increased their discontent.

While farmers and laborers suffered as a result of price rises, manufacturing groups benefited in many ways. They paid relatively less in wages and secured the benefits of price increases. Manufacturers benefited too from the fact that the influx of coin provided the base for a tremendous credit expansion. Obviously, the middle classes were in the ascendant.

Political, Social and Cultural Consequences. By means of the Commercial Revolution the kings in the Atlantic states were able to establish themselves absolutely. They either destroyed the feudal nobility and created a new nobility from the middle classes, or they reduced the feudal nobility to a parasitic class which danced attendance upon the king at his beck and call. With increased funds they built up war-machines based on professional standing armies and used these armies to increase their national domains. They fostered the arts for the purpose of increasing their prestige or defending their claim to rule by divine-right. In all of these activities they leaned heavily upon the support of the middle class, which supported the monarchs at this time because they felt that their chief enemies were the feudal nobility and the Church; these were the enemies of the royal power, too. (They were to shift their allegiance, however, when the royal authority later turned against them.)

It was, of course, the middle class that sparked and dominated the Commercial Revolution. Their money was invested in the joint stock and regulated companies which engaged in most of the overseas commercial ventures; their money created the bank credit that lay at the base of all commercial expansion. As a result, they became self-reliant, highly individualistic men of wealth and leisure, urbane and secular-minded. To build their prestige they placed their power behind the wave of new learning and new art that made up the Renaissance; they became patrons of literature and the arts. In particular, they sponsored literary artists whose writings attacked such churchly notions as running a business *for the benefit of the entire Christian community*, charging a *just price*, avoiding usury, refraining from monopolistic and over-competitive practices and the like; it was precisely the engagement in these practices that had made them a powerful class.

It should not be surprising, therefore, to learn that it was large groups of the middle class that sponsored the rise of Protestantism, which gave some ideological support to money-making activities and did not identify such activities with sinful behavior. Finally, feeling that its new position entitled it to some voice in political affairs, the middle class gave active allegiance to the parliaments that had developed in the medieval era. Through these bodies they were able to exercise some check upon the arbitrariness of royal rule.

CHAPTER THIRTEEN

THE RENAISSANCE

WHAT WAS THE RENAISSANCE?

For many years historians took their understanding of the historical period known as the **Renaissance** from a book written by the great Swiss historian, JACOB BURCKHARDT—*The Civilization of the Renaissance in Italy*. According to Burckhardt, the Renaissance was a spontaneous creation of the Italian people in the fifteenth century (the quattrocento); it was something new that had no roots in the past. From nowhere came a new birth of individuality; from nowhere, an outburst of genius that took the forms of great art and literature. Several concepts distorted Burckhardt's view of the Renaissance: he was primarily concerned with culture and ideas; he, therefore, paid insufficient attention to other factors—religious, political, social or economic; he believed in the "great man theory of history" which blinded him to large movements involving lesser people. In spite of these weaknesses, Burckhardt's study remains a major classic of historical research.

Historians still do not agree on all that the Renaissance was, but most will accept the statement that it was not a "rebirth" so much as a **transitional period between medieval and modern times.** As a transitional period the roots of the Renaissance derive from the medieval outlook; its tentacles stretch toward the dawning era of modern science; in itself it was neither medieval nor modern. Because it was an in-between period it was characterized by criticism of the *status quo*, by restless curiosity about all things, by the raising of questions rather than the answering of them. Such intellectual attitudes inevitably led the men of the Renaissance to place man himself under more intensive examination and it was out of this emphasis upon *man* that the distinctive features of the Renaissance emerged. In this matter, Burckhardt cannot be denied; the Renaissance did burst with creativity and the artists of that period were great men even if they were not the *sole* determinants of the course of history during the Renaissance.

Renaissance Versus Medievalism. There was much in medieval life that Renaissance men openly rejected or disagreed with. While medieval men revered some of the Greco-Roman classics, Renaissance men hailed them all, no matter how pagan, how un-Christian. They made war against medieval Latin and 14th century vernacular and sought to return to the "pure Latin" of Cicero—a virtually unknown tongue. They were optimistic, worldly, and individualistic. They rejected "Gothic" architecture as "barbaric"; they no longer gave unthinking credence to Ptolemaic astronomy which placed man at the center of the universe; they pursued knowledge for knowledge's sake without fearing for their faith; they mocked at chivalry, scholastic philosophy, medieval economics; in short, they affirmed life with enthusiasm and joy.

Causes of the Renaissance. What forces accelerated this drive toward a "new birth?" Many of them lay in earlier developments: contact with Moslem and Byzantine civilizations; the Commercial Revolution with its interchange of goods and ideas; the new learning of the thirteenth century that flowered in scholasticism; the rise of national monarchies bolstered by the Bolognese revival of Roman law; the spread of universities; the near-scientific emphasis of the Nominalist movement within scholasticism; the growth of a wealthy, leisured middle-class seeking prestige as patrons of the arts. These might very well be designated **fundamental causes.** (It is worth re-emphasizing that most of these causes lay, chronologically, *within* the medieval period.) For the more immediate causes, we must turn to the history of Italy in the fourteenth and fifteenth centuries.

THE ITALIAN RENAISSANCE

Political Background. As a result of the struggle between the popes and the Holy Roman Empire, Italy had been fragmented into a large number of independent city republics. Movements to unify the Italian peninsula had been thwarted by successive foreign invasions. Moreover, Guelph-Ghibelline factionalism inside each petty state and almost continuous feuding among the states kept all of Italy in a condition of disorder.

Political instability created the opportunity for powerful individuals and factions to establish themselves as rulers within the states. In this they were aided by the rise of bands of professional soldiers who sold their services to the highest bidders. Those who could afford to hire the mercenaries were the middle class who were reaping wealth from revived Mediterranean commerce. (In fact, most of the inter-state feuding was over trading centers, and trade routes.) To come to power, the ambitious middle class had to destroy the republican forms of government that existed in most of the independent city states. Murder and political assassination became commonplace.

By the 15th century, however, some degree of stability was introduced by a number of successful dictators who were able to keep the power of the state within their families for a number of generations. In Milan the VISCONTI family held power from 1311 to 1450; and then gave way to the family of SFORZA. Florence came under the domination of Italy's most brilliant family, the DE MEDICIS of whom Cosimo and Lorenzo "the Magnificent" were the most noteworthy. There were the DELLA SCALAS in Verona and Vicenza, the CARRARAS in Padua, the BORGIAS in Romagna and many others.

The situation in Venice was somewhat different. There the forms of the republic was retained but actual power was in the hands of a ruling oligarchy who controlled the Senate, the Grand Council and the Doge—a president elected for life. Significant political power was wielded by the Popes in the papal states. Once entrenched, these families began to extend their domains so that by the 16th century Italy had become unified to the extent that there were five powerful and enlarged states: the duchy of Milan, the republic of Venice, the republic of Florence, the kingdom of the Two Sicilies and the Papal States.

IDEAS OF THE RENAISSANCE

The rise of the Renaissance dictators was accompanied by a rationalization of their activities and behavior. One such rationalization was the ideal of *virtù*. A man was to be judged by the bravery and skill with which he achieved his personal goals and by the subtlety and finesse of the means he employed. In pursuit of virtù, conscience was irrelevant. So wrote MACHIAVELLI in *The Prince*.

Machiavellanism. Machiavelli wrote *The Prince* out of a deep sense of frustration with the political condition of Italy—its helplessness before the might of Spanish and French invaders, its lack of patriotism, its dependence upon mercenary soldiers, its state of warring disunity. His dream was of a unified Italy, completely sovereign, untrammeled by church, religion or morals, free to undertake whatever was necessary to bolster its unlimited sovereignty over the lives of its subjects. The end of unity could only be achieved by a patriotic and ruthless prince, possessed of virtù, who by craft and force would reduce the peninsula of Italy to a single sway.

Such a prince, thought Machiavelli, was CESARE BORGIA. Why was Cesare qualified? He took the world as it was and men for what they were—as motivated primarily by evil purposes. He therefore planned to make evil his ally. He did not scruple to break his word when his promise no longer served his purpose; he strove to make himself both loved and feared by giving the appearance of being virtuous but doing all the evil required to maintain himself in power. All means are justified, argued Machiavelli, that serve the end of attaining and retaining political power. Ruse, cunning, artifice, conspiracy—these were the methods of the prince with grandeur of soul, strength of body and mind. Poison to the prince were such Christian ideals as humility, lowliness and contempt of worldly objects.

Such goals were not confined during the Renaissance to princes alone. They can be seen operating in the interesting lives of such Renaissance figures as Pope Alexander Borgia, Machiavelli, himself, the utterly unscrupulous critic Pietro Aretino, the adventurer Castagno, the braggart Benvenuto Cellini and even in the youth of Leonardo da Vinci.

The Perfect Courtier. The ideal of the "very

perfect knight" of chivalry had decomposed by the time of the Renaissance; in its place appeared the ideal of the "very perfect gentleman." BALDASSARE CASTIGLIONE (1478-1529) established this ideal in his book *Il Cortigiano* (*The Courtier*). Who was the gentleman? He was born to a family of good manners or gentility, aristocrats in mind and body, standards and taste. In such an environment he would grow up skilled in sport and the use of arms, a graceful dancer and skilled musician, a master of several languages including Latin, familiar with great works of literature and art, and completely at ease in the company of accomplished women.

Women, said Castiglione, are a necessary part of the environment that makes the gentleman for they refine whatever brute instincts are the natural endowment of man. But women have to be trained in their role of complement to the gentleman and the first requirement was to be feminine in carriage, manners, speech and dress. To be the conversational equals of men, women, too, must undergo the studies that would provide them with ideas on literature, art and statecraft, with facility in many languages. Compared, then, with the medieval ideal of womankind, Renaissance woman was a real woman—rather than an ethereal ideal—and was celebrated as such in paintings of artists like Raphael and Andrea del Sarto both of whom used *live* models for their Madonnas. Gentlemen and gentlewomen, pursuing the ideal of *cortesia* (gentility) inevitably became patrons of the arts.

Art Patronage. Responding to the heightened interest in the remains of classical antiquity, the nobility and wealthy merchants began to collect antiques, to finance projects designed to spread classical, learning, and to give support to local, native artists who possessed unusual talent. The Medici, for example, built a museum for the study of antique art, financed diggings among Etruscan and Roman ruins, invited and supported artists like Bertoldo, Michelangelo, Leonardo and Verrochio to work in the museum on original projects. Lorenzo de Medici was himself exceptionally gifted as a poet and composer.

Artistic Individualism. While the artists appreciated these endowments and made much use of them, they resisted all efforts to form them into guilds or corporations so characteristic of the medieval outlook. The earliest of the great artists worked in guild workshops under the usual guild regulations and restrictions. Gradually the cult of individualism developed; artists of genius established themselves in individual studios and assumed an independent role. They still depended on commissions from the aristocracy and the church, but the subject matter and form of the art-work was to be exclusively their own. The result was that fine art was separated from the crafts; painting, sculpture and architecture became individual liberal arts, each with its own esthetic, or canons of taste and judgment.

As individual artists became recognized, there flocked about them groups of worshipping and imitating students. To bring some kind of order into art instruction, some of the masters began to organize art academies. From the art academies sprang the various schools of art which characterized the Renaissance.

RENAISSANCE PAINTING

Intimations of a change in the medieval mode of painting can be found in the works of CIMABUE (late 13th c.) who first attempted to put individual character into his figures, to give them more substance and to correct the perspective of their surroundings. Some of the faces in his pictures are almost portrait-like.

These trends become intensified in the works of GIOTTO during the *trecento* (1300's). Giotto's perspective is realistic and produces a feeling of depth; his coloring evokes feeling relevant to his theme; he strives not only for portraiture in his faces but for expression of feeling as well; he combines the masses in his pictures for purposes of dramatic composition.

In the 15th century (*quattrocento*) MASSACIO and others brought these trends to completion: the figures are all life-like and exactly proportioned; the perspective is exact; the composition takes on the form of a geometric design (an imitation of the Greek pedimental groups). In the workshop of ANDREA VERROCCHIO and that of DOMENICO GHIRLANDAIO Renaissance realism was brought to a great height. Students in these workshops studied anatomy, mathematics, color grinding and the making of plaster replicas from which to paint. Around these workshops gathered such luminaries as BOTTICELLI, the DELLA ROBBIAS, the SANGALLOS, DI CREDI, PERUGINO and DA VINCI.

Natural man in a natural environment, art as the **imitation of nature,** became the goals of these quattrocento painters. Exact rendering of muscles, draperies and rocks were achieved by direct copy; precise anatomy was combined with exact reproduction of the play of light and dark upon the flesh; new tactile values were achieved by introducing glazes of colors; the atmosphere was given an infinite recession by use of haze. This latter technique was fully exploited by Perugino and a new type of perspective—atmospheric—now appeared. Perugino made use of the fact that some colors recede through being "cold" while others approach through being "warm."

The center for these developments was in Florence and it was the **Florentine school of painting** that produced LEONARDO DA VINCI, MICHELANGELO and RAPHAEL. With technique mastered, these men began to express ideas through the medium of painting. In his earlier works Leonardo experimented with a form of perspective that brought the whole picture forward to a plane directly in front of the viewer, thus increasing attention on the activity within the picture; he also developed further the use of *chiaroscuro* (painting by means of light and dark). In his great works —*Virgin of the Rocks*, the *Last Supper*, the *Mona Lisa*—Leonardo showed mankind and nature in its universal aspects, its permanent features, its inner unities and outer passions.

Michelangelo removed nature from the center of attention and concentrated his gigantic energies upon man alone. In his decorations for the ceiling of the Sistine Chapel there are almost 350 human figures shown in every imaginable position, each a masterpiece in anatomical study, each a superb study in human vitality, creativity, mood and tension. The world surrounding man was tragic; but Michelangelo's men were endowed with the mental and moral power to wrestle with their fates —and to win over them. Thus did Michelangelo transform the Christian epic of Genesis into a pagan epic of man the Master. The work of Michelangelo is the supreme achievement of **Renaissance humanism.** Less convinced that man's life was such an almighty mystery, and far less concerned over man's fate was Raphael. Raphael concentrated upon form and color and so produced great paintings of unperplexed Madonnas, among other subjects. (Botticelli's work, though having many of the characteristics of the Renaissance, were spiritually related to the Gothic, medieval past.)

The Venetian School of Painting. The Venetian school of painting was made distinguished by the work of such artists as the BELLINIS (father and son), MANTEGNA, GIORGIONE, TITIAN and TINTORETTO. These great artists began the tradition of painting on canvas, using brilliant mosaic color schemes and spreading the art of painting with oil and varnish, an art borrowed from the painters of Flanders. The Bellinis and their school exploited the lights from outside the canvas to brighten the tones of their pictures and began the practice of "pointillism" or painting by means of tiny spots of color. They also began the tradition of "Arcadian" paintings—romantic landscapes peopled with gods in contemporary dress. Mantegna experimented with perspective from many angles; Giorgione with composition in depth; Titian with asymmetrical compositions and daring colors. Tintoretto is one of the epoch's greatest masters.

RENAISSANCE SCULPTURE

In 1401, in Florence, a contest was held among sculptors for an assignment to work on the north doors of the Baptistry. Six sculptors were invited to compete; among them were BRUNELLESCHI and GHIBERTI. Brunelleschi's composition was the more medieval of the two. It concentrated upon the drama and significance of the Biblical theme—the "Sacrifice of Isaac," and was less concerned with naturalism, modelling and decoration. Ghiberti— who won the contest—produced a panel cast in a single mold, decorative, impersonal, statuesque, and in a high relief with a unified focus of interest.

DONATELLO applied the rules of Brunelleschi and Ghiberti to single figures and faces in the field of monumental sculpture. Departing from classical standards, Donatello gave life to the figure, movement even underneath drapes, and above all, a sense of realism. LUCCA DELLA ROBBIA infused his classical subjects with lightness and grace; VERROCHIO experimented with action-tensions and lights and shadows. But, as in painting, sculpture reached its height in such works of Michelangelo as his *Moses*, the *Bound Slave*, the *Pieta*, *Dawn* and *Sunset*.

RENAISSANCE ARCHITECTURE

Renaissance architects (Alberti, Brunelleschi, Manetti, Bramante and Michelangelo) returned to the Romans and the Romanesque for their basic forms and decorative motifs. They restored cornices, capitals, pilasters and made use of rusticated (rough on the outside) stone blocks. They made use of column and arch centered about a cruciform transept and nave preferring this-earthly horizontal lines to otherworldly verticals.

They had little sense for the functional in architecture and devoted their greatest energies to the problem of the façade—the outer face of the building. The problem of matching façade to dome agitated Rome early in the 16th century. The Church of St. Peter in Rome had been begun fifty years before and was incomplete. Numerous architects submitted plans and worked upon the problem of relating the great dome to the façade. The eventual solution was a compromise among the suggestions of Bramante, Raphael, Michelangelo and others. The pattern of the dome and façade of St. Peter's became the model for most of the governmental buildings of the western world.

RENAISSANCE LITERATURE

To the history of ideas the Renaissance thinkers brought the doctrines of **Humanism**, which developed from the labors of scholars in translating ancient classics from the Greek to Latin, teaching the methods of classical authors and restoring the monuments of classical antiquity. Out of this devotion to Greco-Roman civilization, appeared a new emphasis upon man as a rational being, capable of vital and creative joy in this life. Such an emphasis upon man compelled a reconsideration of medieval virtues and vices. In the life and writings of FRANCESCO PETRARCA (PETRACH) (1304-74) one can study the conflict that ensued when man first broke from the medieval mold.

Petrach devoted much of his life to the study of ancient Greek and Roman civilization. His "pagan" self was expressed in a series of love sonnets written to "Laura"; his "Christian" self appeared in a series of written dialogues he composed with St. Augustine as his companion.

Less concerned with his "Christian" self was GIOVANNI BOCCACCIO, also a dedicated classical scholar. Boccaccio's best known composition is the *Decameron*, a collection of brilliant, comic, satiric, and sometimes bawdy, tales.

THE DECLINE OF THE ITALIAN RENAISSANCE

The Renaissance movement in Italy came to an end about the middle of the 16th century. Political instability grew worse and at the same time the economic power of Italy was being steadily weakened. Following the "reformation" which resulted in Protestantism, there was a sharp Catholic reaction that effectively stifled expression of Renaissance attitudes.

The Renaissance was essentially an aristocratic movement, a movement that believed in a cultural aristocracy and fostered it. Its "humanism" was not humanitarianism; it was a very special kind of interest in man that Renaissance man reserved for himself. It was the Italian mob that permitted GIRALEMO SAVANAROLA to come to power in Florence. Savanarola was a preacher who, in 1494, began to frighten the citizenry with the wrath that would overtake them if they did not drive from Florence its pagan sinfulness. He became the virtual dictator of Florence. During the period of his rule luxury articles, books and paintings were condemned as immoral and consigned to flames. Eventually the pope himself destroyed Savanarola. But the "mad monk" was a harbinger of things to come.

THE SPREAD OF THE RENAISSANCE

Germany. The hold of Christianity upon the Germans was far too great to permit the humanistic and pagan elements of the Italian Renaissance to take root. The backwash of the secular revolution in Italy appeared in Germany as intensified criticism of the established church.

Painting and engraving advances did make their appearance in Germany in the work of two of the greatest of Renaissance painters—ALBRECHT DURER (1471-1528) and HANS HOLBEIN (1497-1534). Of the two, Holbein was the more secular-minded and devoted much of his matchless talent to portraiture. Both he and Durer, however, painted religious scenes which were startling in their realism and frightening in their somberness and gloom. Mention should also be made of GRUNEWALD whose color and audacious lighting foretold the coming of Baroque, and of CRANACH, a master of the undraped figure.

The Low Countries. In DESIDERIUS ERASMUS (1466-1536) of Holland the Renaissance produced its foremost scholar. He was a professional teacher and writer, familiar with both Latin and Greek, master of the classics in both those languages, and, from his reading of the classics, an admirer of naturalism, tolerance and humanitarianism. All about him Erasmus saw men steeped in ignorance, superstition, and he determined to lead them out of their darkness by the light of reason. Locating much of the ignorance of people as being within the Church, he subjected clerical practices to merciless criticism —though he emphatically refused to enlist in any crusade against the Church. In his *Praise of Folly* he lambasted theologians and monks for their scholasticism, their pedantry and their dogmatism. His program called for a return to a more apostolic form of Christian life. War, science and hate in any form also met with the sting of his criticism.

Flemish painting influenced—and was influenced by—the Italian Renaissance. Where the attention of the Italian painters was upon the classical, the aristocratic or the religious, that of the Flemish was upon the urban, the middle-class and the religious. The VAN EYCKS, MEMLING, and VAN DER WEYDEN achieved a brilliant realism especially in small details, vivid and glowing colors, and the discovery of oil as a painting medium. Somewhat later came PETER BREUGHEL. Departing from the middle-class traditions of his contemporaries, Breughel went into the countryside for his themes and painted humble peasants in their moments of humble glory. The Flemish flair for unashamed realism characterizes Breughel as it does the others.

France. France produced two great writers, true Renaissance figures, to match the achievement in the literary art of Erasmus—FRANCOIS RABELAIS (1490-1553) and MICHEL DE MONTAIGNE (1533-92). Believing it man's supreme obligation to "Do what thou wilt," Rabelais drew his great literary portraits of the two giants, Gargantua and Pantagruel, who did what they wanted. What these two giants wanted most was to subject convention to mockery and hilarity. In no work of literature is there such ridicule of the church, its scholasticism, its monkish practices, its dogma, its prohibitions, its ethics as in the work of Rabelais. Yet for all his fierce anti-clericalism and robust affirmation of the sensual pleasures, it is impossible to charge Rabelais (who was himself a former monk and who remained a "lay priest") with being anti-Christian.

Montaigne in his *Essays* reveals a wonderfully subtle mind which is also of a critical cast. Feeling that no truths were final, that belief and custom are relative to time and place, Montaigne preached a doctrine of no-belief. He advised, underneath his skepticism and cynicism, that men should drop their quarrels over the road to glory or to salvation, and begin to enjoy life to its fullest, exercising restraint only against overindulgence. Happiness is fortified by learning; and learning, by doubt. Accept the universe, stoically, for what it is, and let your neighbor do likewise for there is no cause worth burning a neighbor for. This wisdom is conveyed in one of literature's great prose styles.

England. The English Renaissance, which occurred during the reign of Queen Elizabeth in the 16th century, is one of the world's greatest literary ages. It had been heralded in the previous century by the works of Geoffrey Chaucer, author of the wonderful *Canterbury Tales*. Chaucer was influenced by both the substance and spirit of the Italian tale, with the result that his writings exhibit an earthy robustness within a Christian framework, and a respect for individual eccentricity.

After Chaucer, literary artists began to express mounting confidence in Man, in his power to reason and to interpret both himself and nature. Self-confidence helped to mature the English language which became a superb instrument for expression. Shakespeare culminated this movement—if not the entire Renaissance epoch; but other brilliant poets and dramatists—such as Edmund Spenser, Wyatt and Surrey, Sidney, Greene, Marlowe, Beaumont and Fletcher, Ben Jonson—added greatly to the greatness of the age.

England produced her own humanists as well. In THOMAS MORE she possessed the author of one of the world's most famous accounts of the ideal, "utopian" society, in his book *Utopia*. In More's imaginary perfect state there is no poverty, no oppression of man by man, no war, no disease; men work six hours a day, hold goods in common, devote their leisure to endless intellectual pursuits that make them tolerant, wise, brave and just; all creeds that accept God's existence and the immortality of the soul are welcome; etc. FRANCIS BACON imagined another such paradise in his *New Atlantis*.

The English theatre proved to be the natural locale for the expression of humanist sentiment. It was a link between the intellectual and the mass of people and thus kept the artist close to national rather than aristocratic sentiment. It had a long tradition through the development of Miracle and Mystery plays, plays which enabled the artist to teach through allegory and to combine philosophy with history. Since dramatists could use poetry, they had a medium which could fire the imagination. Excellent poetry can be declamatory, and the theatre served the art of declamation superbly. For these and other reasons the theatre attracted some of the most versatile pens in England. Of these the most versatile and profound was that of William Shakespeare.

Shakespeare's plays can be divided into histories, comedies and tragedies. The main themes of his history plays were the idea of kingship, the sin of rebelling against a king and the problems that arise when a king misgoverns. His purpose was often to hold up the past as a warning to the present; and he expressed the anxiety and the hope of an England ravaged by the civil War of the Roses, but coming to national unity and power.

While concerned with these themes, Shakespeare was centrally interested in man and man's fate. In his comedies, with their magnificent characters and rich inventiveness, and in the great tragedies of his "dark period," Shakespeare was concerned with the human scene and the human predicament and human greatness.

RENAISSANCE MUSIC

In the 15th and 16th centuries music became an independent fine art, developing to a high degree the polyphonic technique, of which the first masters were Flemish. Earliest of the Flemish polyphonists were JEAN OCKEGHEM (1430-1495) and JACOB OBRECHT 1430-1505).

Both technical virtuosity and expressiveness found their supreme expression in the work of JOSQUIN DES PREZ (1450-1521). Des Prez was master of every contrapuntal form and had a particular fondness for canonic imitations. But, all of his tricks of composition were subjugated to the overall design of the piece, a design based both on symmetry or arithmetic proportion and clarifying the words of the text. To achieve the latter, he employed meaningful melodic and harmonic accentuation, purity of cadence, and, always, balance of voices. Josquin's influence was spread widely as a result of music printing which began at the end of the fifteenth century.

The 16th Century. Secular music now became as important as sacred music, developing such forms as the madrigal and the chanson. Along with secular music, instrumental music came into its own during this century—music for the lute, the viol family and the first harpsichords.

Italy. 16th century Italian music was divided between a Roman and Venetian school. The Roman school, a school of sacred music, was dominated by PALESTRINA (1524-1594) whose *Improperia* (Reproaches) has been sung in the Sistine Chapel on every Good Friday since 1560. Palestrina's simple vocal style served the purposes of the church so well that it was given official approval by the Council of Trent (1545-1563). In Venice ADRIAN WILLAERT (c. 1550) and GIOVANNI GABRIELI (c. 1600) continued the high art of Josquin. Willaert began the practice of using a double-chorus and Gabrieli introduced the *concerto* style—a contrast of vocal and instrumental voices.

Germany. German music was also split into two schools—the Bavarian and Saxon. The giant of the Bavarian school was a pupil of Josquin, ORLANDUS DE LASSUS who composed over 2,000 masses, motets, magnificats, madrigals, villanellas, etc. The Saxon school was dominated by MARTIN LUTHER and the chorale (congregational hymn). Luther stressed the moral effects of music and so was worlds removed from the esthetic effects sought by Lassus.

England. English music lagged behind that of the continental states. When it arrived, its prevailing tone was secular and its most popular form was the madrigal. In twenty-five years forty collections of madrigals were composed by such outstanding composers as WILLIAM BYRD (c. 1600), THOMAS MORLEY, and JOHN WILBYE.

English madrigals were almost always set to descriptive words that were underlined by dissonant chords producing sad or joyous moods. England also produced the earliest keyboard music—music written for the virginal. Virginal composers liked dance movements and in an effort to enliven these they employed "variations" around a recurring bass figure known as the "ground bass."

It should be evident from this brief account that Renaissance music cannot in any way be neglected in an account of the magnificent achievements of the Renaissance.

CHAPTER FOURTEEN

THE PROTESTANT REFORMATION

FUNDAMENTAL CAUSES

Between 1517 and 1648 the "universality" of the Roman Catholic Church was shattered beyond repair. Roman Catholicism now had to share its leadership of Christians with a large number of national churches and private sects, each with its dogma, doctrine, ritual and sacramental acts. This momentous schism began as a reformation within the Roman Church but ended as a series of transformations outside it. The political, economic, social and cultural consequences of this schism in Christian thought and practice were explosive in the days of its origin and remain so in our own day, 300 years later. Reform movements within the Catholic fold had occurred previously, as we have seen; they were part of the evolution of the church's structure to meet changing social conditions. Why, then, should the reform inaugurated by MARTIN LUTHER have had such drastic consequences?

Church abuses. The number of church abuses had multiplied, but not significantly, over those that existed at the time of the Cluniac Reform. Many clergymen were ignorant and ineffective as priests; many led scandalous lives and in so doing broke their vows of poverty and chastity. The papal office was held by a number of Renaissance popes notorious for their loose and indulgent living and who were incredibly corrupt. They made a business out of the sale of religious offices and benefices; church offices and dispensations were placed on the auction block and those who won the bids and became church officers got their money back by charging outrageous fees for priestly services.

Still other venerated church practices were converted into profit-making enterprises. Two that figured largely in Luther's protest were the sale of relics and the sale of indulgences. Relics were objects believed to have been used by Christ, the Virgin and the saints and therefore possessed of miraculous power to cure the afflicted and to protect the threatened. Unrestrained and unreproved, relic-hawkers traveled through Europe selling unlimited quantities of holy splinters from the "true" cross or from the "bones" of saints. When the fantastic proportions reached by this traffic were exposed by the Humanists, a great revulsion followed. Even more controversy centered about the sale of indulgences.

An indulgence was a remission of all or part of the punishment for sinning in this life; it was effective in purgatory but not in hell. The practice was an ancient one and in the beginning granted after works of charity, fasting and the like. Church teaching held that Christ and the saints had accumulated a large "treasury of merit" while they were on earth; this treasury was deposited in heaven and the Pope, possessed of "the power of the keys and the authority to bind and loose," could draw upon the treasury to remit punishment both on earth and in purgatory. No indulgence was valid unless the recipient was truly contrite, confessed his sins and was absolved. Since canonical penalties often inflicted hardships and inequities upon helpless people, the church began the practice of commuting penalties into almsgiving. From almsgiving to the sale of indulgences was a natural step for the Renaissance popes who cared little for the spiritual significance of the indulgence and much for its possibilities for fund-raising. In fact, one of the popes turned over the traffic in indulgences to a

banking firm which collected one-third of the "take" as their share of the "profits." When exposed, this, too, caused great indignation among the faithful.

All these things had been before and had brought on reform movements; why should these series of abuses have brought on a schism? The reason must lie deeper. Old abuses gather new force when they occur in a changed environment.

Waves of Doctrine. Disgust with the Pope's exercise of temporal power had stirred JOHN WYCLIFFE (1324?-1384) to denounce it, and to follow this denunciation with demands that the Scriptures be elevated above papal power, and that the clergy be permitted to live secular lives (marriage, etc.) to reduce the amount of corruption that prevailed among them. He thought, too, that the Bible ought to be translated into the vernacular so that all who could would read it.

The fall of the papacy into the "Babylonian Exile" revived Wyclifism after it had been suppressed and found an eloquent spokesman and martyr in the person of JOHN HUS (1369-burned 1415). Humanism added to the amount, not the depth, of anti-clericalism for it did so from within the church. Valla, Mirandola, Lefevre, Colet, Reuchlin, von Hutten and Erasmus were merciless in their exposure of hair-splitting scholasticism, monkish practices of celibacy, poverty and obedience, church practices like worship of saints and relics, confession and absolution (on the ground that research did not reveal these practices among the first Christians). Humanists generally favored a return to a simpler form of Christian practice.

What the Humanists favored the Mystics in the Church (Thomas à Kempis, Meister Eckhart, Heinrich Suso, Johann Tauler, and others) practiced. In "imitation of Christ" they rejected mechanical schemes of salvation for more direct and personal ones. By contemplation, prayer and fasting they tried to come into direct communion with God without any intermediary—that is, without the church. These men were placing considerable reliance upon justification by faith alone and not upon St. James's doctrine of "good works." Emphasis upon man's corruptibility and his need of faith caused a revival of interest in the epistles of St. Paul; Jacques Le Fevre made a translation of them into Latin and John Colet delivered a popular series of lectures upon them. The very bases of church practice were being challenged.

Religion and Nationality. While the Church's power prevailed, criticism had, perforce, to be cautious; why did it suddenly become bold and clamorous? When church critics found secular powers to support them by force of arms, they ceased to be fearful and did not hesitate to draw the conclusions from their criticisms.

Everywhere in Europe, save Germany and Italy, new national states had arisen and were making a strong assertion of secular sovereignty. In France, by the Pragmatic Sanction of Bourges (1438) and the Concordat of Bologna (1516), the kings succeeded in winning for themselves the right to dictate ecclesiastical appointments, jurisdiction and tax levies; by the Statute of Provisors (1351, 1390) and the Statute of Praemunire (1353, 1390), the English kings had made a similar assertion; nor were the Spanish kings far behind the French and English in their demands. These gains against the church stimulated rather than appeased royal appetites. They eyed enviously the vast domains of the church; and they resented the flow out of their countries of vast sums collected by the church in the form of annates, "Peter's Pence," indulgence fees, church court fines, income from vacant benefices, fees for bestowing the pallium upon bishops, etc. They felt that every effort of the church to excommunicate or to interdict was a violation of their sovereignty; they even turned hostile eyes upon the presence in their lands of church courts sharing judicial power with royal courts.

The bourgeoisie (middle class) fully supported the kings, for different reasons. They viewed the vast church holdings as immobilized capital that, if freed, could be used as a base for a great credit expansion; and they bitterly resented being deprived of the fluid capital they had in the form of countless payments to the church. And, since the chief burden of payment fell upon the lowly backs of the peasantry, they, too, echoed the bitter resentment of the kings and the bourgeoisie.

In such an atmosphere, church abuses became the sparks of a revolutionary movement to transform the church. This movement found its voice in Martin Luther whose career is a clear illustration of the causes at work in the Protestant Reformation.

THE CAREER OF MARTIN LUTHER

The Germanies of Martin Luther's time (1483-1546) were hotbeds of anticlerical criticism. Because they were disunified, there was no strong royal power to check the church; the result was that church abuses were magnified in Germany tenfold. Constant protests by the German feudal lords brought no change in church practices. The times awaited the man, and the man was Martin Luther, born in Eisleben in 1483 of peasant-to-bourgeois parentage.

Historical interest in Luther begins with his seventeenth year when he entered the university at Erfurt. Here he studied theology and came under the influence of Okhamist thought, the wing of scholasticism that revived Nominalism in an attack upon the realism of St. Thomas Aquinas. He came in contact with Humanism through the work of Virgil, Cicero, Livy, Ovid, Plautus, Terence and Juvenal—but he did not become a Humanist. His training in Latin, however, stood him in good stead when he decided, later, to translate the Bible into German.

When Luther, at the end of his studies, decided to abandon the pursuit of law and to enter a monastery, his father opposed it bitterly. But some inner need impelled Luther to make this move. The monastery he joined was, significantly, the Augustinian Eremites in Erfurt. (Augustinianism, it will be recalled, placed its strongest emphasis upon man's corruptibility and his complete dependence upon God's grace for salvation.)

Luther proved to be an excellent, though troubled monk, for he could not shake off a feeling of uncertainty in the matter of salvation. He had tried to find relief in the sacraments, but these did not help him. Okham's philosophy brought him some comfort for it was Okham's position that God's existence could not be established (as Thomas had tried) by *reason*; He could only be known through *faith*. God was omnipotent will; the destiny of all men lay in His mind and hands. But try as he might to be perfect, as commanded, Luther did not feel he had won the divine grace necessary for salvation. Then, one day in 1512 or 1513, he was reflecting on the words of St. Paul's *Epistle to the Romans*: "For therein is the righteousness of God revealed from faith to faith: as it is written, the just shall live by faith."

These words brought him a vision of the way out of his disturbed state. By himself, a man can do nothing to win the merits of Christ's sacrifice which washes away the stain of guilt and corruption; striving by good works to be holy in the sight of God will not work; man is saved by *faith* alone, by his unconditional belief in God's love—and that alone. This was to become the Protestant principle of **justification by faith alone.** Conceived in 1513, it was not until 1517 that the radical implications of this position became revealed.

The Indulgence Controversy. In a bull of March 31, 1515, Pope Julius II announced extension of an indulgence for the purpose of completing

St. Peter's in Rome. Behind this announcement lay some exceedingly "shady" deals. Archbishop Albert was chief commissary in the disposal of the indulgences. Though only a youth of twenty-five Albert held *three* benefices—a double violation of canon law: holding of more than one benefice was illegal, and twenty-five was not a canonical age.

To commit these irregularities, Albert had secured special dispensation from Pope Leo X. Pope Leo X had granted dispensation because Albert had paid him 24,000 ducats and had guaranteed him the support of two imperial electors with an election of a Holy Roman Emperor due in the near future. To raise the money, Albert had borrowed from private bankers and to pay off this heavy obligation the extension of the indulgence was to be proclaimed. Half the income from the collections was to go to the pope, and Archbishop Albert and his bankers were to share the remainder.

The whole transaction was kept strictly secret. The terms of the indulgence were liberal: subscribers could name their confessors, the indulgence covered a wide range of cases of sinning, and there was assurance that after proper contrition and due confession full remission of the punishment for the sins would be granted. In Luther's province, a sub-commissariat was granted to John Tetzel, a Dominican prior of Leipzig. Tetzel's promotional activities were unrestrained: he exaggerated the value of the indulgence, he described luridly the anguish of souls in purgatory that could be rescued by purchase of an indulgence, and so on.

For four years (1513-1517) Luther had been convinced that no amount of good works, including the purchase of indulgences, would save sinful man. Tetzel's salesman tactics stirred him to great anger and on October 31, 1517 he nailed to the door of the castle church his historic **Ninety-Five Theses** against selling indulgences and invited all comers to debate with him.

No one responded; but the theses were printed and circulated and stirred considerable sensation in the area. Archbishop Albert, chagrined at the falling off of revenue, notified Pope Leo X of Luther's activities. Leo's response was that the *Theses* were composed by a "drunken German." Now Luther addressed a series of **Resolutions** to the Pope in which he advanced beyond the attack on the sale of indulgences to the assertion that faith predominates over priests in the search for salvation.

The papal curia was now stirred to action and condemned Luther. Luther answered by asserting that the church universal was *the body of the faithful in Christ* with Christ—not the pope—at its head. Luther was made bold in his position by the support given to him by the Saxon elector, Frederick the Wise. With Frederick behind him, Luther traveled to Augsburg to meet formal charges made against him by the papal curia. At the Augsburg meeting Luther added to his original position the statement that infallible authority lay with the Bible alone and that each believer could draw therefrom his own doctrine of salvation.

Luther got safely away from Augsburg. His fully heretical position was now exposed in his debate with Dr. John Eck, a theologian. Luther admitted openly to holding the condemned views of Wyclif and Hus. The papacy, he maintained, was a human not a divine institution and could and did err. On June 15, 1520, appeared the papal bull which condemned Luther as a heretic, gave him sixty-days to recant or suffer excommunication, and threatened any community that permitted Luther to preach with an interdict. On December 10th Luther solemnly committed the bull, a copy of the canon law and some other writings to the flames in a public square outside a gate of Wittenberg.

Between June and December 1520 Luther wrote three pamphlets which rallied secular support to his religious crusade. *An Open Letter to the Christian Nobility of the German Nation Concerning the Reform of the Christian State* denied all forms of papal or priestly supremacy, attacked bitterly all of the church abuses, and asserted the sovereignty of the secular over the spiritual in temporal affairs. *The Babylonian Captivity of the Church* attacked the sacramental system and claimed that only two sacraments, the Lord's Supper and baptism, were valid. *A Treatise on Christian Liberty* declared that all believers are priests and reiterated the doctrine of justification by faith alone.

The "Politicalization" of the Lutheran Revolt. In 1519 Charles V became Holy Roman Emperor. In 1521 he summoned Luther to recant before the Imperial Diet at Worms. Luther refused and was condemned as an outlaw. He was saved from destruction by the Elector of Saxony. While in protective custody Luther, assisted by his friend Philip Melanchthon (a humanist from the University of Wittenberg), formulated the Protestant doctrine. For transubstantiation, he substituted **consubstantiation**: the body and blood of Christ were really present in the Eucharist *along with* the bread and wine; German was substituted for Latin in the services; pope, archbishops, bishops and priests were eliminated; monasticism was abolished and clergy could marry; fasts, pilgrimages, etc. were discarded as inconsistent with the doctrine of justification by faith alone; **predestination** (God knows beforehand the fate of man) and the authority of the Scriptures were stressed. These concepts were given written form by Melanchthon in the **Augsburg Confession** of 1530.

While the church and its secular followers hesitated in their pursuit of the protected Luther, Ulrich von Hutten, a fierce Lutheran partisan, and Francis von Sickingen led the petty nobility in an assault upon the property of the archbishops and rich nobles. It was a desperate assault brought on by impoverishment caused by concentration of landed estates. They were crushed with difficulty in 1523.

A year later the lowest peasantry revolted. They were led by a religious sect called **Anabaptists.** Luther had said that each man can find his own road to salvation through faith and Scriptures. Anabaptism represented extreme individualism in religion: no clergy at all, continuous revelation by God to individuals who had the "inner light," literal interpretation of the Bible, millenialism (the immediacy of the Second Coming and Last Judgment). Belief in religious individualism led them to belief in destruction of all rank and class and thus to a form of "communism." Anabaptists would not pay taxes, serve in armies, take oaths and the like. Their immediate grievances flowed from the dissolution of the old village system caused by the decline of serfdom and the rise of employment for wages. Under THEODORE MUNZER they turned loose their fury into murder, robbery, pillage of ecclesiastical and baronial estates.

In a pamphlet *Against the Thievish, Murderous Hordes of Peasants* Luther himself called for their destruction by striking, strangling and stabbing in secret or in public. They were crushed in 1525 after a year of rebellion. Their violence became, strangely, an extreme pacifism and in more modern times eventuated in the sects of **Mennonites** and **Quakers.** Both of these revolts, however, had taken the pressure off Luther and ensured that his doctrine would survive and spread. Somewhat later, Lutheranism became the official religion of Denmark, Norway and Sweden.

THE SPREAD OF PROTESTANTISM

Switzerland. Switzerland was ripe for religious transformation in the 16th century. It had won its independence from the Hapsburgs (1499), had experienced the full impact of rising capitalism in towns like Zurich, Basel, Berne and Geneva, was thoroughly imbued with contempt for Catholic prohibitions on money-making, had encouraged Humanists to take refuge there from Catholic persecution and was outraged by papal financial exactions.

It was, however, divided into two camps: the Northern commercial cantons and the Southern agricultural ones. Religious reform took easily and rapidly in the North under the leadership of ULRICH ZWINGLI (1484-1531). Zwingli began his career as a reformer and Biblical Humanist. After a deep religious conversion in 1519 he began to preach these doctrines: original sin was not a fatal heritage and man was not thoroughly debased; the Eucharist was merely symbolic and memorial with nothing miraculous about it at all; the church was a *democratic* body of the faithful with Christ as head and Scriptures as law (congregationalism); priests could marry; images in church are forbidden by Scripture—only that literally ordained by the Bible was permitted. Zwingli's ideas lead to a civil war between North and South, and a compromise Peace of Kappel (1531) which permitted each of the cantons to choose its own faith.

Calvinism. Ten years later, JOHN CALVIN (1509-1564) began his rule of the city of Geneva. Church and state were merged into a theocracy; sovereignty rested with representative bodies of clergy: a Congregation or senate and Consistory or assembly. To the latter was assigned the regulation of public morals: every household was placed under inspection; there was to be no dancing, card-playing, theater; the Sabbath was rigidly enforced as was the practice of saying grace before meals; adulterers, "witches," blasphemers and heretics were treated as major criminals; punishment was by branding, flogging, stocks and hanging. What was the theological basis for this extreme puritanism?

Calvin was overwhelmed by a sense of God's omnipotence and man's impotence; man, he held, had been utterly corrupted by Adam's sin. Most men were doomed by their corruption to burn eternally in hell; only a few were "elected" to receive God's grace. Most important, the few who were elected had been *predestined* to election even before they were born. To Calvin, this followed logically from God's omniscience.

There was nothing man could do about his predestined fate. Nor was there any absolute knowledge of who were the chosen. There were simply signs, indications of who were the elect: they were men of strict rectitude, evident moral character, who openly did God's work through study of His Scripture and policing of sinners. Any Calvinist who felt himself among the elect, strove with might and main to deserve his good fortune. Calvinism, thus, was Old Testamentary rather than New, stressed the overpowering omnipotence of God, His Law over His Mercy, outward observance rather than inner assurance. By stressing thrift and hard work, Calvin gave some theological support to the economics of the middle class. Finally, by eliminating all vestiges of a priesthood and making the congregation of the "elect" the sovereign body of the state, Calvin gave a tremendous impetus to the growing historical force of **republicanism** (albeit, in a theocratic form).

In spite of its severity, Calvinism appealed to many intellectuals in many lands. The Calvinists of Geneva soon spread their gospel abroad to influence the **Huguenots** in France, the **Puritans** in England, the **Presbyterians** of Scotland and the **Dutch Reformed Church** in Holland. Through emigration of these Protestants to America, Calvinism became a decisive force in shaping the American heritage.

England. On the European continent, Protestantism rose from below to involve the reigning monarchs; in England it came from the monarchy itself. Church abuses, royal envy of ecclesiastical power, widespread Humanism, Wyclifism and Lutheranism —all had prepared the groundwork for the decisive break with Rome made by the Tudor King HENRY VIII. The immediate cause for the break between Henry and Pope Clement VII was Henry's preference for more than one wife.

Papal delays and Henry's hunger for the church's wealth produced a series of enactments which created an **Anglican Church** fully independent of Rome with the English Monarch at its head. Monasteries were dissolved and their wealth confiscated and seized. In 1539 Parliament passed the **Six Articles** which formulated the Anglican creed: in essence, it made the Anglican an established (state) church; but it retained almost all of the Roman Catholic practices—confession, baptism, masses for the dead, an ordained priesthood, the Eucharist, etc.

While all Protestants welcomed the break with Rome, some were decidedly unhappy with the "orthodox" character of the church established by the Six Articles. During the reign of Edward VI (1547-1553) Protestants were in control of the English government and made drastic revisions in the Anglican church: marriage was permitted for priests, English took the place of Latin in church services; the use of images was abolished; and all of the sacraments but baptism and the Eucharist were abolished. Justification by faith became the official dogma.

Queen Mary (1553-1558) attempted to restore Catholicism completely. She even went so far as to marry Philip II, the Catholic king of Spain and an arch-enemy of the English nation. National feeling against Spain was Mary's undoing and spelled the final defeat of efforts to restore England to Catholicism.

Under Queen Elizabeth I, England took the path of nationalism and Protestantism. An Act of Supremacy (1559) made the monarch the head of the church; an Act of Uniformity (1559) established a Prayer Book printed in English as the basis of worship, greatly simplified the forms of worship, adopted a symbolic interpretation of the Lord's Supper; and final form was given to the creed of the Anglican Church in the **Thirty-Nine Articles** (ca. 1570). As finally formulated, the creed proved quite elastic and open to interpretation. It permitted membership in one church of "high-church" or Anglo-Catholics (who differ from Roman Catholicism only in rejecting the authority of the Pope) and "low-church" Anglicans who were authentic Protestants.

Scotland meanwhile, under the leadership of JOHN KNOX, took the path of Presbyterianism (Calvinism); Ireland remained Roman Catholic. Needless to say, religious issues agitated English political life for many years to come, until, in fact, religious toleration was enacted in the 19th century.

THE CATHOLIC REFORMATION

Even before the decisive Protestant break with Rome, efforts were being made to reform the abuses in the life of the clergy. Unlawful practices were severely punished, unworthy churchmen were dismissed. After the Reformation launched by the Protestants, a number of Popes (notably Paul III, Paul IV, Pius V and Sixtus V—1534-1590 inclusively) began to purify papal practices. Vicious practices were checked, papal finances reorganized and high offices filled with conscientious priests.

As a result of the activities by these Popes, the **Council of Trent** was held (1545-1563). All of the church's doctrines were submitted to the council for review and all were upheld—the Trinity, good works, the sacraments, apostolic succession, the theology of Aquinas, etc. The sale of indulgences was prohibited, plurality of benefices was illegalized, theological seminaries were created in every diocese to raise clerical literacy, an Index was set up to condemn forbidden writings. The reform, among its other effects, gave rise to a new order, **The Society of Jesus,** founded by IGNATIUS LOYOLA.

The Jesuits. Loyola was concerned to return Catholicism to an ascetic path and wrote a book of *Spiritual Exercises* as a guide to this path. The four parts of these exercises were related to the doctrines and ideas of sin, the incarnation and Christ's mission as Savior, the sacrifice on Calvary and the resurrection and ascension. For the practitioner, this meant four steps of instruction—the didactive (or getting the facts), the purgative (or eliminating earthly desires), the illuminative (or acquiring the mystical truth) and the unitive (or joy in God). Loyola's *Exercises* became an important means of winning followers to his proposed order.

In 1540 the order was granted official status. The spiritual exercises and a novitiate of two years was required before one could enter the order. Those accepted then took the vows of poverty, celibacy and obedience. The more able were trained to become masters of theology. After twelve years of study they were ordained priests.

The Jesuits became the master-teachers of their age and obedient wariors for the faith. They conducted missionary activities in the four corners of the earth and founded seminaries and colleges; in Catholic countries they had a monopoly of all education and propaganda; and it was due to their activities that Spain, France, Italy, southern Germany and Poland remained within the Catholic fold and suffered no serious threat from Protestantism.

RESULTS OF THE REFORMATION

Negative Results. Europe was divided into a multitude of hostile sects that, within a short period, became warring sects. Germany endured the Schmalkaldic War (1546-47) when Charles V tried to force all his subjects in the vast Holy Roman Empire into the Roman Catholic faith. The emperor was able to compel a troubled acceptance which did not last. Renewed strife was temporarily settled by the Peace of Augsburg (1555).

By this Peace, each prince could determine the religion of his subjects. Lutherans and Catholics were not to war upon one another, neither were they to permit the existence of any other religion (Anabaptists, Calvinists, etc.) Secularized church property was to remain so, but there was to be no further secularization.

From 1555 to 1618 there was peace. Then the intolerant provisions of the Augsburg Peace, quarrels over secularized property and continued feudal feuds caused a renewal of war. A **Thirty Years War** was fought over the length and breadth of Germany (1618-48). It began when Bohemia, which was Calvinist, revolted against Ferdinand II, the Hapsburg ruler of the Holy Roman Empire. They were spurred to revolt by the German Protestants. The Spanish legions of the Holy Roman Emperor crushed the Bohemians and their German instigators. Christian IV, Lutheran King of Denmark, entered the fray on behalf of his co-religionists. He was defeated by the brilliant generalship of TILLY and WALLENSTEIN. (England had been lending money to the Protestant forces.)

The Protestants defeated, Ferdinand issued an Edict of Restitution which gave back to the church all the lands it had lost since the Peace of Augsburg. The Catholics now began to quarrel over a division of the spoils and this gave Gustavus of Sweden an opportunity to enter the conflict. In an epochal battle at Lutzen (1632) Adolphus met Wallenstein and defeated him at the cost of his own life. With the Catholic Hapsburgs reeling, the Catholic CARDINAL RICHELIEU decided to enter the war for France *on the side of the Protestants.* Here, obviously, was no longer a religious war but a national and political one. This was confirmed by the **Treaty of Westphalia** which concluded the war and the provisions of which were:

—France secured Alsace and Metz, Toul and Verdun.
—Sweden got lands along the Baltic and North Sea coasts of Germany.
—Some German states increased their land holdings.
—The United Netherlands won its independence.
—The independence of the Swiss Confederation was given international recognition.

The religious provisions were:

—The Peace of Augsburg was re-confirmed, but Calvinism was given equal footing with Catholicism and Lutheranism—subject to local determination.
—Protestants won the right to share the rule of the Holy Roman Empire and to retain secularized lands.
—The restoration of Catholicism in Bohemia, Austria and Bavaria was confirmed.

Bitter religious war took place in France too; here it was between Catholic monarchs (Francis I, Henry II), Catherine de Medici, the Guise family and the Huguenots. A massacre of Protestants on St. **Bartholomew's Day** (August 24, 1572) was but one of many such bitter slaughters that featured the French religious wars. Eventually Henry IV brought the wars to an end with the **Edict of Nantes** (1598) by which the French Protestants won liberty of conscience and the right of *private* worship. In 200 specified towns they had the right of *public* worship. They were also granted civil and political rights and were permitted to fortify certain of their towns.

One of the most anguished of the religious wars occurred in the Netherlands. The Dutch provinces of the Netherlands became Calvinist and the Catholic Philip II of Spain determined to exterminate them. He sent the zealous Duke of Alva into the Netherlands with 10,000 troops and the Inquisition. Alva's savagery in suppressing the Dutch has become proverbial, as has the heroic resistance of the Dutch under the leadership of William the Silent. In 1609 the Protestants were able to establish an independent republic and to pave the way for the greatest period in Dutch history.

Bigotry. The religious wars released a wave of bigotry in Europe that was not repeated until Hitler took power in 1933. The Catholic Inquisition destroyed thousands of Protestants by fire; the Protestants, in turn, committed countless atrocities against the Catholics. Both Christian sects, moreover, turned their full fury against the Jews who were either slaughtered, driven into ghettoes or, as in Spain, driven wholesale from the country after centuries of living there.

Both Catholics and Protestants were hostile to the new science that was beginning to find advocates everywhere in Europe. In 1600 GIORDANO BRUNO—an advocate of the astronomy of Copernicus who denied the possibility of miracles—was burned at the stake by Catholics; and MICHAEL SERVETUS—who discovered the lesser circulation of the blood—was burned by Calvinists. Protestants made frontal attacks upon all rationalism and favored literal reading of the Bible as the only source of truth. Finally, art suffered at the hands of both because of its sensuous qualities. Michelangelo's titans were given breeches and skirts by more "moral" artists.

Positive Results. The cleavage in Christianity promoted religious freedom; for any of the sects to survive, some form of mutual toleration had to be established—and it was. Protestantism furthered belief in individualism; individualism, in turn, accelerated the expansion of popular education.

Protestantism hastened the growth of nationalism in the form of the national state. In the course of their struggles, Protestants supported both divine right kings and representative governments; but the direction of their political thought was toward the assertion of the supremacy of the state over the church.

Protestantism encouraged **the rise of capitalism.** They helped destroy the economic power of the medieval church, they disavowed the economic ethics of the medieval church fathers, they advocated thrift and investment.

Finally, insofar as Protestantism was an *intellectual* revolt and had to be met by a Catholic *intellectual* counter-attack, there was wide stimulus to thought in fields other than theological—e.g., in science, in politics, in history. Out of this independent thought was to come the **Enlightenment** of the 17th and 18th centuries.

CHAPTER FIFTEEN

ABSOLUTISM

BACKGROUNDS

Since the Reformation there had come gradually into being in Europe a number of **absolute monarchies.** Fact inspired theory and some thinkers attempted to justify this form of government on philosophical grounds. These thinkers proclaimed the doctrine that **the ruler of a state was bound neither by the laws of nature, nor by any kind** of moral or legal limitation. Here they followed the lead given by JEAN BODIN (1530-1596)—the first modern political scientist—who developed the concept of **sovereignty,** an absolute secular force which bound citizens and subjects to complete obedience.

Bodin did not locate the precise source of sovereignty and thinkers who followed him argued variously that it lay with the nation as a whole, with a ruling élite or aristocracy or with a "prince" or absolute monarch. The new nation-states of Europe seized on this idea in order to free themselves from all restraints by churchmen or nobility. Machiavelli's reasoning gave the rulers of the new nation-states a direction; but rationalization of their absolute powers came to its mature form in the speculations of THOMAS HOBBES (1588-1679).

"Leviathan." Hobbes defined his position in a number of writings, the chief of which, however, was the *Leviathan*. In the dim past, said Hobbes, sovereignty rested with all the people; it was then transferred to a ruler so that he might perform certain necessary functions. Why did this transfer have to take place? Because, argued Hobbes, people in a "state of nature" are "solitary, poor, nasty, brutish" and the like. They are engaged in perpetual strife. In this perpetual war there is no ethics, no standard of right or wrong, of justice or injustice, of private property rights.

There is, however, a rational side to man and this side of him drives him to seek peace, to place a voluntary curb on his impulses. Men set themselves into a harness of government and agree to a transfer of sovereignty—unlimited power to enforce peace, to wage war, to control expression of opinion, to protect property, etc. The ruler must, logically, be absolute in the exercise of these powers; if there were two or more rulers, anarchy would ensue.

James I (1566-1625). Hobbes was a thoroughgoing materialist. But absolutism could also be justified on theological grounds. Before he came to the throne of England, James I wrote *The True Law of Free Monarchy*. James rejected prevailing notions that kings derived their sovereign power from the people. Monarchy was established, argued James, by conquest and passed on through inheritance. Once established, the monarchy was sovereign in Bodin's sense of the term. The law of rightful succession was the only limit on the monarch's sovereignty. To oppose a monarch was illegal, contrary to human reason, to the law of God and of Scriptures. Monarchs are the "agents" of God upon earth. A wicked king is sent as a plague by God for the sins of the people. The King's will is God's will; a king, therefore, can do no wrong when he rules by **divine right.**

SPANISH ABSOLUTISM

Spain was the predominant power in Europe during the 16th century and possessed the resources necessary for establishing an absolutist rule over her subjects. Her army was formidable and had crushed the Moor. This act had made Spain the defender of Christendom. Her ports were crowded with boats hauling precious metals from the New World. Her rulers built an extravagant court that became the center of intrigue in Europe. Spanish intriguing was Machiavellian to the core and every device—military, diplomatic, dynastic, marital, financial—was employed without scruple to strengthen the monarchy at home and to spread its domain abroad. By calculated marriages Spain came into the possession of Hapsburg dominions in Austria, Hungary, and Germany; of Spanish possessions in Spain itself, in Italy and in the New World; of Burgundian possessions, particularly the wealthy Netherlands. Finally, in the persons of Charles V (Holy Roman Emperor)—(1516-1566)—and Philip II (1556-1598) Spain had two talented and devoted rulers. Yet, in spite of its strength, wealth, prestige, lack of scruple and leadership, Spain failed to establish a model of absolutist rule.

Spain's failure was due to her effort to perpetuate the medieval ideal of a united Christendom in an age of expanding nationalism. Her dominions were vast, but lacked unity. Her kings were mighty, but lacked the support of a firm middle-class organized in a national parliament. The power of the monarchs and their tremendous wealth were dissipated in efforts to hold their sprawling lands together and to offset attacks from the powers outside their control. English nationalism destroyed the "invincible" armada; the Dutch began a revolt from Spanish domination in 1568 and held out until victory in 1609; within a few years the Hapsburg wing of the Spanish kingdom was caught up in the center of the whirlpool of the Thirty Years War, a war that drained the Spanish treasury to the bottom and turned Spain into a third class power.

Moreover, Spanish fanaticism and traditionalism made her rulers blind to "modern" trends which were producing a vigorous middle-class. She had the foundations of such a class in the Jews and Christianized Moors within her realm. But her Inquisition-mentality led her to expel these vital elements, these artisans and financiers, and to place her reliance upon effete and corrupt nobility who sought to exploit rather than to build the nation.

During the eighteenth century Spain narrowly avoided being absorbed by France in the **War of the Spanish Succession;** she retained her independence as (virtually) a French satellite. Only her possessions in the New World and the Far East sustained her. When, during the nineteenth century these too were lost, Spain declined into a backward, poverty-stricken land which could not influence the course of world history.

FRENCH ABSOLUTISM

French monarchs in the 17th and 18th century had all of the guile of their Spanish neighbors, their corruptness, their love of power and ostentation. Yet they were able to create the model of absolute government, the classic pattern of it, where the Spaniards failed. The reason for their success was that they accepted and encouraged support of the "bourgeoisie"—the enterprising middle-class. This necessitated that they abandon fanaticism in religion since many of the middle-class had adopted the Protestant faith. In fact, when Henry IV, the first of the Bourbons, came to power in 1589 he was a practicing Huguenot. To secure power he abandoned his Protestantism; once in power he issued the **Edict of Nantes** (1598)—a broad act of tolerance granting religious freedom to both Catholics and Protestants. Having eliminated the burden of being a "defender of the faith," Henry and his "prime minister," MAXIMILIAN DE BETHUNE SULLY, were able to concentrate on forcing the nobility to submit to the royal authority.

Sully. Sully realized that in abandoning the support of the nobility he had to find a substitute in the bourgeoisie. Most of his policies were directed to this end. In reforming the administration of the government he created a new nobility drawn from middle-class ranks, who served as administrators of the king's public and tax policies.

Sully overhauled the financial policies of the royal administration and began a strict system of accounting to improve efficiency. He fostered agriculture by reducing taxes on the peasantry, forbidding the seizure of agricultural tools in the payment of debts, draining marshlands, encouraging scientific tillage and permitting sales of foodstuffs abroad (to build up gold reserves).

Trade and industry also received his attention. New industries were introduced—silk, glass, carpet and leather; protective tariffs were levied; bounties and subsidies were generously granted; roads, canals and bridges were constructed; a merchant marine was built; and raw materials were sought by conquest of colonies overseas. Realizing, too, that France needed peace in this effort to build up her national resources, Sully fathered one of the earliest proposals for a "league of nations" which he called the "Grand Design."

Cardinal Richelieu (1585-1642). A religious fanatic assassinated Henry IV and the succession fell to a child who was named Louis XIII. The regency was in the hands of Marie de Medici, Henry's fanatic, narrow-minded, incompetent but ambitious wife. She almost dissipated all the gains made by Sully in establishing the absolutism of the French monarch by draining the treasury, repudiating the alliance with the bourgeoisie through the Estates General (called in 1614 and not thereafter until the revolutionary year of 1789) and pursuing a pro-Spanish policy that would have reduced France to a second-rate role. In the course of her scheming she selected as an assistant ARMAND DE RICHELIEU, a bishop of the small diocese of Lucon. Richelieu proved to be more guileful, subtle and calculating than the queen-regent; eventually he had her exiled for opposing his policies.

These policies had two objectives: to make the royal power supreme in France and to make France supreme in Europe. To these ends he crushed the Huguenots, not for their religious differences, but because they lived within France as a state within the state, as a potential source of national disunity. Richelieu reduced their power, but did not destroy or exile them since they constituted valuable middle-class support for his designs.

Catholic nobility was similarly reduced by Cardinal Richelieu's policy of destroying their fortified castles, uncovering their conspiracies through an effective system of spies and executing all who plotted against him. They were eliminated from the administrative structure and their places were given to civil servants drawn mostly from the middle-class, who were granted wide powers of taxation, police and justice.

In pursuit of his second aim, Richelieu strove to undermine the power of Catholic Spain and the Catholic Hapsburgs. This meant that he had to give financial and military support to the *Protestant* forces struggling against the Spanish-Hapsburg coalition. Thus, during the Thirty Years War, Richelieu supported the Protestant German Princes, Swedes and Dutch and, in fact, helped turn the tide in their favor. When he died, in 1642, the frivolous monarch Louis XIII was in fact absolute, and France had become a major power.

Jules Cardinal Mazarin (1602-1661). Louis XIII died a year after Richelieu and once again the crown passed to a child, Louis XIV. In charge of the king's government was CARDINAL MAZARIN, an Italian imported and trained by Richelieu as his successor.

Mazarin was a worthy successor and brought to

a completion Richelieu's foreign policy of reducing the power of the Spaniards and the Hapsburgs. In the **Treaty of Westphalia** concluding the Thirty Years War (1648) he secured from the Hapsburgs the cession of Alsace and other advantages; from the Spaniards he got Roussillon and a part of the Spanish Netherlands (modern Belgium). As a final coup, he forced the Hapsburgs to pledge their eldest daughter in marriage to Louis XIV—when, of course, he came of age.

Foreign difficulties were stabilized none too soon for in 1648 came the uprising of the **Fronde** (1648-1652), the last, desperate effort of the nobility to limit the absolute powers of the French monarchy. The nobility were able to rally to their support some middle-class elements, common people, clerics and lesser gentry—all of whom had accumulated grievances. The Fronde uprising was crushed and the absolute power of the monarch was established. The way was prepared for Louis XIV to say truthfully, *"L'Etat, c'est moi,"*—"I am the State."

The Age of Louis XIV. Absolutism reached its pinnacle in the reign of the "Grand Monarch," Louis XIV. BISHOP BOUSSET (1627-1704) stated cogently the case for Louis. Government, argued the Bishop, is divinely ordained as a natural form of organized political society; monarchy is the best of all governments. As a father rules his family, and the father's son rules his by succession, so with monarchs and the nation. The hereditary monarch is a sacred person for he is anointed by the church. As "father" of the people, his power is absolute and accountable to God alone. Against an evil king only prayer is effective. "As in God are united all perfection and every virtue, so all the powers of all the individuals in a community is united in the person of the king."

Louis undertook to complete the centralized administration begun by Richelieu and Mazarin. Ministries of finance, army, navy, public works, etc. were created and staffed by professional civil servants. These officials were stripped of all power to make decisions; all decisions were made by the king and carried out by his subordinates.

Art and literature were also centralized to serve the ends of royal absolutism. Resident at Versailles (the fabulous royal palace) were some of the nation's most gifted men—MANSART, architect of the palace, the Grand Trianon and the dome of the Invalides; GIRARDON, the sculptor; LE BRUN, the painter; LULLY, composer for opera and ballet; CORNEILLE, MOLIERE and RACINE, the great dramatists-poets; LA FONTAINE, fabulist; BOSSUET, philosopher and apologist. Together, these writers, composers, artists and architects made Versailles the cultural center of the world. The French language, French manners and French arts were to conquer Europe as Louis's armies could never do.

Colbertism. Even more than his predecessors Louis realized that he had to cement an alliance between the middle-class and the royal power. In JEAN BAPTISTE COLBERT (1619-1683) he found the perfect instrument for achieving this goal. Colbert was himself the son of a merchant and loyal to his group for he felt that the desires of the bourgeoisie were synonymous with the needs of France. He aimed therefore to reduce government expenditures by eliminating graft, introducing accurate bookkeeping and increasing the number of nobility on the tax rolls; to establish a system of mercantilism through protection, bounties, monopolies, colonies and favorable balances of trade; to open wider the lanes of communication through roads, canals, navies and merchant marine; to secure effective enforcement of mercantile regulations by reorganization of the courts and police administration.

Colbert further sought to bring the same bourgeois efficiency into military affairs and the result was that he introduced strict discipline, regimental differentiation and officer gradation; checked on all contracts; introduced new arms and tactics; and built the most formidable series of fortifications in Europe.

The Decline of French Absolutism. Power corrupts, said Lord Acton, and absolute power corrupts absolutely. There is no better way to explain the decline of French absolutism. Louis, for example, was not satisfied to pursue the century-old French foreign policy of checking Spanish and Hapsburg aggression; instead, he invented an aggressive policy of his own. Every nation, argued Louis, should make an effort to reach its "natural boundaries." (This doctrine was to be re-echoed in American history as the "doctrine of manifest destiny.") In the case of France, the natural boundaries were, apparently, the Pyrenees, the Alps, the Rhine River and the Atlantic Ocean. Determined to secure these for France, Louis waged three wars—the War against the Spanish Netherlands (1667-1668); the Dutch War (1672-1678) against Holland; and the Palatinate War (1689-1697) against a wide coalition made up of the princes of North Germany, Spain, Sweden and the Dutch Netherlands for control of the Rhineland.

Thirty years of war netted Louis Franche Comte and Strasbourg and the bitter enmity of all the

European powers. When, in the War of the Spanish Succession (1701-1713), he sought to annex Spain through a grandson, he was stopped by a coalition of English, Dutch, Austrians and Germans and in the **Treaty of Utrecht** (1713) he had to sit by without protest while Austria fattened on the Spanish Netherlands, Milan, Naples and Sardinia; and England annexed Newfoundland, Nova Scotia, Hudson Bay, Gibraltar, Minorca.

Failure abroad was accompanied by failures at home. The frivolities of Versailles swelled to an orgy of self-indulgence. Intrigue took the place of efficient administration and royal mistresses wielded the power of state ministers. The Catholic Church was bent to his will: Bossuet proved to Louis's satisfaction that the sovereignty of the king is independent of the pope; that a general clerical council is superior to the pope; that the pope could not abridge the privileges of the French church.

Louis then reversed the century-old practice of toleration of religious minorities. In 1685 he revoked the Edict of Nantes and persecuted both Protestants and Jansenists (a Catholic group who believed that beyond the sacraments a believer must experience a "conversion" to be saved). Moreover, increasingly he chose bishops from the ranks of corrupt nobles, thus undermining the integrity of the Catholic hierarchy and causing wide dissatisfaction among the people. Finally, war and regal extravagance drained the treasury and forced the king to increase the tax load on the peasantry. Louis's death in 1704 was celebrated widely throughout France.

Après Moi Le Déluge. Louis XV (1710-1774), great grandson of Louis XIV, was a tragic figure. He foresaw clearly what the fate of France would be if the policies of the Grand Monarch were continued. "After me" he predicted accurately, "comes the flood." It did, in the form of the French Revolution.

But he was unable to act on what he saw. He surrendered to every vice at Versailles. Mesdames Chateauroux, Pompadour and du Barry ruled France. Privileges were accorded the parasitic nobility while burdens were thrust on the peasantry and the bourgeoisie. In spite of approaching bankruptcy, France undertook to fight in two major wars—the War of the Austrian Succession and the Seven Years War. In the latter she suffered her worst defeat and lost all her possessions in Canada and India to England. When Louis XV died, France was already seriously weakened. Then came "Le Deluge."

PRUSSIAN ABSOLUTISM

The **Hohenzollern dynasty** which ruled in Prussia was active in European history from the 15th century onward but did not rise to prominence until the reign of FREDERICK WILLIAM (1640-1688), known as the "Great Elector." Frederick William was able to expand his kingdom by clever diplomacy and success at arms. He established the royal power on an absolutist basis and won common approval by tireless work in building up the economy of Prussia.

Under Frederick William I (his grandson) Prussia's reputation was enhanced. This Frederick William concentrated his energies in building up the famed Prussian army, a rigid military machine, superbly disciplined, professional, and governed by devoted General Staff. Some of the same energy was poured by Frederick into constructing a bureaucracy for administration, as disciplined, professional and devoted. Thus the mentality of the German people was shaped to complete obedience.

Frederick William I was succeeded in 1740 by Frederick II—"Frederick the Great." He won this title by his demonstrated abilities in the War of the Austrian Succession and the Seven Years War.

Mid-Eighteenth Century Wars. Frederick was determined to free Prussia from the control of the Austrian Hapsburgs. In the same year that Frederick became king, Maria Theresa succeeded to the Hapsburg crown. Frederick contracted with Bavaria and France to dismember Maria's kingdom (Prussia was to secure Silesia, France the Austrian Netherlands).

Maria rallied the rest of the Austrian empire to her cause. She found unexpected support, too, in England for at this time England was engaged in the "War of Jenkin's Ear" with France's Bourbon satellite Spain. From being a war over the "Austrian Succession" the conflict spread into a "world war" and was fought in Europe, India and America. It was fought to a stalemate and none of the powers made significant gains—except Frederick II, who retained his aggressively seized Silesia.

Stalemates are not conducive to peace. Three years after the "peace" settlement at Aix-la-Chapelle (1751) the conflict was renewed. But the sides shifted in what was to become a "diplomatic revolution." Austria and France realized that they had a common enemy in Frederick the Great and formed an alliance against him; Russia and Sweden joined them. England, her policy directed toward maintaining a "balance of power" on the continent and toward reducing France to a second-rate power, allied with Prussia. Once more it was Frederick who began the hostilities with an attempt to annex Saxony.

The Seven Years War also resulted in a stalemate in Europe and the Peace of Hubertusberg (1763) re-established the *status quo*. But Frederick had won for Prussia a status of equal rank among European powers. The chief sufferer in the Seven Years War was France. In the **Treaty of Paris** of 1763 England got Canada and all the land that France held near the Gulf of St. Lawrence and east of the Mississippi except New Orleans; all of the French West Indies and all of India except five trading posts which the French were permitted to retain.

Frederick II. In the two decades following the Seven Years War Frederick applied his absolutism to the reconstruction of the Prussian state. He encouraged immigration into Prussia by generous land allotments and travel subsidies; he reduced taxes on the Prussian landlords and then forced them to apply their gains to rebuilding farmhouses and farmlands; he reclaimed swampland and pioneered in the introduction of new crops such as the potato. Having strengthened agriculture, he instituted the practices of mercantilism to foster trade, commerce and manufacturing.

His absolutism—like that of Josephy II of Austria and Catherine the Great of Russia, his contemporaries—was decidedly "benevolent" in that it led to considerable economic gains for the mass of the citizenry. Frederick prided himself on being a philosopher, an accomplished musician, a patron of the arts; he promoted religious toleration and popular education. His concern for rational procedures led him to reform the entire Prussian administration of government and justice; and he succeeded in developing a sound economy.

But the base of Prussianism was still absolutism. Power flowed from a single source—Frederick—and no one dared oppose its course.

AUSTRIAN ABSOLUTISM

Not to be outdone by Frederick, Joseph II of Austria also pursued a course of paternal benevolence to his multinational subjects. In the course of his maturation, Joseph was inspired by the writings of the French *philosophes*. His mother, Maria Theresa, found these beliefs obnoxious and Joseph had to wait until her death in 1780 to make the transformation he sought in the Austrian kingdom.

Once in power, he abolished feudalism in Austria. The serfs were emancipated; feudal tenure was prohibited; the right to buy and sell land and to move freely about the realm was accorded to all. Old feudal governments were replaced by modernized districts under civil administrators. Justice was reformed and equality before the law established. Monasteries were stripped of their surplus wealth and wide social reforms were instituted (e.g., schools, hospitals, asylums, orphanages). Religious toleration became the law of the land and the Jews were finally permitted to remove the "yellow badge" they had been forced to wear, were admitted to Austrian citizenship with all of its rights and privileges.

In the short run, Joseph's reforms failed. The grant of freedom from above had no stabilizing base since Austria had failed to develop an effective middle-class. The result was that peasants revolted, nobles rebelled, churchmen instigated violence, national groups strove for independence—freedom became turmoil. In the long run, Joseph's policies became the pattern not only for Austria but for all the world.

RUSSIAN ABSOLUTISM

Russia entered the rim of Western civilization during the 17th century. Her previous orientation was eastward. Geographically her plains, tundras and forests stretched to the Orient. Nature closed her off from the west for six months of the year. For centuries she was dominated by eastern conquerors—Tartars, Mongols, etc. Her first "westernizers" looked to eastern Byzantium for guidance and when she was christianized Russia adopted the eastern Greek Orthodox faith.

The Rise of Absolutism. The earliest rulers of the Russian land were feudal lords (*boyars*) and upon them fell the task of breaking the Mongolian hold upon Russia. From the ranks of the boyars centered around Moscow arose Ivan III (1462-1505) who effectively broke the power of the Mongols, assumed the title of Tsar (king) and inherited the leadership of the Greek Orthodox faith when Constantinople fell in 1453 to the Ottoman Turks.

This achievement provided a base for expansion of the royal power. IVAN THE TERRIBLE (1533-1584) conquered the Volga basin and began the Russian march across Siberia. It was he that made the first commercial contacts with the West. At home he centralized the Russian state by adopting the Byzantine mode of administration, disinheriting the feudal lords, murdering all opponents and building a national army with the Cossacks as a base. A "time of troubles" followed Ivan's reign and it was not until 1682 when PETER THE GREAT came to the throne that the "westernization" of Russia was resumed.

Peter the Great (1682-1725). Peter was the first conscious westernizer in Russian history. In fact, he began his reign with a study trip into Europe. He studied carefully European methods of production, government, science, medicine, engineering, art, etc., and when he returned to Russia he brought with him a small army of European architects, engineers and technicians of all kinds to help him reconstruct the body and soul of Russia.

Peter's administrative reforms were similar to those adopted in France, Prussia, Sweden and elsewhere: ministries were established for the major areas of government; old feudal localities were abolished and centralized administrative units set up; trained civil servants replaced feudal favorites.

His attention thus focused on the west, Peter built himself a "window on the west" at St. Petersburg on the Baltic and this became his capital. He then plunged into the wars of the west by a series of aggressive attacks upon Sweden in alliance with Denmark and Poland. As a result of these aggressions, Peter added to the already vast Russian realm the territories of Karelia, Finland, Estonia and Livonia.

Catherine II (1762-1796). An amelioration of Russian despotism seemed likely when Catherine II became the Tsarina. Her predecessor, Elizabeth, had substantially fostered art and education in Russia. Catherine seemed determined to complete Peter's program of westernization with benevolence. She established contacts with the great French philosophers; she forced the French language upon the Russian court. But Catherine's liberalism never got beyond the verbal level. In practice she imposed an ever more tyrannical despotism upon the Russian people. They were reduced from serfs to virtual slaves as Catherine strengthened the hand of the nobility, and crushed brutally every effort of the serfs to win emancipation.

Catherine was far more successful in her pursuit of aggressive imperialist policies than in her pursuit of liberal ideals. Together with Frederick the Great and Maria Theresa she participated in the destruction of the Polish state and shared in the partition of its land in 1772, 1793 and 1795. In a series of Turkish wars (1768-1792) she established Russia on the Black and Caspian Seas as well as the Baltic.

By the end of the eighteenth century, then, Russia had become the model of the absolutist state, firmly established on the base of universal slavery and illiteracy and the constant application of terror.

CHAPTER SIXTEEN

THE GREAT INTELLECTUAL REVOLUTION

BACKGROUND

As Western Civilization entered the seventeenth century a number of forces combined to produce a revolution in man's conception of the universe. Man's new view of the universe led to the complete repudiation of Aristotelian thought and to a sharp modification of the church's view of the universe. More and more European thinkers came to the realization that Aristotle's reasoning was inexact; his physics was moral rather than scientific, that is, was divided into *good* motions and *bad* motions, *good* causes and *bad* causes; his classifications were static and were based on supposedly unchanging forms and essences; that, finally, his formulations were useless for they gave to man no control over natural forces. They pointed with scorn to the Aristotelian "scholastics"—engaged in fruitless, impractical discussions; repeating endlessly "proofs" by authorities who were no authorities; quibbling over the forms of knowledge and producing none.

Such were the arguments that flowed from the hostile pens of William of Okkham, Peter, Ramus, Francois Rabelais and Francis Bacon. These critics of Aristotelianism pointed to another mode of thought that had begun to appear with increasing frequency during the late sixteenth and early seventeenth centuries.

This new mode of thought was concerned not so much with the *nature* of objects but with their *behavior* in nature. This required precise observation, exact measurement and only then the formulation of general laws of nature.

Medieval habits, of course, did not slough off easily. The first of the scientists still resorted primarily to reasoning, to mathematical demonstration, to hypothetical formulation. These were the methods employed by Ramus, Bruno, Leonardo, Copernicus and even Galileo. Both Leonardo and Galileo assumed that nature begins with a cause which is imparted to man through his senses, is then transformed by man into mathematical formulae which can then be put to the test of experience. It was this "test of experience," however, that men like Francis Bacon began to insist upon. Copernicus had proved that untested experience was unreliable in the extreme.

Copernicus. In 1543 there appeared a truly revolutionary volume with the title *De Revolutionibus Celestium*. Its purpose was to find some more rational methods for explaining the irregularities observed in the movements of the planets. Its author, NICHOLAS COPERNICUS, was convinced that the Ptolemaic and Aristotelian explanations of celestial movements violated the basic principle that the cosmos operated according to a few simple laws; that the great diversity of movement was only *apparent*; that a few geometrical axioms could be found to abolish all "superfluous causes."

Copernicus began his simplification of astronomy by rejecting the geocentric view of common sense and hypothesizing that the sun was stationary and that the planets revolved about the sun. No sooner was this hypothesis made, then the need for a "staircase" of epicycles to explain celestial irregularities disappeared for the most part, and the movements of the heavens fell into an orderly pattern. The disorderly elements in the Copernican System came from the fact that he retained many of the old, unscientific ideas; he was unwilling or unable to complete his revolution in thought. It took many years to erase these ideas from the Copernican system. But the great contribution of Copernicus was his rejection of "common sense," his insistence on accuracy of observation and method.

Brahe and Kepler. The Copernican hypothesis set men to work to seek supporting data. Without accepting the Copernican theory, TYCHO BRAHE had accumulated a mass of facts about star movements —all without a telescope! Now came JOHANN KEPLER who took Brahe's star-charts and combined them with Copernicus's framework to produce the first masterwork in deriving a few geometrical axioms to explain an infinity of stellar positions.

Kepler derived his planetary laws only after he had shaken off the hold of the idea that celestial bodies *must*—because it is their "nature"—move in perfect circles; he discovered that they moved in "imperfect" ellipses instead. It was Kepler, then, who taught the scientific world to rid itself of all preconceptions, to see what is, and then to search out the uniformities that exist. Using a telescope, Galileo began the long history of verifying the Copernican-Kepler thesis.

Galileo. GALILEO completed the movement begun by Copernicus to see the universe as dynamic, not static. His doctrine of motion took scientific thinking beyond the purely descriptive phase into the explanatory phase. In examining the flight of a projectile he formulated the essential features of the scientific method. Scientific explanation, he taught, consists of stating the conditions of any event and showing how the event depends upon the conditions; resolving the event into its parts (e.g., original impulse, force of gravity, increase of velocity, decrease of velocity, etc.); finally, reconstructing the event in mathematical formulae after which one has a universally applicable *law* for all future events. Science, from now on, was not merely explanatory, but *predictive*.

Philosophical Impact of the Scientific Revolution. It is not easy to reconstruct the impact which these scientific discoveries had upon the minds of men. With a single sweep (it was felt) the scientific conception removed as causes of natural events all supernatural forces. God (they thought) was removed outside the universe. Inside the universe simple mechanical, mathematical forces could account for all phenomena. There was "no purpose" in the world of things; there was not one world but an infinity of worlds (Bruno); the fundamental reality is space, motion and energy (Descartes); the universe was without limit, everywhere displaying inexorable, mechanical law (Spinoza). The road to law was through mathematics and the road to mathematics was through experimentation.

Experimentation. Analyze—systematize, said Galileo. In crude laboratories, men everywhere in Europe began to look deeper into natural phenomena. Torricelli examined the atmosphere; Pascal, liquids; Boyle, gases; Newcomen, steam power; Newton and Huygens, optics; Roemer, the speed of light. Measuring instruments and laboratory tools proliferated—the pendulum clock, the air pump, the barometer, the thermometer, the telescope, the microscope, etc. National interest in experimentation increased and as a result scientific academies were established in all of the major European countries. Scientific journals made their appearance, and international exchange of scientific data was begun.

Isaac Newton. Newton completed what Kepler and Galileo had begun. His major work was the *Philosophiae Naturalis Principia Mathematica (1687)*.

Newton set himself the problem of discovering a mathematics of mechanical motion that would have universal application. What was needed was a mathematics that would measure change, the direction of any movement at any point. Descartes had unified algebra and geometry in the analytic geometry. Newton now invented the calculus and used it to formulate the general laws governing *all* bodies in the universe. The basic law of gravity was the first of the great cosmic laws of the modern world. Its influence was vast for men began to inquire whether the mechanical view of nature did not embrace more than the movement of bodies in space. Were there similar mechanical principles that would embrace with the same degree of certainty the worlds of religion, human nature, mind, society, business, government, ethics and the like?

THE AGE OF REASON

The Exaltation of the Human Mind. Men were overwhelmed, as a result of the Newtonian Synthesis, by the vast power of the human mind. The ability of human reason to discover and, indeed, to create universal law was a new revelation. Analyze—synthesize, said Newton. Thinkers followed this prescription literally and the **Age of Reason and Enlightenment** which arrived by the 18th century was primarily one of intense criticism of existing institutions and the projection of new systems ruled by rational law.

Religion. Of all human institutions in the 18th century, that of religion qualified least under the new scientific standards of simplicity, order, rationality and usefulness. Theological controversy over transubstantiation, consubstantiation, trinitarianism, unitarianism, predestinationism and the like was extremely confusing; religious war was bloody and chaotic; religious authoritarianism was inconsistent with rationalism. Under the influence of such groups as the Socinians, the Arminians, the Rationalists and particularly the Deists, an effort was made to simplify religious beliefs, reduce the element of supernaturalism and to assign a place in the universe to God that would not interfere with its mechanical operations.

These religions taught, among other things, that faith must be made amenable to reason; that man's relation to God must be simplified—hence their emphasis upon unitarianism, the humanity of Christ, the elimination of all mediation between man and God, the essential goodness and perfectability of man and the like. To explain the place of God in the scheme of things these religious rationalists argued that God had created the universe, much as a clockmaker makes a watch; He had wound it up and then departed from the universe. The universe is now running according to the mechanical laws first built in by God; these laws are fixed, eternal, operating within absolute space and absolute time.

Since they are mechanical, these laws can be discovered by human reason. Human reason was created by God on the same basis as the universe. There are no limits to the potentiality of the human mind to discover the universe and its laws. God had intended that the proper study of mankind be man himself.

What remained of religion in this rational framework? Deists conceded that there was a God; that man must live in obedience to His rational will; that reason can discover God's purposes and that, therefore, revelation is unnecessary. In fact, Deists concentrated their attack upon revelation, miracles and therefore upon much that appeared in the Bible. Collins argued that no Testamentary prophecy was ever fulfilled; Woolston and Hume denied the validity of miracles; Voltaire turned his satiric scorn on existing clerical institutions; Hume rejected the idea of immortality; Holbach went further to accept a pantheistic atheism. It did not seem likely at the end of the eighteenth century that religion would recover from these many blows at its foundations. But it did.

Environment. The world of the 18th century was subjected to rigorous examination; it, too, was found wanting. Out of this rigorous examination of the environment of man was born the **social sciences.**

Considerable attention was given to the nature of human nature. Locke, Hume, Hartley, Condillac, Helvetius and Bentham were among the many who attempted to develop a science of man (psychology). Their systems of psychology differed in many ways and any generalization about all of them must be made cautiously. However, most of them conceived of man as a product of nature, one part of which was mind. Like all natural phenomena, man's mind was subject to law. Part of the law of mind was centered in these beliefs: that at birth, all minds were equal; they were all *tabula rasa* (a blank tablet) on which were imprinted the experiences through which they lived; these experiences were outside man and entered into him by way of the senses; sense experience was then regrouped by the mind into ideas according to laws of association.

The important consequence of this psychology was that it placed the primary influence upon men in the environment, the institutions outside of man. From this it followed that if the institutions outside man were perfect then man himself must become perfect. To some, in fact, it seemed that society (environment) perfected itself in the course of the ages (from ignorance to science, for example) and would continue to do so.

Such was the belief of GIOVANNI BATTISTA VICO (1688-1744) who saw all of history as a series of cycles moving from lower to higher stages; and of MARQUIS DE CONDORCET (1743-1794) who saw progress as continuous, a straight line to perfection. But others rejected the concept of the inevitability of progress and argued that no progress would take place until all present institutions were destroyed and replaced by new, more humane ones. It was these latter thinkers who prepared the ideological ground for the upheaval in Europe of the French Revolution late in the 18th century.

THE OLD REGIME

Outside of England, Europe in the 18th century was in the grip of an "Old Regime." Conditions in France were typical, though less backward than, say, in Germany or central Europe. By any standard of perfectability, the form of the French government was clearly outmoded. It was an absolute autocracy centered in a "divine-right" monarch whose will was law. The king's will, however, was capricious and followed no discernible rational principles. He made his caprice into law through an appointed Council of State, and extensive local bureaucracy, a number of courts of the king's law, punitive writs like the *lettres de cachet* (king's orders permitting arbitrary arrest) and, of course, the army and navy.

Rationalists found such a state of affairs unendurable. They were revolted by the worthlessness and extravagance of the decadent and corrupt court at Versailles. Compare this, they said, with the con-

ditions in the country at large. Because of the king's tyranny there were three social castes—three "estates"—the nobility and the clergy as highly privileged and a third estate without any privileges.

The nobility, for example, were men and women no different rationally and naturally from the bulk of mankind; in fact, a good case could be made out that spiritually, morally and productively they were far worse than the most common laborer. Yet these few decadents were privileged (by the king's favoritism) to be exempt from taxes, to monopolize the high offices in the land, to command the armies, to be exempt from military service, to own vast regions of the land of France, to collect all kinds of outmoded feudal dues, to draw expensive pensions from the king's treasury for lackey service to the king's person.

The clergy were regarded as no less undeservedly privileged. They lived the same kind of lives of leisure and wastefulness as the nobility and were of little use to society. This condemnation did not include the impoverished parish priest who ministered to the spiritual needs of the community. The higher clergy were exempt from taxation even though they commanded a large portion of the nation's wealth through ownership of vast estates and collection of the tithe, an annual church tax. They, too, resided at court, received royal pensions and wielded the power of high office.

New emphasis upon a criterion of "usefulness to society" came, in France, chiefly from the bourgeoisie—chiefly those who, though wealthy, were unprivileged. These made up the bulk of the lawyers, merchants, manufacturers, and professional groups in France. Engaged in the process of building up their capital resources, the bourgeoisie were shocked at the waste and extravagance of the court; they resented the fact that they bore a tax load the clergy and nobility avoided; they sought for some reform of the top-heavy bureaucracy and antiquated system of local provinces, each with its power to place tariffs on goods entering their localities. It was unreasonable and tyrannical, they felt, to expect the hard-working useful class of society to support the non-working, useless class.

Most of the attention of the rationalists, however, was directed at the great mass of Frenchmen—the commoners, the artisans, the peasants, sharecroppers and serfs that made up the nation. (By the end of the 18th century, most of the French peasantry were freemen and were far better off than their European neighbors; serfdom was virtually extinct. But in spite of this, the tradition of serfdom and many of the ancient feudal burdens persisted. Freedom did not bring the French peasant status.)

Upon this group fell the chief burden in maintaining the rigid caste system in France. The number of taxes levied upon them, the rationalists felt, was not only unreasonable but inhumane.

England. With the death of Queen Elizabeth in 1603, there came to the throne of England the "wisest fool in Christendom," James the First. "Kings," wrote James, "are justly called gods, for they exercise a manner of resemblance of Divine power upon earth."

James acted on this belief: in the course of his reign he levied taxes without the sanction of Parliament, disregarded protests from that body and dissolved it when it went counter to his will. He undertook personal direction of the national life of England by dictating mercantilist policies, granting monopolies to court favorites, overruling the traditional anti-Spanish foreign policy and undertaking to rid England of the rising number of Puritans who sought to "purify" the English episcopal system of "popish" practices. James acted the traditional part of an absolute monarch; but the English did not for long countenance this high-handed defiance of just government.

Charles I. His successor, Charles I, who came to the throne in 1625, felt the full weight of popular resentment. Charles followed his father's policies. He got into a war with France and needed additional revenue desperately. When Parliament refused to grant him additional taxes, he dissolved Parliament and punished dissenters by quartering soldiers in their homes or by arbitrarily imprisoning them. He then tried personal rule by reviving ancient royal taxes and imposing them upon the English by force.

A revolutionary situation developed as the English rallied against these tyrannical practices. Charles was forced to submit to the national opposition and, in 1628, to sign the historic **Petition of Right** which then took its place alongside the Magna Carta. The king agreed to levy no taxes without consent of Parliament, nor to quarter soldiers in private abodes; he promised to make no arbitrary arrest and imprisonment and not to impose martial law in times of peace.

Charles promptly proceeded to violate all these promises. Once more he imposed outmoded taxes forcibly collected, sold monopolies at fantastic rates, used court fines to swell the national treasury and sought to force his Anglican sympathies upon every dissenting group in the nation. For eleven years he ruled thus without Parliament. In 1640, with a rebellion pouring down upon him from Scotland, he had to convene Parliament.

Cromwell. Parliament set aside all that Charles had decreed and arrested Charles's chief assistants. The result was civil war (1642-1649). On one side of the war were the **Cavaliers**—aristocrats, noblemen, large landowners, Catholics and Anglicans. On the other side were the **"Roundheads"**—merchants, manufacturers, yeoman, Puritans and Presbyterians. By 1646 the Cavaliers were vanquished. However, the Roundheads quarreled among themselves over the restoration of Charles to power and the war continued with the Presbyterians and Puritans on opposing sides. Led by OLIVER CROMWELL, the Puritans won commanding position. They cleansed Parliament of all dissenters and with the "Rump" that remained they abolished the monarchy and on January 30, 1649 beheaded the monarch Charles.

The Commonwealth. Cromwell's government (1649-1660) was called a **Commonwealth.** It began as a republic of Puritan oligarchs but eventually became the dictatorship of Cromwell himself. Cromwell was made Lord Protector for life and the office was made hereditary. He, too, ruled by divine-right; waged brutal war in Ireland and Scotland; tried to harry Anglicans and Catholics out of the land; pursued a strong mercantilist policy; warred with the Spaniards and Dutch; and imposed a puritanical moral code upon all the English—all without benefit of Parliament. He died in 1658 and the rational English now restored (hence The Restoration) the Stuarts in the person of Charles II.

Charles II and his successor James II (1685) learned nothing from the fate of Charles I and Oliver Cromwell and proceeded with customary disregard of Parliament and English liberties to pursue personal foreign policies, to favor one religion above all others, to demand that Parliament support financially their extravagant regimes. Parliament refused and in 1688 came the **Glorious ("Bloodless") Revolution** during which James II was deposed and William of Orange (and his wife Mary) were invited to come over from Holland and become the joint rulers of England *within carefully prescribed limits set down by Parliament.*

The limits of the monarchy were defined in a series of important laws passed in 1689. Parliament decreed that all appropriations of money were for one year only. A Toleration Act then followed which granted religious freedom to all Christians except Catholics and Unitarians. In December came the Bill of Rights which enacted or re-enacted into law the right to a trial by jury, to petition, to freedom from excessive bail, cruel and unusual punishment and exorbitant fines; the king was specifically forbidden to suspend Parliamentary laws or ever to levy taxes without the consent of Parliament. What in essence these laws proclaimed was the supremacy of the people of England through their representatives in Parliament over any ruler. Rational rule was limited rule; only the nation was sovereign.

John Locke (1632-1704). John Locke was the great spokesman for the Glorious Revolution and thereafter for the American and French Revolutions. His *Essay Concerning Human Understanding, Letters on Toleration, Some Thoughts Concerning Education* and *The Reasonableness of Christianity* deeply inspired the thinkers of the Enlightenment. Locke's thinking was practical, tied to human experience.

His ethics followed from his belief that the goal of human life is the pursuit of happiness. Men are born equal in their rights to life, liberty and property for these are indispensable to the pursuit of happiness. Realizing that happiness can degenerate into passion, Locke advocated a belief in reward and punishment in an after-life as social control. Piety should be encouraged by the widest kind of toleration (except for Catholics and atheists!). Thus Locke stressed the need for a favorable environment for the fulfillment of human happiness.

Locke repudiated Hobbes's doctrine that men were in a state of war with one another; in an original state of nature, he said, men lived happily and rationally together. Life, health, liberty, possessions were all secure. To secure these rights, governments were instituted among men according to a social contract based upon natural (i.e, scientific, rational) law. Any government which becomes destructive of these rights, should be altered or abolished. (These were the sentiments that echoed into Jefferson's preface to the Declaration of Independence.) The best protection against an abusive government, said Locke, is a system of checks and balances, one in which legislative, executive and judicial powers are separated and act as buffers to any assertion of absolutism.

Montesquieu. The system of checks and balances was eventually to be written into the constitution of the United States but it was not so much from Locke as from BARON MONTESQUIEU's *Spirit of the Laws* that the details were drawn. Inspired by Locke, Montesquieu turned to the study of history to make a comparison of the republic, the monarchy and the despotism as forms of government. He concluded that the needs of the time and the environment determined the precise form of government that is best for a people. In his own age Montesquieu (misreading the true nature of the English government) felt that the English limited monarchy was the ideal form of government. King, parliament and court were separate and distinct there (so he thought!) and they checked one another so that no one branch could ever assume absolute powers. His influence on the French Revolutionists was immediate and direct.

Voltaire. FRANCOIS MARIE AROUET DE VOLTAIRE was the genius of the era preceding the French Revolution. His creative achievement was prodigious for he was at once dramatist, historian, biographer, philosopher, novelist, poet, pamphleteer, encyclopedist, political scientist, editor and wit. The most distinctive aspect of his life was, however, that he lived most of it as a political exile one step ahead of the police.

Reasons for this are not far to seek. He attacked —wherever he found them—absolutism, privilege, enslavement of body or mind, decayed institutions, incompetence, ignorance, superstition, intolerance. His artillery was the merciless barb, the lampoon, slashing satire and exposé. But what positive program lay behind Voltaire's ceaseless attack on existing institutions? In his *Letters Concerning the English Nation* he supported fully the concept of a limited monarchy, a constitutional king; in his philosophical romances (*Candide, Zadig, The Princess of Babylon,* etc.) he called for the abolition of war, of slavery and of fruitless metaphysical speculation. In philosophical pamphlets he advocated skepticism and rationalism. He turned his fury on all established religion and advanced the deist view of God as Watchmaker. He fought for the abolition of serfdom, slavery, censorship, arbitrary arrest.

He supported the publication of the "Encyclopedia" (under the editorship of Diderot) for the advancement of science. He fought against narrow nationalism in his writings on history and sought to remove divine causation from the study of history and to substitute environmental cause in its place. Voltaire, then, was not as radical as his persecuted life would lead one to believe. His devastating influence arose from the fact that almost any critic of the Old Regime in France—or elsewhere—found somewhere in Voltaire support for his opposition.

Rousseau. More closely identified with the out-

break of the French Revolution was JEAN JACQUES
ROUSSEAU (1712-1778). He came to national attention when he won an essay contest with the argument that man was good by nature and then
corrupted by civilization; to re-establish man in the
world one had to make a return to nature, and
Rousseau would show them the way. He wrote a
series of books describing the way back. The *New
Heloise*, *Emile*, the *Confessions*, the *Discourse on
the Origin of Inequality* and the *Social Contract*
were all, in one way or another, revelations of
"natural man," of man released from the bondage
of civilization to be his natural good self.

But Rousseau's aim was not descriptive, it was
reformative; his essence was revolutionary in the
extreme. His *Confessions* showed how one man
threw over all the trappings of civilized behavior
and lived by the code of bare emotions; the *New
Heloise* glorified unrestrained romantic love. In
Emile he overthrew all theories of education to
permit his pupil to develop naturally through intelligent activity. In his *Social Contract* Rousseau
returned with Locke to a "state of nature" and
there he found man as a pure animal neither good
nor bad.

With the coming of industry and agriculture
equality disappeared; oppressors ruled through laws
over the oppressed. Such a condition was a violation
of the state of nature for ultimate sovereignty over
the lives of people rests with the people themselves.
Whatever laws exist do so · because of a "social
contract" in which the people voluntarily surrendered some rights in exchange for others. No
decision made by a government is valid without
consent of the governed; every citizen from king
to commoner must subordinate himself to the
general will. In the era of the Old Regime this
was revolutionary doctrine.

The Attack on Mercantilism. In its inception,
mercantilism was linked with the rising bourgeoisie;
during the 17th century, however, it had become
a tool in the hands of kings to strengthen absolutism.

Thinkers now arose to challenge the very foundations of mercantilist theory. Mercantilism, they
argued, restricted opportunity to accumulate capital
for expansion of industry and commerce. National
wealth did not consist in the amount of precious
metals held in the national treasury but in the productive capacity of a nation. Increases in productivity were possible only under conditions of
competitive enterprise; any governmental regulation
which interfered with free enterprise was a violation of the *natural laws* of economic growth.

Within the productive sphere the role of government was limited to enforcement of contracts
legally made and protection of property legally
acquired. In all other matters it was incumbent on
the government to pursue a policy of *laissez-faire*
or *hands off*.

Economic philosophers disagreed among themselves where the true source of national wealth lay.
Thus, the French Physiocrats like QUESNAY and
TURGOT thought it lay in land and that therefore
all governmental restrictions upon the free use of
land ought to be removed. But it was a Scotsman,
ADAM SMITH, who, in his *Wealth of Nations*, gave
precise formulation to the modern philosophy of
capitalism outlined above. Needless to say, Smith's
analysis was seized on by the bourgeoisie living
under the French Old Regime and converted into a
political pamphlet for their cause.

By the middle of the 18th century, a profound
revolution had taken place in the minds of men;
the next step was to transfer it to the political
arena. Before it was finished, a new concept had
been born in the world, the concept of democratic
government.

THE BAROQUE PERIOD

During the Enlightenment man's expanding mental horizons, his increasing confidence in his own
creative powers had profound effects in the universe of the arts.

Music. Following the examples of Monteverdi,
the Scarlattis, Cavalieri, Lully and Purcell, Gluck
and Mozart worked out the major forms of **opera,**
widened its musical sphere, adapted it to both tragic
and comic themes and determined its basic instrumental patterns.

In Germanic lands there was hostility to the form
of the opera. To exploit the possibilities of voice
and instrumental accompaniment, German composers turned to the **cantata** and **oratorio.** The
cantata consisted of an instrumental prelude, solos,
choruses in canon form, and a chorale or hymn
tune at the end. The oratorio was a longer and
more dramatic musical form based on texts from
the Old and New Testaments. Instrumental music
served as background accompaniment. Throughout
the period the Passion and the Mass derived from
church services persisted.

Instrumental music developed rapidly; experiment
with forms was widespread. Suites, concerti, toc-
catas and sonatas were among the main forms developed. The sonata was of particular significance

for from its major form developed the symphony.

Of this immensely productive period in the history of music several must be singled out as its greatest masters. GEORGE FREDERICK HANDEL, JOSEPH HAYDN, and WOLFGANG AMADEUS MOZART come immediately to mind. But more even than these geniuses it is perhaps the towering figure of JOHANN SEBASTIAN BACH who best contains and expresses the whole sweep of musical development from the Renaissance to the late 18th century. After Bach music had to take new directions for he seemed to have "exhausted" the old ones.

The future was forced into instrumentation and the ideal vehicle was the symphony. Handel made the first large experiments with an orchestra by introducing horns and early forms of the clarinet. Instrumentation for his oratorios and *concerti grossi* showed that he had a feeling for symphonic form. But it was Haydn who brought the symphony to its first completed form by elaborating the sonata form for full orchestra. He, too, enlarged the orchestra by adding percussion, woodwind and brass instruments. All this was in preparation for Mozart who is both baroque and the transition to the classical period in music. Mozart gave depth to the four-part sonata allegro form, varying the mood of each part and converting the symphony into a monumental art form.

Art. Baroque, then, was not so much one style of expression as the elaboration of many styles to enhance expression. This was particularly true in painting. The period of the Baroque embraced such artists as TINTORETTO, EL GRECO, CARAVAGGIO, RENI, RUBENS, HALS, REMBRANDT, POUSSIN, LORRAIN, VELASQUEZ, VERMEER—to select but a few. This list establishes at a glance the impossibility of attempting to describe Baroque in a single statement that would characterize each of these artists.

Generally speaking these few remarks may be made: In portraiture Baroque artists abandoned idealization for the character-study, the portrait for psychological interpretation; Baroque artists found no theme alien to them and painted everything between the sidewalk and the sky. When the creative spark began to fade late in the 18th century, either overelaboration (roccoco) or flat academicism resulted. But when they were at their height, the Baroque artists exhibited a degree of genius that has not been exceeded since.

Literature. Literary artists during the Baroque period were concerned with fulfilling old forms and inventing new ones. In England Dryden, Congreve, Defoe, Addison, Steele, Swift, Pope, Johnson, Goldsmith and Sheridan dominated the literary world—each in his own time, each in his own sphere. What characterized most of these authors was their rationalism, their "common sense," their wit, their impatience with all forms of fraud and humbug.

Increasing interest in the social environment gave birth to the novel as a literary form. SAMUEL RICHARDSON used the form to propagate middle-class narrow morality; HENRY FIELDING to expose sham and to portray a lust for life; LAURENCE STERNE made it a vehicle for exploration of sentiment and TOBIAS SMOLLET for picaresque adventure.

CHAPTER SEVENTEEN

THE FRENCH REVOLUTION

INTRODUCTION

The French Revolution is a great divide in history. This is not because of the large number of reforms effected in its course; or because of its violence. Other nations had produced similar reforms and greater violence; reforms adopted were later abolished. The significance of the French Revolution is that it directed its appeal to all people to follow its course of "Liberty, Equality and Fraternity." Its call was world-wide, wherever people dwelt under a regime of autocratic absolutism; and its democratic message has retained its validity to our day. As a result, the French Revolution made **democracy** a powerful force in the history of the 19th and 20th centuries. Since democracy could only be realized in the framework of national states, it made **nationalism** into a similar force.

More than any preceding revolution, the French Revolution was inspired by philosophical sources—the great *philosophes* of the Enlightenment. It became inextricably linked, therefore, with the forces of intellectual and religious freedom. These, too, became focusing forces in the history to come. Finally, the French experiment revealed glaringly many of the weaknesses that accompany efforts to establish the democratic way of life.

CRISIS AND REVOLUTION

Revolution is a product of national paralysis. Between 1788 and 1789 the French monarchy entered into a period of crisis, chiefly financial. War, royal extravagance, reckless borrowing, inefficient taxation and the short-sighted inflexibility of the ruling groups had emptied the royal treasury; existing revenues were inadequate to meet obligations of the national debt; existing taxes on the peasantry and bourgeoisie were already crushing.

Potentially prosperous, the French nation was experiencing widespread poverty. Prices had risen because of crop failures; wages lagged far behind prices; business failures were increasing as a result of a British invasion of the French markets; large numbers of wage earners (which included part-time peasant workers) were unemployed. Economists like Turgot, Necker and Calonne, called in to solve the financial crisis did their best to delay collapse by minor economies and major loans. Each realized that France's salvation lay in opening the untaxed wealth of the privileged classes to taxation as the only solution; and for recommending this as national policy, each was dismissed.

At Calonne's suggestion, Louis XVI convened in 1787 an Assembly of Notables. These privileged groups were asked to tax themselves. They refused but did suggest that an Estates General or parliament of the three estates (clergy, nobility and the Third Estate) be called to consider the matter of taxation. The current finance minister, Archbishop de Brienne, coldly dismissed the suggestion of the Notables and undertook to float a new loan.

Popular Reaction. Encouraged by vocal popular support, the *parlement* (court) of Paris (on whose bench sat spokesmen for the bourgeoisie) refused to register de Brienne's new loan, or any loan or tax, unless it was approved by an Estates General. This was subversion and the king moved against the court with troops. But the soldiers refused to arrest the judges and in this act they were supported by menacing mobs in Paris. Uncomprehending and bewildered, Louis was compelled to summon the Estates General. Neither he, nor any Frenchman, foresaw the consequences of this act.

The Estates General. In 1789 the Estates General was only an historical memory since it had not met since 1614. At that time it consisted of three estates—the clergy, the nobility and the Third Estate, each meeting and voting as separate bodies. The least of the three had been the Third Estate. That this was no longer possible was clearly stated in an influential pamphlet written by the Abbé Sieyès. "What is the Third Estate?" asked the Abbé. And he answered: "It is everything. What has it been hitherto in the political order? Nothing! What does it desire? To be something!" Advisers of Louis accepted the truth of the Abbé's formulation and in assigning delegates, the Third Estate was permitted to choose 600 out of a total of 1200.

Elections were held in the early months of 1789 on the basis of almost universal male suffrage. In the course of electoral gathering local communities drew up *cahiers*—lists of grievances which the delegates were instructed to correct. It is interesting to note how un-revolutionary national sentiment was on the eve of the Revolution. The cahiers almost universally proclaimed the delegates loyal to the king and to the idea of hereditary succession. But they did propose hundreds of reforms. In general these reforms centered upon limiting by constitution the powers of the king and the bureaucracy; upon no taxation without representation; upon increased elective local autonomy; upon *universal* taxation; upon humane reformation of the criminal law and its procedures; upon immediate relief of the economic crisis.

Paralysis and Revolution. On May 5th the delegates gathered into a temporary structure called (ironically) the Hall of the (King's) Lesser Pleasures. The first important dispute was on a procedural question: How should the delegates vote? The first two estates insisted on each estate casting a single vote, as in the traditional manner. Realizing that this would place them at the mercy of the privileged groups, the Third Estate insisted on voting by head (one delegate—one vote) in a single body. Third Estate strategy rested on the knowledge that some nobility and many parish priests would vote with the Third Estate to give it a majority.

The result was a temporary paralysis; the first two estates met as separate orders and organized for action; the Third Estate refused to organize until its demands for meeting as a single body were met. The impasse lasted for five weeks. Then, on June 12, the Third Estate organized itself and invited the others to join it. To distinguish itself from the others, the Third Estate, on June 17, assumed the title of **National Assembly** and declared that it had sovereign power to act for the nation. The king's government was set aside. The Revolution had begun.

The National Assembly. On the same day (June 17) the National Assembly began quietly but ominously to reform the state of France. All of the royal taxes were abolished; committees were created to draw up a reformed financial structure and to take steps to relieve the distress among the poor. Louis had not yet acted. On the 20th of June Louis suspended the sessions of the Estates General. The Third Estate, in the form of the National Assembly, withdrew to a neighboring tennis court and there took an oath (The "Tennis Court Oath") not to disband until France had a constitution. This was done with great confidence because by this time many of the parish priests and nobility had joined the National Assembly.

On the 27th of June, Louis seemed to capitulate to the National Assembly by ordering the first two estates to sit with it; he began, however, to gather mercenary troops and to station them in Paris for a showdown. With each new detachment of troops, popular indignation and violence grew. It came to a head when, on July 14, the populace stormed and took the Bastille. Violence now rolled out of Paris into the countryside as enraged peasantry attacked the chateaux of the landed nobility. By the late summer of 1789, France was in the hands of the people; the authority of the crown had vanished. All eyes were turned to the National Assembly which in August had begun to reform France.

The Reforms of the National Assembly. Abolition of feudal privileges. In abolishing the survivals of the feudal past, the nobility in the National Assembly itself took the leadership. One after another the nobles rose to propose destruction of such privileges as exemption from taxation, collection of feudal taxes, monopoly rights, distinctions of rank, vested interests, hunting and fishing rights and the like.

The Declaration of the Rights of Man. Taking its lead from the example of the American Revolution, the French Revolutionists turned to a statement of general principles as a guide to further and more permanent reform. They drew up a **Declaration of the Rights of Man and of the Citizen.**

Three pillars of freedom were erected in the ideological structure. One was **property rights:** men were to be protected in their right to private ownership of property; no one could be deprived of property except in case of public necessity; anyone deprived of property had a basic right to compensation. A second was **personal rights:** these included the basic freedoms; religious toleration; equality before the law; due process of law . . . and the like. A third was **democracy:** sovereignty resided with the people; only the people could delegate sovereignty to government; and the people reserved the right of revolution against tyranny.

Secularization of the church. Church lands were confiscated and were sold in parcels to impoverished peasantry and were also used as backing for a new currency issued to meet the financial crisis. A Civil Constitution of the Clergy was then drawn up which made the priesthood elective civil servants of the state. All clergy were forced to take an oath of allegiance to the state to qualify for the priesthood. The Pope, of course, condemned this feature and prohibited oath-taking. The result was that the French clergy were divided into those who did (juring) and those who did not (non-juring) take the oath.

The Constitution of 1791. To complete their essentially conservative revolution, the French Revolutionists drew up a constitution for France which established a limited monarchy on the principle of the separation of powers. A Legislative Assembly was created with full power to make the law; it was to be indirectly elected by electoral colleges. The executive power was given to the king. As a check upon absolutism the king was shorn of control of the army, church and local government and was removed from the legislative process by being given a veto that could be overridden by the Legislative Assembly.

The Radical Phase. By 1791 the conservative phase of the Revolution was complete. Events soon propelled the Revolution into a more radical phase. To begin with, the economic demands of the impoverished wage-earners were not met; if anything, the situation grew worse due to a currency inflation. Restless, hungry workers had become organized mobs directed by leaders of radical clubs which had begun to flourish in Paris. These clubs reflected the political spectrum which early made its appearance in the National Assembly. Conservatives, those who favored a status quo, concentrated in the **Girondist Party**; Radicals, those who favored complete abolition of the monarchy and a sharp limitation on the rights of the bourgeoisie as well as the clergy and nobility, gravitated to the **Jacobin Party.**

Emigres—those who managed to flee from France to the more hospitable lands of Prussia and Austria and England—had created enough anxiety there to cause the monarchs of these countries to issue an ultimatum to the French Revolutionists to desist in their persecution of church and nobility. National irritation with this unwarranted interference resulted in a declaration of war by the Legislative Assembly on Prussia and Austria. Invasion of France by these two nations created a national emergency. National mobilization of a citizen army to meet the threat of foreign invasion followed. The king and queen actively cooperated with the emigres abroad and, on one occasion, even attempted escape. To the Radicals in France, it seemed that the very Revolution was at stake. In 1792 they moved to take over the government.

THE RADICAL PHASE OF THE FRENCH REVOLUTION

Terror. The radical phase of the French Revolution was distinguished by increased use of terrorization as politcal policy. "Madame Guillotine" became the symbol of this period. Under the loose designation of "enemies of the people" thousands of people were slaughtered. Some were, of course, guilty of treasonable activity, of conspiracy with the emigres abroad and the instigators of civil war at home; some were guilty of no more than association by birth with suspected elements in the population; others were victims of spite, revenge, rivalry and the like. Terror, like power, corrupts; and corruption was no more evident than in the popular jubilation which attended the ceremonies of execution.

Those who used terror were themselves victimized by it. In January 1793 Louis XVI and Marie Antoinette were executed. Only the Girondists opposed this decision. DANTON and ST. JUST, by brilliant oratory, turned the National Convention to this decision. It was not long before the Girondists were made the victims of the terror by the Jacobins led by Danton, ROBESPIERRE and others. This done, it was Danton's turn and he was executed because he felt that it was time to call halt to the terror. Under Robespierre, the guillotine was employed with increasing frequency. But in 1794 he too lost his head though he was almost dead of bullet wounds.

Dictatorship. In September 1792 the monarchy was deposed and the First French Republic declared. An election was then held for a National Con-

vention to frame a new constitution. In 1793 the constitution was published. It was democratic to the core and provided for universal male suffrage, an elected legislature, an executive elected by the legislature, annual elections and the like. But it was not put into effect.

Arguing that the national situation of civil war, foreign war and economic depression was too dire to permit the processes of democracy, the Jacobins set aside the constitution and created instead a dictatorial Committee of Public Safety composed of nine members. This Committee assumed all the powers of government; it sent its agents abroad to check on the loyalty of Frenchmen and to negotiate with foreign governments; it created revolutionary tribunals with virtually unlimited power to try and execute "enemies of the people"; it raised armies and fought the foreign enemies; it nationalized economic enterprise much more effectively than the absolute monarchs of France. For two years there was little but the outer trappings to distinguish Robespierre from Louis XIV.

The fall of Robespierre brought a reaction to terror and dictatorship (the **Thermidorean Reaction**). A new constitution was written in 1795 which returned France to a moderate course. Power was divided between a bicameral legislature and a Directory or executive of five members. Voting was restricted to property owners; age-limits for holding office were raised; two-thirds of the membership of a new legislature had to be chosen from the old. Terror had made men suspicious of democracy.

Reforms. Under the dictatorship some permanent reforms were effected. Price controls stopped the inflation; the metric system was adopted; a commissioin to revise the law code of France began its work by providing for prison reforms, abolition of imprisonment for debts, abolition of slavery in the colonies; public education was expanded with the creation of Normal schools and Polytechnic institutes; a national library was set up; confiscated land was sold to peasants and made France into a nation of small farmers. Above all, the civil war was suppressed and foreign enemies were forced into signing the peace treaties of 1795 which declared an end to foreign efforts to suppress the French Revolution and French efforts to spread it abroad. These accomplishments left permanent effects.

Not so were the efforts of the radical Jacobins to abolish *Monsieur* and *Madame* in favor of *Citizen;* to introduce a new calendar with 1792 as the Year I and with the months renamed to celebrate nature and her wonders; to institute and enforce the worship of the goddess Reason; to inaugurate an official Reign of Virtue and the like.

NAPOLEON BONAPARTE

The Directory ruled France for four years (1795-1799) and then succumbed to a bloodless *coup d'état* unleashed by NAPOLEON BONAPARTE who then ruled France until 1815.

In those five years the Directory so alienated the affections of the French people that they accepted Napoleon as their savior. The Directory was unable to cope with renewed inflation; when it issued a new currency, it could not force popular acceptance of it. Nor could it cope with increasing pressure by the clergy, widely supported by the people, for some restoration of their property and rights. Unbelievable corruption characterized the Directors, each of whom ruled for a price. Peace had been concluded with Prussia, Holland and Spain; but negotiations with England and Austria had fallen through because the Directory insisted upon an extension of France's boundaries to the Rhine.

On October 5, 1795 a Paris mob attacked the Directory and only the quick and ruthless wit of an artillery officer named Napoleon Bonaparte, a Corsican, saved it. On this "whiff of grapeshot" Napoleon marched into history as the prototype of the modern dictator.

What Makes A Dictator? No man in history has been more analyzed than Napoleon, who rose from complete obscurity to become European conqueror. A boundless ambition seems a first requirement. Napoleon had this in abundance.

Recognition of opportunity or rank opportunism coupled with unscrupulous and amoral actions speeded him. He did not hesitate to use artillery against an unarmed crowd, or to enter into a loveless marriage for advancement or to cajole the support of any group that could be useful to him. He permitted himself loyalty to no man; he was his own cause; and this limitless egotism seems a requisite for the temperament of a dictator. Ability, too, is needed; genius is preferable. Napoleon had both military and administrative genius.

The Rise To Power. Having saved the Republic and won the hand of Josephine Beauharnais who had great influence in the Directory, Napoleon in 1796 secured command of the Army of Italy; his instructions were to use his ragged force of 30,000 men to divert the Austrians from the south while the main thrust was made in the North. Napoleon turned this diversionary movement into a major thrust and virtually marched north on Vienna. The Austrians were forced to sue for peace. Acting on the principle that what is done can often not be undone, Napoleon, *without consent of the Directory*, negotiated the Treaty of Campo Formio which forced Austria to recognize French claims to the Rhine, to release her Italian possessions and to surrender Lombardy and Belgium to the French.

This done, Napoleon proceeded with political reorganization of the Italian states into the Cisalpine and Ligurian Republics. He announced himself as the liberator of Italy, the son of the French Revolution and imposed "liberty and equality" on the occupied lands. Beneath this role of liberator lay the more obvious role of terrorist; opposition to French booty-taking was punished with shocking brutality. Napoleon returned to Paris as a conquering hero. What could the Directory do? The army worshipped their commander.

The Egyptian Maneuver. It was clear to Napoleon that the Directory could not long survive. He, Napoleon, must not lend his strength to support their weakness. With keen political astuteness Napoleon therefore proposed that he undertake an Egyptian Campaign as a first step to deprive England of her life-line to Italy. Anxious to get rid of this rising menace, the Directory gave its ungrudging consent to the campaign. In July of 1798 Napoleon evaded the watchful British navy led by Admiral Nelson and landed in Egypt. In the Battle of the Nile, Nelson destroyed Napoleon's fleet and trapped him inside Egypt. Though Egypt fell an easy prey, Napoleon was unable to remove his army from Egypt. He therefore deserted it when news came that France was his for the taking.

A new coalition of powers (England, Russia, Austria, Portugal, Turkey and Naples) had been formed for an attack on France; along the Rhine and in the Italies the French armies were steadily being pushed back. Leaving his scruples in Egypt to follow his star, Napoleon barely evaded Nelson's fleet and returned to Paris as the conqueror of Egypt, as another Caesar. A conspiracy to overthrow the Directory was effected with the aid of three directors and the upper house of the legislature. On November 9, 1799 Napoleon's armed force took possession of the state.

Dictators prefer to act constitutionally. Having seized power, Napoleon wrote a new constitution establishing an elected **Consulate** with himself as First Consul. He created a legislative apparatus but made it impotent. By 1802, Napoleon was ready to throw off the disguise of democracy. He was elected consul for life. Two years later he became Emperor of the French with rights to hereditary succession.

Wherever possible he remained close to popular acceptance. After each coup he submitted the accomplished fact to a popular vote. Since these votes were conducted without free discussion, with no possible alternatives and under army rule, they were overwhelmingly for each of Napoleon's acts. (There is little doubt, on the other hand, that as long as he was successful, Napoleon did command the loyalty of the French people.)

Conqueror. In 1810 Napoleon ruled France, the eastern half of Italy, Belgium, Holland, the Rhineland—directly; indirectly he controlled the vast Confederation of the Rhine (the Germanies), the Grand Duchy of Warsaw (Poland), the Kingdom of Italy, the Kingdom of Naples, Switzerland and the Kingdom of Spain. Within the French orbits lay Denmark and Norway, Prussia and Austria. This overlordship was achieved by conquest in war.

Napoleon's victories at Ulm, Austerlitz, Jena, Friedland are classics of military strategy and are still studied in military academies. His military principles included: simplicity, rapidity, superiority of forces in localized areas, concentration, quick decision on the spot, meticulous study of positions and alternatives, keen perception of the psychology of the opponent, judicious use of all information, material and moral, attention to the most insignificant of details, obedient officers who took no initiative, rigid discipline and self-confidence. Yet, within five years of his position in 1810, his armies were defeated and his kingdom gone. What brought this conqueror so low?

Decline and Fall. Many factors served to bring about the collapse of Napoleon. None was more important than England's dogged resistance and her command of the seas and her ability to inspire and to supply opposition to Napoleon. England's chief weapon was her shops and her chief warrior shopkeepers who produced manufactured goods that were far more durable and cheap than any produced on the continent.

Napoleon hoped to choke off all British trade with the continent. By a series of decrees he placed a paper blockade around Europe and around England; no English ship could deliver goods to Europe; and no non-English ship could deliver goods to England. England retorted with her own blockade on French ships and on foreign ships trading with the French. Europeans felt severely the prohibition on entry into Europe of British goods and evaded Napoleon's **Continental System** by widespread smuggling.

It was the Continental System that led to Napoleon's disastrous Spanish campaign and march into Russia. In Spain Napoleon had to fight a species of guerilla warfare that drained men and supplies and could not be brought to a decision. In Russia he encountered similar warfare accompanied by a "scorched earth" policy and then by bitter winter fighting for which the French were unprepared. Half-a-million men were lost in the **Russian Campaign of 1812.** Moreover, willingness to fight the French resulted from the insurgence of nationalism that arose out of disillusionment with Napoleon's promises of liberation and out of national humiliation resulting from constant defeat at Napoleon's hands. Freedom proved a double-edged sword for the conqueror.

So, too, did Napoleon's efforts to unify such countries as Italy, Germany and Poland. Napoleon's aim was efficiency in French domination. But having tasted the sweets of unification, these countries now demanded the fruits—independence from French domination.

Finally, continual war exhausted the French materially and spiritually. Only a few Frenchmen reaped the benefits of war profits; on most fell the burdens of French taxation and the loss and mutilation of their loved ones. All of these factors collected at Leipzig in 1814 and in the **Battle of Nations** Napoleon suffered total defeat. He was sent to **Elbe** in exile but escaped and for "100 Days" gave Europe a fright until in 1815 he was finally destroyed at **Waterloo.** Once more he was sent into exile on the island of **St. Helena** in the mid-Atlantic. There he "ruled" until he died on May 5, 1821.

NAPOLEONIC REFORMS

Napoleon was a reformer in spite of himself. France had to be a stable base from which to conquer Europe. For this reason he lent himself to any reform proposal that would strengthen his ultimate purpose. Thus he retained the basic structure of the French Revolutionary reforms; any effort to restore the Old Regime would have been fatal to his need for internal unity. The French Revolutionists had abolished the feudal provinces and reshaped France into equalized departments. Napoleon kept this arrangement but centralized it by appointing as responsible to himself the local rulers of the departments. Centralization made for efficiency and economy.

Then Napoleon solved the financial problem. He placed the French currency on a specie basis and established a central Bank of France to issue a uniform currency that proved to be exceptionally stable. The central bank also served as an agency for government loans, a place of deposit and a source of credit to France's rising bourgeoisie. As additional aids to the commercial and mercantile classes, upon whose support he relied heavily, Napoleon built roads and canals, improved harbors and gave direct subsidies to industry. He made Paris imposing by broadening the streets (also for rapid troop movements), fashioning decorative gardens and parks and constructing triumphal arches and columns.

Labor was made obedient to the needs of the bourgeoisie with legislation directed against the formation of unions and the requirement that workers carry passports and were not free to leave their employment without permission.

He made peace with the Catholic Church in a concordat that enabled him to share with the Pope the selection of bishops and lower clergy and to retain control over the clergy through payment of their salaries. Law reform, begun during the period of the Revolution, was brought to completion in the **Code Napoleon** which simplified procedures in criminal and civil actions but in no way reduced the dictatorship of Napoleon over all means of communication. To facilitate the flow of pro-Napoleonic propaganda Napoleon created the University of France, an administrative body that regularized the selection of teachers and the curriculum of the schools of France. Finally, he rewarded devotion to himself by creating the Legion of Honor as the highest state award.

All of these measures were undertaken to consolidate dictatorship. However, when France became democratic again, they were made to serve democratic needs—in this lies their greatness. Napoleon had created better than he knew; his reforms would serve the French people in years to come as a safeguard against dictatorship.

THE IMPACT OF THE NAPOLEONIC WARS ON EUROPE

In conquering Europe, Napoleon transformed it. He provided the impetus which propelled Italy and Germany toward unification. Italians had not known what it was to be unified until Napoleon created the Cisalpine and Ligurian Republics. Germany had been a quilt of small principalities until Napoleon consolidated them into thirty-eight and then unified them into the Confederation of the Rhine. In the course of Napoleon's control steps were taken to shake off the relics of feudalism and to institute modern governmental practices.

The full impact of Napoleon's influence upon Italian and German nationalism was not felt until the mid-nineteenth century. Similarly, Poland, which had been partitioned among Austria, Prussia and Russia in the late 18th century, was given a rebirth in the Duchy of Warsaw. These and many other territorial changes effected by Napoleon were the subject of the Congress that met at Vienna in 1815 to reshape the map of Europe to something like it was before Napoleon had remade it.

The Congress of Vienna. Two problems confronted the **Congress of Vienna**: that of reshaping the map of Europe and that of "containing" the French Revolutionism. The leaders of the Congress —PRINCE METTERNICH of Austria, Tsar Alexander I, the DUKE OF WELLINGTON of England and others— were determined to reap territorial benefits for their own countries, and to arrange it so that no revolutionary outbreak could ever again occur.

How then was the land to be redistributed? France's delegate, TALLEYRAND, proposed a "principle of legitimacy," a principle which would restore all lands to their owners as they were before Napoleon. Thus France would be returned to the Bourbon family, the descendents of Louis XVI; Spain to its Bourbons; Italy to Austria, etc. This was far from satisfactory to those powers instrumental in the defeat of Napoleon who had no European territory before the rise of Napoleon. Led by England these powers proposed a principle of compensation for services rendered. A third principle made its appearance in the form of a demand that buffer states be created to encircle France.

Such "principles" were adopted without any regard for the peoples concerned. Thus it hardly comported with the will of the French people or the Spanish people to have their Old Regimes restored; nor were the Italians happy to be redistributed to the Austrians and to the Pope. German lands were given back to German feudal princes; Holland was merged with Belgium as a buffer state—a merger that satisfied neither people. Compensation was turned into aggressive imperialism when England was awarded Cape Colony, Ceylon, Honduras, Malta, Trinidad, etc. Nationalism was severely violated when Alexander was given the Duchy of Warsaw and Finland as "compensation." The Treaty of Vienna, therefore, created many potential trouble spots over the face of Europe, places of revolutionary infection.

Negligent of the consequences of these territorial arrangements, the great powers at Vienna now formed a **Holy Alliance** and a **Quadruple Alliance** (Russia, Prussia, Austria and England) which would remain permanently armed and ready to suppress revolution wherever it occurred. The job of suppression fell upon the country nearest the source. Thus when an outbreak occurred in Spain in 1820 against the brutal rule of Ferdinand VII, the French were sent in to suppress it; similarly, the Austrians suppressed a Neopolitan revolt for the King of Naples.

Meanwhile, each country undertook to abolish forever the force of liberalism within its own precincts. Following Metternich's example in Austria, complete censorship of the press was instituted, an active system of espionage was launched, universities were placed under direct police observation, student clubs for discussion were prohibited, mass demonstrations were brutally crushed, arbitrary arrest was frequently resorted to, terror was freely utilized. By this means did the powers hope to crush forever the spirit of the French Revolution.

The French Revolution Persists. But all this was easier decreed than enforced. Underground movements spread throughout the European countries dedicated to the overthrow of the **Metternich System** of suppression of democracy and nationalism. Of primary importance to the eventual success of these underground liberals was the defection of England from the Quadruple Alliance. In the decade of the 1820's the Greeks successfully fought their way to independence from the Turkish empire with British assistance. During the same period the Spanish colonies in South America made their bid for independence from Spain under the gallant leadership of SIMON BOLIVAR aided and abetted by England (seeking to take over Spanish trade) and the Monroe Doctrine of the United States. In the 1830's came a series of revolutions and, though for the most part suppressed, these did result in the overthrow in France of the Bourbon Charles X and the separation of Belgium from Holland—in spite of the Treaty of Vienna.

But the great wave of revolutions stemmed from the **French Revolution of 1848.** In the course of these European revolutions, Metternich himself was overthrown in Austria, the second French Republic was established, Italy and Germany established foundations for national unity in Prussia and Piedmont. By the mid-century it was clear that what had been born in the French Revolution could never again be crushed—for long.

CHAPTER EIGHTEEN

INDUSTRIAL REVOLUTION

INTRODUCTION

While the French Revolution was transforming the spiritual and political life of man, an Industrial Revolution was taking place that was to transform his material life. In the middle of the 18th century came the culmination of hundreds of years of experimentation with a new power resource; it took the form of a steam engine. The steam engine was a source of *automatic* power, power for the first time in the history of mankind independent of muscle, wind and water.

No sooner was this accomplished when the pulse of all production, labor, distribution and exchange quickened. Out of this quickening came a rush of material goods that transformed the shape of the earth and the minds of men. At first subtly and then obviously, the impact of the Industrial Revolution made itself felt in the total political, economic, social and cultural life of man.

After 1850, if not long before then, it became impossible to discuss any historical movement without giving full consideration to the results of the Industrial Revolution. As much as any other cause, for example, the Industrial Revolution was responsible for the overthrow of the Metternich System in 1848. Let us turn then to a study of the causes, development and results of the Industrial Revolution.

CAUSES

No nation in history possessed a monopoly on science and invention; the causes, then, for the Industrial Revolution are international. Historically, however, it was England that gave leadership to the movement which became the Industrial Revolution. Why England?

For one thing, the Industrial Revolution required a tremendous outlay of investment capital. England had it. Over the 17th and 18th centuries Englishmen had grown rich in trade and commerce. Agriculture, too, proved profitable after Englishmen had enclosed their fields to convert them into sheep pastures and had applied important discoveries in farming and animal breeding to agricultural production. Viscount Townshend had discovered that turnips restored minerals to the soil; this discovery revolutionized crop rotation and put an end to the wasteful three-field system. Jethro Tull produced an efficient seed-drill that ensured more crops per acre. Robert Bakewell introduced the scientific breeding of cattle and multiplied the number that could be raised for meat. Each of these advances added to the capital store of the English. So, too, did the stable currency, the sound Bank of England, and the many joint-stock devices employed by English businessmen to increase the amount of capital available by the process of pooling.

Labor was also available. English population mounted steadily during the 18th century. Normally this increase would have been absorbed into agriculture. However, the enclosure movement had dispossessed many yeomen, skilled in the use of tools, and had forced them to drift to urban centers where they were available when the first factories were built.

Some role must be assigned to accident for it was not by design that JOHN KAY and JAMES HARGREAVES began an industrial transformation of the British textile industry. Kay had hit upon a "flying shuttle" which sped up the process of weaving to such a degree that spinners could not meet the demand. Out of this necessity, perhaps, Hargreaves invented the "spinning jenny" which equalized the two processes. Men now set about deliberately to make new inventions in these areas and out of this search came, in fairly rapid succession, ARKWRIGHT'S "water-frame" to strengthen the thread, CROMPTON'S "spinning mule" and, following WATT'S invention of the steam-engine, CARTWRIGHT'S "power loom." The pressure was now upon the cotton producer, a pressure that was removed when ELI WHITNEY in-

vented his "cotton gin." Arkwright's "water-frame" was so large that it required separate housing; out of this need the factory was born.

More pivotal than any, however, was Watt's "steam engine." The industrial uses of this invention were manifold. Cartwright hitched it to a loom, Robert Fulton to a boat and George Stephenson to a locomotive. But the boiler and the engine had to be made of sturdy material. Cast-iron would not do. More rapid steel making (an ancient process) had to be devised. Darby found that coke could be used in a blast furnace; Smeaton added an air-pump feature; Cort and Onions simultaneously discovered a reverbatory furnace, the puddling process and rolling mill; Nielson added a hot blast; and it all culminated when Bessemer invented the open-hearth furnace.

Fortunately England possessed the very resources that were necessary in these early stages of the Industrial Revolution: coal, iron, water-power and the like. And, as transport needs mounted, it was England that produced the macadamized road. England also had adequate seaports and inland canals; and—with her far-flung commerce and colonies—there were ready markets.

In England of the 18th century, then, **capital, labor, accident, invention, social necessity, resources and markets combined to produce an Industrial Revolution.** At later dates, the pattern was much the same in all other western lands.

DEVELOPMENT OF THE INDUSTRIAL REVOLUTION

The Industrial Revolution spread out of England slowly; in 1850 the primary productive pattern in the western world was still agriculture and it was not until 1870 that manufacturing began to overtake agriculture.

There are many explanations for this slow progress. Europe, for example, spent the first quarter of the 19th century recovering from the Napoleonic Wars. Many of the countries lacked some one or more of the basic factors required for industrial progress. Social or cultural lag existed in mental outlook and educational system. In the United States wide stretches of free or almost free land acted as a deterrent and prevented large capital accumulation. England's initial superiority gave her a competitive advantage that handicapped other nations. In spite of these many handicaps, however, the Industrial Revolution spread into Europe, particularly into France, Belgium and Germany; Italy and

Russia lagged until the very end of the 19th century.

Stages In The Industrial Revolution. Primary concentration in the first stage (ca. 1750-1850) was upon elaboration of the productive process: discovery of required raw materials, refinement of processes in the extraction of raw materials, extensions of the uses of the steam engine, construction of factories and the development in workers of factory discipline, laying the groundwork for an improved system of transportation and solving the problem of maximizing profits (capital accumulation).

In the second stage of the Industrial Revolution (1850-1900) productive inventiveness continued at a rapid pace; but the other factors of labor, distribution and exchange became the center of concentration. To reduce labor costs and the growing "threat" of labor organization, manufacturers began to invest in machines that would break down production into minute processes and destroy the basis of skilled labor. Symbolic of this trend was the work of the American, FREDERICK WINSLOW TAYLOR (1856-1915), in the field of scientific management. Taylor began experimental studies ("time-and-motion" studies) to set standards of efficient working performance. During this period the corporative form of business organization was elaborated as was the relation of business to banking.

In the field of invention a revolution was effected in transportation and communication. By 1850 the railroad had proved its effectiveness and a rush was begun in all countries to lay track. Problems involved in railroad transport were soon overcome by invention of high powered locomotives, air brakes, standard gauges, signal systems, refrigeration cars, sleepers and the like. Steamboating kept pace with railroading.

More and more industrialism, in this period, began to rely upon pure science. This was nowhere more true than in the field of communications. Out of the work of such men as Franklin, Galvani, Volta, Ampere, Ohm, Maxwell and Faraday came the possibility of communication by electrical impulses. An electric telegraph was invented independently by Carl Steinheil, a German, Charles Wheatstone, an Englishman, and Samuel Morse an American. The telegraph, however, was land-bound until Cyrus W. Field solved the oceanographic problems required to lay a trans-Atlantic cable; this was accomplished in 1866.

Important advances were registered, too, in the field of lighting. The kerosene lamp was perfected in 1784. More useful, however, was the gaslighting device perfected by Murdock, Bunsen and Welsbach in the mid-nineteenth century. Toward the end of this period, electric lighting made its appearance as a result of the researches of Davy, Marks, Edison and many others.

The third stage of the Industrial Revolution had little unity—expansion occurred in every imaginable direction. Invention itself was systematized and accelerated through creation of subsidized laboratories. Of especial note was the rise of the chemist as an adjunct to industry. Upon him fell the responsibility of discovering new uses for old resources and the manufacture of synthetic resources as substitutes for natural products.

Out of the invention of the internal combustion engine and the electric motor whole new worlds appeared: the automobile industry, the industries of radio and television, great hydroelectric plants, the airplane industry and the like. Of equal importance was the development of the precision instrument—a development that gave to the phyicist the same status as the chemist in the industrial world. The engineer, of course, became a key figure as the demand for roads, bridges, communications, building structures, electrical appliances and the like rose.

Mass production became a startling reality when the factory was rationalized through use of assembly lines and standardized parts. Of primary importance was the distribution of this mass production. Problems of transport were solved through further developments of railroad and steamship and the introduction of trucks and airplanes. But the sale of goods required the transformation of advertising into a national industry. This in turn put pressure on the creation of mass media of communication. The linotype machine, typewriter, and rotary press accommodated this need; radio and television enhanced it. Along with the revolution in advertisement of products, came a revolution in the financing of the purchase of goods—installment buying. With exhaustion of resources at home began a worldwide search for raw materials such as rubber, tin, nitrates, manganese, magnesium, chromium, nickel, lead, copper, hardwoods, etc.

With the discovery of thermonuclear power a new and fourth stage in the Industrial Revolution loomed. This stage brought the physicist to the fore. It is too early to project the transformations that will be made as a result of this discovery of a new power-source. The peaceful uses of atomic energy have been probed—chiefly in the areas of medical research, agricultural production, new sources of power and the like. The world is waiting for a new dawn.

RESULTS OF THE INDUSTRIAL REVOLUTION

General. In essence, the Industrial Revolution was a transfer from hand tool to machine process; from muscle-wind-and-water power to steam-gas-electricity-and-atomic power. Manufacturing became a way of life emphasizing compulsory centralization of the labor force around the machine, complete dependence of the labor force upon the machine for a livelihood, impersonalization of the relations between worker and employer and regimentation of the life of the worker to the demands of production. From the factory flowed ever-increasing production and this was reflected in expanding commerce, accumulated capital, national and international corporations, business combinations in the forms of merger, trust, holding company, interlocking directorates, cartels and the like. Increased standards of living resulted and this was followed by rapid increases of population for the most part gathered into urban areas where cultural life blossomed on the nurture provided by increased educational facilities. But culture, too, followed the pattern of standardization; mass media threatened to produce mass minds, mass behavior.

Machine Culture. Mankind came to depend upon invention for innovation; progress was equated with multiplication of gadgets. There was no limit to inventiveness. In the wake of the mechanization of society came many problems affecting human welfare: overcrowded cities, indebtedness, increasing destructiveness of wars, labor-management conflict, and the like.

The Workingman. The brunt of the inhumanity in the machine civilization fell upon the workingman. Skilled workers of the late 18th and early 19th centuries resented and resisted the introduction of the factory system; they became, in fact, "machine-wreckers." Factory processes reduced the workingman to a mechanical unit engaged in some small specialized task that produced fatigue and boredom.

Moreover, in the early period of capital accumulation working conditions were abominable. Factories were hastily and cheaply built; no provisions were made for the health or safety of the employees in matters of ventilation, lighting or provisions for creature comforts. Child labor was brutally exploited in the form of pauper apprentices. Hours of work ranged between 14 and 16 a day. Wages were miserably low.

From impoverished conditions in the factory, workers moved to even worse conditions at home.

Slums made up the bulk of dwelling quarters in factory towns. Crime and epidemic disease were the consequences of these miserable hovels in which workers dwelt. Added to these inadequate conditions of work was the continuous insecurity that hung over the heads of the working people. They were completely unprotected in the face of unemployment produced by technological change or depressions, of illness and accident for which there was no compensation, and of old age—a variable figure depending on the supply of workers available. This, then, was the social lag behind industrial progress.

Overcoming The Social Lag. To overcome the social lag to industrial progress, a humanitarian revolution in the minds of the rulers of mankind had to be effected. Horrible conditions had first to be seen as horrible, and felt as such. This required intensive education through propaganda and agitation, a campaign that was launched by workers' organizations, philosophers like Jeremy Bentham and William Godwin, poets like Shelley and Thomas Hood, novelists like Charles Dickens and George Eliot and politicians like Benjamin Disraeli, William Gladstone, Otto von Bismarck, Andrew Jackson. These men helped to transform the problem of working conditions into a *moral* question.

The result of all this agitation and propaganda was a series of social laws passed by interested governments which set out to reform the conditions under which men labored in factories and mines. In England, for example, between 1802 and 1860, a large number of factory acts were passed. These had the effect of reducing by law the number of hours of work, of discouraging the employment of child labor, of limiting the employment of women, of compelling the introduction of health, sanitation and safety devices in factories. Later legislation in England (1870-1920) freed workers to organize into labor unions and to strike for increased wages and improved working conditions.

Germany, under OTTO VON BISMARCK, took the leadership in framing the first social security laws, laws providing for workman's compensation in the event of accident on the job, for old age pensions, for sickness and unemployment insurance. These laws were eventually introduced into all the industrialized nations of the world.

The Capitalist System. Capitalism came to full growth under the impetus of the Industrial Revolution. It was the primary agency in the transformation of society from a low-producing to a high-producing level. In the course of its development, capitalism moved through several stages. The earliest was the stage of industrial capitalism—where individual capitalists owned the factories as single proprietorships or as partnerships. To a great extent these capitalists relied upon their own resources for expansion. As business grew, however, the single proprietorship and partnership proved to be inadequate as financial vehicles. The result was that capitalists began to depend more and more on the corporation—and the sale of stocks and bonds—as a means for gathering in wealth. Increasingly, in this second stage of capitalist development, industrialists began to turn to the banks for loans for expansion.

This led to the third stage, that of finance capitalism. In this stage industrial and banking elements in the economic process merged to provide industry with a virtually unlimited capital expansion base. In this area, as in the area of mechanization, a social lag appeared.

Ownership and management were divorced, a divorce that produced the possibilities of mismanagement. Mismanagement resulted in practices which strangled free competition by monopolization; which defrauded stockholders through issuance of "watered" stock, or failure to declare dividends; which practiced fraud on consumers through price fixing, adulteration of product and the like; which encouraged corrupt political practices like bribery of legislators. The social lag was somewhat remedied in most countries by government intervention that resulted in anti-trust laws, laws regulating the issuance of corporate securities, pure food and drug laws, income and corporate tax laws and the like.

Abandonment of Laissez Faire. Government intervention in the economic process is the antithesis of laissez faire, the system of ideas under which capitalism grew to maturity. As taught by Adam Smith in his *Wealth of Nations*, the doctrine of laissez faire assumed that there were rational, natural laws that governed economic behavior. Men left alone to pursue selfish ends in the use of their capital and labor would ultimately produce social good. The laws of free trade and of competition, of supply and demand, would determine success and failure in the economic struggle for existence; but the end result would be an increase in the total national wealth.

Smith founded the school of liberal or classical economists, members of which searched for "natural laws" in the economy of capitalism. Thus THOMAS MALTHUS proposed an "iron law" of population and demonstrated that famine, war,

disease and population control are advantageous since population increases geometrically while food supply increases arithmetically. DAVID RICARDO "proved" that wages sink to the mere level of subsistence. Nassau Senior "demonstrated" that hours of work could not be lowered without disastrous consequences to profits. McCulloch "proved" on the basis of and existing "wages-fund" that wage increase to one group had to result in wage decrease for another.

All of this theorizing resulted in a pattern of beliefs that called for abolition of tariffs and subsidies, free contracting, treatment of labor organization as conspiracy, free competition, and no government restraint upon economic free choice. Between 1800 and 1860 the English government, for example, followed this doctrine to the letter. The "corn laws (tariffs)" were repealed, mercantilist regulations concerning the granting of monopolies were removed from the legislative books, laws protecting apprentices were abrogated. We have seen the abuses that followed upon this adoption of the complete policy of laissez faire. (There is little doubt that if we ignore humanitarian considerations, laissez faire did accomplish miracles in production at a time when the resources for such productive effort were limited.)

No country followed England in its application of the policy of laissez faire. From their inception, the classical economists were challenged on theoretical lines. From America and Germany came economic doctrines defending protectionism as a means for hastening industrial advance. Population theorists challenged Malthus when it became obvious that the industrial revolution would extend to the farm and result in fabulous increases in food production. The most serious challenge, however, came from the "socialists" who took the abuses of the capitalist as their starting point and ignored the many efforts being made by governments to correct these abuses.

Socialism. Socialism was as much an *ethical* as an economic discipline; its theories were in part formed out of a preconceived utopian dream in which all men were economically equal and lived in the midst of abundance.

Early socialists like SAINT-SIMON (1760-1825), FOURIER (1772-1837) and ROBERT OWEN (1772-1858) were labelled "Utopians" by later socialists like KARL MARX (1818-1883). This derogatory label was not directed against the ultimate plans of the Utopians, for these plans envisaged the abolition of the capitalist class and the substitution of some form of workingclass ownership and control of the means of production (as socialism is defined). Derogation was directed against the means by which these theoreticians proposed to eliminate the capitalist class.

Saint-Simon hoped to bring socialism by the arts of persuasion and appeal to Christian doctrine; Fourier proposed that workers and others form voluntary socialist societies which he called "phalanxes" where all would work for all; Owen hoped to convince capitalists by his own example to build model socialist communities with their capital. (Fourierism caught on somewhat in the United States in the 1830's and '40's where experiments like Brook Farm and Oneida were tried and failed. Owen went bankrupt after his ventures in capitalist socialism at New Harmony, Indiana.) LOUIS BLANC (1813-1882)—an influential figure in the Revolution of 1848 in France—advanced the concept of government financed socialist communities, a scheme for turning over factories to workers and financing them until they were able to stand on their own feet. In practice this system turned out to be a huge financial dole that almost bankrupted the government.

Karl Marx (author of *Capital* and co-author with Frederick Engels of *Communist Manifesto*) condemned all of these efforts and proposed instead his own brand of "scientific" socialism. He advocated both peaceful and violent waging of a "class war" to overthrow capitalism. His followers, who believed in peaceful "class war" became latter-day socialists; those who favored force and violence to establish a "dictatorship of the proletariat" became communists. Marxism, then, was both a theory about capitalist society and a blueprint for its replacement.

IN SUM

Out of the Industrial Revolution came most of the problems with which men and states are grappling today. Among these are those of healthful and safe living in congested urban areas; of population decline; of the economic and social welfare of the under-privileged; of automation and automatonization; of mass communication and individualization; of the democratization of industry; of the disparity between wealth and equality; of imperialism and nationalism; and finally, of survival in a warring world.

CHAPTER NINETEEN

NATIONAL TRENDS (1815-1915)

ENGLAND

Though by far the most democratic country in Europe in 1815, England was far from being truly democratic. Suffrage was severely limited by property and religious qualifications; most members of Parliament were hand-picked representatives of wealthy rural landlords; representation in Parliament had no relation to population distribution ("rotten boroughs"—electoral districts with virtually no people—continued to send two representatives to Parliament); voting was by open ballot and bribery and intimidation were rife; no woman could vote; the unelected House of Lords shared equal power with the elected House of Commons and could veto any proposal for electoral reform; members of Parliament were not paid—only the very wealthy could afford to be elected. During the century under consideration each of these

abuses was eliminated; by 1928 England was a truly democratic state, made democratic through an evolutionary, not revolutionary, development.

It took almost a century to establish universal suffrage in England. The first break through the Conservative phalanx constructed by the Duke of Wellington came in 1832. **Whigs**, soon to call themselves **Liberals**, took over the government from the **Tories**, soon to become the **Conservatives**, and under the leadership of Lord John Russell and Earl Grey passed the **Reform Bill of 1832**. This bill extended the right to vote to the middle-classes and small landholders; it abolished all rotten boroughs and made representation more consistent with population.

The vote having been granted to them, the middle classes pushed through legislation favorable to themselves—local governments were made elective; public education was extended; Poor Laws were abolished as were the Corn Laws (tariffs). Demands for increased democracy became more vocal. One symbol of this demand was the **Chartist Movement** (1838-1848)—a workingman's group organized to secure universal male suffrage, more equal electoral districts, the secret ballot, a Parliament elected once a year, abolition of property qualifications for office-holding and payment of members of Parliament.

Though Chartism failed as an organized movement, most of its program was eventually adopted. Property qualifications for office holding were abolished in 1858; in 1829 and 1867 religious qualifications were also eliminated. In 1867 the great Conservative Prime Minister, BENJAMIN DISRAELI, pushed through a reform bill which extended suffrage to virtually all of the city workers. Not to be outdone by his rival, the equally great Prime Minister, WILLIAM GLADSTONE, Liberal, in 1884 completed the goal of universal male suffrage by extending the vote to the farm laborers.

Meanwhile, led by EMMELINE PANKHURST and her militant suffragettes, a crusade was launched to extend the vote to women. It was not until after the first World War, however, that limited woman's suffrage was enacted, and not until the "flapper vote" of 1928 that England achieved the democratic goal of universal suffrage for all over 21 years of age who were British subjects. In 1872 the vote was purified by the introduction of the Australian or secret ballot.

As the Industrial Revolution progressed, politics began to concern itself more and more with issues of economic and social welfare. Slow but considerable progress was made during the century in ameliorating the lot of the worker, the impoverished and the illiterate. Each of these moves in the direction of social legislation had been opposed strenuously by the House of Lords. By 1911, the time had come for a reconsideration of the British constitutional system. From the eighteenth century the Prime Minister had slowly emerged as the most important single figure in the British government. (The monarch had become a figurehead completely dependent on Parliament. This is not to say that the monarchy did not serve useful purposes: it served as a symbol of unity for the Empire; it fostered the Englishman's sense of tradition; it could advise public ministers.)

The Prime Minister's importance derived from the facts that he was the spokesman for the parliamentary majority in the House of Commons and, when in disagreement with the majority there,

he could force a new election by dissolving the Commons. Until 1911, however, he had no control over the House of Lords. Led by LLOYD GEORGE, British Liberals forced through in that year a bill which reduced the power of the House of Lords to a suspensive veto. After a stated period of time and certain defined procedures, any bill desired today by the House of Commons can become law whether approved by the Lords or not. Thus England became virtually a unicameral government and responsive to the will of the electorate. In that same year payment for parliamentary members was introduced and it was decreed that there should be an election of Parliament at least every five years.

This century, too, witnessed the expansion of the British empire and the wars fought by England to secure and maintain her colonies. She abandoned the Quadruple Alliance to defend the revolt of the Spanish American colonies; fought an Opium War in 1839 to open China to the trade of England; moved to retain her hold on Canada by making early formulation (the British North American Act 1867) of a dominion (autonomous) form of government; made India into a royal colony after the brutal suppression of the Sepoy Mutiny; fought the Crimean War to prevent Russia's emergence into the warm waters of the Mediterranean (1853-1856); secured strong control over the Suez Canal and eventually over all of Egypt and the Sudan; reduced Afghanistan to dependency; and in the Boer War (1899-1900) won all of South Africa. More "peaceful" penetration had been made of vast sections of mid-Africa.

By 1915 England owned or controlled almost one-quarter of the surface of the globe. Literally, the sun never set on the British Isles where each colonial Englishman was busy with his "white man's burden" to "civilize" the backward peoples to England's imperial needs. Only in Ireland would the matter of domination not settle. While the British, under Gladstone, moved in the direction of relieving the hard economic lot of the Irish, the Irish under the leadership of CHARLES PARNELL and others fought for complete independence.

FRANCE

France, in this century, also took the road to democracy; but it was a difficult road. As a result of the Metternichean restoration, the Bourbons had returned to France in the person of Louis XVIII. Louis was wise enough to realize that the Old

Regime could never be fully restored; that some pretenses in the direction of democracy would have to be made. So he drew up a constitution that was in fact a limited dictatorship. He lived out his normal life.

Less wise was Charles X, his successor. Over-inspired by Metternich, Charles, in 1830, issued an infamous set of **July Ordinances** that destroyed the base of all French liberties. The workers of Paris staged a blood revolution. Charles was deposed. His successor, Louis-Philippe (1830–1848), ruled as a "bourgeois monarch" limited by a constitution that restricted his power but one which also severely restricted the franchise.

Louis-Philippe was overthrown in the Revolution of 1848. A provisional government was set up pending a new constitution that would create a second French republic. In the government was Louis Blanc, the socialist. Blanc managed to get through a scheme of "national workshops"—a parody of his plan for the government to finance worker ownership of the means of production. When these "national workshops" suffered failure, the socialists lost favor and in the election for the presidency of the new republic LOUIS NAPOLEON, a nephew of the great Napoleon, (capitalizing on his uncle's revived fame) was chosen as president. Louis took office in 1848, waited three years and staged a *coup d'etat* (1851) and within a year created the second French empire with himself as emperor.

Where Napoleon I had brought France the fame of conquest, Napoleon III brought it the fame of fashion. Riding a wave of prosperity, Louis used surplus treasury funds to modernize Paris until it became the Mecca of tourists; he fostered many projects which won him the support of the bourgeoisie; he subsidized French artists to the point where French literature and painting received great stimulus; he won the support of the Catholic Church and the French peasantry. Only the working people in the cities suffered during his reign and more and more turned to socialist parties for their salvation.

Dreams of military glory to equal that of his uncle drove Louis into a series of wars, wars overseas that extended French control over Algeria, Indo-China, Mexico and Pacific Islands; wars on the continent against Russia, Austria and Germany. It was this latter, the **Franco-Prussian War** (1870–1871), that led to the overthrow of Louis Napoleon and to the establishment of the Third French Republic. This government which was set up as provisional proved to be the most lasting of the French governments since the French Revolution.

The Third Republic rose out of the revolution which is known historically as the **Paris Commune,** an effort of the workers, intellectuals and socialists to seize the government of France following the debacle in the Franco-Prussian War (1871). When finally constituted this government resembled that of Great Britain in centralization of power in the legislature, in its placement of executive rule in a Premier chosen by the majority party in the lower house (Chamber of Deputies) and in its maintenance of a president chosen by both houses as figurehead with considerable advisory powers. It differed from the British government in that it had a bicameral legislature and in the fact that the presence of many political parties compelled the formation of blocs of parties to secure a majority to choose a premier. Difficulty in securing agreement among the many parties gave France a relatively unstable government apparatus.

Many issues arose in the course of the next quarter-century to challenge the strength of the French republic. In 1886–1889 a "man on horseback," General Georges Boulanger, attempted a coup d'etat and failed. In 1894 began the **Dreyfus Case.** Captain Alfred Dreyfus, an officer in the French army and a Jew, was accused and convicted of treason. Many Frenchmen—particularly the novelist EMILE ZOLA—were convinced that Dreyfus was innocent, a victim of a combined monarchist-clerical plot against the Republic. A long battle was fought and won (1906) to free Dreyfus. In the course of this battle, the royalist-clerical parties of France were so thoroughly discredited that the republic became solidly founded and democracy extended.

In 1901 the Associations Law secularized education and in 1905 a Separation Act separated the church and state by abolishing Napoleon I's Concordat with the Pope. After 1905 a series of laws brought to French workers the same social security protections (accident and sickness insurance, old age pensions, etc.) that were already enjoyed by the workers of England, Germany, and other countries. Of considerable importance for the future was the growth of the French Catholic Party pledged to accept republicanism and a program of social welfare as a check to the growing socialist influence. One drawback in the democratic state thus created in France was the absence of woman suffrage. Women, in fact, did not secure the right to vote until the reconstruction of the French

Republic following liberation from the Nazis in 1945.

ITALY

Italy was but a geographical expression in 1815. Spanish Bourbons ruled Sicily and the southern half of the Italian boot as the Kingdom of the Two Sicilies. The Pope owned and ruled a vast domain in central Italy known as the Papal States. Petty princes ruled over three large states—Parma, Modena and Tuscany. Austria owned the even larger northern states of Lombardy and Venetia. Only the Kingdom of Sardinia which consisted of the island of Sardinia and the large northwestern state of Piedmont were ruled as an *Italian* nation. The Congress of Vienna had stamped its approval on this disunity.

Risorgimento. Out of the embers of the preceding Revolutionary epoch there had risen everywhere in Europe a **spirit of nationalism** among people who spoke the same language, had a common history and tradition, occupied a memorial land, shared the same customs and cultural heritage. In Italy scholars led the way by reviving memories of the glories of ancient Rome, the great contributions of Dante and the Renaissance masters to world culture, and they called for a rebirth, a *"risorgimento,"* of Italian splendor.

Of prime importance to the realization of this goal, they preached, was the violent overthrow of all foreign rulers in Italy and the establishment of a united nation. Moving from preachment to action, scholars helped to organize secret societies pledged to overthrow the Austrians as a beginning. In 1820 and again in 1830 attempts were made, but they proved abortive. Major obstacles appeared in the opposition to unity by the foreign overlords, the petty princes, the Pope (supported militarily by Louis Napoleon after 1848) and the quarrels among the Italian revolutionaries themselves.

JOSEPH MAZZINI (1805-1872) led one group. An impassioned poet and dreamer, Mazzini inflamed and then organized Italian youth into a movement called **Young Italy** dedicated to a direct assault on foreign masters in Italy and to the immediate and unconditional establishment of a free democratic society in a united land. Young Italy was opposed by Vincenzo Gioberti who proposed a united Italy under the presidency of the Pope. A third group, the party of the Sardinians, proposed that unification be made to center around the already established Kingdom of Piedmont.

During the Revolution of 1848 Piedmont's king, Charles Albert, had led an attack on Austria in the hope of rallying all of Italy to the cause of national unity. Albert was deserted by his southern allies and defeated by a revived Austria led by Field Marshal Radetsky. During the debacle which ensued, radical nationalists under Mazzini and Garibaldi seized Rome. They were ousted from power by the zealous Louis Napoleon's troops in 1848. All efforts at unification of the Italian peninsula collapsed—for the time being.

Count Cavour. The Revolution of 1848, however, brought a constitution to Piedmont, a new king—Victor Emmanuel II—to the throne, and CAMILLO DI CAVOUR (1810-1861) into the ministry of the government of Piedmont. Cavour conceived and executed the plan which made Italy into a united nation by 1861.

His plan was simplicity itself: he would build up Piedmont's economic and military potential and then ally himself with some strong European power at the price of removing Italy's enemies from control of Italian land. Italy's middle classes were strengthened by curbs on church property, favorable commercial treaties with neighboring states, construction of railroads, etc. The standing army was enlarged and improved. When the Crimean War broke out, Cavour joined it as an ally of Britain and France. The choice was wise for it enabled Cavour to befriend Louis Napoleon and to win from him a defensive alliance against Austria.

Cavour then provoked Austria into a war (1859) in such a way that Austria appeared the aggressor. Napoleon intervened and the Austrians were routed at the battles of Magenta and Solferino. At the moment of victory Napoleon negotiated with Austria. Piedmont secured only Lombardy from this maneuver. Nationalism swept down the peninsula and as a result the people of Parma, Modena and Romagna (in the Papal States) revolted, overthrew their princes and allied themselves with the enlarged Piedmontese state. (France took Savoy and Nice for herself in this operation.)

At this point (May 5, 1860) GIUSSEPPE GARIBALDI (1807-1882) appeared with his "red shirts"—a tiny army—in southern Sicily. Within months the Kingdom of the Two Sicilies was his. These were also turned over to Piedmont. In 1861, Italy was a united nation; only Venetia and Rome were in foreign hands. Cavour died in 1861 but his successors followed his policy of uniting with a powerful neighbor against Italy's enemies. Thus Italy was Germany's ally when Bismarck attacked Austria in 1866. This brought her the province of Venetia. Then, finally, when the Franco-Prussian War came in 1870, Italy was once again Germany's ally. France's desperation forced her to withdraw her Roman garrison. The Italian state moved in and occupied Rome. Unification was complete—except for the Tyrolean north. This became, in Italian propaganda, *Italia Irredenta* ("unredeemed Italy"). It did not become Italian until after the first World War.

GERMANY

No less than Italy was Germany a geographical expression in the year 1800. She was made up of more than 300 states organized within a Holy Roman Empire which was in fact neither holy, nor Roman, nor an empire. In spite of this fragmentation, Germany had achieved considerable greatness —in philosophy and poetry (Liebnitz, Lessing, Kant, Schiller and Goethe); and in music (Bach, Handel, Haydn, Mozart and Beethoven). Germans spoke a common tongue; they shared a common history; they practiced common customs and honored common traditions. All that made for a single nation was present among the people. Napoleon had intensified this feeling of unity by scrapping the Holy Roman Empire (1806), by consolidating the more than 300 states into 38, and by combining these 38 into a Confederation of the Rhine with himself as protector. Within the Confederation feudalism was abolished, legal equality and religious toleration established.

Napoleon's interest in German unity was secondary to the maintenance of his own power. It was left for Prussia to take the leadership in German unification. To do this, Prussia had to first clean her own house and after the humiliating defeat at Jena administered to her by Napoleon, the Prussians made themselves into a modern state by abolishing serfdom, reorganizing the governmental apparatus and fostering a new spirit of nationalism. Prussian aims for German unity were thwarted, however, by the Congress of Vienna of 1815. This body kept the form of the Confederation of the Rhine but substituted for Napoleon's strong leadership a weak confederation of rulers over whom Austria dominated.

There were other obstacles to German unification besides that of Austrian domination of the German Confederation. There was religious dissension between the Protestant north and Catholic south; political differences between the autocratic north and more liberal south; economic disagreements between an agricultural east dominated by the *Junkers* (landed proprietors) and a more industrialized west; and, as in Italy, there were petty princes more interested in their small domains than in national unity.

As a result of the work of OTTO VON BISMARCK (1815-1898) these obstacles were overcome and in 1871 Germany emerged as a united nation, a pivot in world affairs. A number of factors paved the way for Bismarck's great work. In the period from 1815-1848 Germany's cultural development was tremendous. Germans became leaders in historical research, musical composition, philosophy, and scientific research. The Industrial Revolution spread rapidly at the same time—railroads proliferated, resources were tapped, factories sprang up, etc. Reflecting this growth the German states cooperated in a *Zollverein* (tariff-union) for goods passing within the German states. Efforts by Prussia to create a constitutional German state under Prussian leadership were made during the Revolution of 1848. This failed and convinced Prussian leaders that unification would not come peacefully. Bismarck said as much: "Not by speeches and resolutions of majorities are the great questions of the time decided—that was the mistake of 1848 and 1849—but by blood and iron."

Otto von Bismarck. Bismarck became the chief minister of Prussia in 1862 and immediately set in motion a plan to unify the Germanies. For this purpose he strengthened Prussia's military arm; in this he ignored Parliament's objection. At the same time he began preparing for prolonged wars by carrying through a policy of state economy and efficiency that made Prussianism a byword for these practices.

When ready, he turned to the problem of eliminating Austria from the German Confederation. This was done by a series of deft political maneuvers that began with an Austro-Prussian War against Denmark (1864), continued into a quarrel between the allies over seizure of Schleswig-Holstein from Denmark and ended with war between Prussia and Austria. In seven weeks Austria was crushed and in the Treaty of Prague ceded Venetia to Italy, Holstein to Prussia and accepted ouster from the German Confederation. Exactly as Bismarck had foreseen! Meanwhile, in the course of the war, Bismarck had annexed the North German States and formed a North German Confederation with a constitution that made Prussia unconditional ruler. Even more devious was the maneuver to unite the south German states to this union. This was done by forcing France to declare war on Prussia in the same way that Austria had done. In the case of France, Bismarck started the trouble by promoting the cause of a Hohenzollern for the throne of Spain. Since this would surround France with Hohenzollerns (the ruling family of Prussia) Napoleon objected strenuously. In the course of his objections, Napoleon sent an ambassador to the Prussian King at Ems to demand that a promise be given that no Hohenzollern would become king of Spain. The Prussian king sent Bismarck an account of this meeting in an **Ems Dispatch.** Bismarck edited this dispatch so that, when published, it became "a red flag to the Gallic bull." France declared war and was crushed in ten months after a long, bitter siege of Paris. In the Treaty of Frankfort (1871) France had to cede to Prussia Alsace-Lorraine, had to pay a billion-dollar indemnity for the cost of the war, and had to suffer an army of occupation until the indemnity was paid. More important, however, was the fact that during the war the south German states joined with Prussia in a union that was consolidated in 1871 as the German Reich with Kaiser William I at the helm.

RUSSIA

In 1815 Russia was the largest state in Europe with the greatest amalgam of peoples—Great Russians, Ukrainians, Poles, Rumanians, Finns, Letts, Germans, Lithuanians, Tartars, Mongols etc. etc. The prevailing religion was Greek Orthodox; but there were large islands of Protestants, Catholics, Jews, Mohammedans and Buddhists. More than ninety per cent of the people were attached to the land and, until 1861, had the legal status of serfs. In that year, Tsar Alexander emancipated the serfs legally, but introduced a system of village-land ownership that reduced the free peasants to virtual economic slaves. This universal poverty laid the economic base for the revolution that came once in 1905 and again in 1917. In other European countries the Industrial Revolution took the pressure off landed poverty by absorbing surplus farmers into factories. But in Russia the Industrial Revolution did not arrive until very late in the 19th century and then advanced slowly.

Throughout the 19th century Russians were ruled by Tsars, the most absolute rulers on the continent. It was not until after the Revolution of 1905 that the Tsars granted the people a legislature. Tsarist rule produced the most corrupt bureaucracy on the continent, corruption that took its toll in burdensome taxes, wars, and bitter persecution of minorities. For, in an attempt to secure some degree of national unity, the Tsars fostered the spirit of **Panslavism,** the union of all Russians (and non-Russians) who spoke a Slavic language. Those who were non-slavs were forcibly Russianized and made to adopt the Russian language and the Greek Orthodox faith. Nationalist opposition to these policies resulted in brutal pogroms conducted by vicious Cossacks against helpless men, women and children.

Repression bred opposition and throughout the nineteenth century Russian intellectuals experimented with forms of opposing the Tsar's absolutism—ranging from advocacy of terrorism to advocacy of constitutional monarchy. A small, but very determined minority, were Marxists who planned revolution against Tsarism.

War came easily to Tsarist Russia for the great geographic fact in Russia's life was that she was landlocked. Her northern Baltic ports were frozen half a year and she was kept from entering the warm Mediterranean by the Turkish Empire which controlled the Bosporus and the Dardenelles. It became Russia's driving ambition to destroy Turkey and extend her dominion over these gateways to the Mediterranean. Since Turkey included within her empire many Slavic peoples in the Balkans, Russia could pose as protectors of the Slavs and Greek Orthodox religionists and provoke Turkey into war. The Turks gave the Russians every excuse to intervene as their treatment of their Christian subjects was bestially brutal.

Therefore, when the Greeks revolted against the Turks, the Russians, in spite of their allegiance to the Metternich System, aided the Greeks. This brought England, too, to the aid of the Greeks as England was determined that Russia would not capitalize her aid into seizure of the Dardenelles. England's maneuver succeeded. The Russians tried again in 1853 to destroy Turkish power in the Balkans. This time England came to Turkey's aid and the **Crimean War** resulted.

For reasons of self-interest France and Piedmont joined with England. Russia was defeated and lost control of Rumania, the Black Sea and the Danube. After particularly brutal slaughter of her Christian subjects, Turkey was again attacked by Russia in 1877. This time the other Christian nations were unable to come to Turkey's support and the Russians were permitted to defeat the Turks. In the Treaty of San Stefano following this defeat the Russians virtually forced the Turks out of Europe and destroyed Turkish control over the Dardenelles.

Now England intervened; by threatening war, she forced Russia to set aside the Treaty of San Stefano and to meet at a **Congress of Berlin** (1878) for a revision. At this meeting, Bismarck played the part of "honest broker"; the other powers had to consent to the destruction of the Turkish Empire in Europe. Serbia, Montenegro and Rumania were granted their independence. Austria received Bosnia and Herzegovina (in modern Yugoslavia). Bulgaria was divided into autonomous and dependent parts. England took Cyprus. But nationalism would not down, and in 1885 most of Bulgaria became an autonomous state. Once more, Russian hopes for an outlet to the Mediterranean were thwarted. In 1912 Russia unleashed a number of Balkan Wars out of which came the creation of Albania. Thwarted again, Russia made another plunge in what was to become World War I. After 1880 Russia's great opponent to her expansionist efforts was Austria-Hungary.

AUSTRIA-HUNGARY

In the case of Germany and Italy, nationalism had proved to be a unifying force; in that of the Turkish Empire and Austria-Hungary it was disruptive. Next to Russia, Austria-Hungary contained the largest amalgam of nationalities in Europe. Austria proper was inhabited by Germans; Hungary by Magyars. In the dominions controlled by these two ruling groups were Italians, Czechs, Slovaks, Poles, Serbs, Croats, Yugoslavs, Rumanians, etc. Each of these submerged nationalities had its own tongue, history, customs, traditions, religion—all the factors making for unity. In the first half of the century Austria ruled the empire through the oppressive tactics of Prince Metternich. In 1848 came the Revolution which swept Metternich from office and momentarily threatened to fracture the entire empire. When this was followed in 1859 by defeat in the war with France and Piedmont, the ruler Francis Joseph (who came to power in 1848 and ruled thereafter until 1916) granted the people an illiberal constitution, one that the Hungarians refused to accept. With the disastrous defeat by Prussia in 1866, Austria made an agreement with the Hungarians for a joint rule in the empire.

Thereafter Austria and Hungary pursued different tactics in keeping the submerged nationalities under control. Austria permitted a considerable degree of local autonomy and freedom to pursue national and religious differences. Hungary carried on a policy of "magyarization," a policy designed to suppress free expressions of differences. The breakup of the Turkish empire and the policy of Russian Panslavism placed considerable pressure on the Austro-Hungarian state.

Encouraged by Russia all Slavs now strove for national independence. Freed Slavic nations like Serbia began to make efforts to unite with Serbs in the Austro-Hungarian empire to form an enlarged state with a water outlet on the Adriatic Sea. To prevent Serbian expansion to the sea Austria-Hungary seized Bosnia-Herzegovina in 1908 and aided in the creation of Albania in 1912. Serbian-Austro-Hungarian complications were two years later to spark off the first World War. The European state-system came to completion at the end of World War I. From the Austro-Hungarian empire emerged the states of Czechoslovakia, Yugoslavia in full, and Rumania, Poland and Italy in part.

THE LESSER STATES

Spanish decline continued through the 19th century. The United States of America delivered the final blow to Spain's overseas strength by defeating her in the Spanish-American War of 1898 and stripping her of Cuba, Puerto Rico and the Philippines.

For a short while, liberalism succeeded in curbing the Spanish monarchy. Under a liberal constitution Spain nonetheless became a pawn in the power politics of a small group of military and political dictators. In these circumstances, radical movements grew inside Spain and toward the end of the century brought about universal male suffrage. High illiteracy, however, negated these efforts at democratization.

Portuguese history was an echo of Spanish; the monarchy continued in that land until overthrown in 1910, when Portugal became a republic. Belgium separated from Holland in the Revolution of 1830. Thereafter both states prospered and extended democratic privileges to the people gradually.

Most democratic of these lesser States was Switzerland. In 1874 this nation was the first to adopt the practice of the **referendum,** a means by which the people could pass on legislation. This was followed in 1891 by the **initiative,** a means by which the people could introduce legislation by petition. Denmark did not become fully democratic until King Christian IX's power was curbed in 1901 by a law making the upper house of the legislature elective and another extending the suffrage. Finally,

Norway, in 1905, proclaimed its independence of Sweden (a union that had been effected by the Congress of Vienna in 1815). Both countries permitted universal male suffrage by 1907.

On the eve of the first World War it seemed to many that western civilization had created the best of all possible worlds. Everywhere in Europe—even in autocratic Russia—the French Revolutionary ideas of liberty, equality and fraternity were finding concrete expression in the spread of suffrage, of parliamentary government, of the basic freedoms of speech, press, assembly and petition. Most of Europe had secularized church property and separated church and state, particularly in education. Free public education was expanding as the demand for increased literacy made itself felt. All nations were experimenting with forms of social security introduced by Bismarck in Germany. Labor was winning collective bargaining rights and making itself felt as a political force through unions and political parties.

World War I, however, shattered the comparatively serene surface. Imperialism played a major role in releasing this universal holocaust.

CHAPTER TWENTY

IMPERIALISM AND WORLD WAR I

INTRODUCTION

Imperialism, or empire-building, is as old as recorded history. Throughout history strong nations have been impelled by political, economic and dynastic forces to conquer their neighbors and to subject them to some form of involuntary servitude. The Egyptians, Mesopotamians, Assyrians, Persians, Greeks and Romans all followed the course of empire-building. During the medieval period in the history of Europe Mongols, Mohammedans, Turks and Tartars extended their territory forcibly, far from their native lands. And when Europe emerged from medievalism, it, too, began a westward and eastward expansion that resulted in the carving-out of large empires overseas. Thus Portugal, Spain, Holland, France and England entered the 18th century with holdings in North and South America, Asia and Africa. Russia confined her expansion to the eastward stretches of Siberia.

These modern nations came as conquerors and wherever they settled they imposed direct or indirect political and economic control on the native peoples. Such control resulted in huge streams of native wealth flowing out of these "backward" areas to the "mother" country. Early in the 19th century, however, came a lull in imperialist expansion. European energy was consumed in the Napoleonic wars, in coping with the revolutions and nationalist upheavals of the first half of the century, in building up a capital base for the Industrial Revolution and in experimenting with the new doctrine of laissez-faire. As democracy developed, nations had to wrestle with the moral problem involved in the subjection of peoples to authoritarian and, indeed, absolutistic rule.

IMPERIALISM

About 1875 territorial aggrandizement became the dominant drive of the large European powers, and of the United States of America. No one cause can account for this phenomenon. The Industrial Revolution was certainly a most important factor. As industry expanded so did the need for raw materials, many of them unavailable in the industrialized lands. This caused a search for basic materials, particularly for such materials as rubber, tin, petroleum, tungsten, etc.

As mass production mounted, nations began to seek potential "outlets" for surplus goods; colonies could be excellent dumping grounds for these goods and in many cases imperialized markets were the "margin of profit" for manufacturers. Similarly with surplus capital that now began to accumulate. Investments at home rarely brought the rate of return that could be gained by investment in colonial areas where labor was cheap and monopoly assured by government fiat.

Accompanying these economic motives for imperialism were equally strong political, social, psychological and religious ones. Nationalism virtually dictated that each nation should seek some "place in the sun"; national pride was fostered by each new splatter of color on the map that showed national expansion; national propaganda led to widespread belief that each nation was engaged in a civilizing mission. Very popular, though little founded in fact, was the prevailing argument that all nations, riding the crest of tremendous population increases, needed outlets for "surplus" population. Enough people did emigrate to the colonies to make this fiction seem a fact. Also there was the revival in this period of missionary activities that opened wide new worlds to the West.

Finally, imperialist expansion was strongly advocated by military leaders in all nations as the best means for securing naval bases and an adequate supply of strategic raw materials. To the support of these military men came the geographers who developed anew the doctrines of geopolitics, the science of national security that determined what heartland and fringelands were vital to "defense" —even though they were inhabited by other peoples. Geopolitics became power-politics, politics supported by military force. In reality, it was a "scientific" rationale for world conquest or domination.

Methods and Forms of Imperialism. International trade, investments and loans are not imperialistic but are part of a normal process of international intercourse. They become imperialistic when they are used as excuses for territorial conquest or for establishing exclusive economic control. During the late nineteenth century it often happened that rulers of undeveloped areas borrowed heavily from the investment bankers of the west. In exchange for such loans favored concessions were made to European investors. If such rulers defaulted on their debts or were unable to protect the investments in railroads, mines, etc., it often happened that the rulers of the powerful investor nations sent troops into that area to "protect" the lives and property of their nationals. It was at this point that imperialism began. Under foreign control these areas lost their political freedom and the right to exploit their own national wealth.

Out of this pattern emerged four forms of imperialist control: the **colony** or direct political control where the powerful nation openly ruled the undeveloped area as a possession; the **protectorate** or indirect political control where the powerful nation ruled the undeveloped area through a native puppet; the **concession** or exclusive direct control over some particular resource; and the **sphere of influence** or indirect economic control over the whole of the undeveloped area. These basic forms intermingled freely. The imperialist test for any of them was the degree of freedom retained by the undeveloped area.

IMPERIALISM IN AFRICA

In 1870 Africa was known to Europe on the fringes only. North Africa was a settled abode; the French had already taken Algeria. The west coast was lined with trading posts; here, too, France was in possession only of Senegal. At the southern tip, England held the Cape Colony. The vast interior of Africa, peopled with primitive tribes still in the earliest stages of civilization, was a "dark continent."

The first light shed on the African interior came as a result of the incident of DAVID LIVINGSTON and H. M. STANLEY. Livingston was a missionary working inside Africa. A rumor spread that he had disappeared. To check the rumor Stanley undertook to find Livingston; he did. However, Stanley went on to exploit his discovery of Africa and returned to interest bankers in the possibility of investment in the African interior. In 1878 King Leopold II of Belgium convinced Belgium bankers to underwrite the International Congo Association, a private venture in the purchase of Congo land for the exploitation of rubber resources. African native chiefs, without the slightest sense of private property, traded tremendous regions for trifles.

When this venture became known, land fever struck Europe. German and French investors landed in Africa to buy up land against the possibility of discovering valuable resources. Bismarck, in 1885, made a feeble effort to regularize this traffic in African land, but the tide could not be contained. Until 1908, the Congo was in the control of the private corporation. A report of the abominable labor practices employed to exploit the land forced the state of Belgium to take over the Congo as a territorial possession. It remains such to this day.

English Imperialism in Africa. England had a southern base for imperialist expansion in Cape Colony. In 1875 she established a northern base in Egypt when Benjamin Disraeli purchased an important block of stock in the Suez Canal. Thereafter the unwise ruler of Egypt, Ismail Pasha, placed himself heavily in debt to both England and France. Unable to pay, Ismail was then forced to submit to control of the Egyptian treasury by British and French citizens. When he finally balked at these restrictions, he was forcibly deposed and England and France ruled Egypt under a "condominion."

A native revolt against foreign occupation gave

the imperialists the excuse for complete military occupation. (France had withdrawn because of a cabinet crisis and England had gone it alone.) A protectorate was then created in Egypt. This proved an ample base to begin southern operations into the Sudan. France became the chief obstacle to this move.

French Imperialism in Africa. Following Stanley's methods in the Congo, Frenchmen began to "buy up" large areas in what was to become the French Congo, Dahomey, Senegal and the Ivory Coast. Then, in 1881 the French began to operate from their Algerian base eastward into Tunisia and southward into the great Saharan sands. By 1898 they had linked their central African possessions with the northern ones and began a wide eastward movement to take in the Sudan. Here they came flush against the British.

The Fashoda Affair. A French expedition under Captain Marchand moved from the French Congo region eastward to the upper (southern) region of the Nile. Great Britain sent France a note claiming that area as a British sphere of influence and to reinforce this claim dispatched the famed General Kitchener to the Sudan. With war hanging in the balance, the matter was resolved by the action of the French minister Delcasse who ordered the French troops withdrawn when England agreed to grant France unlimited rights in central Sudan. Delcasse, we shall see, had his reasons for seeking British friendship at this moment. English holdings now stretched almost halfway down the east coast of Africa.

The Boer War. Meanwhile CECIL RHODES, Prime Minister of Cape Colony from 1890 to 1896, had begun a sweep northward along the east coast in an effort to join with the Egyptian-Sudan bloc and to effectuate his dream of a Cape-to-Cairo Railroad that would make all east Africa England's (and Rhodes').

But there resided in South Africa a group of Dutch emigrants called Boers who resisted every effort of the British to extend their possessions northward. The Boers resented British rule in Cape Colony, especially after 1833 when the British made slavery illegal. They therefore migrated out of the Cape Colony over the Vaal River to the Transvaal region. Each time the British moved northward, the Boers moved on. In 1881 they decided to stop moving and fought and defeated a British force at Majuba Hill. Discovery of Kimberly diamonds (1870) and Rand gold (1886) brought thousands of English to South Africa. Cecil Rhodes was one

such. To fulfil his imperialist dreams, Rhodes had to eliminate the Dutch. He almost provoked a war in the Dr. Jameson raid on the Boers, but failed. War came in 1899. It took three years before thousands of British regulars were able to conquer the Boers. In 1902 South Africa became British and extended far northward to include Rhodesia.

German Imperialism in Africa. Only German East Africa lay between an effective union of northern and southern British ownership of east Africa. Under Bismarck's influence Germany had been very slow to enter into the African imperialist scramble; but the tide could not be resisted. Karl Peters had begun in 1884 to gather up eastern African lands and these became German East Africa, the region lying between British Uganda and British Rhodesia. Directly west of British South Africa the Germans gathered in a tremendous state, German Southwest Africa; south of the Congo they won Kamerun. By 1900 the Germans were challenging France in North Africa by making a bid for Morocco. It now becomes somewhat easier to understand why the French and British preferred not to fight it out over the Sudan; Germany was in the way of both.

This led these two countries to conclude an anti-German **Entente Cordiale** in 1904 which included among many provisions one of granting to France a "free hand" in Morocco and to England a "free hand" in Egypt and the Sudan. Imperialism was obviously propelling the major nations into a world war.

To complete the African picture, one ought to mention Italy's success and ambition. Italy had managed to secure control of two territories west of the free state of Ethiopia, Italian Somaliland and Eritrea. Now she coveted the North African province of Libya (won in 1912 by conquest) and the free state of Ethiopia. In her effort to take Ethiopia she suffered a humiliating defeat at the hands of the natives at the Battle of Adowa (1896).

IMPERIALISM IN ASIA

International tension was multiplied by an extension of imperialist grabbing to the Asiatic continent. Imperialist conquest of Asiatic territory had begun in the 16th century during the era of discovery and exploration. By 1900 virtually all the Pacific Islands had been gathered into western hands, the chief beneficiaries being the Dutch who controlled the East Indies, the Germans who had the Carolines by purchase from Spain and the Americans with their conquest of the Philippines, Guam, Samoa, etc. In the 18th century England had taken possession of the subcontinent of India and after the Sepoy Mutiny of the natives (1858) had made that land into a crown colony. Meanwhile the Russians had reached the Pacific in Siberia and the French had moved into Indo-China. Lying between these foreign holdings was the ancient kingdom of China which now became the field for imperialist expansion.

The Partition of China. Why was this great state so easy a prey for the western powers?

China lacked political unity; her many provinces were loosely bound into an empire under a weak Dowager Empress. Western powers found it easy to divide and rule. China regarded western civilization as barbarian and by means of tariffs closed her ports to all trade with the western world. In her religious beliefs, China glorified her ancestral past and followed rigid codes of behavior that did not permit adaptation to modern times. Her industries unexploited, without an efficient national army, her standard of living among the lowest in the world —China collapsed at the first western blows. These blows were first administered by Great Britain.

The Opium War (1840-1841). England made a rich business of producing opium in India and selling it to the Chinese as a narcotic. When the Chinese government finally prohibited this grotesque trade, the British declared war and in a short time forced the government to its knees. The **Treaty of Nanking,** signed after this war, became the model for all future treaties wresting land and concession from the Chinese. England secured Hong Kong as a possession; China was forced to pay England an indemnity for the damage inflicted on England during the war (!); five "treaty ports" were opened —that is, ports through which British goods were permitted to pass freely and in which the British were permitted to control the tariffs; the British secured the right of extraterritoriality, that is, the right to use British courts for offenses committed by British subjects in China. Needless to say, other nations quickly followed suit.

The Westernization of Japan. Japan, too, until 1850 clung to its feudal past. Hatred for foreigners extended to such a point that even shipwrecked sailors were slaughtered when they sought refuge on Japanese shores. Feudal lords led by a *shogun* kept the *mikado* or emperor, chained to the past. The Opium War jolted Japanese considerably and created a group within Japan that began to investigate the reasons for the collapse of China. These were the groups that welcomed Commodore Perry, an American, when he sought to compel the Japanese government to obey humane international standards with respect to shipwrecked victims.

The Japanese, led by the Emperor Mutsuhito, not only accepted Perry's proposals for international fair treatment, but took up his further proposal that the Japanese modernize themselves on western models. In the incredibly short period of thirty years the Japanese transformed themselves. They abolished feudalism, created an industrial revolution, built a modern mechanized army and an efficient state apparatus to support it and, inevitably, joined in the scramble for possession of the world's resources overseas—for Japan, an overcrowded island with few natural resources, had all the motives for such expansion. What was a more likely area than China across the sea, an area which might disappear if the western powers accelerated their rate of conquest? The Japanese decided to move in rapidly.

Battles over China. As early as 1875 Japan began to meddle in the islands off the coast of China and in Korea. When China tried to protect Korea, Japan declared war (1894) and by 1895 had forced China, in the **Treaty of Shimonoseki,** to pay an indemnity, to cede Formosa and the Liaotung Peninsula with its naval base at Port Arthur and to surrender claims to Korea, thus permitting it to become a Japanese sphere of influence.

Aware of the threat to them of this new imperialist star on the Far Eastern horizon, the great powers set aside the Treaty of Shimonoseki and proceeded to carve up China to suit their own needs. Russia helped herself to Manchuria, the Liaotung Peninsula (which she wanted as a terminus for her projected trans-Siberian Railroad) and Korea; Germany took the valuable port of Kiaochow and the whole hinterland of Shantung as a sphere of influence; England, alarmed at Germany's action, grabbed the more northerly section around Weihai-wei where she could also keep an eye on Russia; France took what was left in the most southerly area of Kwangchowan. Japan and England both felt somewhat out-maneuvered and in 1902 concluded an alliance of friendship—that is, a defensive alliance which in case of war committed either to the support of the other.

The United States. Acquisition of the Philippine Islands by the Spanish-American War (1898) had made the United States a factor in the politics of imperialism in China. Fearful that the partition of China in 1898 would permanently exclude her from any trade with China, the United States circulated a note among the imperialist powers demanding that they keep the door open in China—more technically, that there be free entry for all goods at all Chinese ports and that only Chinese-made tariffs have the force of law.

This **"open-door policy"** became expanded as a result of the **Boxer Rebellion.** Chinese enemies of westernization made one last desperate effort to destroy western imperialism. Organized by religious leaders as the "Patriotic Order of Harmonious Fists" they opened attacks on railroads, factories and foreigners resident in Chinese cities. To counter-attack, the western powers, including the United States, organized an international expeditionary force which suppressed the rebellion with excessive brutality. Fearful of the effects of the presence of armed forces in China, the United States once again circularized the powers and sought to force them into a pledge to protect the territorial integrity of China, in other words, not to subdivide China politically.

Japanese Conquests Continue. Ignoring the "open-door policy," Japan, in 1904, suddenly attacked Russia to challenge the latter's possessions in China. She won military success but at great economic expense and, when virtually exhausted, she accepted (as did the Tsar who was faced with revolution at home) Theodore Roosevelt's offer of good offices to settle the conflict. At the **Treaty of Portsmouth** (N.H.) Russia had to recognize Japan's sphere in Korea and had to turn over Port Arthur, the southern half of the island of Sakhalin, the Liaotung Peninsula and southern Manchuria to Japan.

Humiliation swept through China as she watched, helplessly, two foreign powers quarrel over her territory. This humiliation permitted DR. SUN YAT SEN to organize his **Young China** movement into an effective fighting force. In 1911, Dr. Sun succeeded in overthrowing the decadent monarchy and establishing a republic in China. Between 1911 and 1921 it became apparent to China and to the rest of the world that the chief aggressor in the Far East was destined to be Japan for in 1914 the Japanese presented to the weak Chinese government Twenty-One Demands which would have turned all of China into a Japanese province. It was only the post-war action of the United States that prevented this outrage from being committed. Japan was able to maneuver at this time because the western powers had to remove their Far Eastern forces to commit mayhem on one another in the first World War.

THE FIRST WORLD WAR

The basic causes of the first World War were the rival imperialist ambitions among the western powers, their excessive nationalistic pride, the armaments race that developed in the face of political and economic rivalry, the struggle of suppressed peoples for independence, the geopolitical drive to reach "natural boundaries" and the absence in the world of any effective world organization that might have prevented war through peaceful settlement of disputes. These fundamental causes worked themselves out in a series of international events the primary effect of which was to create two great systems of alliances that opposed each other in a menacing **balance of power.**

The Triple Alliance vs. The Triple Entente. The **Triple Alliance** of Germany, Austria-Hungary and Italy (and allied satellites) was born from Bismarck's desire to isolate France so that she could never wage a war of revenge against Germany after her ignominious defeat in the Franco-Prussian War. By promise and perfidy Bismarck secured a secret defensive alliance with Austria-Hungary, a "gentleman's agreement" with Russia, an alliance with Italy directed against France, English neutrality, Serbian and Rumanian allegiance, and Turkish friendship.

To each of these nations Germany promised diplomatic support for nationalist aspiration—no matter how contradictory these promises were. Thus Russia and Austria-Hungary were bitter rivals in the Balkans as were Serbia and Austria-Hungary; Italy had many grievances against Austria-Hungary with respect to *Italia Irridenta;* Rumania and Turkey could not be friends. Yet Bismarck accomplished the impossible as long as Germany pursued a non-imperialist policy of its own. When William II overrode Bismarck and began an aggressive policy of imperialism, economic rivalry and arms supremacy, the grand alliance fell apart. Out of its pieces was born the **Triple Entente.**

Russia was the first to leave and to join France in a Dual Alliance in 1894. When Germany rejected Russia's request for large modernization loans, France granted them in exchange for a military convention that amounted to a defensive alliance. (This agreement, incidentally, was as much directed against England as against Germany, for England was threatening France in the Sudan and Russia in Persia and the Far East.)

By 1900 a number of factors compelled England to reconsider her policy of "splendid isolation" from continental affairs. Germany had begun to construct a formidable navy and to challenge England's markets in all parts of the world. She was the chief obstacle to the union of British territories in east Africa. Now she proposed to construct a Berlin to Baghdad Railroad through Turkey which would possibly destroy England's trade advantage in the Near East and India. The result was the **Entente Cordiale** with France (1904), a settlement of all territorial differences and an implied defensive alliance. Russian-English differences over Persia and the Far East were finally settled in an entente that settled differences in Persia and Afghanistan by division of those territories. By 1907 the Triple Entente was complete and faced the Triple Alliance in a delicate balance of power.

International Crises. War approached by a series of international crises in North Africa and the Balkans. In 1905 France began a series of familiar maneuvers westward from Algeria into Morocco, an area that Germany had selected as her own hunting grounds. The Kaiser promised the Moroccan ruler support if he resisted French overtures and then went on to demand that the "Moroccan Question" be submitted to an international conference. Such a conference was held in 1906 at Algeciras and Germany forced through a policy of the "open door" in Morocco to France's chagrin.

In 1911 an uprising in Morocco gave the French an excuse to move in with troops. The Germans sent the "Panther," a gunboat, to challenge French occupation. War hung in the balance. At that moment English warships began to maneuver around the "Panther," and Germany decided that the time was not ripe for a challenge. In exchange for a part of the French Congo Germany gave France a "free hand" in Morocco.

Attention was now focused on the Balkans. In 1908 a group of humiliated **Young Turks**, resentful of the slow disintegration of the Turkish Empire, undertook a revolution. Austria-Hungary took advantage of this situation to annex Balkan territory. Russia, fearful of Austro-Hungarian moves, had secured a promise from her that she would support Russian moves in the Dardenelles area in exchange for Russian support for Balkan seizures by Austria-Hungary. This was the infamous "Buchlau Bargain."

Austria-Hungary violated the bargain by annexing Bosnia and Herzegovina without support for Russia's territorial ambitions. Russia was infuriated and resolved to make war on the first occasion that presented itself. She began to provoke Serbia into anti-Austrian activities. At the same time Russia continued maneuvering against Turkey by organizing a Balkan League (Montenegro, Serbia, Bulgaria and Greece) for an assault on Turkey. This assault came in 1912 and 1913 in two Balkan Wars. Once again Austria frustrated Russian ambitions by creating the buffer state of Albania. Europe became a "powder magazine."

The spark that blew it up occurred in **Sarajevo**, Bosnia when the Austrian Archduke Ferdinand was assassinated by a member of a secret society for the creation of a greater Serbia. Austria delivered an ultimatum to Serbia to stop all anti-Austrian propaganda, to suppress all anti-Austrian publications, to dismiss Serbian officials implicated in the assassination plot, to permit Austrian police forces to enforce the ultimatum. Serbia temporized and on July 28, 1914 Austria declared war on Serbia. On July 30 Russia mobilized. On July 31 Germany warned Russia to cease mobilizing; Russia refused. On August 1 Germany declared war on Russia and sent an ultimatum to France to remain neutral. France temporized. On August 3 Germany declared war on France and began to pass through Belgium whose neutrality had been guaranteed by all the European powers. On August 4, when Germany refused to respect Belgian neutrality, England declared war. The holocaust was on. Who was responsible?

The Military Phase. From 1914 to 1918 the greatest war in history to that date was fought. Before it was over, thirty nations had become participants, 65,000,000 men bore arms, 8,500,000 soldiers were killed, 29,000,000 were wounded, an inestimable number of civilians were destroyed and some $200,000,000,000 had ben expended.

After initial German successes, the war settled down to a stalemate fought in "no-man's lands" from fixed trenches along the western front. Following an initial push to Paris, the Germans were stopped at the Marne; thereafter they were held in spite of such mighty pushes as the one at Verdun.

Allied counter-attacks came similarly to grief. Efforts of the Allies to take Turkey in the Gallipoli campaign were repulsed. The Austrians were checked in the Balkans. Italy deserted the Triple Alliance for the Allied cause but proved more of a handicap than an aid particularly following her defeat at Caporetto. In only one direction did the war move to a completion, that of Germany's assault on Russia. Then came the Russian revolution, and the Bolsheviks, who seized power from the democratic liberals in November of 1917, decided to seek peace. In 1918 they signed the **Treaty of Brest-**

Litovsk which ceded Poland, Lithuania, Courland, Bessarabia, the Caucasus, Finland, Estonia, Latvia and the Ukraine to the Central Powers.

Germany did not win the war chiefly as a result of the entry of the United States in 1917. Provoked by unrestricted submarine warfare, sabotage, plots with Mexico and German sabre rattling, and led by economic stakes in the Allied cause and effective Allied propaganda in the United States, America declared war on April 6, 1917, resolved to make the world safe for democracy and to fight a war to end all wars. So did Woodrow Wilson frame the goals of the Allied cause. Entry of men and material from America in 1918 gave the Allied powers the strength to mount a final offensive in 1918, one that broke through German lines and forced the Germans to sue for peace on November 11, 1918.

The Versailles Treaty. Vision and reality met in battle on January 18, 1919 when the victorious powers met to determine the fate of their conquered enemies. The vision was in the person of Woodrow Wilson, President of the United States, who had boldly announced in January 1918 his **Fourteen Points** for an enduring peace. Wilson foresaw a post-war world where secret diplomacy would be outlawed; where the seas would be free; where all economic barriers to international trade would be removed; where armaments races would end; where imperialism would be eliminated on moral grounds; where national aspirations would be respected; where closed waters, such as the Dardenelles, would be forever open; and where a league of nations would be established to settle once for all all international disputes by conciliation, arbitration and judicial settlement. It was a splendid vision, one that captured the imagination of people all over the world.

The reality was in the persons of LLOYD GEORGE of England, CLEMENCEAU of France and ORLANDO of Italy who comprised a "Big Three" determined to make the Peace of Versailles a vengeful and profitable one at the expense of the conquered nations. What emerged was in the nature of a compromise between the vision and the reality.

Germany, Austria-Hungary, Turkey and Bulgaria were punished. Germany ceded Alsace-Lorraine back to France, Eurpen and Malmedy to Belgium and a corridor through West Prussia for Poland to reach the sea. Schleswig was returned to Denmark; Lithuania secured Memel; Danzig became an internationalized "free city"; the Saar was placed under the political control of the League of Nations and the economic control of France for fifteen years after which there was to be a plebiscite held in which the Saarlanders could vote for a permanent political settlement of their fate. Germany lost all of her Pacific holdings to the League of Nations which received them as "mandates" and which distributed them to the victorious powers for education and eventual release as independent states. (Such was Wilson's plan for the eventual elimination of imperialism.)

Germany was then stripped of all military power —armed forces, navy, fortifications—and had to submit to occupation of her territory to ensure enforcement of the terms of the treaty. At the same time, Germany was declared to be guilty of having provoked the war and was therefore made to bear the expense of repairing the damage. Reparations costs ran to some sixty billion dollars. As immediate payments on this reparations bill, Germany was stripped of railroads, capital equipment, livestock and coal. Out of the treaties of St. Germain, Neuilly and Serves with Austria, Hungary and Turkey respectively came the birth of many new nations and additional mandated territories to be granted to the victorious powers.

The League of Nations. In exchange for many concessions to the nationalist and imperialist aims of the victorious allied powers, Wilson demanded that as Article I of the Versailles Treaty appear a covenant for a League of Nations to which all the victorious powers would belong and which would be given sufficient power to end all future wars.

To some degree this was accomplished. An international organization was framed which would include an Assemlby of all the member nations, each with a single vote; an executive Council of permanent big-power members and non-permanent elected members to enforce decrees of the Assembly; a World Court for the judicial settlement of disputes; a Secretariat for arranging meetings and recording results. The covenant also provided for a mandate system to eliminate imperialism. It was projected, too, that the League would form committees to alleviate some of the basic economic, health, education and communication problems of the world.

That there would be an end to war seemed a realizable hope in the year 1919. Countries were already projecting a series of disarmament conferences that would reduce the burden of maintaining powerful armed forces. Nationalism had been satisfied in the creation of the "succession states" of Poland, Czechoslovakia, Austria, Hungary, Yugoslavia and others. Imperialism would end as mandatory nations fulfilled their obligations to their territories and prepared them for the status of independent nations who would then join the League. International anarchy was to end with the establishment and growth in the power of the League of Nations and the World Court. International co-operaiton was to replace economic rivalry. What causes for any future war were possible?

But twenty years later came a second, and even more terrible, war. What went wrong with the vision?

CHAPTER TWENTY-ONE

THE SHAPING OF THE MODERN WORLD

SOVIET RUSSIA

In March 1917 the Tsar was overthrown and a liberal democratic state set up under the leadership of Prince Lvov and Professor Miliukov. Instrumental in this overthrow were the numerous "soviets" or local government that had made their appearance during the stages of the first revolution. In the elected Soviets the Bolsheviks (communists) led by Lenin had no control.

In the first All-Russian Congress of Soviets held in June of 1917 Kerensky Social Revolutionaries and Menshevik socialists-groups favoring democratic processes of government—were voted control of the government. Even after the Bolsheviks had seized control of the government of Petrograd in November 7th they could not secure approval from a constitutional assembly called in January 1918 to confirm the seizure. This constitutional assembly was freely and democratically elected. However, when it voted down Bolshevik proposals with respect to making peace, distributing land and disarming all of the Russians but the workers, it was abruptly dismissed and in its place was created a dictatorship under the leadership of Nicolai Lenin, Leon Trotsky and Joseph Stalin.

Many circumstances played into the hands of the Bolsheviks to enable them to maintain and to consolidate their power. They voluntarily signed the Treaty of Brest-Litovsk with Germany in which they surrendered a considerable portion of European Russia. Moreover, they published secret treaties that revealed many of the imperialist aims of the warring allied powers.

Frightened by the success of the Bolsheviks, the Allied powers dispatched an international force to aid the "White Russians" in their effort at a counter-revolution. Since these "White Russians" contained many of the elements of the hated Old Regime the Allied intervention was strongly opposed.

Meanwhile, the Bolsheviks set up the Cheka—secret police and revolutionary tribunals—which destroyed not only elements of the old regime but *all* opposition to Bolshevism. At the same time, to give meaning to their "socialist" revolution, the Bolsheviks temporarily turned factories over to workers' committees, distributed land to the peasants, as much as each could work, nationalized all industry without compensation, confiscated all Tsarist obligations to domestic and foreign lenders and removed money as a means of exchange.

Consolidation. In 1919 a Supreme Economic Council was created to make plans for the eventual creation of complete state ownership and operation of the means of production. The productive system collapsed and in 1921 there was desperate poverty.

In 1921, therefore, Lenin ordered a "new economic policy" to be instituted. The base of the new economic policy was state ownership of about 85 per cent of the means of production. In the remaining 15 per cent the Communists permitted foreign investors to invest funds at high rates of interest. Opposition abroad was considerably disarmed by this maneuver; Western nations were led to believe that Russia would some day return to the family of capitalist nations. In 1924 Communist Russia was officially recognized by Great Britain, France and Italy. Not until 1934 did the United States follow suit.

The "Plan" was fulfilled in a series of "five-year plans" launched by JOSEPH STALIN in 1928. All foreign influence in Russian industry was abolished. A state planning commission drew up goals for a five-year increase in industrialization, mechanization and electrification of state owned industries. Every type of incentive was used to increase worker productivity; this was needed, for productivity increase was linked to a decrease in consumption—the surplus being used to purchase basic machinery abroad. Meanwhile, the process of forcible collectivization of farms was begun.

Thus straitjacketed the Russian economy did move into the high gear of production. Opposition to collectivization was so strong, however, that Russia suffered another severe food famine in 1934. A second five-year plan eased the consumption picture somewhat; a third was just begun when Russia was attacked by the Nazi forces. Her industrilization, considerably aided by American "lend-lease," stood her in good stead and enabled her to make a rapid recovery after the war.

Dictatorship. Protest in Russia could find no effective means of expression once the Bolsheviks had imposed their dictatorship. All political opposition was suppressed. The "purge" and staged trials became an institution by which Joseph Stalin periodically eliminated potential rivals.

Yet the Communists could not forever ignore the need for some form of national consent. In 1936 they granted a constitution which constructed a tremendous facade of republican institutions that were designed to conceal the dictatorship. A bicameral legislature representing all the people and their nationalist divisions was created; an elective ministry headed by a premier was set up as executive. An extensive "bill of rights" was added. But the realities in these political forms are evident in the facts that in Soviet elections only one party is permitted, that only members of the Communist Party may hold high office, in the control which the state holds over all means of communication, in the secret police, in the use of secret trials and summary executions, in the absence of all debate at the meetings, when called, of the legislature, in the rigid control of ingress and egress from Russia itself, in anti-religious official attitudes and propaganda, in the strict control of education.

FASCIST ITALY

BENITO MUSSOLINI, founder of Italian Fascism, came to power by a coup d'etat on October 28, 1922. He and his "Black Shirts"—a private army—"marched on Rome" and took possession of the state apparatus. Only the complete breakdown of the democratic apparatus of the Italian government could have permitted this to take place. This breakdown was due to Italy's multi-party system that, at the crucial moment, was unable or unwilling to

form a government to counteract this coup. A breakdown in government was the result of accumulating difficulties resulting from widespread postwar depression, unemployment, radical efforts to seize factories, peasant revolts, etc.

Once in power, Mussolini destroyed all opposition and civil liberty, ruled by terror and secret police, resorted to political assassination and prepared Italy for a series of wars that would make the Mediterranean an Italian lake. Both industry and labor were harnessed to state purposes. Industrialists had no choice but to produce what the state required; labor was denied every form of free action on its own behalf. Both were organized into "corporations" (hence the "corporate state") and these were directed by state-appointed bureaucrats. Propaganda and militarization took the place of education. From earliest age, the youth were organized as military cadres and taught implicit obedience to the dictates of *Il Duce* ("The Leader").

The economy felt the artificial stimulation of increased war production and Mussolini was able to secure a surplus which enabled him to make Italy somewhat more self-sufficient by the draining of marshes, improvement of railroads, large hydroelectric and reclamation projects, subsidies for overseas trade, construction of a merchant marine, etc. But the intent of this program of reform was war and renewed imperialistic attacks on those powers which held territories overseas—particularly England and France.

NAZI GERMANY

ADOLPH HITLER's coup came in January 1933. As in Italy, the normal process of democratic government had broken down when the major parties in the Reichstag were unable to agree on a government bloc. Few governments were more democratically oriented than Germany under the Weimar Republic, a government created to replace that of the German Kaiser. When faced with large scale unemployment and dissatisfaction resulting from the world depression in 1933, the radical and liberal parties were unable and unwilling to combine to suppress the threat of the author of *Mein Kampf* and his private army of Brown Shirts.

Adolph Hitler was a master of vicious propaganda; he exploited every grievance of the Germans by centering them upon a few scapegoats—the Treaty of Versailles, the Jews, the German need for *lebensraum* (living space). To justify the use of these scapegoats, he constructed out of a long history of racist theorizing (DE GOBINEAU, HOUSTON STEWART CHAMBERLAIN) the doctrine of the racial superiority of the German Nordic. He convinced the German people by ceaseless dinning through every means of communication that they were the only source of civilization, that they stood in dread danger of corruption and bestialization through intermingling with inferior race, that they must save the world by conquering it for humanity and civilization, etc.

At best one might say that the German people had little inkling—though the unspeakable brutality of the Nazi Storm Troopers must have been evident to them from the day Hitler took power—that these false and vicious doctrines were soon to be translated into furnaces that would burn up more than 6,000,000 people whose only crime was that they were of different religions and nationalities from the ruling German cliques.

After 1934 Hitler became *Der Führer* ("the Leader"). The German state was completely totalitarianized. Industry and labor were organized in similar fashion to that of Mussolini. Capitalism was retained but placed at the beck and call of state needs. War production was immediately begun in preparation for a series of adventures to test the democracies' will to resist and eventually for a bid for world conquest. German freedom disappeared and the Gestapo and the Storm Troopers combined to produce absolute terror.

THE WEAKENING OF THE DEMOCRACIES

World War I proved to be empty victories for the democracies. In 1921 and again in 1931 they suffered depressions of unparalleled dimensions. England, in particular, found that economically she was slipping into the place of a second rate power in the face of American and Japanese competition. Unemployment, exhaustion of native resources, mounting taxes which destroyed considerable investment capital, the failure of Germany to produce any sizeable reparations, widespread strikes among the transport workers and coal miners—all of these factors helped keep successive British governments reeling. In 1923 the first Labor government, under Ramsey Macdonald, was elected; but it was no more able to manage the various crises than the Conservatives.

With the onset of the Great Depression England experimented with a coalition government of Conservative and Laborites. The great achievement of this government was the final abandonment of England's free trade policy for a policy of imperial preference and the Statute of Westminster. The latter was virtually a declaration of independence for all British dominions. It created the British Commonwealth of Nations for the dominions, a system which permitted any dominion to leave the Empire when it wished and if it stayed within the Empire to enjoy absolute local autonomy. (No dominion has left the Commonwealth except Ireland, which in 1922 became Eire, a free state without any political ties to England.)

As the Fascist menace rose to challenge England's position, England began a rearmament program that stimulated the economy to slow revival. Out of the general feeling of helplessness that England felt, however, was generated her policy of "appeasement"—a policy associated particularly with Prime Minister Neville Chamberlain. This policy had as its central aim the strengthening of Fascism to a point where it could successfully attack Communism. In the struggle which ensued, England hoped, both would destroy each other.

French difficulties were similar to those of England with this addition—under the impact of economic crisis the normally unstable French Governments became even more so. France felt keenly Germany's inability to meet her reparations payments since France had been the chief sufferer among the western powers of the first World War. High taxes and shortages of goods produced an astronomical inflation in France in 1926. Unemployment, loss of foreign markets, colonial difficulties and the threat of both Germany and Italy to her security kept France off balance throughout the two decades and made her a leading exponent of appeasement. She, more than any, sought to direct Hitler's power eastward toward Russia.

Finally, the United States withdrew completely from the arena of international responsibility. She rejected the League of Nations, refused to enter the World Court and adopted a series of neutrality laws that were designed to remove her physically from direct or indirect participation in any future European conflict. The world depression of 1931 struck the United States with especial force. Unemployment mounted to 16,000,000, factory production fell by fifty per cent, emergency relief drained the treasury and forced the policy of government borrowing that was to become the greatest government debt in history following the second world war. These difficulties intensified America's desire to remove itself from the arena of world affairs and to concentrate upon her own revival.

Finally, the hope of the democracies resided in the League of Nations; but it proved to be a weak vessel. Weakened by the requirement of unanimity for any decisive action, by the provision in the covenant permitting an aggressor to leave the League after two years' notice, by the absence from the membership rolls of both the United States and the Soviet Union—the League had proved itself incapable of coping with any threat to the peace involving a major power. Its successes were on the fringes of international politics.

Lack of confidence in the League was reflected in the successive disarmament conferences that were held outside League auspices. Though none of these conferences was an unqualified success, the earliest ones—particularly the Washington Arms Conference of 1921-1922—did manage to provide for a cessation in the armaments race for a ten-year period. Japanese ambitions in the Far East were effectively curbed by a Nine-Power Treaty and a Four-Power Treaty which made her sign support for the open door policy, for preservation of China's territorial integrity and for the integrity of the Pacific island possessions of the western powers. (Japan freely violated all these commitments since no effective check was provided for to ensure that she fulfilled them.) Even the idealist Kellogg-Briand Peace Pact which "outlawed war" was negotiated by America and France outside the League. Moreover, both France and England placed their reliance on the construction of a wide system of security alliances (the Little Entente, the Locarno Pacts, etc.) rather than on the force of the League. International anarchy was as prevalent with the League as in the days before the League. With this state of affairs in the world there was no reason for the aggressive fascist nations to hesitate in their new imperialist policy . . . the second factor leading to World War II.

THE NEW IMPERIALISM

The old imperialism was, for the most part, directed against helpless, undeveloped areas; the new imperialism unleashed by the powers of the Rome-Berlin-Tokyo Axis was directed against strong, advanced nations. In 1931 Japan began what she called a punitive expedition against Chinese bandits, an expedition that ended with the conquest of all of Manchuria. When the League investigated this aggression through the Lytton Commission and condemned the actions of Japan, Japan left the League, and converted Manchuria into the puppet state of Manchukuo. From this as a base, Japan in 1933 spilled over into the province of Jehol.

It was now Hitler's turn. In 1935, Hitler ordered general conscription and then marched his troops into the Rhineland. Both these actions had been forbidden in the Treaty of Versailles. The French met this threat with the construction of an "impassable" Maginot Line; Hitler built the "Siegfried Wall" opposite it.

In 1936, Generalissimo Francisco Franco, aided and equipped by both Mussolini and Hitler, began an assault on the Spanish Republic with the avowed purpose of setting up a fascist regime in Spain. Spain became an experimental laboratory for the use of Axis weapons and troops; pursuing the policy of "non-intervention" the democratic nations stood aside while these tactics were being employed. After a gallant but hopeless defense, the Spanish Republic collapsed in 1939. Once again the democracies gave evidence that they would not resist fascist aggression until it was directed against themselves.

In 1936, Mussolini began his assault on Ethiopia to revenge the defeat at Adowa and to outflank England on the east coast of Africa. Worried now, England attempted to force the League to adopt sanctions against Italy, particularly sanctions on the sale of oil. But United States oil companies took this as an opportunity to capture the Italian market. As a result, Italy proceeded unchecked until Ethiopia was hers.

Meanwhile, Hitler's "Fifth Column" of Nazi Austrians had begun to agitate for *anschluss* (union) of Germany and Austria. The Austrian Chancellor Schussnigg resisted Hitler's demands. As European eyes focussed on this crisis, the Japanese, in 1937, began their plunge into the deep south of China, a plunge that Chiang Kai Shek—China's President and Generalissimo—could do no more than delay. With attention shifted to the Far East, Hitler on March 11, 1938, simply walked in and took over Austria without a struggle. Within weeks Austria was nazified by the well-organized fifth column which had been in secret preparation for many years.

A few months later Hitler, at a Nuremberg Conference, began agitating for the Sudetenland of Czechoslovakia—a section of Czechoslovakia that contained many German-speaking people. This demand led to a remarkable series of meetings in which England's Chamberlain and France's Daladier granted to Hitler his demands upon Czechoslovakia because this was the only way to achieve "peace in our time" and because this was to be Hitler's "last request!" In the face of this complete acquiescence, Hitler took over all of Czechoslovakia and permitted Poland and Hungary small slices bordering their lands.

Italy, early in 1939, took over Albania. This was no sooner done, than Hitler began to agitate for a return of the Polish Corridor to Germany. This was absolutely his last demand. But in August of 1939 came a "diplomatic revolution" that changed the international situation overnight.

THE DIPLOMATIC REVOLUTION

From 1933 to 1939 relations between Russia and Germany had deteriorated sharply. Hitler had made "bolshevismus" the chief target of his international attacks; he had openly admitted his intention to conquer the Ukraine. His persistent attacks on Russia had encouraged appeasers to believe that a war between the two totalitarian states was imminent. Russia, herself, had produced many symptoms of anxiety. She had dropped the cause of world revolution for peaceful co-existence; communist parties in other countries were advocating a "united front"; in 1934 Russia entered the League of Nations and took the leadership in organizing an anti-Fascist coalition.

It is hard to calculate the shock, then, which the democratic world suffered when in August, 1939 Russia and Germany announced that they had signed a "non-aggression pact." Undeclared was the agreement of Hitler and Stalin to partition Poland. For Hitler this was the signal to begin his assault on the western powers using the very materials and resources granted him by the western powers. How appeasement had backfired! England and France solemnly warned Hitler that any move on Poland would mean war. On September 1, 1939 Hitler attacked Poland. France and England fulfilled their pledge to Poland and the Second World War began.

THE SECOND WORLD WAR

Poland was crushed by Hitler in five weeks; the Nazis unleashed the *Blitzkreig* tactic, a combined bombing and armored vehicle attack that was both mobile and paralyzing. Poland's allies lent her no assistance. Russia now moved to collect its dividends on the Nazi-Soviet pact. Lithuania, Latvia, Estonia, the Rumanian provinces of Bessarabia and Bukowina, and (1940) Finland were conquered by the Red Army.

In April 1940 the Nazis overran Denmark and Norway. British failure forced Chamberlain out of office and Winston Churchill became Prime Minister on May 10, 1940. On that very day came the Nazi attack on the Low Countries and France. France fell in one of the most ignominious defeats in military history on June 21, 1940. Collaborationists like Laval set up a new French government at Vichy; Italy formally entered the war by an assault on British positions in North Africa; England was without allies; the United States began to drop its aloofness as Roosevelt began his campaign to win Americans to the support of England. Such were the consequences of the fall of France.

Germany now began its air assault on England and against meager opposition. Hitler's air blitz on England failed. The small Royal Air Force proved marvelously effective and destroyed 3,000 German planes; British morale grew sturdier with each attack; supplies, protected by the British navy, began to pour in; American aid grew mountainously especially after the passage of the Lend-Lease Act; Hitler was forced to pull his Italian ally out of difficulties in North Africa and the Balkans and this diverted his energies eastward.

In June 1941 Hitler attacked Russia without warning in a hope to break through the Caucusus into India and to join there with the Japanese who had already advanced far into Southeast Asia in the direction of eastern India. Initial successes brought the Nazis to the gates of Moscow and far south to the city of Stalingrad. On December 7, 1941, Japan attacked the U.S. naval base at Pearl Harbor. America now entered the conflict.

In 1942 the counteroffensive against the Axis powers began. Russia destroyed the Nazi army at Stalingrad and began an offensive that carried her to Berlin in 1945. England defeated the Nazi-Fascist forces deep in Egypt at El Alemain and took the offensive that ended only when the British met the American forces who had landed in western North Africa to spring a trap on the Nazis. The U.S. began its island-hopping campaign that brought her to the perimeter of the Japanese Islands. No assault had to be made on these islands for the dropping of atom bombs on Hiroshima and Nagasaki convinced the Japanese military that further resistance was useless. Russia completed the demolition of the Japanese by destroying its Manchurian armies.

From North Africa Anglo-American forces

crossed over to Italy and began a northward assault on German-held positions. But the greatest water-borne assault in history came on D-day— June 6, 1944—when Anglo-American forces invaded Normandy and continued rolling until all of western Germany had fallen. Victory in Europe came on May 7, 1945; Victory in Japan came on August 14, 1945. The most devastating war in the history of mankind was over. Its total cost in money, lives, disease, broken bodies, broken minds will probably never be fully calculated; its effects upon the political, social, economic, psychological and cultural institutions of the civilized world are as yet incalculable. Yet it, more than any other phenomenon, shaped the frame and features of the world today. We can do no more than indicate some of the vectors that have revealed themselves since 1945 and wait for their unraveling in the future.

THE POST-WAR WORLD

"One World." World War II was fought on a high ideological level. In August 1941 Churchill and Roosevelt met to frame the "Atlantic Charter." The nobility of the cause of the united nations was framed in the words of this document, words that bear repetition especially today. The allied nations agreed that

> they will seek no aggrandizement, territorial or otherwise;
> territorial changes will be made in accord with the freely expressed wishes of the people concerned;
> people will choose the form of government under which they will live;
> they will see to it that people who have forcibly lost their self-government will get it back;
> with due respect for existing obligations, they will see to it that all States have access, on equal terms, to the trade and raw materials of the world;
> they will get all nations to collaborate to improve labor standards, economic advancement, and social security;
> they will establish a peace in which men may live out their lives free from fear and want;
> they will assure freedom of the seas; and
> they will disarm aggressors and will remain armed themselves until permanent security is established.

Out of this drive for world peace came the United Nations organization.

THE UNITED NATIONS

A United Nations Organization had been projected simultaneously with the issuance of the Atlantic Charter. At the Moscow Conference—and other military meetings during the war—the need for such an organization was officially proclaimed and the basic principle of the equality of states was announced (1943).

At Teheran (1943) a planning committee was projected. It met at Dumbarton Oaks (1944) and consisted of the Big Four—the United States, the United Kingdom, the Soviet Union and China. Ninety percent of the Charter of the United Nations was hammered out at Dumbarton Oaks. The remainder was completed at Bretton Woods (N.H.) where an International Bank for Reconstruction and Development and an International Monetary Fund to stabilize world currencies were set up; at Yalta where the formula on the voting procedures in the Security Council was agreed upon and each of the great powers was granted an absolute veto on all matters except procedure; and at San Francisco (April-June 1945) where the addition of the important Article 51 was made, the article that provided for regional pacts for individual or collective self-defense pending action by the Security Council.

Purposes. Article I of the Charter of the UN sets forth its major goals: "To maintain international peace and security, and to that end: to take effective collective measures for the prevention and removal of threats to the peace . . ."; and "To achieve international cooperation in solving international problems of an economic, social, cultural or humanitarian character . . ."

Membership. All independent, peace-loving nations are eligible if they accept the obligations of the UN and are willing and able to carry them out. On January 1, 1957 there were over eighty member nations.

Structure. There are six main organs of the UN: **The General Assembly** composed of all member states. Each state may send five delegates but each state is entitled to only one vote. On most matters a two-thirds vote prevails. The Assembly must meet at least once a year but may meet in special session. After the creation in 1947 of an interim committee called the "Little Assembly" one may now say that the General Assembly is in continuous session.

The Security Council. This was to have been the leading organ of the UN. It consists of eleven members, five (U.S., U.K., USSR, France and China) with permanent seats and six elected by the General Assembly for two-year terms. It is in continuous session and has the primary responsibility for maintaining peace and security; all other members of the UN are bound to carry out its decisions. But its decisions have been few since each of the permanent members has an absolute veto on all substantive matters. Its *potential* power remains virtually limitless.

The Economic and Social Council (ECOSOC). ECOSOC's 18 member council is chosen for staggered three-year terms by the General Assembly. It is charged with carrying out programs of international and social improvement. The most spectacular accomplishments of the UN have been in the work of this organ through its many specialized agencies whose titles clearly indicate their functions: The International Labor Organization (ILO), the Food and Agricultural Organization (FAO), the United Nations Educational Scientific and Cultural Organization (UNESCO), the International Civil Aviation Organization (ICAO), The International Bank for Reconstruction and Development (IBRD), the International Monetary Fund (IMF), the International Telecommunications Union (ITU), the World Health Organization (WHO), the International Trade Organization (ITO). Through these organizations particularly does the light of "one world" shine through.

The Trusteeship Council. This organ supervises territories previously administered by the League of Nations as mandates as well as such territories that nations have voluntarily placed under trusteeship with the UN. Six UN members are at present charged with advancing the political and economic development of 20,500,000 people in eleven African and Pacific areas. The Council sends out questionnaires, hears reports, listens to complaints from natives and sends out on-the-spot investigating committees—unless the trust-holding power designates its trust territory as "strategic."

U.N. Successes and Limitations. Since 1945, the United Nations has scored many successes. It caused Russian withdrawal of troops from Iran (1946); it halted Civil War in Greece and set up the U.N. Balkan Commission; it created the independent states of Israel, Indonesia and Libya; it fought the Korean War to a truce; it halted intense religious battles between India and Pakistan over the disputed territory of Kashmir; it halted similar strife in the Israeli-Arab War of 1948-9; it stopped a tripartite invasion of Egypt by England, France and Israel in 1956 (caused these nations to withdraw from Egyptian territory). In 1948, the General Assembly adopted the Declaration of Human Rights, a world charter of human civil liberty; and in the same year approved the Genocide Convention to protect any ethnic group from extinction. The U.N. sponsored GATT., a general agreement on tariffs and trade to limit world economic nationalism.

U.N. limitations, however, were evident in the rapid increase of regional agreements for collective security (NATO and the WARSAW PACT); the constant use of the veto power by the Soviet Union in the Security Council; inability of the U.N. to establish a permanent international armed force; existence within the U.N. of political blocs (American, Soviet, Afro-Asian), inability to act on such matters as suppression of the Hungarian revolt, etc.

THE COLD WAR

Communist Imperialism. By 1947, the "One World" built during the war was replaced by a so-called Cold War between two power blocs: a Western bloc headed by the United States and an Eastern bloc headed by the Soviet Union. Conflicting military and economic goals were the basic causes of the Cold War. Russian satellite states were created in Albania, Bulgaria, Hungary, Rumania, Czechoslovakia, Poland and East Germany. Yugoslavia, under Marshall Tito, broke from her satellite status but retained a Communist form of government. Estonia, Latvia, Lithuania, the Karelian Isthmus of Finland, Finnish Petsamo, Bessarabia and the eastern provinces of Poland were absorbed into the U.S.S.R. itself. The Chinese Communists drove Chiang Kai Shek off the mainland on to Taiwan (Formosa) and assumed control of China; later, the Chinese Communists conquered Tibet. Chinese Communists aided in the formation of Communist North Korea. In each of these conquered or absorbed territories, the Communists instituted political dictatorship and economic totalitarianism modeled after the Soviet state. Efforts at protest or revolt in Czechoslovakia, Poland, East Germany, Hungary and Tibet were crushed. The Communists inspired hostilities in Greece, the Philippines and Malaya; and major wars in Korea and Indo-China. They were constantly active in the Middle East and Latin America, and important inroads were made in Indonesia and Africa. Meanwhile Russia's military power was enhanced by the successful firing of a thermonuclear bomb and by the launching of a 3000-pound space missile. Soviet diplomats combined the diplomacy of threat with an increased program of foreign aid to backward nations. Through shipments of military equipment, Communist prestige increased in the Middle East and in Africa.

Counterattack. The Western counterattack to Soviet-bloc expansion evolved with events and took three forms.

Containment. In 1947, President Truman called for an end to Communist expansion and in the **Truman Doctrine** offered American military, economic and financial aid to any nation under attack or threat of attack by Communist-bloc nations. Subsequently, the United States intervened directly and unilaterally to counter Communist attacks or threats in Greece, Turkey, Korea, Indo-China, the Philippines and Malaya. This was followed by the formation of a series of defensive military alliances designed to "contain" Communist expansion.

On April 4, 1949, the North Atlantic Treaty Organization (NATO) was formed. Original members included Belgium, Canada, Denmark, France, Greenland, Iceland, Italy, Luxemburg, the Netherlands, Norway, the United Kingdom and the United States; subsequently Greece, Turkey and West Germany were added to the alliance to form a community embracing more than 400,000,000 people. NATO, located in Paris, is composed of a ruling Civilian Council and a Military Council, with a Supreme Commander who controls motorized infantry divisions, air and naval fleets, complex and instantaneous communication systems, suppliers and, of course, conventional and atomic weapons. In its first decade NATO was able to overcome difficulties created by the failure of member nations to meet personnel quotas, forces withdrawn for non-NATO operations (French withdrawal of troops for use in Indo-China and Algeria), competition among members for favored posts and commands and non-NATO rivalries among members (England vs. Greece vs. Turkey over Cyprus; England vs. Iceland over North Atlantic fisheries). The most serious threat to NATO, however, was the demand by President De Gaulle of France for complete parity with the United States and England in Mediterranean commands and over control of atomic weapons (the latter forbidden by the United States without the consent of Congress). As a result, the United States was forced to move all its French-based atomic equipment to other sites.

Less effective than NATO was the alliance formed in Southeast Asia (SEATO) among Australia, New Zealand, Pakistan, the Philippines, Thailand, France, England and the United States. This alliance is purely consultative and it suffers considerably from the absence of India, Burma, Indonesia, Taiwan (the Republic of China) and Japan.

Least effective is the Middle East Treaty Organization (METO) organized by England but financed by the United States. It includes only Turkey, Iran, Pakistan and England (Iraq having dropped out in 1959) and is merely consultative; moreover, Egypt and the Arab League are violently opposed to it. Because these multilateral alliances have been strengthened by bilateral agreements between the United States and countries across the world, American troops are provided with military bases along the fringe of the Communist world. That the United States has not abandoned unilateral action is evident in the 1957 adoption of the **Eisenhower Doctrine** which provides for armed assistance to repel Communist aggression in the Middle East, if requested by a Middle Eastern nation.

Strengthening Europe's Economic Defenses. The United States launched its Marshall Plan (1948-1952) to remove the ruins of war, to rebuild Europe's economy and to reduce the effectiveness of the Communists throughout Europe. This economic and financial aid was distributed in Europe by the **Organization of European Economic Cooperation** (OEEC). European cooperation within the OEEC was the first step in a move toward European integration. In 1946 Belgium, the Netherlands and Luxemburg organized a tariff union (Benelux) within the OEEC. In 1949 a Council of Europe was formed to examine the possibilities of political unity of the OEEC powers. Then in 1952, France, Italy, West Germany and the Benelux nations adopted the Schuman Plan which integrated the economies of these six countries into a coal and steel community under a unified high authority which planned the production, the distribution and the labor forces available for the making of steel. In 1957, Euratom was created to promote common production of nuclear energy; and in 1959, the Schuman Plan nations began Euromarket designed to eliminate all tariffs within the community and to adopt a common tariff against all nations outside the community. England proposed a wider free-trade area to embrace all Western Europe. Finding no approval for this plan by Euromarket, England began to organize its own free-trade area to include itself, Sweden,

Norway, Denmark, Austria, Switzerland and Portugal.

Strengthening Non-European Economic Defenses. To offset Communist inroads into the more backward areas of the world, the United States and its allies have begun large-scale programs of economic aid to these areas. Technical assistance to improve control over natural resources was made available under President Truman's Point Four program and a similar United Nation's project. Loans and grants-in-aid were provided for Southeast Asia in the British-sponsored and American-financed Colombo Plan; and to all the rest of the world in the United States' **Development Loan Fund** and **Agricultural Trade and Development Loan Funds** (which distributes America's farm surpluses to needy nations). Other sources of loans for approved projects were the **American Export-Import Bank** and the **International Bank for Reconstruction and Development.** Billions of dollars and pounds poured into these backward areas have successfully halted important Communist gains, and have kept the governments of these nations, generally inclined to Communism, on a neutral path.

Support for Former Enemies. Since enemies of Communism are not necessarily friends of democracy, the Western powers have taken active steps to obtain necessary allies. Thus, Marshall Tito, heading a Communist state in Yugoslavia, was aided by loans and military support to defy the Soviet bloc and retain his independence; Generalissimo Franco, heading a Fascist state in Spain, was encouraged to be friendly to the Western powers by a defense agreement with the United States in which air bases were exchanged for military and economic aid. Similarly, Japan, having been effectively democratized, was permitted to rearm, admitted to the United Nations, granted large sums of rehabilitory aid, and made a defense bastion in the Far East. Most significant, however, was the treatment accorded to Germany.

The Yalta and Potsdam agreements of 1945 provided that both Germany and its historic capital, Berlin, were to be partitioned until the country was completely demilitarized, denazified and democratized. When this was accomplished Germany was to be reunited as a minor power. Unilateral Russian action, however, in changing Germany's boundaries within the eastern zone, in blockading Berlin, and in converting the Russian zone into the satellite nation of East Germany, caused the Western powers to take positive steps. West Germany became an independent state; the German General Staff was recreated; West Germany was militarized and admitted to NATO. The Western powers maintained their position in West Berlin despite the efforts of Russian Premier Khrushchev who threatened to turn West Berlin, located well within the territory of the East German state, over to East Germany, and conclude a separate peace treaty with East Germany.

East and West met at the conference table at Geneva in 1959 in an attempt to solve the problem of a united Berlin and a united Germany.

BASIC PROBLEMS CONFRONTING THE WESTERN ALLIANCE

Revival of Nationalism. Since World War II, Asiatic and African people have shown a grim determination to drive former colonial powers from their territories, to seize control of their own governments, to bring all means of production under their own political control, and to assume independent roles in the council of nations. These movements are nationalistic, not democratic; political control in the liberated areas has, for the most part, been synonymous with control of the army. The chief result of this wave of nationalism has been the loss of much of the English and French empires. England has lost effective control over India, Pakistan, Ceylon and Ghana (which remain in the Commonwealth as dominions); Burma, Palestine, Malaya, the Sudan, the Suez Canal, Jordan, Iraq and Cyprus. France has surrendered Tunis, Morocco, Guinea and Indo-China; she was forced to grant autonomous status to Madagascar, Senegal, French Sudan, Mauritania, Chad, Gabon and Middle Congo, and is in a bitter battle to integrate Algeria with France proper. Holland surrendered Indonesia. The liberated Afro-Asian nations have, since the Bandung Conference in 1955, united as a powerful third force, dedicated to playing East against West and West against East in an attempt to secure their own power and independence.

Most serious, however, is the situation in the Middle East. Nationalist uprisings have endangered Western oil resources in Iran, Iraq and Saudi Arabia. Confiscation of privately owned property by Arab nations seriously threatens the Western position in the area. In 1956, the Egyptian government seized and nationalized the Suez Canal. In the same year,

Israel launched an attack upon Egypt with the declared intention of wiping out bases of Egyptian raiders and compelling Egypt to reopen the Suez Canal to Israeli shipping. This gave the occasion to England and France to follow suit with the declared intention of protecting the Suez Canal from destruction in an Egyptian-Israeli war.

Since the creation of Israel by the United Nations in 1948, the entire Middle East has been like a tinder box. The Arab League's permanent declaration of war against Israel (which it does not recognize) has led to a continuous series of border raids, boycotts and bars to Israeli shipping in the Suez Canal. Communist arms shipments and the granting of commercial loans to finance such projects as the Aswan Dam have increased the Soviet influence in the Middle East. "Arab Nationalism" has grown with the merger of Egypt and Syria into the United Arab Republic. Revolutions directed against Hussein in Jordan and Kassem in Iraq have contributed to the general unrest.

THE PROBLEM OF WORLD DISARMAMENT

The Cold War was accompanied by an intensified arms race which concentrated on producing thermonuclear bombs, intercontinental rocket-driven missiles, atomic-powered submarines, and world-wide communication defense systems against surprise attacks. The Russians have successfully launched their man-made earth satellites (Sputniks) and although the United States has put several satellites in orbit, it is generally conceded that the Russians are further advanced in this important area of research. Meanwhile, the air grew steadily more contaminated with radioactive fall-out. These developments forced continuation of the first disarmament talks begun in 1946.

Halting Bomb Production. Agreement on cessation of bomb production was stalemated by American insistence on a fool-proof inspection system to augment any treaty providing for a stoppage of bomb production and by Russia's insistence upon a paper prohibition immediately, modified inspection, and a big-power veto provision such as operates in the Security Council.

Limitation of Bomb Testing. Russian and American scientists drew near to permanent agreement on the elimination of atmospheric tests, means of checking on elimination through the use of space satellites, and limiting tests to underground and underwater areas.

Avoidance of Surprise Attacks. Both sides accepted the principle of "open-skies" inspection and defined areas of inspection; but disagreed on which areas and the American proposal of accompanying "on the ground" inspection.

Peaceful Uses of Atomic Energy. Following President Eisenhower's proposal of an atoms-for-peace program, an International Atomic Energy Agency was set up for the diffusion of information about peaceful uses of atomic energy, for distribution of fissionable materials, etc. An international congress held in Geneva proved most valuable for all the participants.

CHAPTER TWENTY-TWO

THE WORLD SINCE 1959

THE UNITED NATIONS

There are 121 nations represented in the General Assembly, and the Security Council has been raised from eleven to fifteen members to accommodate the growing number of states. The hopes that created the UN were still alive in the late 1960's, twenty years after its founding: it is still a forum for world opinion. Yet in many respects it is more shadow than substance; everywhere in the world nations are beating their plowshares back into swords. Through the sixties there has been the constant threat of war: between Israel and its Arab neighbors; between civil factions in the African states; between Indonesia and Malaysia (until the Indonesian Communists were removed in 1966); between India and China over a border strip; between India and Pakistan over Kashmir; between the U.S. and the U.S.S.R. over Berlin and Cuba. There has been war in Vietnam since 1945; Turkey and Greece fought in Cyprus; there is a popular demand for war between England and the secessionist Rhodesia. The result has been the greatest arms race in history. France and Communist China have become members of the "nuclear club."

Successes. What it was permitted to do, the UN did well. Under the brilliant leadership of Dag Hammarskjöld (killed in an air accident in 1961) and U Thant the truce between the Arabs and the Israelis was maintained, although uneasily. The UN kept order in the Congo when Belgium's withdrawal in 1960 precipitated violence. In 1964 bloody civil strife between the Greeks and the Turks tore the island of Cyprus apart. Britain turned the matter over to the UN and another military mission established order there. The UN mediated international disputes between Laos and North Vietnam in 1959, between Sarawak and Sabah, and between Lebanon and Syria. Through all of the disorder of the sixties the specialized agencies continued to render substantial aid to children, to the sick, and to the illiterate and the impoverished.

Failures. Basically, national sovereignty predominates over international solidarity in the UN. War and insecurity prevail over peace and security in the minds of statesmen. Where self-interest has not prevailed, regional blocs have, for within the General Assembly there exists a Russian Communist bloc, a Chinese Communist bloc, an American bloc, an Asian bloc, an Arab bloc, etc. Each pursues narrow interests and utilizes the UN podium for propaganda against its enemies. The American bloc has effectively kept Communist China out of the UN, thus making the organization somewhat less than universal. Russia's vetoes have crippled the Security Council on many occasions. The UN has been financially starved—the 1965 session, for example, was unable to vote any activity since its members were $100 million in arrears. The decision of the World Court that assessments must be paid was ignored, as was a U.S. request that the defaulters (notably France and Russia) be stripped of the right to vote in the General Assembly, as the Charter requires. Then the U.S. reserved to itself the right to refuse to pay for any action it disapproved of. Many UN members rely on agencies outside the UN; hence, the proliferation of mutual defense treaties (NATO, the Warsaw Pact, etc.), summit meetings, and unilateral action, as the U.S. took in the Dominican Republic and in Vietnam.

THE WESTERN ALLIANCE WEAKENS

Gaullist France. To end parliamentary rule by party blocs, the Fifth French Republic was established. The power of the presidency was increased and Charles de Gaulle, the wartime hero, was elected President. De Gaulle had for some time preached that colonial imperialism was dead, that the Cold War was over, and that France must assume the role of a Third Force between the U.S. and the U.S.S.R. By 1962 almost all of France's former colonies were independent, although they remained members of the French Community, a kind of loose French commonwealth of nations. With

this as his base of operations, de Gaulle began to disengage France's connections with the U.S. He attempted, but unsuccessfully, to woo West Germany from its position as a virtual American satellite by means of a Franco-German Entente which would recognize France's leadership of Europe. West Germany's rejection of this offer has caused strained relations between the two powers. Furthermore, de Gaulle did all but withdraw from NATO: he removed French troops and ships from NATO contingents; he ordered the supreme headquarters of the NATO command to leave France by 1967. He further alienated the U.S. by recognizing Communist China, by trading with Cuba and North Vietnam, and by refusing to allow England to enter the Common Market. (England, he said, was not a European power but an American satellite.)

NATO. The United States had hoped that by 1969, when the 20-year alliance would be up for renewal, NATO unity would have been cemented by three auxiliary units—the Common Market, a European Parliament, and a Multilateral Nuclear Missile Force. De Gaulle shattered these hopes by vetoing England's entry into the Common Market, by rejecting the political unity of Europe, and by refusing to give West Germany nuclear weapons of any kind under any conditions. West Germany herself has been an unhappy member of NATO. She refused to buy munitions in the U.S. to help the U.S. maintain a favorable balance of trade. In fact, America's insistence that she spend the money she promised here caused the fall of the Erhard government in 1966. Moreover, with France virtually out of the NATO command, West Germany is reluctant to have French troops stationed in West Germany.

Other troubles confronting the NATO alliance include the falling-out between two of its members, Greece and Turkey, over Cyprus; the U.S.'s support in the UN for independence for Angola and Mozambique, two colonies belonging to Portugal, our NATO ally. There are numerous other examples, but what they all add up to is a NATO alliance which is less solid and less committed than it has ever been.

Common Market Difficulties. France, West Germany, Belgium, the Netherlands, Italy, and Greece are members of the Common Market, officially called the European Economic Community. Since these countries are also members of NATO, the affairs of the two groups are closely linked. There is little doubt that the Common Market was responsible for the "economic miracles" that occurred in the first half of the 1960's. With tariffs cut some 60 per cent within the Common Market, trade doubled among its members and jumped

50 per cent with the outside world. Economic growth rate leaped, unemployment was reduced, much foreign capital entered the market seeking investment opportunity, and living standards rose dramatically. There was much resentment in the U.S., however, because the common tariff discriminated against imports from America. In 1961, England, a member of the European Free Trade Association (another economic community known as the "Outer Seven"), applied for membership in the Common Market, but was blackballed by de Gaulle.

Other problems affecting the Common Market include inflation resulting from a vicious price-wage cycle, and the inability to think in common about agriculture since each nation is concerned with protecting its own farmers—France wants low tariffs because French farmers are efficient producers, while Germany wants protection for the opposite reason.

THE TWO GERMANIES

Germany remains what she has been in modern world history: a threat to world peace. This is true despite the fact that the Western Allies still occupy her land, that she is basically disarmed, that her foreign policy is not solely her own, and that she is divided into two sovereign (but still unrecognized) states—the Federal Republic of Germany (West Germany) and the German Democratic Republic (East Germany).

The West German government is a coalition between several major political parties: the Christian Democrats, the Christian Social Union, and the Free Democrats. This bloc has brought West Germany to its high position in the Western world. It is a member of NATO; it has a small but well-armed and well-equipped army; it is a member of the Common Market and the Western European Union. It moved up the industrial ladder until by the mid-1960's it was second in world automobile production, fourth in steel output, and fifth in coal mining—all resulting from a prosperous, free-enterprise economy that was managed along Keynesian lines. East Germany, on the other hand, had become a Communist state, but nonetheless an industrial one, with an average industrial output higher than Russia's and only $400 per capita below West Germany's. The tremendous difference between the two Germanies was the availability of consumer goods—very little in East Germany and very much in West Germany. In a sense, here was a classic example of competition between the two systems involved in the Cold War.

Why, then, is Germany a threat to world peace? First, any talk of unification involves the possibility of

civil war between two systems, a war that must engage the partisans of each and could develop into a world war. This tension is evident in the fact that none of the Western powers will recognize East Germany as a sovereign state. Another symbol is the Berlin Wall, built in 1961 to halt the flow of thousands of refugees from East to West Germany. To emphasize the significance of the wall the Russians have a number of times prevented the Allied Occupation Forces from entering Berlin across East Germany, an action that has always led to an American-Russian confrontation with all the tension that such an action involves. Additionally, the West Germans have never accepted the territorial division worked out between the East Germans and the Poles in a boundary known as the Oder-Neisse Line. This is a potential German-Polish conflict similar to that over the Polish Corridor before World War II.

The West Germans have grown increasingly dissatisfied with the limited position assigned to them by the U.S. They want to be free of the cost of maintaining Allied troops on their soil (although they want the support of these troops); they want to enter the "nuclear club"; to compete freely in the world's markets; and to conduct an independent foreign policy. Even more ominous has been the appearance of a Nazi-like party, the German National Democratic Party, with a new brand of supernationalism, anti-Semitism, etc. The party is supported, particularly in Hesse and Bavaria, by ex-Nazis and by the lumpen German middle class with its low level of national frustration. A flare-up is not inevitable, of course, but the elements for an explosion are certainly apparent.

COMMUNISM IN EUROPE

Russian. Nikita Khrushchev was the Soviet guiding spirit from 1955 to 1964, when he was summarily relieved of his duties by the "collective leadership" of Alexei Kosygin, Chief Secretary of the Communist Party, and Leonid Brezhnev, Premier of the U.S.S.R. Khrushchev had achieved much during his dictatorship. His public denouncement of Stalin and Stalinism and the "cult of personality" resulted in the reappearance of free criticism and experimentalism, particularly among Soviet intellectuals. Many of Stalin's victims were restored to public life, the infamous labor camps were closed, and an end was put to arbitrary arrest and imprisonment. An important by-product of this anti-Stalin movement was Khrushchev's policy of co-existence, which led to a detente with the West, an increase in East-West trade, the nuclear test-ban treaty, the "hot line" between Moscow and Washington, summit conferences, and polycentric relations with the satellite states (giving them more equitable trade advantages, permitting more numerous degrees of national Communism, etc.). Under Khrushchev, Russia experienced a rapid increase in population and a high rate of economic growth from 1955 to 1960 (although it fell sharply thereafter). Khrushchev started to decentralize industry to increase small plant efficiency and to permit some experimentation with "capitalist" forms of production based on supply-demand markets and profit-making.

With a firm base in industry and electronics the Soviets under Khrushchev moved into first place in the space race. Their defense program gave Russia equality with the U.S. as a nuclear power capable of totally destroying its enemy with missiles. After the secrecy and mystery surrounding Russian dictators, Khrushchev's bouncing personality, his frequent visits abroad, his willingness to debate with all comers, his geniality commingled with his Stanislavsky rages, gave the Soviets a new and generally favorable image in the eyes of the world. Why then was he suddenly made into an "unperson" in 1964?

An editorial in *Pravda* explaining his dismissal accused him of "hare-brained scheming, bragging and phrase-mongering." In more conservative eyes, Khrushchev was guilty of re-creating a cult of personality, of placing his relatives in advantageous jobs (nepotism), of acting without dignity (beatnikism), and of failing to envision the consequences of his decisions. Impetuous agricultural proposals failed to overcome Russia's cattle and grain deficits. Decentralization, too hastily introduced, had fostered conflict between party leaders and industrial managers. Soviet writers, given a finger of freedom, demanded the whole hand and when denied published their writings abroad. Polycentrism got out of control, particularly in Albania and Romania, the former linking with the Chinese and the latter with Tito's Yugoslavia. Western powers stepped up their efforts to pry the satellites loose from the Russian grip. More important, however, was the fact that Khrushchev contradicted his own policies: he crushed the Polish, East German, and Hungarian revolts with Russian tanks; while pursuing coexistence, he continued to arm Russia; he obstructed disarmament talks, exploded summit meetings, built missile bases in Cuba, threatened the U.S. with thermonuclear annihilation if she intervened in Laos, Vietnam, or Cuba, disrupted the UN, etc. It was Khrushchev, too, who began the schism between the Soviet and Chinese Communists.

Khrushchev's successors, Kosygin and Brezhnev, attempted to restore the earlier, more enigmatic, image of Russia. Stalin's name was made respectable again; the mass media were purged of Khrushchev's relatives and friends who held leading posts; censorship was again imposed on Soviet intellectuals. They did, however, continue Khrushchev's industrial experiments (decentralization, consumer choice, profit-making). In agriculture they returned to the old collective farm system, although they increased fringe benefits for farm workers ($2 billion in debts canceled; pension plans introduced; prices increased). Their foreign policy took a much harder line: assuming anti-American leadership over the Vietnam crisis by virtually replacing Communist China in North Vietnam; winning over to their side of the Chinese-Soviet schism all of the Communist parties of the world except the Albanian; translating coexistence into a policy of international mediation, as in the Tashkent Agreement settling the Pakistani-Indian War of 1965; strengthening the Soviet position in the Middle East with a strong anti-Israel posture which included economic and military aid to members of the Arab League.

Polycentrism in Eastern Europe. Communists control East Germany, Bulgaria, Czechoslovakia, Hungary, Poland, and Romania. In form, each of these countries is like the Soviet Union—Communist Party rule over the façade of a democratic state; government ownership and operation of all means of production, distribution, and exchange; and production by state planning commissions. In each, there is an emphasis on self-sufficiency in industry and agriculture. Between 1948 and 1963 the nations of Eastern Europe increased their steel production fourfold and established quite respectable gains in such items as coal mining, production of electricity, etc. Standards of living have risen and a variety of consumer goods have become available, although they are quite expensive by Western standards. Since 1963, however, rates of economic growth in many of these countries have declined because of over-centralization of bureaucratic control, over-expansion of industry in relation to agriculture, defense expenditures, black markets in overpriced consumer goods industries, and too much reliance on economic aid from Russia. Within the common market of the Communist states (Comecon) the satellites have insisted upon mutual economic assistance, integration of the economies of the different states, and wider use of investment funds. Romania, for example, refused to be assigned the role of feeder-nation in oil, chemicals, and foodstuffs; she wanted to share in large, mechanized industrialization. Poland would like to do more of its business with countries outside the Communist bloc. All the countries are insisting that the Russians supply the capital for large-scale projects affecting more than one state, and Russia has acceded to this by setting up projects for interstate communications, pipelines, etc.

One should not, however, drop the label of "satellite" too soon. The Soviet hold is still very powerful in Eastern Europe. The countries all follow Soviet foreign policy, subscribe to the Warsaw military alliance pact, are members of Comecon, and have Russian-built industries and thus are dependent on Russia for spare parts, etc.

MOSCOW VERSUS PEKING

Russia no longer has a monolithic control over world Communism. What are the reasons for the great schism between the Communist giants, Russia and China?

To the Chinese, the Russian policy of coexistence represents an abandonment of the revolutionary core of Marxism-Leninism for the purpose of appeasing the West. The Chinese say that this policy has led the Soviet Union to imperialistically dominate the smaller Communist states; to cooperate with American imperialism in Southeast Asia; to surrender to hollow American threats; to prop up bourgeois nationalist powers like Egypt and India; to treacherously turn upon its fraternal ally, China, by giving India military aid when China merely "rectified a border problem"; and to block the efforts of the world proletariat to free themselves in wars of liberation. To the Soviets, the Chinese policy of world revolution is simply infantile leftism. It ignores the fact that a thermonuclear war can be mankind's last, and that any "war of liberation" can escalate rapidly in that direction; it lacks faith in the ability of socialist systems to outcompete capitalism peacefully and bring about peaceful revolutions in the world; it is unaware of the many strains already affecting capitalism—NATO differences, American unilateralism, difficulties in the Common Market—and it underassesses the revolutionary potentials in peace efforts such as the test-ban treaty.

It seems to have been the Chinese rather than the Russians who precipitated this break. China's grievances against the U.S.S.R. were numerous: Stalin, they claimed, appeased Chiang Kai-shek; Russia never surrendered to China the Chinese territory seized by the Russian tsars; Russia refused to China the economic aid that would have made her a first-class power in a short time and rejected China's request for atomic weapons; Russia disgraced Communism with its retreats whenever a showdown arose and tried to destroy Mao Tsetung with its attacks on "cults of personality." This ideological dispute has created one of the most serious threats to world peace in modern times and could precipitate a major world crisis.

OTHER WORLD DANGER SPOTS

Middle East. The possibility of war in the Middle East has been present since 1948: Israel versus the Arab League, specifically Jordan and the Palestine Liberation Organization, a group of Arabs displaced from Israel who now live in Jordan as refugees. The wars between the Israelis and Arabs—the Sinai Campaign of 1956 and the Six-Day War of 1967—demonstrated Israeli military superiority and the effects of Arab disunity. But they solved none of the problems of the area. Furthermore, the Middle East reflects another typical confrontation between West and East, with the U.S. and Britain supporting Israel and the Communists helping the Arabs.

Vietnam. The civil war in Vietnam between the Communist North Vietnamese and Vietcong on one side and the South Vietnamese, increasingly supported by American troops and equipment on the other, has developed into a major threat to world peace. Vietnam was a French protectorate from 1884 to 1954, when France withdrew following a crushing defeat by the pro-Communist Vietminh (now called Vietcong) at Dienbienphu. In July 1954 a cease-fire agreement was signed at Geneva. It called, among other things, for the partitioning of Vietnam into northern and southern zones and eventual free elections. South Vietnam opposed the elections, however, because it was obvious that the majority of the Vietnamese would choose a government headed by Ho Chih Minh, the guerrilla leader supported by Communists. A succession of South Vietnamese governments, many riddled with corruption, rose and fell, largely supported by American economic, military advisory, and political aid.

While there was no direct military intervention by the U.S. during the Eisenhower and Kennedy administrations, President Johnson escalated active American participation until by the end of 1966 more than 350,000 U.S. troops were in combat, extensive bombing operations were carried on in both North and South Vietnam, and the U.S. assumed supervision of the entire military operation. Partial cease-fires took place during the Christmas-New Year's holidays of 1965 and 1966, during which the search for peace formulas was intensified, with UN Secretary General U Thant and Pope Paul VI offering assistance. But no easy peace seems likely since both the U.S. and North Vietnam have established fairly rigid conditions before they will agree to negotiate.

Certain significant facts have emerged from this war. Despite the most intensive bombing in military history and the use of the latest developments in weaponry by the U.S., the North Vietnamese have been able to infiltrate the South in ever-increasing numbers. In addition, the American ground forces have been unable to wage successful guerrilla war against the Vietcong. Therefore, while American troops have been able to hold urban enclaves along the coast, they have not made much progress in the interior. This seems to justify Mao Tse-tung's theory that in any future conventional war the country can defeat the city, as was the case in China.

China. Communist China retains its pivotal spot in the Far East. Her industrial potential has grown steadily in spite of the withdrawal of Soviet aid. She has entered the "nuclear club" with sophisticated thermonuclear weapons. Her difficulties are tremendous—constant economic crises in food, military weakness in the air and at sea, and cultural backwardness. Yet she was able to fight the U.S. and fifteen other nations in Korea; she aided wars of liberation from Indochina to the Congo; attacked the islands of Quemoy and Matsu in the face of the American fleet; and became the center of anti-American and anti-Russian propaganda. Her recent foreign policies have been disastrous, and her influence has almost disappeared in Africa, but she still commands support within the Communist movement all over the world and in non-Communist states such as Pakistan, which turned to her when American and Russian military aid was given to India in the Indian-Pakistani war over Kashmir in 1965.

Africa. The problems here are characterized by the sudden growth of independent states from what had been British and French colonies. Almost every newly independent country is plagued by the lack of real leadership since so few natives were given the opportunity or training while the countries were under colonial rule. Many new African states are torn by tribal sectionalism. In attempting to unify they have been forced in many cases to surrender the concept of democratic government to rule by military juntas. In addition, a very wide gap prevails between national aspirations and the economic capability of fulfilling them. Despite their enormous wealth in natural resources, Africans by and large lack the skill and training to exploit this wealth—hence there is a prevalence of poverty, illiteracy, and sickness, conditions that sap the energy of the people and require constant assistance from outside sources such as the UN, the U.S., Soviet Russia, Communist China, etc.

The policy of apartheid (strict separation of the races) is another problem that Africa faces. It is practiced in the Union of South Africa and in Rhodesia and has its origins in the Nazi principle of racial inferiority. Not only does it permit a brutal kind of segregation and discrimination against colored peoples, but whites suffer too because of the absence of civil liberties and the imposition of strict censorship, arbitrary arrest and imprisonment, and trials that become mockeries of the concept of justice. There is not much opposition to these policies by the West because there are substantial Western investments in both countries. Even many black states appease South Africa and Rhodesia because these countries are their market for export or their sources of raw materials.

To solve some of their problems, the African states have united into an Organization of African Unity (OAU) pledged to non-interference in one another's internal affairs, to the elimination of white rule in South Africa, Rhodesia, Southwest Africa, Angola, and Mozambique, to peaceful settlement of African disputes, and to intra-African trade and military assistance. To win the support of the OAU states, rich Western and Eastern nations are sending technological aid in the form of machines and personnel. While in many states a form of African socialism prevails, foreign investment under state control is welcomed. Still, outside the white-controlled areas African progress is very slow in spite of aid from the outside: there are lingual and tribal barriers; dictatorship by military junta; territorial disputes; the virtual absence of skilled labor and a professional class; low standards of living; and the persistence of colonialism. With time, training, and understanding these barriers will be overcome.

INDEX